Imperial Formations

School for Advanced Research
Advanced Seminar Series

James F. Brooks
General Editor

Imperial Formations

Contributors

Jane Burbank
Department of History, New York University

Frederick Cooper
Department of History, New York University

Fernando Coronil
Departments of Anthropology and History, University of Michigan

Nicholas Dirks
Department of Anthropology, Columbia University

Prasenjit Duara
Department of History, University of Chicago

Adeeb Khalid
Department of History, Carleton College

Ussama Makdisi
Department of History, Rice University

Carole McGranahan
Department of Anthropology, University of Colorado, Boulder

Peter C. Perdue
Department of History, Massachusetts Institute of Technology

Irene Silverblatt
Department of Cultural Anthropology, Duke University

Ann Laura Stoler
Department of Anthropology, New School for Social Research

Imperial Formations

Edited by Ann Laura Stoler, Carole McGranahan, and Peter C. Perdue

School for Advanced Research Press
Santa Fe

James Currey
Oxford

School for Advanced Research Press
Post Office Box 2188
Santa Fe, New Mexico 87504-2188
www.sarpress.sarweb.org

James Currey Ltd
73 Botley Road
Oxford OX2 0BS

Co-Director and Editor: Catherine Cocks
Manuscript Editors: Ann D. Brucklacher, Margaret J. Goldstein
Design and Production: Cynthia Dyer
Proofreader: Margaret J. Goldstein
Indexer: Bruce Tracy
Printer: Edwards Brothers

Library of Congress Cataloging-in-Publication Data:

Imperial formations / edited by Ann Laura Stoler, Carole McGranahan, and Peter C. Perdue. – 1st ed.
p. cm. – (School for Advanced Research advanced seminar series)
Includes bibliographical references and index.
ISBN 1-930618-73-5 (pbk. : alk. paper)
1. Imperialism–History. I. Stoler, Ann Laura. II. McGranahan, Carole. III. Perdue, Peter C., 1949-

D210.I45 2007
325'.32–dc22

2007005550

British Library Cataloguing-in-Publication Data

Imperial formations. - (School for Advanced Research advanced seminar series)
1. Imperialism - History
I. Stoler, Ann Laura II. McGranahan, Carole III. Perdue, Peter C., 1949- IV. School for Advanced Research (Santa Fe, NM)
325.3'2

ISBN-13: 978-1-84701-200-5 (paper)

Manufactured in the United States of America.
Library of Congress Catalog Card Number 2007005550
Paper ISBN 13: 978-1-930618-73-2
First edition 2007.

Cover illustration: Chinese soldiers march outside Potala Palace, Tibet, © AP Images, 2007.

Contents

Preface

If "the pulse of teaching is persuasion," as George Steiner contends, then its strongest pulse, as we were to learn in this collaborative work, is generated by mutual persuasions that course in unexpected ways.[1] This project began in a graduate seminar at the University of Michigan in the fall of 1995. The class was Ann Stoler's "Culture and Historical Methodologies," which centered on the politics of colonial historiographies and followed "The Colonial Order of Things" offered the previous semester. Frederick Cooper and Ann Stoler's edited volume *Tensions of Empire* was in the final stages of production, and students read its introduction in manuscript form. Those students from anthropology, history, and sociology whose work was situated in former Ottoman, Russian, and Chinese imperial domains were simultaneously excited and agitated by what they read. Rather than embrace the focused critiques of European empire, a number of seminar participants, Carole McGranahan and Theresa Truax most vocally, forced us all to turn those critiques on their head: how might these critiques of European empire serve to help us understand imperial forms elsewhere? Were other imperial polities subject to the same structures of dominance as European ones? Would an expanded focus on other empires confirm or challenge the European model of what constituted the prevailing technologies of imperial rule?

If taken with the idea of thinking across metropole and colony, discussions were vexed by a persistent undertone in the literature that the only *true* forms of colonialism were European ones. All others—be they Chinese, Japanese, or Russian—the argument seemed to be, were not so much derivative of these forms but set aside as different from them. Nor was this disinterest solely geographic. Imperial and colonial practices in socialist states seemed to challenge claims that colonialism was a specific product of the liberal state. McGranahan and Truax initiated a more formal and public response, organizing a panel on colonial studies beyond the European liberal state for the annual American Anthropological Association (AAA) conference in 1996. Tor Aarestad presented on the Soviet Union, Judy Farquhar and Jim Hevia on China, Maureen Feeney on Vietnam, Beth Notar on southwest China, Theresa Truax on Uzbekistan, and Carole McGranahan on Tibet. Nicholas Dirks and Ann Stoler were willing targets—and the discussants.

It was five years later that McGranahan, still disquieted by the Eurocentric slant of colonial studies, suggested a more extended and intensive conversation with other interlocutors, as an advanced seminar at the School for Advanced Research. Our SAR proposal on "Empires: Thinking Colonial Studies beyond Europe" addressed the plurality of empire *and* the analytic and political consequences of comparing imperial projects beyond those of Europe. We targeted non-European empires, socialist states, empire beyond colonialism, temporal questions about modernity, and traces of empire in the present. Refiguring the prototypes for empire led to a set of pointed questions: If liberalism and bourgeois respectability were such key features of nineteenth-century European empire, then what were the equivalent social, political, and moral anchors of other empires? Did empire and its aftermath look wholly different when liberalism and the bourgeois project were not the cornerstones of rule?

We specifically invited anthropologists and historians who worked on European empires, as well as those who did not, seeking to spark dialogue across multiple empires, disciplinary commitments, and theoretical trajectories. Eleven of us—Jane Burbank, Fred Cooper, Fernando Coronil, Nick Dirks, Prasenjit Duara, Adeeb Khalid, Ussama Makdisi, Peter Perdue, Patricia Seed, and ourselves as organizers—gathered in Santa Fe in the fall of 2003. For five days we debated and discussed empires from unconventional—or so we thought—perspectives: a historian of China commenting on France, an anthropologist of

Latin America discussing Japan, a historian of Russia remarking on China, an anthropologist of Southeast Asia commenting on the Ottoman empire. Those working outside colonial studies scholarship were asked to directly engage those within it. In an unusual twist for an SAR advanced seminar, the majority of the participants were historians, not anthropologists. Ten of the original participants appear in this volume. After Santa Fe, Patricia Seed withdrew from the group, and we invited Irene Silverblatt to bring her work on the Spanish genealogy of modern inquisitions into conversation with our project.

If the questions we raised over a decade ago motivated the design of the initial project, the contemporary issues around imperial comparisons have reframed those questions and set them in new directions. As we collectively demonstrate in this volume, yes, critiques of empire can travel beyond Europe, but—in the spirit of *Tensions of Empire*—so too can they turn back to challenge the given attributes of European imperial formations. The chapters herein empirically and theoretically address head-on whether or not it makes sense to consider European and non-European, capitalist and socialist, modern and early modern, colonial and noncolonial forms of empire in the same analytical frame. Not surprisingly, given our diverse intellectual trajectories, our motivations and questions were not all the same. Some authors were more focused on the intricacies of their particular historical cases, others on articulating broader models for scholarship. Some sought to directly intervene in colonial studies' agenda; others, newly in dialogue with colonial studies, worked primarily outside of its orbit. We were also clearly convening in a time when the political grounds and academic stakes of empire had shifted.

As our authors so clearly demonstrate, thinking empire beyond Europe has both retrospective value and immediate relevance. Our assessments of the layers of empire, of imperial geologies, are designed to confront confusions of empire in the present. We see the popular assumption that contemporary political rationalities are continuous with earlier empires as itself a political stance not just a historical argument. In the face of such simplifications (and disavowals) of empire in the present, we suggest that a return to specific histories bears on understanding the imperial present. One collective move we make is to conceptualize degrees—degrees of tolerance, of difference, of domination, and of rights—as an integral part of the imperial project. This attention to degrees and gradations, to layers of rule and organization, of rhetoric and experience unsettles monolithic views of empire without sacrificing the recognition that appearance as a monolith might be a desired imperial strategy.

Imperial Formations is not without its own tensions. Seminar participants disagreed about some basic issues. Some held to the all-consuming power of colonial structures, while others contended that people were using these structures to other ends. The cultural labor some contributors considered so crucial to reproducing dominance was not as key an issue for others. Some participants insisted more strongly than others that a fundamental violence of empire is lodged in opaque and changing vocabulary. Do imperial categories—of caste, gender, race, or sovereignty, for example—themselves structure and produce violence, or is violence not produced out of these categories but alongside or independent of them?

In asking these questions, our motives were often dual: to reconsider our general and specific understandings of empires and to contemplate how to best intervene in debates about contemporary empires, including that of the United States. If most authors address the first issue overtly, the second manifests as a more subjacent concern, working to shape current debates on empire by providing clear models for history and analysis, and by thinking through—as we detail in the introduction—empires not as things but as processes, as states of being, becoming, and deferral. As with the original graduate seminar that inspired this project, our SAR seminar raised questions that we were not able to sufficiently answer. In engaging across disciplines, periods, regions, and scholarships, what results is less a finished product than a working concept for rethinking empires and refiguring imperial terrain.

Carole McGranahan and Ann Laura Stoler

1. George Steiner, *Lessons of the Master,* Cambridge, MA: Harvard University Press, 2003: 26.

Imperial Formations

1

Introduction

Refiguring Imperial Terrains

Ann Laura Stoler and Carole McGranahan

> For us, an agricultural colony [*colonie*] is a rural institution that extends its benevolence to all those who have access, whatever their title, and where the benefits are shared.... That obligation may consist of the work of clearing or of ordinary cultivation, of more or less demanding service, or the obligation of a simple stay, it basically does not matter: the rule applies to all, to obey is required of all. Each contributes according to their ability, according to the contract or obligation they hold. Everyone who inhabits a colony is a colon whatever role they play, whatever work they perform, whatever particular rights are granted to them.
>
> —*A. de Tourdonnet*[1]

In the early and mid-nineteenth century, a *colon*—a term that would be more firmly fixed later in the century to overseas settlers throughout the French empire—conveyed multiple referents. *Colon* could refer to a "pioneer settler" in Algeria, as one might expect, but as frequently to a member of a state-run establishment for paupers in central France, a penal colony inmate in New Caledonia, or an orphan child in a rural residential shelter in Provence.[2]

The semantic slippage displayed in the French treatise on the "agricultural colonies of education" quoted above captures a feature of colonization that contemporary studies of colonialisms and empires have since lost or discarded, namely that different notions of a colony and who its members were coexisted, were contested, and were actively compared. Imperial expansion and modes of confinement, resettlement of delinquents, pauper programs, and the recruitment of empire's pioneers were not separately conceived and executed projects with wholly different architects and different names.[3] The spectrum of meanings implicit in the words *colonie* and *colon* was diffused across overlapping collaborative projects. Government planners and social reformers themselves were concerned that the term *colonie* covered such a wide range of institutional arrangements.[4] They too asked whether pioneer colonies should be treated alongside long-settled agricultural ones, whether colonies of rescue for foundlings, of punishment for criminals, and of education for industrial and agricultural pioneers were not all forms of social relief designed to moralize those who would inhabit them.[5]

The social etymology of *colonie* draws us to something else: a strikingly broad scope of imperial comparison developed through the exchange of principles, practices, and technologies between empires in their metropolitan regions and far-flung domains.[6] If etymologies highlight the careers of words, social etymologies reveal the contexts of these comparisons. Social etymologies register which practices these concepts illuminated and gathered into commensurable form. As the epigraph above suggests, French blueprints for agricultural and pauper colonies drew on strategies of empire, strategies that scholars have often presumed followed European models. However, French observers in the nineteenth century, for example, also considered initiatives by Catherine II and her successors in Russia to be exemplary efforts to create a reasoned empire through colonization.[7] As France turned to Russia, Russia in turn looked to the American West for models of settlement and expansion.[8] Such borrowings that stretched from France to Russia and Russia to the United States of America mark a competitive politics of comparison that accelerated circuits of knowledge production and imperial exchange.[9]

Yet, for students of European empires, what constituted the objects of comparison is perhaps more arresting than the comparisons themselves. French planners admired both the programs that housed abandoned children in rural "colonies" on the outskirts of St. Petersburg and Moscow as well as those that recruited the urban poor and foreign workers to colonize Russia's steppes and vast eastern territories.[10]

Russian programs to house orphaned children were relevant both to making an orphaned underclass productive in France and to producing from that group "colonists" suitable for North African homesteads. Envisioning three stages of physical acclimatization and moral education, French planners proposed "preparatory colonies" for children one to twelve years of age (outfitted with nursemaids and a bovine population), "colonies of transition" for those aged twelve to fourteen, where adolescent bodies might be first "bronzed by the sun in Provence, Roussillon or Languedoc," and finally "colonies of application," where those aged fourteen to twenty-one would be primed for cultivation of the soil and already equipped for a disciplined cultivation of the self.[11]

Such a range of comparisons is dissonant to students of European colonial cultures for it references and revives long-buried connections. What were once politically tethered terms—components of related but diverse reformist state projects—now appear as mere homonyms dislocated from each other and from the commensurabilities that once linked them. Much of the scholarly space in which studies of the colonial are profiled and concentrated, the field of "colonial studies," with its abiding focus on late nineteenth- through mid-twentieth-century European empires, misses those untidy connections. Its default model of empire fails to address the fact that ambiguous terms and opaque criteria for intervention have been fundamental structural features of European and non-European imperial states alike. Indeed the reference to "refiguring" in our title is intended to address a refiguring of several sorts: of our approaches to and understandings of empire, shifting both our analytics and the scope and scale of imperial forms to which we pose our queries.

The fact that French commissions on the education of impoverished children could look at once to the Saratov colonies on the Volga and to Crimean colonies in the Russian south alongside those established in the Amur basin on the Chinese frontier underscores the inclusive and changing breadth of their comparative frames.[12] This dynamic, nonstatic quality demands that we attend less to what empires are than to what they did and do, for these transformative practices altered their relations with other empires and with their own subject populations. Cross-imperial knowledge acquisition and application included a poaching of practices, a searching for new technologies, an invigorating of categories of exception and difference, and a competing for status. Such cross-imperial scrutiny shares recognition of the portability of practices and ideas, be it in form or in goal, across imperial systems and within them.

French social planners and state officials did not imagine that all these sorts of colon were the same. In this mid-nineteenth-century moment, when officials were as preoccupied with getting rid of certain segments of the metropolitan population as they were with conquest, some distinctions were in flux, and others were not yet operative. That historians offer discrepant and confused accounts of the numbers of colon who left for Algeria between 1848 and 1851—and the conditions under which they did so—is itself instructive. According to some, "14,000 Parisian workers" were sent by decree in September 1848, followed by three thousand "republicans" after the 1851 coup d'état of Louis Napoleon.[13] Others state that in 1851 the Second Republic arrested nearly fifteen thousand people, of which six thousand were "deported Republicans."[14] How many of those arrested were also deported as "political undesirables" is hard to say: "disorder" in Paris led to 450 political deportations to the Algerian penal colony of Lambese, and deportations to at least six former *colonies agricoles* newly converted into *colonies penitentiaires* (penal colonies).[15] Colonists from Malta, Italy, and Spain as well as "other Parisian workers encouraged...to emigrate voluntarily" were added to the mix of French soldiers established in *villages-militaires* in 1840.[16] Thousands more were recruited under an intensive colonization program to make colon out of a lethal mix of unprepared urban poor alternately referred to as the unemployed (*les sans-travail*), the insurgent (*les revoltés*), and the rootless and dispossessed (*déraciné*). The changing connotations of colon reflect this movement of people and projects. Here the colony emerges less as a geographic space than as a political one with directionality.

How ethnic, religious, and social differences mattered varied, as did the management of these differences. Administrative attention to social differentiation and the complex taxonomies intended to secure it did not necessarily congeal only around racial distinctions or instill the intensities of political anxiety associated with late nineteenth-century European colonialisms. In the 1850s, frames of imperial reference were mobile and migratory, moving across geographic and political space as well as institutional arrangements. This was true of Ottoman and US empires as well as European ones.[17] As social imaginaries and political arrangements shifted focus from empire and emperor to empire and nation, they were joined by new programs and policies of containment and expansion. Paradoxically, these new projects required both the production and protection of social categories and social kinds, and often anxious defense of such distinctions by those they privileged.

In this volume we see analytic purchase in staying close to the specifics of these arrangements. Still, our collective effort is as much about what such imaginaries afford for thinking beyond the skewed templates that have guided study of imperial governance, forms of sovereignty, and their acquisitive states. We begin, therefore, with a French genealogy, not to dwell in iconic European models but rather to underscore what has shaped both scholarship on empire and its frames of reference. Scholars from many quarters now stress the problems inherent in taking Europe as either a historical or conceptual paradigm for how empire—if not the world—works.[18] The strong undertow of European history and its epistemic frames has methodological consequences as well. Challenging this pull requires more than acknowledging its ubiquity. It requires new assessments of what have been treated as defining coordinates of imperial rule. A number of the essays included here question both earlier imperial logics and the contemporary analytics in which past coeval empires such as the British and Ottoman or Dutch and Japanese are not considered equally (or even) imperial.

The critical points raised by our brief turn to the ambiguities of the term *colonie*, then, are not confined to the French context. First, these ambiguities capture a range of social experimentation that would later be rendered as incommensurate kinds. Etymological entries for *colon* (cultivator, pioneer, colonist, settler, boarder, camper) convey a truncated genealogy of the social forms represented by the term.[19] Second, these ambiguities suggest a differently circumscribed meaning and space of "colonization" that would later be narrowed in common convention. Third, such ambiguities counter the prevailing narrative of "Western Europe as the ultimate model of the advanced and enlightened civilization."[20] Instead, they move toward a shared analytical space for forms of rule not predicated on a West versus the Rest dichotomy or on a Victorian India model.

ON AN ANALYTICS OF IMPERIAL FORMATIONS

We focus less on empires than on imperial formations. The term "imperial formations" is common, but the analytics of our choice is not. We think here of Louis Althusser and Etienne Balibar's use of "social formation" to signal the "concrete complex whole comprising economic practice, political practice, and ideological practice at a certain place and stage of development."[21] We include cultural practice in this configuration to stretch our concerns to a broader set of practices structured in dominance. Raymond Williams's sense of a "formation" as a social form suggesting "effective movements and tendencies" that have "variable and often oblique relations to formal institutions" also motivates us here.[22] We take up the notion of imperial formation as a critical analytic to underscore not the inevitable rise and fall of empires, but the active and contingent process of their making and unmaking.[23] Our interest lies less in institutions and fixed ideologies than in the prevalence of blurred genres of rule and partial sovereignties. Empires may be "things," but imperial formations are not. Imperial formations are polities of dislocation, processes of dispersion, appropriation, and displacement. They are dependent both on moving categories and populations. Not least, they are dependent on material and discursive postponements and deferrals: the "civilizing mission," imperial guardianship, and manifest destiny are all promissory notes of transformation. As states of deferral, imperial formations manage and produce their own exceptions, which can be easily named: conditions of delayed sovereignty, temporary intervention, conditional tutelage, military takeover in the name of humanitarian intervention, or violent intervention in the name of human rights. Imperial formations thrive on deferred autonomy, meted out to particular populations incrementally, promised to those in whose lives they intervene. They create new subjects that must be relocated to be productive and exploitable, dispossessed to be modern, disciplined to be independent, converted to be human, stripped of old cultural bearings to be citizens, coerced to be free.

Imperial formations are not steady states, but states of becoming, macropolities in states of solution and constant formation.[24] Several of the tacit notions that have informed characterizations of European colonialisms over the last two decades distract us from appreciating the features that imperial forms may share. One such problem is a fixation on empires as clearly bounded geopolities, as if the color-coded school maps of a clearly marked British empire were renderings of real distinctions and firmly fixed boundaries. As Thongchai Winichakul has observed, however, imperial maps were a "model for, rather than model of, what they purported to represent."[25] Imperial ventures are and have been both more and less marked, opaque, and visible in ways that scholars of European empires have not always registered or sought to see.

It is not coincidence, however, that some models of empire have a tunnel vision quality to them, for such perspectives are, in part, scripted and endorsed by imperial states themselves. Rather than considering empire as a steady state, we posit these formations as ongoing polities of dislocation, dependent on refiguring spaces and populations, on systemic recruitments, transfers, and promotions of governmental and nongovernmental agents, on the reassignment of native military forces away from their colonies of origin, on a redistribution of peoples and resources in territories, contiguous and overseas.[26] Imperial formations may present themselves as fixed cartographies of rule. This volume insists that they are not. At any one time, the designated boundaries were not necessarily the sole force fields in which imperial formations operated or their limits of governance and authorization.[27] With this in mind, we turn attention in this volume to a range of imperial actors—to people on the fringes of empires as well as at their centers, to designated subjects as well as colonial administrators, to those with companion and countervailing motivations to empire, and to those who reside at the categorical edges of the imperial.

Gradations of sovereignty and sliding scales of differentiation are hallmark features of imperial formations. The British empire was not merely "in" India;[28] its historical coordinates pass through Wales, Scotland, Protestant Ireland, the Caribbean, and the Americas.[29] Nor was the French empire, as Frederick Cooper contends in this volume, located in the colonies; the French empire was a single but differentiated France, in which Napoleon's continental expansion was part of an older and more recent pattern of expansion overseas. As Ann Stoler has argued, "blurred genres of rule are not empires in distress but imperial polities in active realignment and reformation."[30] The insight that different "semblances of sovereignty" characterize the relationships of both domestic native American peoples and the inhabitants of US overseas territories, as legal historian Alexander Aleinikoff holds, has a wider relevance than just to the United States.[31]

What is striking in the historical record is not the absence of these liminal and disparate zones but the exceptional treatment and scholarly misrecognition of them. Ambiguous zones, partial sovereignty, temporary suspensions of what Hannah Arendt was later to call "the right to have rights," provisional impositions of states of emergency, promissory notes for elections, deferred or contingent independence, and "temporary" occupations—these conditions lie at the heart of a broad range of imperial projects.[32] If the expanse of spatial sovereignty is unstable so are the terms for the inclusion and exclusion of peoples. Imperial formations are founded on sliding scales of basic rights, as Jane Burbank shows so clearly in the case of Russia.[33] Such conditions required constant judicial and political reassessments of the criteria for affiliation, distinctions that invariably exceeded any clear division between ruler and ruled.

Sometimes empire-states were intent to establish their order by clarifying borders but as often they were not. Agents of imperial rule invested in, exploited, and demonstrated strong stakes in the proliferation of geopolitical ambiguities.[34] The observation invites a re-viewing of what counts as imperial expansion and what does not. Those terms signaling the unclarified sovereignties of US imperial breadth—unincorporated territories, trusteeships, protectorates, possessions—are not the blurred edges of what more "authentic," nonvirtual, visible empires look like, but variants on them.[35] Uncertain domains of jurisdiction and ad hoc exemptions from the law on the basis of race and cultural difference are guiding and defining imperial principles, as students of colonial history should know well.

Edward Said's insistence that specific empires claim to be unlike all others critically identifies discourses of exceptionalism as part of the discursive apparatus of empires themselves.[36] We extend Said's insight: imperial states by definition operate as states of exception that vigilantly produce exceptions to their principles and exceptions to their laws.[37] What scholars have sometimes taken to be aberrant empires—the American, Russian, or Chinese empires—may indeed be quintessential ones, consummate producers of excepted populations, excepted spaces, and their own exception from international and domestic laws.

As we expand our notion of imperial force fields to early modern forms of empire, to imperialisms without colonialism, to empires by other names, and to imperial formations outside of Europe, efforts to do so without sacrificing historical specificity and theoretical validity come with risks. If so many of the elements long considered imperial are called into question here, the reader might rightly ask, What are the attributes that still mark something as imperial?

There is consensus on some points, but differences in emphasis remain. In this volume, most of the contributors agree on inequitable treatment, hierarchical relations, and unequal rule.[38] Fernando Coronil insists that empire is a concept that identifies "relatively large geopolitical formations that establish dominion by hierarchically differentiating populations across transregional boundaries."[39] All agree that the forms of domination and exploitation go beyond economic exploitation and geopolitical domination, that empire-states, as Frederick Cooper writes, "determine the forms in which opposition could gain a foothold and the terms in which (cotemporaneous and our current) analysis of colonization could be articulated."[40] Jane Burbank turns to the vast "organizing capacity" of imperial states, to the scope and scale of intervention, violent or otherwise. A hierarchical sense of difference organizes and also informs imperial practice. As Ussama Makdisi demonstrates, American missionaries in the Ottoman Middle East believed in "the righteousness of their cause [and] the inevitability of their triumph."[41]

One thing that these perspectives share is an emphasis on how knowledge is organized and conceived. Imperial projects are predicated on and produce epistemological claims that are powerful political ones. Coronil aptly sums up a prevailing premise of new scholarship on empire: it is "the privilege of empires to make their histories appear as History."[42] Just how they do so may vary, but "modalities of representation predicated on dissociations that separate relational histories, that reify cultural differences and turn difference into hierarchy" are critical epistemological features with deep political effects.[43] Dissociated histories sometimes appear blatant, once identified, as in the case of Haiti's part in the French Revolution;[44] sometimes the lineaments that connect remain harder to track, as Peter Perdue argues for the unintended endorsements of subsequent racial politics by successive Qing emperors[45] or as Nicholas Dirks contends in the case of the missed importance of empire for the development of modern sovereignty.[46] But as the cases in this volume underscore, imperial polities are not, as we once imagined them, based on fixed forms and secure relations of inequity: they produce unstable relationships of colonizer and colonized, of citizen to subject, and unequal struggles over the forms of inclusion and the principles of differentiation.[47]

There is nothing comprehensive about this list of imperial attributes, nor is definitional satisfaction the goal of this particular volume.[48] In fact, we focus in some sense on the very opposite; namely, on disparate nomenclatures as well as shared ones, on contexts in which "national interest" and "human rights" are the terms that replace and efface imperial intervention; on situations in which unequal rule corresponds to the imperial attributes mentioned above but those polities call themselves by other names. The varied terms empire-states give to their interventions and forms of sovereignty may stymie scholarly attempts at definition, but these creative vocabularies too are part of the imperial game.

Claiming exceptionalism and investing in strategic comparison are fundamental elements of an imperial formation's commanding grammar. As we expand the imperial forms to which we look, it is increasingly clear that overt comparison and claims to exceptionalism went hand in hand.[49] At the same time that architects and agents of empire sought comparison, they claimed exceptional status for the imperial ventures of which they were a part. In the cases of the Ottoman, Chinese, Dutch, US, and Russian empires most notably, searches for comparison and claims to exceptionalism were not contradictions but compatible conventions. Comparison provided the legitimating grounds for exceptional status, immunity, and exemption from international law—hallmark features of imperial statecrafts. Thus our widened perspective underscores the common emphasis on exceptionalism across imperial time and space. Alongside the inclination to appraise and compare, to borrow and share across empires, was—and is—the claim to exceptionalism that occupies academic projects as much as imperial states.

THE POLITICS OF IMPERIAL COMPARISONS

The lexical intricacies of *colonie* provide insistent reminders that some of these features taken to be fundamental to late nineteenth-century European empires at an earlier moment were particular, distinct, and not long entrenched. Those features that provide the template of European colonial empires and the scholarship about them—sharp distinctions between metropole and colony, an abiding preoccupation with race over other exclusions, the incessant proliferations of distinction in the pursuit of profit—look less like imperial universals when considered across a thicker swath of imperial ground.[50] Our goal, however, is not to simply turn universals into particulars, but to question the logic supporting universal claims. We specifically, therefore, bring together scholars of European and non-European empires—British, Chinese, Dutch, French, Japanese, Ottoman, Qing, Russian, Soviet, Spanish, and US—to reexamine the theories and imaginaries, the histories and politics upon which our understandings of colonies and colonialism, empires and imperialism have been and continue to be worked out.[51]

We use the term "colonial studies" with a specific body of literature in mind: that which developed out of Edward Said's enabling challenge in the late 1970s to put specific forms of cultural production and regimes of truth at the creative center of imperial politics. We are less concerned with Said's intervention, one that pointedly included US empire in its purview, than with subsequent scholarship that has focused almost solely on the ways in which certain European states—France, England, and the Netherlands most notably—framed their imperial projects.[52] Several of the contributors here—Dirks, Cooper, and Stoler—are among those whose work at one time steered colonial studies in that prevailing direction.[53] Anthropology and history were not the only disciplines interested in European colonialisms. The impetus came from postcolonial theory as well, from cultural studies, English departments, and philosophers whose take on empire derived from an unacknowledged and often unexamined European prototype.[54] Many analyses are still wed to this constricted model, not least new studies of non-European empires and the sorts of relations those polities establish with their subject populations.

Insisting that the structures of imperial rule should not be drawn solely from late nineteenth-century Europe invites entry into far wider geographic and historical fields.[55] Imperial agents themselves employed ideas from earlier or other polities, albeit often with different intentions and results. While they modeled their practices on those of other polities, their modeling was less a wholesale replication of practices than a selective bricolage. Such administrative work entailed a refunctioning of practices in different places and to different ends. Imperial architects talked about models, but comprehensive borrowing was rarely what they had in mind.

What might be awkwardly termed "modular modeling" is a more accurate description of what imperial agents actually did in specific contexts and at specific times. This term implies piecemeal projects that partially adopted certain practices while carefully leaving other parts behind. What they retained is of as much interest as what they discarded. The modular quality of political forms, a characteristic Benedict Anderson has identified in the making of nineteenth-century nationalisms and that Frederick Cooper and Ann Stoler have used loosely to describe the fashioning of new colonial projects, captures such comparative labor in the uneven stratigraphies of the imperial formations themselves.[56]

Attention to modularity foregrounds convergence and counter-intuitive comparisons: a French empire that looked to Russia and Australia, a Russian one that looked to Spanish Creole communities in Latin America, a Qing empire that looked to the Ottomans and the Portuguese, and an Ottoman empire that was keenly aware of American missionary activities in Hawai`i. Attention to such lateral, oblique, and global visions does something more: It undercuts both developmental and linear models. It allows us to think with multi-dimensional movement rather than with the one-dimensional clarity of maps; with different densities of concern and with different surfaces coming into contact.

Comparison, however, was strategic and situational, relevant and revelatory in some times, irrelevant and to be avoided at others. Our analytic turn, thus, does not aim to resurrect a comparative imperial studies based on national character, as Cooper and Stoler, among others, criticized over a decade ago.[57] Nor are we intent to provide a model or formula for how these comparisons should be carried out. Rather, our sights are set on developing questions that treat comparison as an *active political verb.* Those questions might include when comparisons are enlisted and set aside, for what reasons, by whom, and to what effect. What commensurabilities are required and what differences are effaced? What kinds of new knowledge are mobilized in making new comparative claims? Such questions do specific analytic labor: they demand reflection on the work that comparison does as an act of governance and as a located political act of analysis.[58]

Inviting attention to the politics of comparison does not mean that we expect these comparative ventures to be pursued in parallel ways. Nor do the contributors here do so; in fact, some do not explicitly compare at all. Some attend to comparison and convergence at the same time. Some look more to shared imaginaries and intentions, others to shared structural consequences and economic effects. Nor is there consensus as to whether we should be comparing those policies envisioned but unrealized, or those that were effectively enforced.

We call for an appreciation that the shifting references for what constitutes comparison are at once historical and political issues.[59] They are not benign. The fact that some contributors found their materials more amenable to comparison than others is also due to the nature of archival formations themselves. Dutch authorities who sought comparisons with Australia's colonization of its hinterlands or with Spanish authorities in the Americas rarely did so across the board. Comparisons were invoked to legitimate acts of violence and interdiction and to counter specific social reforms. Thus the will to compare on the part of scholars may be thwarted by the nature of archival organization, by the idiosyncratic contexts and events for which comparative frames were enlisted in the techniques of governance.

THE NATIONAL, THE GLOBAL, THE IMPERIAL

If colonial studies has produced a representational archive of empire that seems to mimic that of well-bounded nation-states, it has also generated debate about the relation between empire and nation. Frederick Cooper argues that we have overemphasized the national impulse for empire,[60] while Prasenjit Duara contends that we have not recognized that impulse enough.[61] Duara argues that as developed in Manchukuo, the prevalent modern imperial form is empire without colonialism, that is, empire beholden to a nation-state project rather than to an expansionist or territorial one. For the most part, empire has been viewed as an extension of nation-states, not as another way or even a prior way of organizing a polity. Irene Silverblatt counters with the argument that nations and nationalism were "born from colonial processes."[62] Cooper also sees it otherwise: even those model empires of western Europe were not simply extensions of a home polity.[63] In the case of France, he maintains that empire was not seen as a monolithic or even coherent project, but as a series of projects, of relationships with different peoples and polities. Inclusion and differentiation were not stable across French imperial territories, but widely varied and subject to debate.

The common notion that imperial formations build on old differences and foster new ones underwrites much of recent imperial historiography. Yet empire-states are not always invested in escalating differences between social groups. Using the case of Ottoman religious tolerance and American missionary intolerance, Ussama Makdisi contends that neither Ottoman nor American colonial sensibilities were secular, liberal, or modern. If the Ottomans tolerated difference, Peter Perdue shows how Qing China accommodated difference through a series of shifting paradigms for civilizing projects. In the case of Russia, Jane Burbank contends that the right to difference grounded imperial organization. In assessing that logic, Burbank suggests that we pay more attention to what constitutes an imperial habitus, "the unrecognized self-reproducing and adjusting field of practiced empire."[64] Adeeb Khalid, however, argues that what looks like colonial difference in the Soviet Union may be part of several different state projects, only one of which—the imperialism of benevolence—is indebted to empire or its state practices.

It is not only nation-state projects that get melded with imperial ones. Those policies, personnel, and practices of multinational corporations and globalizing technologies can become so entangled and embedded that they seem indistinguishable as well. However, there is a newness to globalization that no one would want to disavow in its present form. But imperialism is not globalization. We do not suggest that emergent forms of global networks reiterate familiar networks from earlier nineteenth- and twentieth-century imperial forms. Those emerging now are animated by new forms of global consumption, marketing, and communication and should not be reduced to earlier forms that depended on different technologies of production and exchange. What Arjun Appadurai calls "the rush to history," the refusal to reckon with what is located in *this* moment, should grab our collective attention.[65] We wrestle here with how new innovations make room for and may build on specific recuperations, longer genealogies of which they are a part. As Inderpal Grewal similarly observes, US strategies for accumulating global power were dual—first, the generation of new forms of regulation across "transnational connectivities," and second, the recuperation of "historical inequalities generated by earlier phases of imperialism,"[66] such as "older colonial legacies" surrounding racial categories.[67] As Foucault reminds us, however, the word *legacy* can conceal more than it reveals. We press such connections and recuperations to identify which features of earlier imperial forms were most durable and then ask why.[68] In the present day, such connections are made not only through the traces of past imperial circuits but also through new transnational routes and global networks.

EMPIRE BEYOND EUROPE

We are not alone in questioning European models of empire and their late nineteenth-century templates. Recent works in the burgeoning field of empire studies take as their vantage point the Qing rather than the British,[69] move from Saint Petersburg through the Americas to the Russian steppe rather than from Amsterdam to Batavia,[70] or start in Korea, Manchuria, or Taiwan and look to Japan.[71] Such studies do not just rein in European models. Rather, these vantage points reset our temporal clocks at the same time that they redirect our geographic attention. The Qing empire is historically deep, cotemporaneous with not just modern Dutch and French empires but with the early modern Spanish empire in the Americas.[72] This temporal stretch of empire demands a rethinking of colonialism's "modern" roots, as Laura Hostetler and Irene Silverblatt respectively argue for Qing China and Spanish Peru.[73] Geographic shifts generate new questions about imperial practices and effects. How does our understanding of the civilizing mission change upon recognition that the civilizing mission is as Chinese a marker of empire as it is a European one?[74] Does the politics of sympathy that so characterizes the benevolent projects of European colonial reforms produce similar distributions of sentiment or wholly different ones in other locales?[75] In posing these questions, our goal is not so much to provincialize Europe or a European form of empire[76] as it is to push our clarifications of imperial formations outside *and* inside of Europe.

Attention to imperial formations during their moments of transition is also on our agenda. Empires may be simultaneous or successive, that is, geographically adjacent such as Portuguese Macau and British Hong Kong or temporally successive such as Burma under the British and the Japanese. In such imperial configurations, cooperation appears as valued a strategy as comparison and competition. We clearly see this in Tibet, where cooperation, comparison, and competition were all tactics "against empire, not just of it."[77] British imperial reach in Tibet turned into American imperial shepherding, both of which engendered Chinese imperial action; on the against-empire side, non-colonized Tibetans residing in India drew on pan-Asian anti-imperialist models (from India, China, and Japan) to critique British rule there.[78] New work on such multiplicities of empires includes Korean experiences in writing history between successive periods of Chinese and Japanese reign,[79] Mongolian experiences of a community split between independent Mongolia and the People's Republic of China (PRC),[80] simultaneous Indian experiences of rule by the British, French, and Portuguese,[81] and Eritrean and Somali experiences under Italian, British, and Ethiopian rule.[82]

What changes as empires shift? As Sudan, for example, transited from Ottoman rule to shared Egyptian and British colonialism, with brief interludes of Belgian and French rule,[83] the Sudanese people (themselves a diverse population) lived with and through these changes that were not of their own making. Complications and contradictions not only plague imperial rule but also get played out between metropole and colony. For the Sudanese, Egyptian anxieties surrounding their status as "colonized colonizers" had real effects felt in everyday life, in administrative decisions, as well as in relations between the two countries today.[84] The crafting of an everyday of empire is a joint but not shared project, one that continues beyond any supposed "end" of empire. Certain imperial dispositions and categories more easily outlast the legal and political forms of empire than others. Turning to this particularly shifting ground of empire, to an exploration of how colonized peoples maneuvered within and between empires, suggests a new set of questions. How did ordinary people conjugate the dislocative tense of empire? To whom did it matter when street names changed but property lines did not? What imprint did successive empires leave on a population? As with Sudan, Tibet's twentieth-century history is one of multiple empires—British, Chinese, and American.[85] For both Tibet and Sudan, our histories are written in and of the geopolitical haze generated by a century or more of competing (and at times cooperating) imperial interventions. In both cases, current political situations require an analysis of empire in the present tense as well as the past imperfect one.

In Taiwan, a similar politics of dislocation has a different set of consequences. Drawn into the imperial realm of the Qing empire, colonized by Japan, and claimed by the People's Republic of China, Taiwan is not widely recognized as independent, nor is Taiwan a member of the United Nations.[86] This erratic genealogy is not alone in unsettling attachments to and estrangements from communities in and out of Taiwan. The very categories of empire and colony are similarly disruptive to contemporary Taiwanese reckonings of imperial pasts. Neither Japanese nor Qing colonialism in Taiwan was recognized as such by European states. Ironically, despite Japan's efforts at global political significance through colonial rule in Korea,[87] Japanese colonialism was not considered equal to European colonialism by Western viewers. As a consequence, "decolonization" was not applied in the Japanese context. With no explicitly named decolonization process for the Japanese empire as there was for European empires,[88] there was also no public discourse on empire and its aftermath in either Taiwan or Japan (or in Taiwan and Qing China).[89]

In China, as elsewhere, imperial vocabularies have a particular politics. Successive polities—Chinese, Mongol, Manchu/Qing—are unproblematically labeled "empires." Twentieth-century China, however, can neither comfortably be considered "colonized" in the time of European empire nor "colonizer" as the People's Republic of China.

Tani Barlow explains this trend as one generated as much by claims of both successive Chinese regimes and multiple European empires to exception status as by Cold War academic politics (as played out in the "Fairbank School" of China scholars).[90] The defining of China as neither colonized nor colonizer reproduces the idea that colonial empire is a European domain. A new generation of scholars argues, however, that twentieth-century China was not outside the European imperial sphere, that is, not "outside the 'real' colonial world."[91]

Colonial histories rarely play out as originally intended. Peter Perdue contends that the Qing emperors ironically laid the groundwork for current tensions of national and racial difference in the People's Republic of China.[92] Despite the pan-Qing adherence to a model of universal culturalism, Perdue argues that added together, different policies of each emperor contributed to the fashioning of a "racial definition of the state and the people it ruled."[93] This contradiction within the Qing empire has its parallel in the visible complications and contradictions of the British colonial project in Qing China.[94] In his studies of British imperial "pedagogy" in China, James Hevia maintains that China was not peripheral to European colonizing or globalizing forces.[95] Where Hevia claims that China was an important part of the European colonial world, and Perdue contends that Qing China was an imperial power (and not just a "Chinese" empire habitually set apart from others), Laura Hostetler maintains that Qing China was a colonial power as well as an expansionist imperial one.[96] How might we analyze these parallel British and Chinese colonialisms? Was the "colonial" of Western activities in nineteenth- and early twentieth-century China the same as that of the Qing empire, which ruled from 1644 through 1911? Is it that familiar features of administration and organization—the naming and managing of difference, the claims to exceptional status, the strategies of comparison—mark each? Or is it not so much this similarity that matters as it is the deployment of these features, the means through which they are put to specific ends?

The Manchu Court's interest in European knowledge systems complicates the received historiography of Chinese–European interactions.[97] The Kangxi Emperor's techniques and philosophies of rule were neither Manchu nor Chinese nor best understood as European. Instead, Hostetler suggests that Qing practices of geographic and ethnographic mapping are best understood in a temporal continuum—as early modern as opposed to indigenous or modern.[98] Assigning a temporal classification to these practices places Qing and European imperial technologies within the same analytical and historical realm, rather than within a binary or derivative cultural or geographic framework. Qing China was not isolated from the rest of the world but, as with other imperial formations of the time, participated in, responded to, and shaped similar world forces.

Such specific histories should direct how we write about empire and what we do and do not assume about its shared features. As the nation form increasingly "captured" history,[99] imperial histories became nationalized in manners that obscured specific aspects of imperial formations or even obscured them altogether. The nation "erases" empire in service to new strategies for managing difference, highlighting national unity, for example, rather than imperial variations among a state's population.[100] Moreover, the historiographies one must write with—and against—are rarely confined to any single empire. As Fernando Coronil demonstrates, current articulations of US imperialism are often contingent on the claims and effects of other imperial formations.[101] One such effect was the enabling of mid-twentieth-century US imperialism by the period of European decolonization.[102] For both the United States and the People's Republic of China, the anticolonial and anti-imperial rhetoric associated with decolonization deflected charges of imperialism at the same time that it facilitated new imperial projects.[103] Yet not all anti-imperialism generated a new imperialism. In the Soviet Union, Adeeb Khalid sees not a socialist empire but an "activist, interventionist state that seeks to sculpt its citizenry in an ideal image."[104] Khalid's argument regarding common Soviet citizenship builds his case against Soviet empire and is parallel to other arguments that citizenship is not possible within empire.[105] Carole McGranahan takes a different stance—that while it may rarely be a genuine privilege of empire, citizenship "does not rule out colonization."[106]

THE PRODUCTION AND PROTECTION OF DIFFERENCE

Students of European imperial formations have long taken the construction of difference and consolidation of distinctions as central to the political viability and organization of those polities. But from a non-European center, that hallmark feature is more open to question. All empires are composite polities of varied human social forms, but not all are invested in producing differences to the same degree. New studies of Chinese, Russian, and Ottoman empires set our sights on a different tension: that between the production of difference and its protection, resting less on exclusion alone than on a principled tolerance of religious, cultural, and linguistic variations. The production of difference in the Ottoman case operated in different manners and over a far greater span of time than did the nineteenth-century European empires that have so preoccupied colonial studies.

Imperial formations practiced tolerance and discrimination to different degrees. This statement would be less striking were it not for the fact that studies of European empire rarely imagine the concept of "tolerance" as a relevant one. Ussama Makdisi traces a genealogy of tolerances that turns conventional historical accounts on their heads. Ottomans accommodated religious difference, unlike US imperial agents, who more often refused different forms of faith. Here the "politics of comparison" is played out at several critical levels: one, between Ottoman and US agents of empire but also among different and seemingly incommensurate US imperial ventures themselves. US officials and missionaries viewed their choice of strategies in the Middle East in direct light of what they could not accomplish among Native Americans in the 1830s.

As importantly, Makdisi's essay confronts the task of thinking creatively about convergent and dependent histories. It is not only that failed efforts in one place open the possibility for another venture: traces of that earlier, seemingly distant Native American history are plaited through the later Ottoman one, the knowledge of one shaping how historical actors once knew and how historians today can know the other. Makdisi's essay demonstrates the vast gap in understandings of religious difference between Ottoman communities and Protestant missionaries. The Ottomans embraced tolerance of different religious communities under assumptions of hierarchy, rigid separation, and no crossing of boundaries. Missionaries, on the other hand, based on their experience with Native Americans in the United States, assumed uncritically the superiority of Anglo-Saxon peoples. They embraced a transformational ideology that stressed the need for total conversion from one faith to another and saw the Ottoman empire as filled with oppressed people who longed for liberation from their backward, stagnant religious and social environment. Focusing on the ambiguous case of one individual, As'ad Shidyaq, who seemed to have converted to Protestantism, Makdisi's account underscores the dramatic intersection of different visions of what imperial subsumption entails.

Imperial formations neither imagined uniform sorts of rule nor subscribed to uniform vocabularies. Thus they demand that our analytic lexicon stretch to these shifting spaces as well. Jane Burbank argues that what constitutes a "composite state" or "composite empire" in Russia does just that, offering a compelling vocabulary with which to think about the enduring and varied politics of difference and particularity that guided some imperial polities more than others.[107] Key to her analysis is recognition of a differential distribution of rights based on the granting of privilege by the state to the various groups that comprised it. The tsarist state kept control of a polity containing extraordinary degrees of cultural difference without creating comprehensive classifications coherently organized around religion, ethnicity, territory, or language. Equally, its legal codes allowed local courts to recognize a range of customary practice. Stressing imperial practice instead of official ideology, Burbank highlights the great diversity of the empire instead of the later monotonal autocracy of a centralizing ideology dominated by Moscow.

The accommodation of difference, the importance of legal categorizations of subjects' privileges, and the "ongoing tension between universalizing, homogenizing ends and pragmatic differentiated practices" are key issues that empires beyond Europe bring into relief. What Burbank calls the "pragmatic politics of social inclusion" ensured long life for the Russian empire in ways that demand we ask why and how people chose to participate in it. Even rebellions against the imperial order, for example, often only claimed to reassert privileges guaranteed by the tsar and did not try to overthrow the tsarist state. The persuasions and comforts of habitus explain this in part, but most provocatively, Burbank posits an "imperial social contract" that may account for the enduring qualities of an empire-state, a social contract that not only allows but also actively supports social particularity.

If from a Russian perspective, one could hold "difference as normal," from a Soviet perspective it was decidedly not. Adeeb Khalid, impatient with the quick rush to write Soviet history as an imperial one, makes a strong case, from the vantage point of Central Asia, for why an expanded notion of empire may be neither accurate nor appropriate. Khalid demonstrates how the Soviets broke sharply with tsarist accommodation by introducing, with great violence, a radical modernizing project designed to pull all the Soviet Union's diverse peoples toward common Soviet citizenship in pursuit of the ultimate goal of building communism. He denies, however, that this developmental project was Russian imperialism. Throughout Central Asia, Soviet goals overlapped with those of many native intellectuals. Unlike the historiography on European empires in which the distinction between citizen and subject is more often taken for granted, Khalid reminds us that the threshold between the two is wider and more ambiguous than is often acknowledged.

Khalid identifies a critical distinction between imperial technologies of rule that operated in nineteenth-century Russia and those used by a Soviet macropolity. He asks not how to assess empire outside of Europe, or how to reassess European empires, but when and why the category of empire is historically applicable. "Where," he queries, "does empire end and other forms of nonrepresentative or authoritarian polities begin?" Khalid's skeptical approach to the current vogue of colonial and postcolonial theory in Russian studies provides welcome pause to our overall project. External domination is not a guaranteed indicator of imperialism, nor do once imperial polities seamlessly morph into new imperial formations. Thus territories once colonized by Russia were not simply converted into Soviet colonies under the USSR. Instead, Khalid argues that the genealogy he traces for the Soviet state is not an imperial but a modernist one in which the "activist, interventionist state…seeks to sculpt its citizenry in an ideal image."[108] Khalid's attention to the politics of the label "empire" in the tsarist/Soviet context further focuses our attention on post–World War II, Cold War framings of imperialism. As he states, the "lines connecting empires to mere states are not easy to discern."

Why has the passage from empire to nation produced such a violently racist ideology? Peter Perdue asks this critical comparative question, but in a way that students of European imperial history might pose quite differently. He looks at how Han Chinese writers in the 1900s drew new sharp distinctions between themselves and their Manchu rulers, mobilizing a virulent form of racial nationalism. Three converging global processes supported their project. These were the latent discourse of racial exclusion in the Chinese classical heritage, as reinterpreted by activist scholars and students at the end of the Qing Dynasty, global ideologies of scientific racialism, transmitted from Europe and the United States to China via Japan, and the experiences of Chinese overseas students and migrants in Japan, Southeast Asia, and the United States.

Chinese discussions of "barbarian" nomads had always alternated between visions of racial exclusion and cultural inclusion. The Qing Dynasty, as a Manchu conquest dynasty bringing both central Eurasian and Han peoples under a single imperial gaze, faced these tensions of empire in particularly heightened form. The late nineteenth century and first decade of the twentieth century sharpened the contradictions so much that the Manchu empire could not survive. Anti-Manchu mobilization was not simply a passing moment in Chinese nationalism but one of its foundational principles. These imperial contradictions, which echo European racial discourse since the sixteenth century, still persist in the nationality policy of the People's Republic of China today. Even though modern China perceives itself as heir to a two-thousand-year-old continuous imperial tradition, this tradition contains tensions in its ideology and practices that are fully recognizable as characteristics of more recent imperial formations across Eurasia.

RETHINKING BOUNDARIES, IMAGINARIES, EMPIRES

Imperialism is not always a colonial endeavor. Indeed, Prasenjit Duara contends that empire without colonialism is the "new imperialism" of the twentieth century. In his formulation, imperial strategies of the United States, the Soviet Union, and Japan depart from the organizing strategies of European colonial empires. Instead of colonial polities marked by difference and extraction, this new imperialism creates or incorporates peripheral states, modernizing and developing these regions in service to their own global aspirations. If Duara's specific case of Japanese Manchukuo fits this model, its extension to the

United States cannot sidestep difference or extraction so quickly, nor remain solely in the twentieth century. Fernando Coronil pushes us back further, calling for a renewed analytics of earlier American imperial formations. The multiple configurations of US imperialism index an imperial agility not beholden to the obligations of a publicly acknowledged empire. As Coronil argues, this flexibility is evident in a historical trio of imperialisms—colonial imperialism, national imperialism, and global imperialism—that may coexist within any one imperial power. These forms are not historically prior to one another. In the present world, he contends, all three forms are operative.

What sort of subjects does an empire without colonialism produce? What does it mean, as Carole McGranahan asserts, that "to be an imperial subject was not necessarily to be a colonial one?"[109] It is not just a matter of a direct versus indirect relationship to empire, nor a question of one status being more pernicious than the other. Both categories signal an imposed relationship to empire, an imposition that persists even as the categories and relationships themselves shift. In Latin America, Fernando Coronil suggests that the relationship to empire is experienced as "a common sense understanding of reality" in that US imperialism is an unmarked category.[110] As imperialism folds into everyday life, it is simultaneously diffuse and tangible. This does not always mean it is subtle. A short list of US imperial domains alone—Okinawa, Puerto Rico, Guam, the Philippines, and Iraq, to name but a few—provides evidence of this. It is not only the United States or other postcolonial empires that create and maintain noncolonial imperial subjects; European colonial empires did as well. Relationships to empire are never of one's own choosing, but there are individuals, whole communities even, who did choose to "live in someone else's empire."[111]

British India is one example: in the early twentieth century, the Himalayan hill town of Kalimpong had a diverse community of colonized and noncolonized peoples (along with a range of British citizens, Europeans, and Americans with varied connections to the empire). Tibetans resident in Kalimpong were imperial but not colonial subjects and thus were both safeguarded from and disadvantaged by a colonial list of rights and regulations. McGranahan's narrating of the dilemmas of Tibetan noncolonials in British India emphasizes the "troubled importance" of the imperial–colonial gap for subjects and imperial agents alike. McGranahan suggests that these sorts of imperial experiences are "out of bounds," that is, askew to received notions of where imperial interests lie. The noncolonial and other supposedly peripheral spaces of empire are not easily factored into standing discussions of colonialism, yet the unease they introduce is itself an important facet of imperial projects and scholarship. Given that the imperial boundaries were never limited solely to directly colonized territories, studying empire out of bounds should sharpen rather than dull the extent to which analytic frameworks capture imperial effects.

Categorical boundaries for such imperial formations extend in several different directions. In the period following decolonization, certain spaces opened for imperial subterfuge while others closed. Empire did not necessarily go away (as the terms *decolonization* and *postcolonial* each imply), but reorganized itself in forms publicly contrary to the classic European model of the nineteenth and twentieth centuries. As McGranahan specifies, decolonization provided a cover for new imperial formations, allowing them to refuse the labels "imperial" and "colonial." For Tibet, imperial formations of both the People's Republic of China and the United States fit this category. China's current rule of Tibet is certainly imperial, if not colonial, yet Chinese disavowals of either category go mostly unchallenged. If China established its anti-imperial stance as an anticapitalist one, then the United States asserts its anticolonialism in developmental terms. "Interventions" by the United States on behalf of development and democracy may be a different sort of imperialism, but one no less influential for Tibet than the interventions of British officials in earlier decades. For example, CIA efforts to support Tibetan resistance against China drew Tibetans into the orbit of yet another global power, whose interests were not the same as their own. Like many of the authors contributing to this volume, McGranahan zooms in on local manifestations of imperial force fields, showing how grand plans hatched in metropolitan centers turned into quite different projects on the ground and in the minds of Tibetan actors.

Such domestic disconnect might itself be a historical project, what Prasenjit Duara calls the "fault lines" of empire. In considering how Japanese interpreted the possibility of the incorporation of non-Japanese as equal citizens, calls for assimilation ran up against claims of the primacy of blood and race. This story—one familiar also to China, as Peter Perdue demonstrates—blurs boundaries between empires and nations. Duara sees imperialism as both a goal of nationalism and an important means of its formation. His focus on different forms of affiliation with empire underscores one of our central claims: that gradations of sovereignty are the rule of empire-states, not the exception. Duara places Manchukuo, the independent state established by Japan in northeast China in 1931, beyond the nominal borders of the Japanese empire or the Chinese nation-state. In this out-of-bounds sense Manchukuo resembled Tibet. In the realm of international geopolitics, what was Manchukuo? Was it a nominal nation not recognized by any state except Japan, a "client-state" lying between full colonies such as Korea and truly independent nations under military rule, or an inalienable part of China taken over by alien military conquest? Japan's multiple forms of domination in East Asia show many similarities to European forms elsewhere.

The developmental state was also an important component of many imperial formations. Japan set up Manchukuo as an independent nation but imposed on it programs of industrialization and agricultural development to serve its own military needs. Some Chinese, however, endorsed the Japanese project and worked with it to serve their own goals. Manchuria, a region that had only recently been colonized by Han Chinese prior to Japanese colonization, became a frontier space of experimentation, where imperial promoters invoked discourses of civilization, pan-Asianism, racial war, and pseudokinship to mobilize East Asians in a common enterprise. In Duara's view, Japanese practice actually recognized and promoted difference, in the form of popular religion and local ethnicity, more actively than did the Chinese nationalist regime, which tried to suppress both ethnic and religious diversity to strengthen a centralized state.

Such imperial circuits, the exchange of tactics and practices among imperial officials, past and present, persist with or without our debates over categories and classifications. Fernando Coronil asserts that imperial circuits were never rooted only in empire but also in the spaces between regions, in the networks of capitalism that linked empire to imperial territories as much as to colonial ones. Capitalism, he argues, is central to imperial formations in their present and past forms. Other volume authors, especially McGranahan (but also Perdue, Duara, and Khalid), find significant imperial activities beyond the bounds of European capitalism. Coronil's arguments, however, hinge on using capitalism to reassess categories of empire, to see where and how capitalism interlocks with imperialism as a political formation defined by domination, be it political or economic, formal or informal. Here it is not so much a question of the form of a given imperial formation but its effects among people trying to "make sense" of their "experiences of inequality, exploitation, and domination."[112]

Of the many blueprints available for assessing imperial formations and effects in the present, Coronil turns to September 11. Specifically, he thinks through the differences in September 11s—9/11/1973 in Chile and 9/11/2001 in the United States. If the September 11, 1973, overthrow of Salvador Allende with US complicity draws our attention to imperialism, the September 11, 2001, attacks in the United States draw our attention to empire. Coronil urges us to tend to both, to continue asking how much US imperial domination is founded on the denial of that history. His argument extends beyond the Americas to ask how to make the concept of imperialism "useful" in the present. As a first step, he suggests a broadening in chronological as well as geographical terms. In extending empire's temporal scope backward to sixteenth-century Spain and forward to the twentieth-century United States, those empires without colonies assume "singular relevance for considering the present."

NEW GENEALOGIES OF EMPIRE

Perhaps one of the most important contributions of colonial studies over the last decade is to reverse the trajectory that imagines the modern as a European invention. More than just "laboratories of modernity," as Gwendolyn Wright once called the colonies,[113] colonial situations demand a recasting of the relationship between empire and the modern. The contributions here take that impulse in new directions. Empire primed the modern state through expectations, habits, and tribulations. Bureaucracy, sovereignty, nationalism, and other attributes of the modern state were developed—at least in part—through imperial practices abroad and in response to the anxieties they often generated in Europe.

Rethinking statecraft is one critical way of unbracketing imperial practices from what has been cordoned off as European history proper. In so doing, this rethinking challenges claims to what constitutes the originary modern. New work on the Spanish empire pulls our modern genealogies back from the nineteenth century and south of northern Europe, while work on cornerstone empires such as those of Great Britain and France shows how empire threatened rather than merely supported or proved a training ground for the European state.

Irene Silverblatt sees the Spanish Inquisition as a key source of modern practices of statecraft.[114] The Inquisition, as implemented in colonial Peru, developed a large bureaucratic institution stuffed with paperwork as it attempted to purify the empire through well-documented legal procedures. At the same time, the Inquisition reflected deep-seated fears about disloyalty of subject populations as it mobilized the "pure-blooded" colonial elite against those with suspect allegiances. Hannah Arendt argued that totalitarian states in twentieth-century Europe used racial ideologies to support bureaucratic state interests in a racial system that could be traced back to Inquisitional Spain;[115] Silverblatt relocates those racial practices in colonial Spanish policies in Peru. The contest for control over the dreaded outsider, the heretic, or the racial alien, which lies at the heart of modern state formation, expressed itself very early in European colonial history.

Indeed, Silverblatt argues that we must trace modernity back to the seventeenth century to fully grasp the effect of colonialism on the European state. Shifting our focus from Britain and France to Spain and Portugal reveals that "the mix of 'civilizing,' bureaucracy, and race thinking at the heart of modern experience" developed out of the empires of southwest Europe.[116] Challenging this northern European dominance of the imperial form upsets genealogies of modernity that start both earlier and elsewhere. Silverblatt is careful to show the multiple ways that practices of the Spanish Inquisition fashioned a modernity suitable for Europe and the colonies, albeit one that has been overlooked in favor of other times and other empires, and of our experiences and relations.

Nicholas Dirks "writes empire back into the history of the West" in yet another fundamental way.[117] Suggesting that our understandings of sovereignty have been dislocated from their imperial underpinnings, he traces the expansion of the East India Company on the South Asian continent and the discussions in Parliament about the relationship between company authority and Crown control. Edmund Burke, as both political theorist of imperial relations and the prosecutor of Governor-General Warren Hastings for corruption in India in 1788, emerges as a critical figure enunciating the doctrines that closely linked British sovereign rule in India with the "ancient constitution" at home. Scandal was key to the development of the idea that empire was dangerous to British sovereignty and that the company needed to be reined in for sake of the fledgling nation. Dirks contends that this sense of empire as crisis for sovereignty has dropped out of our understandings of modern sovereignty.

In undoing common assumptions of British empire in India as the archetypal imperial form, Dirks sketches a new view of just how contentious imperial projects in India were for the metropolitan British state. The building of empire was neither orchestrated by officials in London nor consonant with their ideas of what empire should look like; instead, empire had an unexpectedly influential role in the shaping of modern Britain. In Dirks's formulation, however, imperialism and capitalism worked together to craft modern Britain in unforeseen ways. Rather than paving the way for the nation-state, imperial realities (if not ideals) threatened to disrupt the very bedrock of national sovereignty. Using the trial of Warren Hastings to demonstrate this potentiality of empire, Dirks further contends that attention to the erasure of empire evident in the trial and in the histories it has generated allows us to reanimate the story of both empire and sovereignty then and now.

As we have insisted, imperial formations generated ambiguous conceptual frames, social categories, and geographies on which they thrived. As Frederick Cooper writes, they were a "space that was neither sharply differentiated nor wholly unitary."[118] Such gaps and openings provided room—small though it may have been—for maneuvering within and beyond structures of domination and difference. Taking two points at the beginning and the end of France's trajectory between revolution (the Haitian-French Revolution, 1789–1804) and decolonization after World War II, Cooper shows that at both times French leaders were not thinking of France as a singular nation-state ruling dominated colonies, but as one presiding over multiple units, each with a different relationship to ruling institutions. Not only could the terms of incorporation and differentiation be manipulated to preserve the imperial polity, but some of the most important critics and opponents of the colonial status quo hoped that those structures could be manipulated in different ways, not turning empire into nation but into a more egalitarian form of multinational polity. In between, one does not find a stable relationship of colonizer to colonized, of citizen to subject, but unequal struggle over forms of inclusion and differentiation.

As importantly, Cooper argues that views of France as the epitome of modernity—modern empire, modern nation, modern state—fail to adequately explain nineteenth- and twentieth-century French history. Holding that "France became national at the same time as its colonies," Cooper takes on the project of "provincializing France." This is not, he argues, a new project, nor one derivative of recent work in postcolonial studies, but an endeavor to be recommenced. In the 1940s in both Senegal and France, progressive local leaders and colonial officials sought to reframe French empire to advance new ideas about the plurality of imperial community. The awkward fit between the multiple allegiances of empire and the homogenizing impulses of nationalism was put to use by elites such as Senegalese political activist and president Leopold Sedar Senghor. During decolonization, Senghor and others effectively invoked French ideals of citizenship to promote their power within the French imperial system (as well as at home). Cooper suggests that the historical reassessment of both empire and nation that this case requires must be routed through Napoleon's France just as much as through French Morocco, Algeria, or Senegal. It is France, as much as its empire, that needs to be rethought.

WRITING IN THE IMPERIAL PRESENT

We write in a time in which the concept of empire appears and disappears as a political analytic. Urgently called upon and debated when the war in Iraq began, empire was then almost abruptly left aside, despite the war's continued virulence. But such has been the strategic invocation of empire at other times as well. Those large territorial states that do dominate different cultures and suppress resistance from them (e.g., China in Tibet and Xinjiang, Russia in Chechnya, Israel in Palestine) have claimed and continue to claim these territories as essential parts of the nation, not as imperial possessions. Some might argue that there are few colonies left.[119] But we do not concede that point so quickly. Imperial vocabularies have narrowed over time, such that the French range of meanings for *colonie* with which we began appears merely metaphorical in the present, rather than definitional or operational. The histories behind the terms often tell different stories. Discarding the term *colony*, therefore, also "discards the histories that have found quiet refuge within it."[120] In its contracted, singular form—of formal, often overseas settler colonies—the colonial is the target of critiques from all sides.

Anticolonial sentiment of the twentieth century cleared the way for the quiet persistence of colonies officially sidelined by the narrower model. As a result, several volume authors—especially Prasenjit Duara—suggest that empire without colonization is the prevalent twentieth-century model.[121] In this dual formulation—of empire without colonies and of colonies as a singular form—US global hegemony is the case par excellence. While current US actions in Afghanistan and Iraq are the impetus for much of the renewed debate about imperial formations, part of our collective motivation is to provide a framework within which to consider American empire in a broader range of imperial formations and in a specific genealogy of American imperialism that well predates the Cold War.[122]

How to imagine the history of imperial formations to work as effective knowledge today remains the pressing question, for some more than others. Frederick Cooper urges us not to become caught in marking out genealogies but "to look at what possibilities were available to people at different moments in history and not only to see where those concepts in use today come from."[123] Others hold fast to an insistence that genealogies of a longer *durée* provide a more telling history of the present. Fernando Coronil endorses the latter, calling for attention to the imperial effects on people subject to the organizing power of contemporary imperial forms.

Most papers in this volume do both, tracking imperial possibilities and practices as well as the spatial and temporal genealogies that inform them. Some authors work up close, in the familiar quarters of everyday lives amid imperial projects or inside the muddle of imperial projects themselves—Makdisi's missionaries and converts, Perdue's emperors and authors, McGranahan's rebels and soldiers, Cooper's intellectuals and officials, and Dirks's politicians. Others track imperial formations at broader levels, assessing constructs, intentions, and consequences across wider geographic, historic, or institutional sweeps—Burbank's detailing of rights and inclusions, Khalid's analysis of the interventionist state, Duara's outlining of a developmental imperialism, Coronil's scrutiny of imperial effects and persistence, and Silverblatt's tracing of a new colonial biography for modern torture. In the context of specific empires, volume authors address analytic questions that are shared but are not one and the same.

Despite the range of topics covered in this volume, some issues slip through. Questions of gender and race are minimal; the voices of imperial subjects are few. We had not anticipated how easily the project would move away from the microsites of rule, those arenas of the domestic and intimate that have so transformed our understanding of imperial governance, of how and where it takes place. No simple answer explains this slippage. As we collectively worked to assess imperial formations, not just as historical polities but as a flexible analytic term—one relevant and at work well beyond (and before) nineteenth- and twentieth-century Europe—this project on refiguring the imperial took root at a different level. If our labor here tends more toward the institutional or the familiar than the domestic or intimate, our questions in general (and some of our collective findings) open to both, to an institutional *and* intimate analytics of imperial formations representative of the multiplicity of communities caught within and between empires.

Analyzing such systems of imperial domination via "their significance for subjected populations, rather than solely by their institutional form or self-definition,"[124] is as much an ethnographic venture as it is historic and textual. Sitting down with imperial agents and subjects, as Carole McGranahan does with former CIA agents and Tibetan guerrilla soldiers,[125] is not the same as reading their stories in the archives. A different set of seductions is involved in each venture such that these are complementary but not interchangeable projects.[126] Effective histories of contemporary empire need both. Catherine Lutz makes an appeal for more ethnographies of contemporary empires, arguing astutely that "empire is in the details."[127] As Ann Stoler has long argued, such details are deeply embedded in the changing social and affective lineaments of the everyday.[128] The "human and material face and frailties of imperialism" at home and abroad haunt the present in ways that create new methodological demands: to recognize both the complex interiorities of those living in and off empire and the creative terms of critique of those living under the imperial spotlight or in its shadows.[129]

One thing is clear: more examples from a wider field are not enough to unsettle prevailing models. Stockpiling cases is hardly the point. Collectively, if differently, we seek to reconceptualize what constitutes imperial forms and to ask what advantages are gained for whom by doing so. Rather than rush to distance ourselves from a field declared as fraught with traps, we have chosen instead to pause, to take advantage of this moment when efforts to rethink empire are not coming only from the North Atlantic center but taking place in many locales, among people with different stakes and political agendas.[130] We stay resolutely concerned with the politics of comparison to foreground the relational quality of imperial formations and the uses to which knowledge of them is and should be put.

Notes

1. Translated from Tourdonnet, *Essais sur l'éducation des enfants pauvres*, vol. 1, 26. The quote reads: *"Pour nous, une colonie agricole est une institution rurale qui étend ses beinfaits sur tous ceux qui y ont accès, à quelque titre que se soit, et dont les bénéfices leur appartiennent, dans less et dans les limites de la fondation, sou la condition d'un devoir à accomplir. Que ce devoir consiste dans un travail de défrichement ou de culture régulière, dans un service plus ou moins assujetissant, ou dans une simple obligation de séjour, peu importe au fond; la règle s'applique à tous, l'obéissance est de rigueur pour tous. Chacun contribue dans la mesure de sses forces det de ses aptitudes, selong la teneur de son contrat, s'il y en a, ou des obligations que lui impose son admission; chacun percoit proportionnellement aux droits communs à tous, ou aux droits spéciaux qui lui sont réservés. Tout individu qui habite la colonie est colon, quelque rôle qu'il y joue, quelque treavail qu'il doive exécuter, quelque droit particulier qui lui sont attribué."*

2. See Tourdonnet, *Essais sur l'éducation des enfants pauvres*, vol. 1, 26.

3. On the Portuguese expansion of empire through "criminals, sinners, orphans and prostitutes as colonizers," see Coates, *Convicts and Orphans*.

4. For two different treatments of the relationship between penal colonies, colonial expansion, and the people who inhabited and moved between them, see Price, *Convict and Colonel,* and Redfield, *Space in the Tropics.*

5. While we highlight pauper, penal, and settler colonies here, leper colonies were of equal importance in this frame of reference. See Anderson, "States of Hygiene."

6. In using the term "social etymology," we look to Michel Foucault's notion of "historical ontology" and Ian Hacking's elaboration on this notion in *Historical Ontology,* page 5. What intrigues Hacking about Foucault's use of "historical ontology" is how it points to "the beings that become-things, classifications, ideas, kinds of people, people, institutions," with emphasis on knowledge, power, and ethics. With "social etymology" we think particularly of the enduring social relationships of power that remain buried and suspended in political terms.

7. On Russia's new "framework of comparison," see Sunderland, *Taming the Wild Field,* 45.

8. Bassin, *Imperial Visions.*

9. For a discussion of some circuits of knowledge production in a US context, see Stoler, "Tense and Tender Ties."

10. Tourdonnet, *Essais sur l'éducation des enfants pauvres,* vol. 1, 16-17.

11. Tourdonnet, *Essais sur l'éducation des enfants pauvres,* vol. 2, 179-80.

12. Tourdonnet, *Essais sur l'éducation des enfants pauvres,* vol. 2, 17.

13. Verdes-Leroux, *Les Français d'Algérie,* 195.

14. Montagnon, *Histoire d'Algérie,* 180.

15. Verdes-Leroux, *Les Français d'Algérie,* 195. J. P. T. Bury's count is fifteen thousand arrested. Four hundred and fifty of these were deported to Algeria. See Bury, *France,* 77.

16. Ruedy, *Modern Algeria,* 69; Belvaude, *L'Algérie,* 36.

17. See Ussama Makdisi, this volume.

18. Representative of much of this literature is Chakrabarty, *Provincializing Europe.*

19. *Colon,* as used in the mid-nineteenth century to refer to children housed in rural assistance programs, is wholly absent from the lists provided in the three etymological dictionaries consulted here. A possible vestige may remain in the term *colonie de vacances* for children's (usually rural) summer camps.

20. Bassin, "Inventing Siberia," 771.

21. Althusser and Balibar, *Reading Capital,* 313.

22. Williams, *Marxism and Literature,* 117.

23. As an analytic that focuses on the formative and transformative aspects of

empire, we see our notion of "imperial formation" as related to, but differing from, Mrinalini Sinha's concept of an "imperial social formation" as a "mode of analysis that is simultaneously global in its reach and conjunctural in its focus." We thank an anonymous reviewer of an earlier version of this introduction for pointing out Sinha's use of a similar vocabulary of which we were both unaware. See her "Mapping the Imperial Social Formation," 1078, 1082; "Teaching Imperialism as a Social Formation"; and *Colonial Masculinity.*

24. The following section draws on Stoler, "On Degrees of Imperial Sovereignty," which in turn drew on insights of participants in this conference.

25. Winichakul, *Siam Mapped,* 130

26. Anthony Pagden makes a similar point that empires consist of and rely on mobility; see his *Peoples and Empires.*

27. As Carl Schmitt once noted, "every true empire around the world has claimed such a sphere of spatial sovereignty beyond its borders…a space far exceeding the boundaries of the state proper." Schmitt, *The Nomos of the Earth,* 281.

28. Nor, as Nicholas Dirks contends in this volume, was sovereignty safely located in London or even solely in England.

29. Armitage, *Ideological Origins,* 6-7.

30. Stoler, "On Degrees of Imperial Sovereignty," 138.

31. Aleinikoff, *Semblances of Sovereignty.*

32. Arendt, *Origins of Totalitarianism,* 296. See also, for example, Sandars, *America's Overseas Garrisons,* esp. 142-145 on Guantánamo's history; Hernon, "The Falklands," 43-48; and Richardson, *When Allies Differ.*

33. Jane Burbank, this volume.

34. For an argument that this is part of a new "new imperialism," see Prasenjit Duara, this volume.

35. For an example of a protracted contest over degrees of sovereignty, see Osborne, *"Empire Can Wait."*

36. As Said noted, "Every single empire in its official discourse has said that is not like all the others, that its circumstances are special, that it has a mission to enlighten, civilize, bring order and democracy, and that it uses force only as a last resort." Said, *Orientalism,* 2003, xxi.

37. Stephen Rosen, professor of national security and military affairs at Harvard's Olin Institute for Strategic Studies, makes a similar point when he argues that "the organizing principle of empire rests on the existence of an over-arching power that creates and enforces the principle of hierarchy, but is not itself bound by such rules." Rosen, "An Empire, If You Can Keep It," 53.

38. These are some of the attributes Ronald Suny provides in "Learning from Empire."

39. Fernando Coronil, this volume.

40. Frederick Cooper, this volume.

41. Makdisi, this volume.

42. Coronil, this volume. See also Partha Chatterjee, *Nationalist Thought and the Colonial World* and *The Nation and Its Fragments;* Guha, *History at the Limit;* and Mignolo, *Local Histories/Global Designs.*

43. Coronil, this volume.

44. See Dubois, *A Colony of Citizens* and *Avengers of the New World.*

45. Peter Perdue, this volume.

46. Dirks, this volume.

47. Imperial polities might also be imperial in some realms of their domains and not others. As Adeeb Khalid argues in this volume, the Soviet Union can rightly be considered imperial in relation to its external empire but not in his estimation in relation to its internal domains.

48. For a volume that productively explores some of the definitional quandaries of empire in relationship to contemporary political interventions of the United States, see Calhoun, Cooper, and Moore, *Lessons of Empire.*

49. As Selim Deringil argues in the case of the Ottoman empire, imperial officials considered the Ottoman state "somehow sui generis and [therefore it could not]...be compared to any other polity." Deringil, *Well Protected Domains,* 5; see also his "'They Live in a State of Nomadism and Slavery.'" For a comprehensive review of American exceptionalism in a range of historical fields, see Tyrell, "American Exceptionalism." Also see Kramer, "Empires, Exceptions, and Anglo-Saxons." An argument that "the Netherlands does not belong among the imperialistic powers" is discussed by van Goor, "Imperialisme in de Marge?"

50. For a description of some features that have defined understandings of European colonial empires, see Stoler and Cooper, "Between Metropole and Colony," and Catherine Hall, *Cultures of Empire,* 1-36. For a history of theoretical approaches to European colonialism, see Wolfe, "History and Imperialism."

51. For a comparable approach, see the collected essays generated by the Colonialism and Its Discontents conference at Academica Sinica in Taiwan in 1997. As conference organizer Allen Chun argues, "understanding colonialism as an abstraction must begin by understanding colonialism as a concrete, historical experience. Moreover, this is the only basis for understanding colonial experiences comparatively, as well as for understanding what may be considered colo-

nial violence in political regimes not literally defined as colonial (given the conventional definitions of European colonialism)." See his "Introduction: (Post)Colonialism and Its Discontents," 382.

52. On Edward Said's own attention to U.S. empire, see Stoler and Bond, "Refractions off Empire."

53. We think here of a number of key monographs and edited volumes, such as Dirks's *Colonialism and Culture;* Cooper and Stoler's *Tensions of Empire;* and Prakash's *After Colonialism* (which expands the purview to Latin America), and the dense body of work in subaltern studies focused on South Asia and the British empire, including *Subaltern Studies,* vols. 1-10, and *Subaltern Studies,* vol. 11.

54. Bhabha, *Location of Culture;* Said, *Orientalism* and *Culture and Imperialism;* Spivak, *A Critique of Postcolonial Reason;* and Robert Young, *White Mythologies* and *Colonial Desire.*

55. In addition to the cases highlighted in this volume, see also recent and forthcoming works on other European empires, such as Ben-Ghiat and Fuller, *Italian Colonialism;* Palumbo, *Place in the Sun;* Steinmetz, *Devil's Handwriting;* and Wildenthal, *German Women for Empire.*

56. See Anderson, *Imagined Communities,* and Stoler and Cooper, "Between Metropole and Colony."

57. Cooper and Stoler, *Tensions of Empire.*

58. While not advocating a formal comparative model, our project could be considered in dialogue with George Steinmetz's notion of "critical realist" comparison. As he outlines it, "a critical realist comparative research strategy... [compares] across mechanisms and across events. Empirical phenomena may be selected for comparison for explicitly political or 'interested' reasons or because they are believed to be relevant to uncovering or illuminating the causal mechanisms and structures of interest." Steinmetz, "Odious Comparisons," 393.

59. For a fuller treatment of the politics of comparison, see Stoler, "Intimidations of Empire" and "Tense and Tender Ties."

60. Cooper, this volume.

61. Duara, this volume.

62. Irene Silverblatt, this volume.

63. See also Dirks, this volume, for a rethinking of nation and empire in the British context.

64. Burbank, this volume.

65. Appadurai, "Globalization and the Rush to History."

66. Grewal, *Transnational America,* 21-22. Grewal defines "transnational

connectivities" as constituting webs of "connections that move along historicized trajectories."

67. Grewal, *Transnational America,* 209.

68. Silverblatt, for example, pushes us to reassess "our sense of modernity," contending that we must "trace its elementary forms back from the nineteenth century to the seventeenth." See Silverblatt, this volume.

69. On the Qing empire, see Crossley, *Translucent Mirror;* Elliott, *Manchu Way;* Hostetler, *Qing Colonial Enterprise;* Millward, *Beyond the Pass;* Perdue, *China Marches West;* and Teng, *Taiwan's Imagined Geography.*

70. New works on the Russian empire include Barkey and von Hagen, *After Empire;* Bassin, *Imperial Visions;* Brower and Lazzerini, *Russia's Orient;* Burbank and Ransel, *Imperial Russia;* Hirsch, *Empire of Nations;* Khalid, *Politics of Muslim Cultural Reform;* Northrop, *Veiled Empire;* and Sunderland, *Taming the Wild Field.*

71. On Manchuria and Japan, see Duara, *Sovereignty and Authenticity;* Matsusaka, *Making of Japanese Manchuria;* Tamanoi, *Dreaming Manchuria* and *Crossed Histories;* and Louise Young, *Japan's Total Empire.*

72. See Lewis, *Hall of Mirrors;* Mallon, *Peasant and Nation;* Mignolo, *Local Histories/Global Designs;* Seed, "Taking Possession and Reading Texts," *American Pentimento,* and *Ceremonies of Possession;* Silverblatt, *Modern Inquisitions;* Thurner, *From Two Republics;* and Thurner and Guerrero, *After Spanish Rule.*

73. Hostetler, *Qing Colonial Enterprise;* Silverblatt, *Modern Inquisitions* and this volume.

74. As argued by both McGranahan and Perdue, this volume.

75. Rai, *Rule of Sympathy.*

76. Chakrabarty, *Provincializing Europe.*

77. McGranahan, this volume.

78. McGranahan, this volume.

79. Schmid, *Korea between Empires.* Gi-Wook Shin and Michael Robinson contend that colonial and postcolonial studies of Korea are a matter of "theory run[ning] ahead of history." See their preface and introduction, along with accompanying essays, in *Colonial Modernity in Korea.*

80. Bulag, *Mongols at China's Edge.*

81. For the literature on British India, starting points include Cohn, *Colonialism and Its Forms of Knowledge;* Dirks, *Castes of Mind;* and Guha, *Dominance without Hegemony.* In comparison, English-language scholarship on Portuguese and French colonies in India is still scant; see Coates, *Convicts and Orphans;* Miles, *Imperial Burdens;* and Siqueira, "Postcolonial Portugal, Postcolonial Goa."

82. On Italian colonialism in Africa, see Ben-Ghiat and Fuller, *Italian Colonialism;* Hess, *Italian Colonialism in Somalia;* Negash, *Italian Colonialism in Eritrea;* and, Palumbo, *Place in the Sun.*

83. Powell, *Different Shade of Colonialism;* Sharkey, *Living with Colonialism.*

84. Powell, *Different Shade of Colonialism.*

85. See McGranahan, this volume.

86. On these points, see Teng, *Taiwan's Imagined Geography.*

87. Dudden, *Japan's Colonization of Korea.*

88. For a detailed examination of the decolonization process of European colonies, see Muriel E. Chamberlain, *The Longman Companion* and *Decolonization.*

89. Ching, *Becoming "Japanese";* Teng, *Taiwan's Imagined Geography.*

90. Barlow, "Colonialism's Career in Postwar China Studies."

91. Hevia, *English Lessons,* 26.

92. Perdue, this volume.

93. Perdue, this volume.

94. Hevia, *English Lessons* and *Cherishing Men from Afar.*

95. Nor was China outside the US imperial realm at the time. See Scully, *Bargaining with the State from Afar.*

96. Hostetler, *Qing Colonial Enterprise.*

97. Moving beyond, or at the very least alongside, a story of European imposition and Chinese resistance, we find a series of relationships between Qing rulers and Europeans abroad. The Kangxi Emperor (1654-1722) was a cosmopolitan ruler in a noncosmopolitan society, an intellectual drawn to global currents of technology and information in a society that prized Chinese cultural epistemes and scholarly pursuits. His coterie included Jesuit European as well as Han Chinese advisers and administrators.

98. Hostetler, *Qing Colonial Enterprise,* 21.

99. The idea of "capture" is taken from Duara's *Rescuing History from the Nation.* See also Partha Chatterjee, *Nation and Its Fragments,* and Dirks, "History as a Sign of the Modern."

100. Perdue, this volume.

101. Coronil, this volume.

102. McGranahan, this volume.

103. McGranahan, this volume. See also Duara, this volume, for a perspective that reaches back further in terms of "new" imperial projects.

104. Khalid, this volume.

105. Steinmetz, "Return to Empire."

106. McGranahan, this volume. See also Cooper, this volume, for a discussion of the range of concerns with imperial citizenship in the French context.

107. See Burbank, this volume, and Suny, "Learning from Empire."

108. Compare with Enrique Dussel, who argues on the contrary that colonialism is the "underside of modernity." Dussel, *Essays: The Underside of Modernity.*

109. McGranahan, this volume.

110. Coronil, this volume.

111. McGranahan, this volume.

112. Coronil, this volume.

113. Wright, "Tradition in the Service of Modernity."

114. Silverblatt, *Modern Inquisitions* and this volume,

115. Arendt, *Origins of Totalitarianism.*

116. Silverblatt, this volume.

117. Dirks, this volume.

118. Cooper, this volume.

119. On contested and continuing European colonies in the present, see Aldrich and Connell, *Last Colonies.*

120. David Bond, personal communication.

121. As Duara argues, "the costs of direct colonial rule increased while the conditions for indirect rule were enhanced."

122. See Bender, *Rethinking American History;* Briggs, *Reproducing Empire;* Go and Foster, *American Colonial State in the Philippines;* Kaplan, *Anarchy of Empire;* Kaplan and Pease, *Cultures of United States Imperialism;* Love, *Race over Empire;* Rafael, *White Love and Other Events;* Stoler, "Tense and Tender Ties"; and Trask, *From a Native Daughter.*

123. Frederick Cooper, personal correspondence.

124. Coronil, this volume.

125. McGranahan, this volume

126. On the seductions of the ethnography of empire, see Gill, *School of the Americas,* and Lutz, *Homefront.*

127. Lutz, "Empire Is in the Details."

128. See Stoler, *Race and the Education of Desire, Carnal Knowledge and Imperial Power,* and *Haunted by Empire.*

129. Lutz, "Empire Is in the Details," and Stoler, "Toward a Charmless Colonial History."

130. In Russia, for example, a new generation of scholars critiques conventional approaches to Russian empire in favor of a critical, poststructural approach. See Gersimov and others, "In Search of a New Imperial History."

Part 1
The Production and Protection of Difference

2

Bringing America Back into the Middle East

A History of the First American Missionary Encounter with the Ottoman Arab World

Ussama Makdisi

Neither Ottoman nor American history is normally considered an integral part of colonial studies. This omission reflects not only the tendency of colonial studies to focus on Europe's colonies as the exclusive center of inquiry but also the hegemonic self-representation of US and Ottoman historiographies in which colonialism is at best seen as a marginal or late chapter in the unfolding story of the nation-state.[1] In what follows, I bring together Ottoman and US history to understand how the first American missionary assault on the Ottoman empire represented a collision of manifestly different and complex imperial formations, racially articulated in an expansionist American republic and religiously elaborated in the Ottoman domains. Specifically eschewing the language of a clash between an undifferentiated Islam and a monolithic West, I outline how American missionaries, shaped by their ambivalent embrace of certain white triumph over American Indians, responded to the difficult realities of a new Ottoman frontier that they had opened but could not dominate. In the face of an unanticipated defeat by natives who refused to conform to their millennial fantasy or their location in a missionary worldview that regarded the Ottoman "heathen" in a substantially similar way to the American Indian "heathen," the missionaries sought to transform actual defeat into moral victory. They first fabricated a story of martyrdom of the first Arab convert to American Protestantism and then, *later,* integrated this story into a broader narrative of Anglo-American ascendancy. These stories presupposed not only an orientalized reading of the East but an idealized reading of America as well.

To appreciate the complexity of this initial clash of cultures is first and foremost to appreciate the richness of a missionary encounter in which the historical and historiographical cards are not, as is so often the case with missionaries operating in European colonies, overwhelmingly in Western hands.[2] Put more boldly, to understand American missionaries in the Orient, indeed to understand this early American mission history overseas, one has to acknowledge the intersection of a settler/colonial American logic defined by the opposition of white to American Indian with an intricate imperial Ottoman logic defined by the opposition of high to low as well as Muslim to non-Muslim. Furthermore, making sense of American missionary documents, their representations and silences, requires a plunge into unfamiliar, in this case Ottoman, waters. Ottoman Arab history, contrary to the assumptions of American missionaries and indeed much of US diplomatic history in the Middle East, was not the setting for the triumphal unfolding of "American" liberal and democratic values, but an active stage upon which American history, with its passions and prejudices, was dialectically played out.

Ottoman society, after all, was not formally colonized by European powers, although it was subject to pressures similar if not identical to those in colonial India and Africa. Moreover, the Ottoman empire embodied a mature non-Western imperial tradition that viably, if defensively, competed across the nineteenth century with ever more dominant Western imperial powers. How this non-Western imperial tradition was "read" by American missionaries in the 1820s, who were themselves emerging out of the crucible of US colonialism against the Native Americans, offers a fascinating study of the dynamic of a premodern, non-Western imperial tradition that came into unexpected confrontation with American missionaries. In this encounter, the American missionaries could not depend on any of the certainties that defined outright European colonialism or on their own American colonial background with the Native Americans. That is, they could neither tacitly nor openly count on the coercive mechanism of a colonial state to pressure natives into conversion; nor could they avoid the fact that they stood face to face with a literate, if in their eyes false, multireligious culture that, in the 1820s, was still fully confident of its abilities to withstand, and even repel, Western encroachment. Simply put, the Ottomans were not Tzvetan Todorov's Aztecs.[3]

Nowhere was this encounter more vividly and tragically illustrated than in the exemplary story of a Maronite Christian subject of the Ottoman empire, As'ad Shidyaq, who became the first Arab convert to Protestantism in the Ottoman empire and who died for his beliefs in the late 1820s. Shidyaq's conversion and death occurred at a pivotal moment in Ottoman history. The empire already faced tremendous Western pressure following Napoleon's invasion of Egypt in 1798 and the outbreak of the Greek War of Independence in the 1820s. Major military reforms, including the bloody abolition of the Janissaries in 1826, had taken place. Further, the doctrine of religious equality that would become the mantra of modern Ottoman imperial identity from the mid-nineteenth century until the end of empire had not yet been elaborated. More specifically, Shidyaq's story revolved around the violent meeting of two very powerful currents of American and Ottoman history. The first current was represented by an American missionary view that unconstrained individual freedom of choice would lead inevitably to homogenous evangelical Protestantism at a time of "hardening" racism in American society and seemingly inexorable westward expansion in the United States. The second current emerged out of an Ottoman Arab accommodation of religious difference, one that regarded the stability of different religious communities, and their mutual recognition, as a guarantee of order and harmony in an unequal, multireligious society.[4]

What is at stake in the following history is an attempt to delineate fundamentally different Ottoman and American missionary understandings of how religion operated in the world. The Ottoman imperial understanding saw religion as the foundation of a long-established and *accepted* coexistence, a belonging to an utterly unequal multireligious and ethnic imperium. While the *theoretical* imperative was to maintain the achieved order and to preserve and uphold a status that had supposedly already been secured, the *practical* imperative was compromise and acceptance of the limits of Muslim Ottoman power as well as the ambivalent location of minorities within the empire (this is quite different from insisting that Jews and Christians were simply "oppressed" and "second-class" subjects, as much of the literature on Ottoman minorities has emphasized).[5] On the other hand, an aggressive American missionary religiosity was born out of a remarkably victorious colonial American experience with Native Americans. This missionary view was defined by a refusal to accept compromise regarding sacred truth, a refusal to coexist with different forms of faith or to allow any "perishing soul" to be deprived of Christian "benevolence," and a powerful belief that the world could be remade here and now in evangelical and "civilized" terms. The perfect order, in other words, had yet to be achieved, but missionaries firmly believed in their duty to hasten its arrival. By framing this early nineteenth-century encounter as a clash between the temporalities of Ottoman tolerance and American missionary intolerance, neither of which was secular or liberal, this study seeks to sharply question a central assumption that has dominated the politics of comparison in which Ottoman studies has been mired and in which studies of American missionaries in the Middle East have consistently been written: namely that missionaries were harbingers of "modernity" to a stagnant Ottoman empire.[6] Rather than compare Muslim and American cultures as if they were plotted on a single evolutionary line in which America leads a reticent Middle East into a uniquely Western modernity—one that is often assumed by historians to be a completed project in the West but incomplete, failed, resisted, or subverted in the East[7]—it seems far more reasonable to undertake, in however preliminary a fashion, a history that reveals the complex dynamism of both missionaries and the worlds upon which they impinged.

THE PREHISTORY OF THE "MARTYR OF LEBANON"

Hailing from a New England in the grip of the Second Great Awakening, the Protestant missionaries of the American Board of Commissioners for Foreign Missions arrived in the Ottoman empire in 1820. They chose Beirut as the main station for their mission to Syria in 1823.[8] Missionaries such as Jonas King, Isaac Bird, and William Goodell—the latter two accompanied by their wives Ann and Abigail—unleashed a direct assault on what they perceived to be the falsehood of Islam and the errors of Eastern Christianity. They loudly proclaimed a notion of one true faith, which urgently had to dismantle all other religions to pave the way for the Second Coming of Christ. Such an aggressive interpretation of faith signaled a provocative challenge to, if not immediate rupture with, conventional notions of the relationships among faith, society, and politics in the multireligious Ottoman empire.[9] This missionary optimism, and this belief in the necessity of making everyone believe the same thing, could not have found a more opposite situation than in the Ottoman Arab world of the early nineteenth century. In this world, where the majority of the population was Muslim, referred to by the missionaries as Mohammedans, there were also Jews, whose "dereliction," the missionaries proclaimed, "is not to be perpetual" and whose putative salvation had prompted the original mission to Palestine,[10] as well as Greek Orthodox, Greek Catholics, Nestorians, Maronites, and a host of other Christian communities that the missionaries referred to contemptuously and collectively as "nominal" Christians.

As an ostensibly orthodox Islamic dynasty superior to all other empires, the dynamic of pre-Tanzimat rule had been to conserve (but also to overlook) what was held to be largely immutable religious and ethnic differences among subjects and to maintain an imperial distance between the center and the tribute-paying peripheries of the empire. In the large cities of Damascus and Aleppo, Muslim and Christian subjects of the Ottoman sultan were certainly not equal in rights, obligations, or responsibilities. Christians and Jews were tolerated under the terms of the so-called Pact of 'Umar, which established the social inferiority of the *ahl al-dhimma* (literally "the people of the contract"), non-Muslims in a Muslim society, allowing them to maintain their own customary practices, property, rituals, and freedom of worship in return for extra taxes (*jizya*) and loyalty to the state, while also confirming Muslim precedence in any shared public space.[11]

Although Muslims were legally superior to *dhimmi* Christians and Jews, the Ottoman sultans did grant each minority community full autonomy to run its own internal affairs in return for loyalty and taxes.

The state did not normally compel religious change, except for those who desired to be identified as members of the ruling Ottoman elite.[12] Every hierarchy of every community of the empire had a stake in the supposedly divinely ordained Ottoman social order, in which stability and harmony were guaranteed by having each person know his or her place in society, just as each community was meant to know its place.

This was particularly the case in rural areas such as Mount Lebanon, where As'ad Shidyaq was born and lived until the arrival of the missionaries. Neglected as a backwater by Ottoman rulers, the villages and small towns that comprised Mount Lebanon were governed by a nonsectarian hierarchy of Druze and Maronite elite families and presided over by a ruling emir named Bashir Shihab. Before the coming of the American missionaries, Protestantism as such was unknown in Mount Lebanon. The area had, however, a large Christian population composed mostly of Maronites but also of Greek Orthodox and Greek Catholics.[13] Indeed, long before the United States was founded and the idea of the American Board of Commissioners was conceived, the Maronite Church had been the object of sustained papal concern.[14] The Latinization of the Maronite Church from the sixteenth century onward occasioned bitter disputes within the Maronite ecclesiastical community, but by the beginning of the nineteenth century, the Latinizing reformers, led by Patriarch Yusuf Hubaysh, had consolidated their control of the Maronite Church.[15] They successfully created a mythology of Maronite "perpetual orthodoxy": a supposedly unshakeable and ancient fealty to Rome that defined the Maronite Church. This increasingly pronounced Maronite identification with Rome in ecclesiastical affairs was not seen as a threat by the Ottoman government or by the other communities in the region. In part, this was due to an Ottoman indifference to ecclesiastical affairs. To a greater extent, however, it was due to the fact that the social order in Mount Lebanon was marked not by religious discrimination but by a rigorously upheld distinction between elites and commoners of every village. This division between high and low, between supposedly knowledgeable elites and ignorant commoners, defined all arenas of political, religious, and social life in Mount Lebanon. The accommodation of religious difference, in other words, presupposed a strict and unalterable hierarchical delineation between different classes of society, each of which was expected to defer to and obey the classes above it, the highest being the Ottoman sultan himself, who, in theory, benevolently ruled over a vast multireligious empire.[16]

There was both a price paid and a benefit gained from such religious toleration. On the one hand, tolerance allowed for a kind of coexistence within the framework of an avowedly Islamic Ottoman empire, a situation that was largely unimaginable to Western travelers and missionaries, who had long understood Ottoman "toleration" as a mask for an underlying and dangerous "fanaticism."[17] On the other hand, the social order was assumed to be unchangeable; while political, economic, and social changes certainly occurred, they were always justified as a return to tradition, as conservation of rather than repudiation of tradition. Education was scant, and what little intellectual activity occurred did not interest, let alone trouble, the Ottoman authorities. Indeed, the Maronites had long been the prime beneficiaries of this Ottoman order, as evinced by the increase, during the Ottoman era, in the number and size of the Maronite monasteries that dominated the landscape of Mount Lebanon. Whereas they had once been confined to inaccessible monasteries such as Qannubin, by the time Yusuf Hubaysh assumed the patriarchate in 1823, Maronites could proudly point to the monastery of Bkirke as their own prominent and quite visible monument to Ottoman order. Although Patriarch Hubaysh lamented to Rome about being surrounded by a "sea" of infidels, he was quite able and willing to work within a social order that mandated interaction with these same infidels, for he shared their same broad cultural values: no unmediated access of the common man to knowledge; total submission to authority; and certainly no proselytizing or other action that might disturb the divinely sanctioned order of things.

What little formal education there was in this rugged land was limited to parochial village schools and institutions such as the Maronite seminary of 'Ayn Waraqa. It was established in 1789 and intended for a tiny minority of aspiring Maronite clergy who occasionally decided to work for secular rulers, Druze or Maronite, rather than dedicate themselves to a life of the cloth. As'ad Shidyaq was one such man. Shidyaq's family was prominent but not powerful. His grandfather had been a subdeacon in the Maronite Church, hence the family name Shidyaq, which means "subdeacon" in Arabic.[18] One among five brothers (and two sisters about whom the historical record is otherwise silent), the ten-year-old As'ad was taught Syriac, the liturgical language of the Maronites, and Arabic grammar and script by his older brother Tannus and was soon employed as a copyist. He showed such promise in Arabic and Syriac that Tannus enrolled him in 1814 in the 'Ayn Waraqa, where he perfected his Arabic and Syriac and learned logic, rhetoric, and natural and theological sciences. Upon his graduation from the seminary, Shidyaq unexpectedly left the clerical path (the Maronite Church had sponsored his education with the expectation that he would serve it faithfully thereafter) to become a private secretary to various secular Druze and Muslim notables before finally returning in 1823 to the newly elected Maronite patriarch, his former teacher at 'Ayn Waraqa, Yusuf Hubaysh, to plead for employment. Patriarch Hubaysh, however, berated Shidyaq for abandoning his ecclesiastical calling and provided him with little work. In 1824, a disgruntled Shidyaq left the patriarch to return to his village, Hadath, and was soon engaged to be married.[19]

It was at this moment that the American missionaries appeared in As'ad Shidyaq's life. Jonas King, Isaac Bird, and William Goodell were all graduates of Andover Theological Seminary. From Andover they joined the American Board of Commissioners for Foreign Missions, which was founded in 1810 as part of a reaction to a growing liberalism in religious life in America—particularly the rise of Unitarianism in New England and the growth of Catholic immigration to the United States.[20] The American Board insisted, however, that its missionaries represented "American Christians." Bird and his fellow missionary Goodell departed for the Holy Land knowing two things for certain: that they undertook a task of both urgency and magnitude to save a "multitude of perishing souls" in dire need of salvation and that their own country was uniquely poised to carry out this formidable burden. "From a continent but recently discovered," they were told upon their departure to the East by the board, "you carry back the knowledge of the Scriptures and of salvation to regions where flourishing churches once stood, but where the power of religion has long ceased to exist. As our Christian community cannot go in a body to deliver the message of their Lord, they send you to deliver it for them."[21] As an American missionary, Bird saw his duty in both religious and national terms: to evangelize in stagnating biblical lands for the brotherhood of Christ and to do so with the knowledge that a vibrant Christian America showed the peoples of these lands an image of their own evangelized future. If the first impulse explained the mission, the second defined its elaboration. The missionaries believed utterly in the common nature of humanity, but they were also convinced of the elect nature of America and Americans.

In the Orient, the missionaries drew not only on a narrative of reformation—as Jessup's subsequent comparison of Shidyaq to Luther and Cranmer underscored—that assumed the *righteousness* of their cause, but they also drew on their own experience of Anglo-Saxon expansion in North America, which assured them of the *inevitability* of their triumph. The American Board firmly believed in the inevitable ascendance of an American-led Protestant Christian civilization that could benevolently encompass all humanity. Such optimism defied the realities at hand in the early nineteenth-century United States. In the case of the American Indians, for example, the board was well aware that the situation in the 1820s was grim because "national sins" by "wicked and unprincipled white people" had brought the Indians to the brink of physical extermination.[22] Indeed, the American Board's own experimental Foreign Mission School at Cornwall, Connecticut, which sought to assimilate Indians to a white way of life, was forced to close down in 1827 following a local uproar when two Indian students married white women.[23] Racialism of the sort traced by Reginald Horsman had become so prevalent in the 1820s United States that the domestic missionary enterprise was severely constrained.[24] It is no coincidence, then, that the American Board's mission to the Ottoman empire arose with, and the As'ad Shidyaq affair developed alongside, the travails of the domestic missionary enterprise to the American Indians, not just in northern states such as Connecticut but also in the South in such places as Georgia, culminating in the Indian Removal Act of 1830.[25]

Colonization, ethnic cleansing, and the closing of one domestic frontier had given birth to a new frontier overseas, one that was as yet unencumbered by colonizing imperatives. Poignantly, Levi Parsons, the original missionary of the American Board to Palestine, insisted that it was the Indians who had urged him to embark on a mission to the Holy Land.[26] The missionaries, however, were anything but "cultural imperialists" as they settled the biblical lands. Rather, they were a lonely band who rekindled a foundational myth of their Puritan ancestors—to civilize and reform natives overseas—at a time when it was increasingly impossible to do so in the United States. They also represented a belligerent opposition to both a liberal turn in nineteenth-century New England religious and intellectual history and a far more widespread racist turn across the United States, which precluded any hope of a civilizing mission to Native Americans.[27]

The missionaries, nevertheless, felt an equal sense of urgency about the prospect of the spiritual extermination of the "perishing souls" of the Orient upon the Second Coming of Christ. Men like Jedidah Morse, one of the founders of the American Board and also the corresponding secretary for the American Society for Promoting the Civilization and General Improvement of the Indian Tribes within the United States, prophesied that the reign of the eastern and western antichrists was set to end in 1866.[28] The establishment of the mission to Palestine and Syria coincided with a period of tremendous upheaval in the Ottoman empire. European encroachment, beginning with Napoleon's invasion of Egypt in 1798 and continuing with the Greek War of Independence of the 1820s, had forced both the Ottoman government and Ottoman society more generally to grapple with Western-style reform and had encouraged the missionaries to take on the mantle of reform. Like other Westerners, the missionaries enjoyed rights of extraterritoriality in the empire. The United States was still largely unknown, so the missionaries, who were protected by the English consulates and closely identified with British missionaries, were described locally as "the English," or *al-Inkiliz*. The missionaries, moreover, were initially welcomed by the various Christian leaders, including the Maronite patriarch, but when it became clear that the Americans were not simple pilgrims on their way to Jerusalem but missionaries who intended to convert the Maronites (among others), the local churches turned against them.

When the Maronite patriarch, in particular, heard that the missionaries had started distributing unauthorized editions of the Bible, he anathematized them, encouraged no doubt by the stream of missives that arrived from the Vatican's Propaganda Fide.[29] He ordered their books burned but could do little else since the missionaries operated under English consular protection and hence were not subject to Ottoman law. In every communication to the Propaganda Fide, for example, Patriarch Hubaysh underscored how he had immediately recognized the danger inherent in the missionaries and how his anathemas against them had been unhesitatingly obeyed by the "entire" Maronite community. That the truth of the matter was quite different—for many Maronites did continue to communicate with the missionaries, and Patriarch Hubaysh had in the first instance welcomed the missionaries—did not prevent the patriarch from presenting an image of a homogenous, orthodox, but poor Maronite community.

The missionaries, in turn, escalated their contest with the Maronites in January 1825 by dismissing the authority of the "papists" and urged the patriarch to accept the fact that it was the missionaries, not Rome, who desired "to propagate Christianity, such as it was in the first ages and among the first disciples."[30] The upshot was that while many individuals in the Ottoman Levant were undeniably intrigued by the missionaries—by their dedication, their novelty, their printed books, and most importantly their schools (the missionaries opened the first school for girls in the Ottoman empire in 1834)—the majority refused to contemplate conversion to Protestantism. The missionaries, in short, had no trouble filling their schools in this era of increasingly apparent European hegemony; they did, however, have trouble producing conversions, which the missionaries understood as not simply a change in religion but also an abandonment of stagnant and corrupt native culture. This situation was particularly evident with the "nominal" Christians of the Orient, whom the missionaries regarded as more corrupt and more contemptible than Muslims.[31]

THE TRIBULATIONS OF AS'AD SHIDYAQ

It was in this context that the As'ad Shidyaq affair unfolded. When Jonas King in 1825 wrote his polemical "Farewell Letter," in which the young American missionary outlined to his "friends" in Palestine and Syria why he could not become Roman Catholic, the twenty-seven-year-old As'ad Shidyaq took it upon himself to rebut the Protestant charges against Maronite and Catholic dogma. In the process, however, Shidyaq himself rebelled against Maronite dogma, particularly against the notion of the infallibility of the pope and the worship of saints. Although he never declared himself a Protestant and insisted that he was still a Maronite, Shidyaq was nevertheless summoned in January 1826 by the Maronite patriarch to the monastery of Dayr ʻAlma in Mount Lebanon. There, he was interrogated by the patriarch about his allegedly "heretical beliefs."[32] Shidyaq was repeatedly questioned by the patriarch who could not decide how to deal with Shidyaq's crisis of faith. He alternated between asking Shidyaq to state that his belief was that of the Roman Catholic Church, accusing him of being bribed by the "English" and then promising him suitable employment if he renounced the missionaries, declaring Shidyaq to be *majnun* (crazy), and thinking of him as a victim of the poisonous doctrines of the missionaries. At times, the patriarch fulminated against Shidyaq and forbade any priest to discuss matters of faith with him, only to contradict himself shortly thereafter and engage in a theological debate with his erstwhile student. At no time in this initial confinement was Shidyaq physically beaten or tortured. This process went on for three months until, finally, in March, Shidyaq escaped to the Beirut house of Isaac Bird, who immediately asked him to record his story, as proof of Eastern intolerance to be sure, but also as evidence that a "convert" had finally been made.[33]

No sooner had Asʻad Shidyaq recorded his narrative in March 1826 than his family persuaded him to leave the missionaries. Shidyaq did so at the end of March and, according to the missionaries, was forced almost immediately by his family once more to Dayr ʻAlma. There Shidyaq, who reminded the patriarch that "my name is Christian; my church is Catholic and I am a Maronite of ancient stock," begged permission from the patriarch to preach against the severe "ignorance" that he felt prevailed in Mount Lebanon. Shidyaq condemned the hypocrisy of the supposedly knowledgeable Maronite clergy who declared theft to be the greatest of all sins, while they ignored the manner in which other sins—which in various places in his diary he specified as lying, greed, covetousness, and accumulation of worldly power—were committed and, worse, forgiven with impunity. Shidyaq, moreover, now turned against the practice of confession, for it assumed that a person lived in several, constantly shifting states of blessing and sin. Humans had only two states, he declared: an initial physical birth from the mother's womb and a second spiritual rebirth by the grace of God. He explicitly repudiated the patriarch's ecclesiastical authority by insisting that the common person, hitherto defined by ecclesiastical and secular authorities as inherently passive and ignorant and constructed politically and religiously as a quietist obedient subject, was capable of autonomously interpreting and receiving "living" faith.[34]

In the face of such unmitigated defiance, and in the face of Shidyaq's determination to publicly evangelize, the patriarch had Shidyaq moved to the remote monastery of Qannubin at the end of April 1826. Three times Shidyaq tried to escape, after which and because of which he was finally tortured: beaten, isolated, and chained. By December 1826, the patriarch referred to him only as the wretch and as *rab shayul,* the Syriac term for "lord of hell."[35] His handwriting, preserved in the surviving documents in the Maronite patriarchate, visibly deteriorated. Then, in 1828, after the missionaries were forced to abandon temporarily their stations in Syria due to an upsurge in the Greek War of Independence, all contact with him ceased.[36] As'ad Shidyaq vanished. He was literally annihilated by the Maronite Church, which at the time categorically refused to treat his "Protestantism" as an intellectual, spiritual, or moral position. Since then—with the notable exception of encyclopedist Butrus al-Bustani's *Qissat As'ad Shidyaq,* published in 1860—there has not been a single Arabic history dedicated to the Shidyaq affair. Abandoned by his own community, As'ad Shidyaq was embraced by the Americans. He first became known to American readers through the pages of the *Missionary Herald* and later through widely distributed memorial pamphlets in the United States, which described him as the victim of a veritable "Syrian Inquisition" and as "the Martyr of Lebanon."

FORESHADOWING MARTYRDOM

On one level, therefore, the missionary narrative of As'ad Shidyaq's martyrdom begins with his defiance of the patriarch and can be read as a tale of sincere concern for one man's fate. Indeed as fragments of Shidyaq's story began to appear in the *Missionary Herald* in 1826, the readers of the journal were treated to a gripping tale of his courage and resistance to Maronite bigotry. As'ad Shidyaq, in fact, became one of the very few natives whose name and history appeared in the *Missionary Herald.* Most others of the local population were referred to only as "native helpers" or as "hopeful converts." Further, his celebrity as a "martyr" starkly contrasted the almost complete silence about Shidyaq in the missionary archives *before* his troubles began. From being considered a native babe in Christ before his tribulations, As'ad Shidyaq was suddenly elevated into a "suffering brother" in Christ.[37] With each issue, more news was published on the fate of As'ad Shidyaq, until finally in June 1827, just over fourteen months after Shidyaq's initial confinement, the *Missionary Herald* announced the following to its readers:

> That he will escape from the hands of his enemies except by death, is possible, but we fear, not very probable; that, overcome by pain, and broken down by oppression, he should, like Cranmer, recant, though it would grieve, it should not greatly surprise us; but, that he will, through the divine assistance, persevere to the end, and be a distinguished monument of evangelical piety rekindled upon the ancient altars of Christianity, is what we are entitled to hope, and what all should make an object of their continued and fervent prayers.[38]

For the readers of the *Missionary Herald,* a quintessential missionary drama seemed to be unfolding: the Maronite Church may have broken Shidyaq's body, but the missionaries hoped that they had won his soul—even as Shidyaq still languished, alive but out of the reach of the missionaries.

On another level, however, the narrative of As'ad Shidyaq begins much earlier: with the glaring incommensurability between the mission's perception of a static and corrupted Holy Land and the dynamic, historical reality of Muslim, Christian, and Jewish interaction in the Ottoman empire.[39] Although the missionaries studied the different communities of the empire and recorded detailed and important information about their customs and manners, they believed that Jews, Christians, and Muslims interacted only on violent terms—as if they were all constantly involved in a perpetual clash of civilizations. Unable or unwilling to comprehend a living multireligious society, they recorded only a segregated society composed of entirely separate and entirely debased Christians and Jews groaning under what the missionaries described as an unremitting Mohammedan despotism. The missionaries prepared themselves to suffer, and even to be martyred for the cause of Christ, precisely because they thought they were entering an Islamic Ottoman empire in which their message of salvation would fall on oppressed, but grateful, Christians and Jewish ears.[40]

When the Jews and Christians did not convert as expected, the missionaries were disappointed; however, they were quick to point out in letters back home that this was because the Ottomans did not recognize the Protestants as a separate community.[41] A more likely basis for their disillusionment lies in the fact that from the very beginning, the missionaries refused to abandon their unshakeable conviction that an individual with the freedom to choose, to be "rational" as they put it, would inevitably choose to be a Protestant. They could not accept that the vast majority of Christians and Jews, despite whatever inequities they may have faced legally or politically in the Ottoman empire, were quite content to be who they were, at the same time as many among them were interested in the secular aspects of missionary education.[42] A seemingly endless wait for the anticipated flood of converts, the opposition of local churches, and the fact of Ottoman rule led to increasingly evident missionary frustration. Goodell lamented in September 1826:

> It is a great grief to us that we can do nothing directly to diminish the political evils of the country, nothing to insure protection for the innocent or to bring the guilty to justice, nothing to abate national guilt by being instrumental in promoting a national reform. In this respect, our circumstances are widely different from those of our brethren at the Sandwich Islands or among the Indian tribes of the West, whose labors have a direct and efficient bearing on the body politic, and an influence more or less powerful on the minds of those who enact laws and who control the opinions and practices of others.[43]

A significant point of reference for most missionaries in the Levant was, as Goodell's admission illustrates, the American encounter with and the Christian triumph over the "heathen" Indians. The only choice Indians seemed to have was to be "civilized" (that is, to be Christianized) or to be physically exterminated.[44] The idea of being "civilized" without also being Christianized had never been a viable option for the Indians. The missionaries, therefore, did not contemplate it for Arabs either.

For precisely this reason, even on the rare occasion a native Arab did show genuine interest in Protestantism, as did As'ad Shidyaq in 1825, the missionaries invariably found themselves trapped between the contradictory impulses that defined their mission: on the one hand, the missionaries believed utterly in the common nature of humanity, and implicitly, at least, they presumed the potential equality of all people; but, on the other hand, they also were just as convinced of the elect nature of America and Americans, who had to lead the rest of the world to salvation. It was not good enough to profess Protestantism. One had to become a Protestant, which for the missionaries meant abandoning a "nominal" native spirituality and jettisoning the native culture and politics that legitimized that spirituality, including how women were treated in the home, how Arabic was written, and how the government itself was run. Indeed, the first indications of As'ad Shidyaq's rebellion against the Maronite dogma were treated with suspicion by the American missionaries. Isaac Bird, for example, confided on January 6, 1826, that "we questioned Assad closely with regard to the state of his heart, and were rather disappointed at the readiness, with which he replied, that he thought he was born again. He can hardly be supposed to have acquired yet, even speculatively, very clear notions of what is regeneration; and it would seem quite as consistent with Christian humility and a true knowledge of his sinfulness, if he should speak of himself with more doubt and caution."[45] Bird conflated an explicitly theological stance on regeneration applicable to Americans and Arabs alike with an equally explicit paternalism reserved for natives alone. He refused to accept both Shidyaq's sincerity and the independence of his judgment, in large part because he considered Shidyaq too early down the path of spiritual and cultural amelioration.

For Bird and the other missionaries of the American Board, the mission to Syria represented one more step in a modern history of evangelism that had begun over a century before as an "errand into the wilderness."[46] Because the missionaries understood conversion to mean a process of spiritual transformation that they themselves had already completed by the nineteenth century (and accordingly had become missionaries "for propagating the gospel in heathen lands," as the act of incorporation of the American Board of Commissioners stated[47]), they intertwined a discourse of native spiritual rebirth within a framework of religious and civilizational progress. The missionaries sallied forth from a place "where the correctness of religious faith characterizes a riper age—where mind is inquisitive and active and well informed —where Christian institutions have retained their purity—where social intercourse is based upon sound principle—where conscience is unconstrained, minds unshackled, and liberty, full orbed, sheds her golden beams upon the happy land."[48] The missionaries, in short, interpreted the dynamic of their encounter with natives as a cultural and spiritual reconquest, which not only resurrected a familiar trope of Oriental despotism but crucially celebrated the United States temporally and geographically as the very pinnacle of human progress from which missionaries descended voluntarily to uplift, reform, and civilize those others who lived in a corrupted place and age. There could be no hint of equality, in the missionary mind, between such utterly antithetical societies or peoples.

THE RESPONSE OF A MULTIRELIGIOUS SOCIETY

This inability on the part of the missionaries to reconcile humility and primacy was compounded by the fact that the missionary encounter was anything but stable. Because the missionaries assumed that history and genuine Christianity had somehow left the Orient behind, they were unable to appreciate just how fast, and just how tenaciously, the supposedly stagnant Eastern churches, including the Maronite Church, would react to the threat they posed. The Maronite refusal to allow independent interpretation by As'ad Shidyaq was more than simple church domination over an allegedly superstitious flock. It was as much an expression of a relatively recent Maronite embrace of Roman Catholicism. Further, it was tied to an ardent Maronite conviction that to survive as a minority in a multireligious Ottoman empire meant preserving the supposedly unchanging boundaries of faith that separated Maronites from others. Indeed, as early as 1823 Patriarch

Hubaysh had denounced the "deceit and innovation [*tajdid*] instigated by these devious and deviant ones [the missionaries]."[49] He understood innovation to be ecclesiastical heresy, a deviation from the correct path charted out by the Roman Catholic Church, but also, implicitly, social and political heresy incipient in a missionary project that reduced the guardians of secular and religious knowledge in Mount Lebanon into purveyors of ignorance and despotism.[50]

The patriarch framed the encounter with the missionaries as a struggle between two rival intellectual and elite forces, the first represented by the wise patriarch backed by the will of God, and the second by cunning missionaries unleashed by Lucifer himself. The two battled for the putatively passive minds of the general Maronite population. While Patriarch Hubaysh insisted that the perpetual orthodoxy of the Maronites made them intrinsically immune to the temptations of the missionaries, he recognized a danger that the missionaries could lead the "simple" ones astray.[51] The Maronites, in other words, could not independently become heretics but could be made to become heretics if the false doctrines propagated by the missionaries "corrupted" their minds. The same conceit, of course, defined the social order of Mount Lebanon. Chroniclers and Ottoman authorities constructed the trope of the common peopple as inherently passive tax-paying subjects who might, on occasion, be stirred into rebellion by shadowy conspirators but who would never autonomously be moved to rebel.[52] For this reason, the patriarch and other Eastern Christians appealed to the Ottomans to suppress the missionaries.

While the Ottoman authorities may have been initially willing to tolerate missionary activity among the distant and marginal Lebanese Christians, Patriarch Hubaysh appealed to the Maronite community, to the Propaganda Fide in Rome, and to local Ottoman authorities to help him resist what he described as the insidious and destabilizing power of the well-funded foreign missionaries.[53] He recognized that As'ad Shidyaq threatened to leave the Maronite community exposed and unprotected by the rituals of social custom, political order, and hospitality that (in David Urquhart's words) "covered a multitude of sins."[54] For this reason perhaps, the patriarch often seemed more preoccupied with what As'ad Shidyaq publicly proclaimed than with what he truly believed, for it was the public proclamation and not inner belief that made Shidyaq break with or partake in, and hence become rebellious against or complicit in, the myth of perpetual orthodoxy and the myth of perpetual obedience to the Ottoman sultans. The patriarch pointed out that to allow Shidyaq to become a "heretic"—to become evangelized—was not simply to admit the malleability of Maronite faith and the porosity of Maronite religious boundaries. It was also to admit, implicitly, the instability of supposedly stable social and political boundaries, for if one did not respect the hierarchy of God, who was to guarantee the hierarchy of the shadow of God on earth, namely the Ottoman sultan?[55] The patriarch understood, correctly, that to open interpretation to any individual, regardless of rank, was to undermine the very basis of Ottoman order as it then existed. Or, as Emir Bashir put it February 1827 to a brother of As'ad Shidyaq, it was "to pull down all sects of religion."[56]

The missionaries ultimately found themselves locked in a rapidly escalating war, a war of metaphorical annihilation in which neither the Maronites nor the missionaries recognized the legitimacy of the other. Through the case of As'ad Shidyaq, the missionaries were dealt a stunning evangelical defeat. By isolating Shidyaq and making the Maronites and local Ottoman authorities accept his persecution as necessary (or at least having them turn a blind eye to it), the patriarch successfully transformed what the American missionaries presented as an apolitical spiritual and benevolent mission into a political battle. The patriarch turned As'ad Shidyaq's case into a struggle between being one of the heretical "English" and being a religiously and politically faithful "Maronite": between being, on the one hand, an insidious outsider having no religion or place in local society, and being, on the other hand, religious, that is, a quiescent and obedient Maronite with a name, a family, and a standing in multireligious Ottoman society.

The lack of any formal Ottoman response to American missionary proselytizing among the inhabitants of Mount Lebanon (and the tentativeness of the response to missionary activity in Aleppo) underscored the contradictions of premodern Ottoman tolerance.[57] On the one hand, this situation reflected what Bruce Masters has called Ottoman "official ambivalence" to changes within Christian minorities that did not undermine the sultan's sovereignty or tax base, an ambivalence underscored by "the prevalent response of Muslim religious scholars to cases involving the defection of an individual Christian from one sect to another [which] was to invoke the saying ascribed to the Prophet, 'Unbelief constitutes one nation' [*al-kufr mi lla wahida*]."[58] On the other hand, the lack of an initial Ottoman response was just as much an indication that the state did not interfere in the internal affairs of Christian communities, which were an integral part of the Ottoman order of things. To a much larger extent than historians have appreciated, the Maronite response to the American missionaries drew very much on a shared Muslim–Christian understanding of the world. The Maronite patriarch read the missionary intrusion in social Ottoman terms as much as in ecclesiastical Roman Catholic terms.

The patriarch thus contended that while missionaries may have tried to manipulate the "minds of the simple ones," and although they resorted to all manner of "deceit"—from distributing Arabic sermons and wandering among the people posing as benefactors of the poor, to bribery, and to buying and burning Bibles printed in Rome and replacing them with free copies of their own idolatrous books—they were destined to be frustrated by one of the oldest Christian churches in the world.[59] The patriarch thus spoke of engaging in a jihad against the American missionaries. He appealed to secular Maronite and Druze elites to expel the American missionaries, and in the early 1840s (when the Ottoman state made its direct presence in Mount Lebanon felt) he appealed directly to the Sublime Porte against what he called a foreign intrusion and in terms of coexistence—of a hierarchical social order that included all religious communities, the tranquility of which depended on the subordination of supposedly ignorant commoners to men of knowledge.[60] The patriarch warned the Ottoman authorities of the dangers posed by the arrival in Beirut "of a group of Biblishiyyin [Bible men] from America…who have taken to different ways to overturn the peace and tranquility of these parts, and to steal from them all calm and security, their goal being first to seduce to their sect any whom they can seduce from the different nations so that they can later carry out their designs."[61]

The patriarch expressed the paradox of a Maronite world caught between two masters, Rome and Istanbul, each demanding a different discourse of obedience, religiously consistent with Rome yet socially distant from it, and religiously distant from the Ottoman Arab Muslim environment yet socially cohesive with it. If Sultan Selim emphasized Muslim purity in the face of Napoleon's invasion of Egypt in 1798, the Maronite patriarch repeatedly avowed Maronite purity in the face of a putative American invasion.[62] Both pointed to a shared temporality that contradicted that of evangelical discourse: ideal order had already been achieved, and this order had to be protected and restored. Rather than looking forward to the Second Coming of Christ, the orientation in the Maronite case was to the safeguarding of an already achieved "perpetual orthodoxy," even as it reconciled itself to living in an impure world among impure communities. Against the new ideology of evangelism predicated on mass conversion came a first round of improvised if not harmonious Ottoman–Maronite defense, one that was as yet unsure precisely how to deal with a new reality of constant Western intrusions in an age of Western-dominated modernity.

CONSTRUCTING A NARRATIVE OF MARTYRDOM

The missionaries found themselves operating in an Orient that was radically out of place with what they had imagined. Despite their initial fears, they were personally secure and safe; at the same time, they were unable to produce a single Arab convert. To be so tantalizingly close to the object of their most fervent desire—the Holy Land—and yet to be so far from achieving what they had set out to achieve—the conversion of the millions of "perishing souls"—was the epitome of what we might call a kind of Protestant missionary purgatory. The missionaries, in a very real sense, seized upon the As'ad Shidyaq affair as a golden opportunity to escape this purgatory. No matter that Bird had initially doubted Shidyaq's sincerity; once the patriarch made his move, the missionaries quickly transformed him into a convert and a martyr.

In 1833, the readers of the *Missionary Herald* were provided with a dramatic conclusion to the hagiography of a convert. Two years before, Mehmed Ali, the ruler of Egypt, had sent his son Ibrahim Pasha to invade Syria. The Ottoman empire appeared on the brink of collapse, and a zealous Scottish merchant by the name of Robert Tod offered to use his influence with the conqueror of Syria to force the Maronite patriarch to reveal what he had done to As'ad Shidyaq. Tod asked Ibrahim Pasha to provide him with an escort of troops, and with them he marched to the distant monastery where Shidyaq had been imprisoned.

But he was disappointed, for he found no trace of As'ad Shidyaq. As Tod described the encounter with the Maronites at Qannubin:

> They then begged me to be seated, but I declined. They entreated. I replied, that my mission prevented my accepting anything at their hands. They nevertheless continued entreating and brought sherbet and pipes, neither of which I would receive. "What," said they, "do you take us for Mohammedans? We are Christians. There is no poison here," (drinking part of the sherbet). They once more offered it to me, but I again declined it. I stood in this manner about half an hour, surrounded by priests and servants, who all kept silence, when the patriarch was at length announced. I advanced to meet him. On coming up he appeared troubled, but recovering himself, he began complimenting me in a profuse and vapid manner. I attempted to interrupt him, but in vain: he kept on. Then suddenly retiring, for what reason I know not, he again appeared, and we all went underneath the awning. Here he again renewed his compliments, but I succeeded in interrupting him, saying that I wished to speak with him one word.
>
> "Speak," said he.
>
> "By the authority from Emir Besheer I require at your hands Asaad Esh Shidiak."[63]

The Maronite patriarch insisted, under Tod's imperious interrogation, that As'ad Shidyaq had long since died of a fever, leading Tod to conclude that Shidyaq must have died under the cruel torture of what the American Board would refer to as the Syrian Inquisition.[64]

Tod's account of his visit, in effect, transformed a resounding defeat—the imprisonment of Shidyaq and the failure to convince other Maronites thereafter to risk conversion—into a highly symbolic victory. Tod's narrative regained the initiative for the missionary cause after it had been lost to the Maronites during the battle over As'ad Shidyaq's body. That modern troops could be led by an evangelical Protestant into the heart of the Maronite patriarchate, that they could force the patriarch and his obsequious clergy to submit to a humiliating search, that they could brandish the enlightened authority of secular powers against the Maronites, were critical elements in the rewriting of the Shidyaq affair. These elements became part of a larger narrative of the inevitable triumph of a modern missionary movement over its supposedly medieval opposition. The image of the Inquisition —which as Edward Peters has suggested was itself a largely Enlightenment invention based on Reformation-era myths[65]—was used to script the story of As'ad Shidyaq as an encounter between self-avowedly rational missionaries and their irrational opponents. Although As'ad Shidyaq was not publicly executed, although his suffering was not openly witnessed, and despite the patriarch's adamant statement that Shidyaq died of a fever and the fact that Tod searched Qannubin in vain, the missionaries continued to insist that Shidyaq had met a martyr's fate. Jonas King, for instance, claimed that "if he died because of the horrible sufferings in a dungeon, without door or window, or in a five by four cell with a small hole for a window, or if he was massacred by his inexorable persecutors—enemies of the truth of the Bible which they profess to believe in, we do not know. However it may have been, he was a veritable martyr, and rested firm in his faith till the very end."[66] As early as 1828—before Shidyaq's fate had been ascertained but after he had been imprisoned at Qannubin—Rufus Anderson, then the assistant secretary for the American Board, wrote to Bird to urge him to memorialize As'ad Shidyaq:

> What should you think of preparing speedily from the materials in your possession, a brief memoir of Asaad Shidiak, to come into the series of Sabbath School Books? If you will prepare such a memoir I will see that it is carefully printed. Its sale will be a matter of certainty. Our M. Paper, No. VII, consisting of your journals respecting Asaad has been well rec[eived]. But what is needed is a narrative more continuous and popular in its form.[67]

This work entailed a "simple narrative" in which Shidyaq's own words would be eclipsed by a simple missionary martyrology. As the century progressed, the missionaries published several versions of the story of As'ad Shidyaq, each increasingly shorn of historical context to the point where the story could be summed up in the single phrase: that of the "first Protestant martyr."[68]

As'ad Shidyaq, the convert, the martyr, in this sense was an invention. First, his story rationalized, and at the same time it obscured, the failure of the mission—it made it possible for the missionaries to claim that if only As'ad Shidyaq had not been tortured there would have been many more converts. His martyrdom kept alive the fantasy the missionaries entertained of converting those who already considered themselves Christians. Missionary William Goodell, for example, wrote in September 1826 that Shidyaq's "blood would be like good seed sown in prolific soil."[69] Because his memorialization was directed entirely at an American audience, Shidyaq's example was meant to inspire fellow believers in the United States to continue to believe in, and contribute money to, an ever fitful missionary enterprise.

Second, and above all, As'ad Shidyaq was presented and was considered by the missionaries to be the model of the true native convert. Their memorialization of Shidyaq reconstituted the concept of martyrdom from a price that missionaries themselves might have to pay for their evangelical zeal to an inherently native act—a native witness to true faith that, in missionary eyes, could only be fully represented in American Protestant religious and cultural forms. That As'ad Shidyaq spoke and wrote in Arabic, that he identified until the end with the Maronites, that he partook in myriad cultural practices that the missionaries deemed incompatible with civilization, were henceforth passed over in silence by his missionary memorialists because they believed that he had been martyred for his Protestant faith. As they made As'ad Shidyaq exceptional, they also made him an exception to their cardinal rule that equated Protestantism with American spirituality but also with American culture and practice. Through his martyrdom, As'ad Shidyaq was an example for natives to follow; through his Arab Ottoman culture, he was not. For the missionaries, no native would ever measure up to Shidyaq's sincerity and integrity because no native could ever be sufficiently American enough spiritually or culturally.

Third, and perhaps most importantly, the "simple narrative" of Shidyaq presaged, and evolved into, another supposedly simple narrative about the transformation of an entire society. The missionaries, in other words, presented themselves, and have been represented by mostly sympathetic historians, as pioneers of the East who transformed local hostility into an enduring partnership that reformed the

Ottoman empire and that continues to reform the post-Ottoman Arab world despite formidable obstacles.[70] The missionaries claimed to be leading the region from a moribund fanatical past to a future marked by religious tolerance and freedom. When the Ottoman state, therefore, formally declared the equality of Muslims and Christians in the 1856 reform decree following the Crimean War, American missionaries presented the famous British ambassador Stratford Canning (Lord Stratford de Redcliffe), himself an evangelical Protestant and a champion of the missionaries in the empire, with a memorial of gratitude on March 4, 1856. This memorial concluded:

> We cannot, however, close this inadequate expression of our views and feelings on the subject, without alluding to the necessity of the continued experienced counsel, and the friendly encouragement and assistance too, which the enlightened Western Powers, and especially England, will have to afford the Government of Turkey in introducing and supporting these principles, which are so far beyond the conceptions of an ignorant and fanatical population. The temptation of yielding to circumstances, and of sacrificing the principles of justice and truth to popular prejudice, will be great and constant. The very novelty of the moral principles now to be introduced into the administration of the spiritual interests of society, as well as the depth and extent of their bearings, will, for some time to come, render experienced counsel and cooperation from abroad a welcome service, even to the most vigorous Government, in carrying out the intentions of the benevolent Sovereign, and in meting out equal justice to the various religious denominations and to individuals, without respect of persons or of traditionary fanaticism.[71]

The underlying assumption of this genealogy of tolerance was shared by both Canning and the American missionaries. They firmly believed that the principle of "equal justice to the various religious denominations and to individuals" was a natural outgrowth of (Anglo-American) Christian civilization and morality, whose antithesis they clearly identified as an unchanging local Muslim (and Maronite) tradition.

Obscured in this genealogy of modern tolerance was any appreciation of the enduring legacy of premodern Ottoman tolerance. This tolerance had been generated almost exclusively from the exigencies of Muslim imperialism and from the ambivalent yet dynamic relationship that reconciled the Ottoman empire's non-Muslim subjects to Muslim Ottoman dynastic rule and integrated them into it. These same exigencies led to a never declared but always understood idea of compromise, a realization of the limits of power, and hence a reading of a multiethnic and religious empire as an already achieved ideal Muslim (or Maronite) order that occasionally was disturbed only to be set right. Nothing could have been more alien to the expansive and expectant American missionary attempt to fundamentally reshape the world.

Equally important, the limits on the principles of "justice and truth" in contemporary Britain and the United States were also obscured by this genealogy of tolerance. That ideas of equality were as fraught with tension in the antebellum United States and in Great Britain as they were in the Ottoman empire (if not far more so in the case of the United States) was not only lost on the missionaries but considered utterly irrelevant to the issue at hand. They could conceive of the question only as a uniquely Muslim problem of fanaticism with a uniquely Western Christian solution of tolerance. Thus any resistance to the logic or practice of reform, any deviation from the course of Christianization and civilization, was immediately identified by the missionaries and by Canning as evidence of the "bigotry of old times," unable or unwilling to accept "modern civilization" and "Christianity."[72]

Historians of the Ottoman empire, and specifically those studying the missionaries to the Middle East, have tried repeatedly to refute this genealogy of tolerance as something inherently foreign to the Ottoman Muslim tradition. They have illustrated the complexity and transformations regarding the nature and limits of Ottoman treatment of minorities.[73] But they have, by and large, passed over the question of what was occurring at precisely the same time in US history. In other words, historians of the Ottoman empire have, wittingly or unwittingly, affirmed the central assumption that has animated a spurious politics of comparison between the Middle East and the West—one that views Middle Eastern history as the problem to be analyzed, leaving uninterrogated key episodes of American and Western history—from surging anti-Catholicism in the United States to increasingly stark racial thinking and policies in both European empires and the United States—that utterly refute the notion that liberal tolerance was an accomplished fact in the West. The idea, of course, is not to caricature American history in the manner that Ottoman and Middle Eastern history has often been, and is still being caricatured, and still less to "defend" the Ottomans by pointing to the obvious discrepancies between the rhetoric and reality of freedom in the American past. It seems clear, however, that the only way out of this impoverishing historiographical pitfall, which compares the assumed with the actual and which leaves untold at least half the story of a cross-cultural encounter involving American missionaries and the Ottoman empire, is to enlarge dramatically the scope of inquiry. We must examine how relevant history unfolded simultaneously, if distinctly and unevenly, in the Ottoman empire and the United States to compare historical process with historical process and to understand the implications of their juxtaposition brought about by the missionary intrusion into the Ottoman empire. That is, we must literally unravel history's different strands, first woven together by these missionaries in a so fervent, if tendentious, a manner. We are still at the very beginnings of this endeavor.

Notes

1. This is only just beginning to change in Ottoman history; see Deringil, "'They Live in a State of Nomadism and Savagery,'" and Makdisi, "Ottoman Orientalism." For US history, see also Stoler, "Tense and Tender Ties," and the roundtable debate that follows in the same issue of the *Journal of American History*.

2. Jean and John L. Comaroff struggled with this problem in their classic two-volume history of nonconformist British missionaries among the southern African Tswanas. See their *Of Revolution and Revelation*, vols. 1 and 2. For a similar problem, see also Catherine Hall, *Civilising Subjects*.

3. See Todorov, *Conquest of America*.

4. Here I am building on the phrase "pre-modern accommodation of difference," which Bose and Jalal, *Modern South Asia*, suggest for Indo-Islamic cultures before the arrival of the British as an alternative to either an anachronistic sense of liberal multiculturalism or an ahistorical sense of age-old communalism or sectarianism.

5. See Reynolds, "Difference and Tolerance in the Ottoman Empire," in which Aron Rodrigue enjoins scholars to forgo the misleading language of post-Enlightenment majority and minority in the Ottoman empire. Rodrigue also rejects nationalist thinking and repudiates romantic thinking about the Ottoman empire as a place of "harmonious coexistence."

6. I am here indebted to Ann Laura Stoler's discussion of the "politics of comparison" found in her reading of US historiography. See Stoler, "Tense and Tender Ties."

7. Chakrabarty, *Provincializing Europe,* 42–43.

8. For the classic study of this mission, see Tibawi, *American Interests in Syria.*

9. Deringil, "'There Is No Compulsion in Religion.'"

10. Salibi and Khoury, *Missionary Herald,* vol. 1, 6.

11. Masters, *Christians and Jews in the Ottoman Arab World.*

12. Deringil, "'There Is No Compulsion in Religion.'"

13. The Greek Catholic sect arose in the eighteenth century after Catholic missionaries succeeded in proselytizing a large number of Greek Orthodox followers in cities such as Aleppo. See Masters, *Christians and Jews in the Ottoman Arab World.*

14. See Heyberger, *Les Chrétiens du Proche-Orient.*

15. Patriarch Yusuf Hubaysh rose through the ranks as a dedicated Latinizer, and it was during his tenure as patriarch that the Maronite Church finally abolished the tradition of mixed monasteries and also introduced a reformed liturgy. He also oversaw the establishment of the Maronite seminary of 'Ayn Waraqa, marking it as the foremost center for the reformed education of aspiring Maronite clergymen. Yet Hubaysh's election as patriarch in May 1823 was controversial: he was not yet the required forty years old and did not have an outright majority of votes cast by the Maronite bishops. As a result, the Propaganda annulled his election, only to have the pope confirm it on May 3, 1824. Energetic but initially insecure in his position, Patriarch Hubaysh was confronted almost immediately with the arrival of the American missionaries. See Dib, *Histoire de l'Eglise Maronite,* 22.

16. Makdisi, *Culture of Sectarianism.*

17. Rycaut, *Present State of the Ottoman Empire,* 98–99.

18. al-Shidyaq, *Kitab Akhbar al-a'yan fi Jabal Lubnan,* vol. 1, 111–21.

19. This information is taken from al-Bustani, *Qissat As'ad al-Shidyaq,* 11–15.

20. Phillips, *Protestant America and the Pagan World,* 3; Ahlstrom, *Religious History of the American People,* 393–97; Elsbree, *Rise of the Missionary Spirit in*

America, 84–98. Eighteen of the board's twenty-six members in 1813 were college educated. Five of them were college presidents (of Yale, Bowdoin, Middlebury, Union, and New Jersey). The board also included governors of Connecticut and Rhode Island. Field, *America and the Mediterranean World,* 88.

21. American Board of Commissioners for Foreign Missions, *Instructions to the Missionaries.*

22. American Board of Commissioners for Foreign Missionaries, "Memorial of the American Board of Commissioners for Foreign Missions to the Honorable Senate and House of Representatives of the United States in Congress assembled," in *First Annual Report of the American Society for Promoting the Civilization and General Improvement of the Indian Tribes in the United States,* 1824 (Milwood, NY: Kraus Reprint, 1975), 66.

23. Hutchison, *Errand to the World,* 65–67; Andrew, "Educating the Heathen."

24. Horsman, *Race and Manifest Destiny,* 202–07.

25. The American Board was among the minority that unsuccessfully led opposition to Andrew Jackson's policies of Native American expulsions. See Hutchison, *Errand to the World,* 64; Horsman, *Race and Manifest Destiny,* 205; Phillips, *Protestant America,* 71–73; and Andrew, *From Revivals to Removal.*

26. Obenzinger, *American Palestine,* 33.

27. It was, for example, reaction to the appointment of the liberal Henry Ware to the Hollis Professorship of Divinity at Harvard in 1805 that led in 1808 to the establishment of Andover Theological Seminary, from which most of the first American Board missionaries were drawn. Yale was another bastion of conservatism under Timothy Dwight.

28. Elsbree, *Rise of the Missionary Spirit in America,* 129.

29. Archives de Bkirke (archives of the Maronite Patriarchate, Lebanon). Drawer of Yusuf Hubaysh, Somaglia to Hubaysh, August 28, 1824. The Bibles distributed by the missionaries were reprints made by the British and Foreign Bible Society, printed in Rome in 1671, with the Apocrypha omitted. For more information, see Tibawi, *American Interests in Syria,* 27.

30. Salibi and Khoury, *Missionary Herald,* vol. 1, 483.

31. Papers of the American Board of Commissioners for Foreign Missions, 16.5, Communications for the Mediterranean, 1817–1837, William Goodell to Jeremiah Evarts, September 15, 1826; Tibawi, *American Interests in Syria,* 41; Obenzinger, *American Palestine,* 50.

32. al-Bustani, *Qissat As'ad al-Shidyaq,* 20–48.

33. Salibi and Khoury, *Missionary Herald,* vol. 1, 407; American Board of Commissioners for Foreign Missions, *Report of the American Board of Commissioners for Foreign Missions, Compiled from Documents Laid Before the Board at the Eighteenth Annual Meeting* (Boston: Crocker and Brewster, 1827), 43.

34. This information is drawn from what appears to be a diary left by As'ad Shidyaq during the first month of his second confinement at Dayr 'Alma. See Archives de Bkirke, fragments of a diary of As'ad Shidyaq, April 6, 1826–April 25, 1826.

35. al-Bustani, *Qissat As'ad al-Shidyaq,* 56; Salibi and Khoury, *Missionary Herald,* vol. 1, 467.

36. The missionaries departed Beirut for Malta in May 1828. They returned two years later, in May 1830.

37. American Board of Commissioners for Foreign Missions, 16.5, Communications for the Mediterranean, 1817–1837, William Goodell to Jeremiah Evarts, September 15, 1826; Bird, *Bible Work in Bible Lands,* 196–97.

38. Salibi and Khoury, *Missionary Herald,* vol. 1, 467.

39. For more general American attitudes toward the Islamic world at this juncture, see Bencherif, *Image of Algeria,* 1–71; Sha'ban, *Islam and Arabs;* and Allison, *Crescent Obscured.*

40. Salibi and Khoury, *Missionary Herald,* vol. 1, 5–7, 290.

41. Salibi and Khoury, *Missionary Herald,* vol. 1, 430–31; vol. 2, 22–25.

42. By 1826 the missionaries had opened seven schools, including one for girls. According to figures in the eighteenth annual report of the American Board, the total number of students was 350, of whom 30 were girls.

43. American Board of Commissioners for Foreign Missions, 16.5, Communications for the Mediterranean, 1817–1837, William Goodell to Jeremiah Evarts, September 15, 1826.

44. Wallace, *Jefferson and the Indians.*

45. Salibi and Khoury, *Missionary Herald,* vol. 1, 440.

46. Miller, *Errand into the Wilderness;* Hutchison, *Errand to the World,* 4–5; Phillips, *Protestant America,* 19.

47. American Board of Commissioners for Foreign Missions, *Memorial Volume of the American Board of Commissioners for Foreign Missions* (Boston: ABCFM, 1861), 405.

48. Salibi and Khoury, *Missionary Herald,* vol. 1, 368.

49. Archives de Bkirke, drawer of Yusuf Hubaysh (1823 encyclical against the Bible men).

50. This notion of innovation echoes the Islamic concept of *bid'a.* It is men-

tioned as well in edicts of local secular authorities against Protestant proselytization. See Salibi and Khoury, *Missionary Herald,* vol. 2, 6. Catholic counterreformation persecution of Protestants also charged Protestants with innovation, so it may well be that the Maronite Church was drawing simultaneously on Ottoman and Catholic discourses of innovation. See Gregory, *Salvation at Stake,* 177.

51. Archives de Bkirke, drawer of Yusuf Hubaysh (1823 encyclical against the Bible men).

52. Makdisi, *Culture of Sectarianism,* 49.

53. Archives de Bkirke, drawer of Yusuf Hubaysh (report of Patriarch Hubaysh to the Apostolic See), December 23, 1831; Salibi and Khoury, *Missionary Herald,* vol. 1, 469; vol. 2, 6.

54. Urquhart, *Lebanon,* vol. 1, 208.

55. Since this project is still at its beginning, the question of the precise Ottoman reaction to the case of As‘ad Shidyaq is unclear. According to a copy of a *ferman,* or imperial edict, preserved in the papers of Isaac Bird, the Ottoman sultan forbade Muslims to read the subversive books from *bilad al-afranj* ("the land of the Franks," or Europe). See Isaac Bird Papers, Manuscripts and Archives, Yale University Library, New Haven, Group 82, Box 2/Folder 24, ferman dated Sevval 1239/June 1824. A similar situation occurred nearly a century earlier, when many of the Greek Orthodox community of Aleppo defected to form the Greek Catholic Church. The Greek Orthodox patriarch appealed to Istanbul to prevent the rebellion. At the time, while local Ottoman authorities wavered between accepting the autonomous civil status of the Greek Catholics and rejecting it, the central government generally sided with the Greek Orthodox establishment. Finally, in the 1820s, the Ottoman authorities formally recognized the civil status of the Greek Catholics in Syria as a result of the Greek War of Independence. The civil status of the Arab Protestants was not recognized until 1850. For more information on the Greek Catholics, see Masters, *Christians and Jews in the Ottoman Arab World.*

56. Salibi and Khoury, *Missionary Herald,* vol. 2, 6.

57. It appears that it was only when the Greek Catholic community in Aleppo complained about American attempts to cause "sedition" and "unrest" among the sultan's subjects that the Ottoman government forbade the circulation of all Bibles and Psalters printed in Europe, on the basis that they caused "apprehension, disputation, and disturbance" among the people. The missionaries ignored the prohibition. Tibawi, *American Interests in Syria,* 28–29.

58. Masters, *Christians and Jews in the Ottoman Arab World,* 81–85.

59. Archives de Bkirke, drawer of Yusuf Hubaysh (1823 encyclical against the

Bible men).

60. Makdisi, *Culture of Sectarianism,* 29.

61. Archives de Bkirke, drawer of Yusuf Hubaysh (1841 draft petition to Sublime Porte).

62. Karal, *Selim III,* 49; Tibawi, *American Interests in Syria,* 27.

63. Salibi and Khoury, *Missionary Herald,* vol. 2, 331.

64. Salibi and Khoury, *Missionary Herald,* vol. 2, 27.

65. Peters, *Inquisition,* 155–56.

66. King, *Extraits d'un ouvrage écrit vers la fin de l'année 1826 et au commencement de 1827,* 182.

67. American Board of Commissioners for Foreign Missions, 2.01, Preliminary Series, Volume 1, Rufus Anderson to Isaac Bird, June 20, 1828.

68. Thomson, *Land and the Book,* 129.

69. Salibi and Khoury, *Missionary Herald,* vol. 1, 436.

70. For example, Field, *America and the Mediterranean World.* For more information on American attitudes toward the Middle East, see McAlister, *Epic Encounters.*

71. National Archives, Kew, Foreign Office, Great Britain, Series 424/9, Correspondence Respecting Christian Privileges in Turkey 1851–1856, Lord Stratford de Redcliffe to the Earl of Clarendon, March 6, 1856, Enclosure, "Address," Constantinople, March 4, 1856.

72. National Archives, Kew, Foreign Office, Great Britain, Series Canning to Aberdeen, March 27, 1842.

73. Masters, *Christians and Jews in the Ottoman Arab World;* Deringil, "'There Is No Compulsion in Religion.'"

3

The Rights of Difference

Law and Citizenship in the Russian Empire

Jane Burbank

If we focus on the structure of states, rather than their names, Russia presents itself as a particularly enduring imperial formation. An imperial mode of rule was successfully configured on the territories of sixteenth-century Muscovy and endured as the foundation of Muscovy's successor states—imperial Russia, the Union of Soviet Socialist Republics, and the Russian Federation. The Russian kind of empire was more successful in the long run—that is, up to the present—than those of its imperial rivals in the modern era. Unlike Great Britain, France, the Ottomans, and the Habsburgs, Russia did not lose the most extensive and valuable of its imperial territories in the twentieth century. Siberia, with its vast resources, remains a part of Russian political space.[1]

The organizing principles of empire were not, in themselves, a cause of the three catastrophic breakdowns on Russia's territories of institutionalized state authority—the Time of Troubles (1598–1613),[2] the revolutions of 1917, and the suicide of the Soviet regime. Each of these crises was precipitated by elite desertions at the very highest levels of authority, rather than by colonial or national rebellions. Indeed, it could be argued that habits of imperial governance helped the state survive these disastrous collapses by providing structures, imagination, and the will to reconfigure an empire-state. Both in the formative years of innovating communism and during the disintegration of Soviet power, would-be and actual state leaders employed shared conceptions of the state, its tasks, and its relationship to citizens, as well as a common language—all deriving from the experience of empire. The habitus of empire provided each generation of rulers with a powerful means to stitch most of the country together again.[3] By shifting the level of our inquiry from ideologies (whether of scholars or of states) to practices—to the integument of polities—we can investigate the organizing capacity of the empire-state form.

In this chapter, I focus on the configuration of rights in imperial Russia. I draw attention to conceptions of rights asserted and employed by rulers and subjects and examine the significance of the "imperial rights regime" for politics, law, and society in Russia. The underlying principles of the Russian rights regime may be compared with those of other empires, enabling exploration of the impact of different foundational attitudes regarding rights upon imperial polities. The Russian rights regime was based on the state's assignment of rights and duties to differentiated collectivities. I argue that the practice of allocating particular and various rights to groups defined by acknowledged social differences inhibited the formation of a democratically minded public and a politics based on equal citizenship. At the same time, the imperial rights regime provided imperial subjects with a normalized and legal framework for connection to the state and the exercise of collective authority. Inclusion and difference were not antagonists but partners in the habitus of empire based on differentiated rights.

UNDER THE UMBRELLA OF IMPERIAL LAW

Russia became an empire-state by both conquest and law. The Grand Princedom of Moscow emerged as a spreading center of political control through piecemeal, often violent, incorporation of bordering territories and the people living on them. The wide dispersal of low-level resources over a large space uncoveted by any other great power conditioned the formation of the Russian polity. The center could afford to add on new regions bit by bit, but the populations of incorporated regions did not have the resources—social or economic

—to resist incorporation, nor could they conceive of uniting against the center. Both territorial expansion and ad hoc imperial governance—the administration of regions as separate units through distinct regulations—were cheap and possible. From the eighteenth to the twentieth century, the extension of Russian political control into the wealthier spaces of central Europe, Central Asia, and the Caucasus —also piecemeal and often violent—did not fundamentally alter the imperial mentality built into the Russian administrative system from its beginnings.[4]

Governance for leaders of this empire was about control over resources—land, its products, and labor—and the social order required to secure them. Administration, rather than law, was the primary imperative of Russian rulers, but law entered the picture as soon as the imperial state asserted its claim to define the rights and obligations of people living on its terrain. Building on the tight connection established by Muscovite law between state and subjects in the most vital aspects of their lives—status, resources, and individual dignity[5]—leaders of the expanding empire asserted their sovereignty through decrees and regulations. Military might or the threat of its use may have established imperial borders, but ruling by force alone was beyond the capacity of the governors.

Legislation addressed the imperial population in two ways. First, elites with the power to serve or undermine the Russian empire had to be themselves served or undermined. Thus a part of imperial law defined rights and obligations of local elites. In the seventeenth century, for example, Polish nobles in areas ceded to Moscovy were ordered to "possess their estates...in accord with...imperial commands and the grants and privileges of the Polish kings."[6] The language of this decree reflects the tsar's superior power over property rights as well as the state's incorporation of privileges that had been earlier assigned by other rulers. Edicts of this kind expressed the basic bargain of noble politics. Elites received certain rights, by category, in return for their service (military, administrative, economic) to the state.

A second kind of legislation addressed imperatives of maintaining order and acquiring resources at a different social level. If tribute and taxes were to be collected, the organizing and reproductive capacity of local populations had to be sustained. Legal regulation enhanced social stability and productivity, and the incorporation of distinctive customs and laws into official governance became an element of imperial statecraft.

That legal practices concerning marriage and property were not identical across the empire did not pose a problem for this strategy. A foundation of Russian legal thinking was the assumption that all peoples possessed their own customs and laws. This lesson was learned by negative experience on occasions when imperial authorities tried to impose Russian legal institutions in conquered areas.[7] A more efficient method was to validate earlier legal regimes by bringing them into the imperial fold. Over time, the empire produced a series of regulations and decrees that asserted the particular rights and obligations of whole groups of people, defined by territory, confession, ethnicity, or even work. This cumulative and malleable kind of legalism corresponded to real differences in social norms and legal practices throughout the empire as well as to the crasser needs of rulers. The multiplicity of legal regimes legitimated within the empire both asserted the superior authority of Russian rule and allowed populations to do a great deal of governance themselves. Drawing "customs" in under the umbrella of law expressed an imperial social contract: the empire enforced an array of local judicial practices—a cheap way to keep the peace—in return for tribute and taxes.[8]

For the rule makers, imperial legal culture had the following qualities. All people of the empire were governed by Russian law, emanating from the emperor. All rights and duties were created by this law; there were no natural rights. Rights and duties were assigned differentially to variously defined groups. The particular content of laws regulating many aspects of social life depended upon "customs" and "laws" of different groups. What was "natural" to Russian conceptions of law was not the possession of rights by individuals but the practice of social regulation by groups. It was expected that peoples would have "their" collective customs and rules, developed prior to Russian conquest or annexation. Russian imperial law accommodated particular social institutions extant in the population, did not homogenize them, but legalized them selectively within the whole opus of imperial legislation. The law recognized and incorporated particularity while retaining its claim to be the ultimate source of justice.[9]

This expansive approach to legal regulation could be described as "legal pluralism," although the term itself is controversial and variously defined. The Russian empire conforms to what has been called the lawyer's kind of legal pluralism: "the recognition by the state...of the existence of a multiplicity of legal sources which constitute its legislation."[10] Russian rulers recognized an array of local religious and customary practices within their enormous polity and legalized these sources of authority by integrating many kinds of local courts into the legal system. The point is not that multiple systems of social norms operated outside the Russian law—this is always the case even in the most conventionally law-based states—but that Russian law assigned legal power to courts and other local authorities, such as religious leaders, whose decisions in many cases could be made, legally, on customary or confessional principles. Imperial law thus included several different procedural and normative regimes. "Otherness" was a fact of life for law, as administrators and conquerors gathered their collective subjects under the imperial legal umbrella. The task facing imperial legislators was to attain completeness in their rules, to include all subjects with their diverse customs, not to enforce uniformity.

DIFFERENCE IN A LAND OF UNCERTAIN "WE'S" AND MANY "THEY'S"

In Russia the acceptance of difference in legal practices and in historically established "customs" was enfolded in an ideology of imperial prerogative concerning rights. Rights belonged to peoples because and only because they were allocated to particular groups by the state. "Difference" was a foundation of the empire's existence, essential to the process of defining and allocating rights. Rights could not be had except through the state and through official identification as a member of one or another kind of group. The recognition of "natural" social collectivity—not "natural" individuals—went hand in hand with the imperial practice of assigning rights to groups. The state kept for itself the authority to assign, reassign, and take away rights and privileges from the groups that comprised the empire's population.

If differentiated collectivities were units of the polity—the groups of people to whom particular sets of rights were assigned—how were these groups defined? Religion, ethnicity, territory, status, sex, age, occupation, and culture were available and cross-cutting categories for imperial lawmakers. Although Russian elites were as engaged as their western European and other contemporaries in efforts to catalog, characterize, and classify the "peoples" of their empire, their efforts did not produce one single regulatory scheme or map of civilization. Even under the strong influence of German ethnographic science and Herder's romantic nationalism, Russian scholars and officials—often the same people—emphasized the multiplicity of the empire's "peoples," celebrated their diversity, and, for the most part, arrayed them in magnificent displays of imperial heterogeneity. For example, the message of early nineteenth-century projects for a national museum was not the glory of conquest over natives or even the progress that Russia brought to them but the wondrous creations of the "various tribes who inhabit areas of our fatherland, and who are distinguished among themselves by their ancestries, customs, languages, and religions." All of these were to be preserved and displayed to the public to enhance awareness of the "fatherland" and its enormous family.[11] The similarity between this nineteenth-century vision of grand diversity and the proud displays of "our native peoples" in Soviet times signals the positive appeal of composite empire to Russia's self-image makers over two centuries.

Students of colonial empire will find such imperial representations of diversity familiar and may interpret them as displays of inferior status and claims to cultural hegemony typical of any colonial power. After all, the terms "our native peoples" and "our fatherland" both suggest that some undefined "we" claimed power over a motley array of "others." Certainly a tension existed throughout the imperial period between the legitimation of different heritages and practices and the prospect of transforming them into different, better, perhaps more unified behaviors and beliefs. Further, some native people could be treated better or worse—even much worse—than others at different times. But note that in the Russian version of empire, there was no national or metropolitan "we" confronting an inferior peripheral "they." For one thing, there were multiple "they's," and for another, what a "we" might be was unclear in a number of respects.

First, consider the possible "they's." A classificatory impulse permeated Russian elite thinking from the eighteenth century, but the creation of a single, fixed, and ethnicized geography proved to be impossible.[12] A satisfying alignment of peoples, spaces, and confessions could not be had. Nations (in the eighteenth-century sense), religions, and territories were not alike in their distribution; settlements, migrations, and long-term, long-distance contacts continued to mix people up; most importantly, perhaps, this unbourgeois polity did not acknowledge permanence of property rights. It was not in the rulers' way of thinking to draw up eternal territorial boundaries and to localize government in a final fashion in "national" or "ethnic" hands. Acknowledging the importance of letting locals use their own "laws" for certain purposes did not mean a commitment to thoroughgoing federalism or to equal treatment of all subjects. Quite the contrary. Keeping multiple maps of "they's" in play was fundamental to the flexibility and tactics of imperial rule. Religious, ethnic, territorial, and status-based categories were all possible objects of legal attention and manipulation.[13]

Another obstacle presented itself to aspiring builders of absolute civilizational divides and hierarchies: Russians were also "they's." Or at least some of them were. The question of who Russians were bogged down in ethnographic confusion in the mid–nineteenth century. Neither the leaders of the Ethnographic Division of the Imperial Geographical Society, nor historians working with surveys of local material culture, language, and folklore could produce a "scientific" analysis of Russianness. Too many "Russian" peasants did things in too many different ways for would-be systematizers. Very thick description and expansive research projects on a multitude of "peoples" and their many ways of being became the hallmarks of imperial (and later Soviet) ethnographical investigations of Russians and the other natives of the empire.[14]

One reason that Russians could not be securely attached to a hegemonic "we" was serfdom, which until 1861 subordinated half of the peasant population to their landlords (not all of them Russian). Another was the estate system, which endured until the end of the Romanov empire. Both before and after emancipation, most Russians were peasants and taxpayers, not members of a civilizing and nontaxpaying nobility. The lived divide between estates, between nobles and peasants with their very different rights regimes, meant that commonality as Russians and as a dominant people was hard to think of in the present. There was little in the political imagination of Russian elites that would compel them to see themselves and peasants as equal members of a national community or to construct institutions that would reflect such shared membership in an ethnicized "we." Even those who hoped for a more uniformly governed polity imagined extending "Russian" law and culture over everyone—both Russian peasants and non-Russian peoples—rather than consolidating the power of Russian ethnics over others.

Besides, many of the most powerful administrators, military leaders, and advisers to the emperor were not Russian anyway. The political economy of the empire was based from its earliest days on cooptation of high-ranking and powerful local elites into a serving and ruling class.[15] Some of the highest-ranking families in the realm were originally Tatars or Poles; over time, these great landed families became the "Russian" aristocracy. Even in the beginning of the twentieth century, half of the titled members of the State Council came from non-Russian families.[16] One consequence and cause of the imperial rights regime was the absence of a nationalized "we" both in the metropole and among authorities dispatched to govern the enormous realm.

A multiplicity of differences was fundamental, not problematic, for the workings of Russian empire. The Russian imperial rights regime took shape in a polity based on awareness, acceptance, and manipulation of "difference" but not upon categorical divisions of an ethnic or racial sort between the rulers and ruled. A division into "self" and "other" made no sense for elites in a society of many "others" and little sense of "self." The human heterogeneity of the polity was a given for Russian leaders, but just what constituted grounds for classification and division and what was thought to be gained from differentiated governance shifted over time. Governance based on differentiated collectivities provided a framework for social life and had a profound effect on the political imagination of both rulers and subjects.

THE IMPERIAL RIGHTS REGIME

What did governance based in law and on differentiated collectivity mean for subjects? First, for ordinary people, as well as elites, imperial law was a source of rights. Rights, like obligations, were assigned to people through their status as members of collective bodies. The empire's legal codes spelled out the rules for social life by addressing particular groups. It was by belonging to a collective, with its assigned rights, that an individual gained the possibility of engaging legally in many of the most fundamental aspects of social life. Marriage, buying property, changing one's place of residence, and bequeathing land and goods were not simply regulated but regulated according to the estate, confession, ethnicity, or territorial location of the individuals concerned.[17]

Individuals living in the empire thus possessed rights through their inclusion in a particular category of imperial subjects addressed by imperial law. These rights were no less rights for having been assigned to groups. Moreover, the particularity of imperial legislation, and its concern for local custom, meant that a variety of norms and sanctions relating to basic social institutions were not only tolerated but legalized within the imperial system of governance.

The right to be married by the rules of one's own faith was offered to most subjects of the empire. The laws on marriage in the Russian Civil Code display the habits of collectivist thought, communal particularity, and state-assigned rights characteristic of imperial governance. Book 1 of the Civil Law Code, entitled "On Family Rights and Obligations," sets forth the rights and obligations of marriage possessed by the empire's members. These rights were defined differently according to the religion of the spouses. The first three chapters of the marriage code are titled "On Marriage between People of the Orthodox Faith," "On Marriages of non-Orthodox Christians among Themselves and with Orthodox People, and on the Registration of Marriages of Sectarians," and finally "On Marriages of non-Christians among Themselves and with Christians."[18] The law assumed that every person seeking marriage was either a Christian of a particular denomination or a non-Christian member of a "tribe" or a "people" (*narod*). No place was made in the legal code for a person without a religion, nor was it conceivable to Russian lawmakers that a church, "tribe," or "people" would not have marriage rules.[19]

Imperial marriage law both recognized differences in marriage practices and made some universalizing assumptions. The law assumed that there were social concerns—such as marriage—that all "peoples" would address according to their particular ethical beliefs and regulating practices based in religion, custom, and law. Equally foundational was the notion that all individuals belonged to one or another group and would participate in a group's regulatory practices. When individuals wanted to marry someone of another faith, it was critical for the law to establish how the intersection of two moral regimes could be achieved and whether marriages of this type should be allowed. There were no "civil" marriages outside religious authority, in our terms, but from an imperial perspective, all marriages attained a legal force by virtue of their regulation by religious authorities recognized and empowered by imperial law.

In accord with the imperial prerogative of differentiated governance, the rules for marriage were not uniform: Orthodox Christians, non-Orthodox Christians, and non-Christians could marry under laws particular to their religious groups. The Civil Code was far more specific in its regulations of Orthodox and non-Orthodox Christians than it was for non-Christians. Non-Christians had the right to "marry according to the rules of their law or customs, without the participation of civic authorities or Christian spiritual administration." This right devolved authority generously and far outside the state.[20]

The marriage code spelled out relationships between religious status and other potential sources of rights and obligations. For the Orthodox, religion explicitly trumped other collective categories. The first statute in the Civil Code declared, "People of the Orthodox confession of all estates [*sostoiania*] without distinction, may enter into marriage with each other, without soliciting for this a special permission from the administration, nor a discharge from the estate [*soslovie*] or societies, to which they belong."[21] This statute, which explicitly addressed the postemancipation right of Orthodox people of different estates to marry each other, was followed by a series of "limitations and exceptions" upon this right of the Orthodox to marry. Some of these restrictions applied to all Orthodox subjects. For example, marriage over the age of eighty was forbidden, as were fourth (consecutive) marriages. Most "limitations and exceptions" that affected a person's right to marry were based on a prolific variety of other collective conditions, such as belonging to a particular monastic group, being of a certain age and sex, serving in the military or the civil service, having been convicted of a crime, or coming from a certain province or area of the empire. Orthodox Christian natives of the Caucasus, for example, could marry earlier than other Christians.[22]

In accord with this imperial vision of a confessionally clustered society, many of the marriage code's statutes addressed the problematic, diverse, and numerous interfaces between people of different faiths. This is an area where the governors' tendency to privilege Orthodox Christianity over other faiths is visible. Orthodox and Roman Catholic subjects were forbidden to marry non-Christians, and "Protestant marriages with Lamaites and pagans" were also not allowed. A large section of the Civil Code was devoted to regulating marriages between Orthodox and various non-Orthodox Christians and to ensuring the primacy of the Orthodox faith in these unions.[23] The imperial state aspired to include multiple social norms within the law, but also to sustain oversight and manipulative capacity through its ultimate authority over all subjects.

Marriage rules are only one example of how legal pluralism enabled people from different social spheres to use legal rights for their own ends. Procedures such as adoption, inheritance, transfers of property, and contracts were all addressed by imperial law, which made "exceptions" or referred to special regulations that covered particular categories of people. The law's asserted authority over all rights and their use was enhanced by its incorporation of distinctive ways to legitimate transactions. Under the rubric, "On the means of acquiring rights to property," statute 699 of the Civil Code declares, "rights to properties [*imushchestva*] are acquired only by means defined in the laws."[24] This statute is followed by others that specify various property regimes recognized for different categories of people and different regions, for example, for members of the rural estate, for Cossacks, for rural inhabitants of the Grand Princedom of Finland, for certain transactions in Siberia, and for the western and Baltic provinces.[25]

Imperial law thus extended civic possibilities to its subjects in the most fundamental aspects of their lives. Because all marriages were legalized indirectly through the law's recognition of a variety of religious authorities, the empire's people could enter into legally defined unions and gain rights associated with marriage such as inheritance, family support, and protections from certain affronts. Because property transactions had to take place in accordance with the law, the empire's subjects possessed the legal means, at various instances and through various rules, to acquire and manipulate property.

In addition to acquiring rights and social possibilities through the imperial rights regime, subjects of the empire gained protections of these rights through the law. The empire's criminal laws defended the multiple collectivities of the polity and the state itself against outlawed behaviors. Both criminal and civil legislation asserted the state's ultimate authority over rights, crime, legal process, and punishment, while making way for differentiated and localized legal practice.

Criminal law in the late empire was both all-encompassing and differentiated. The empire's Criminal Code asserted the state's primacy in defining criminality. Statute 1 of the Criminal Code declares as a "general principle" that "a criminal action is one forbidden and punishable by the law at the time it is undertaken." Because all crimes must be defined by law, people could not be punished for actions that had not been forbidden by the state. In a more positive sense, the empire's criminal laws offered subjects and communities the protection of law by providing an array of official institutions through which justice could be sought. Church and military regulations, exile, treasury and administrative codes, and other "special regulations and legislation" were empowered to define and punish certain kinds of crime committed by people belonging to particular groups.[26]

For criminal cases, jurisdiction was determined by the application of these codes and regulations concerning region, status, ethnicity, confession, or activity. In some regions, the Criminal Code was not to be applied to "actions punishable according to the customs of non-Russian tribes." For example, with legally defined exceptions, criminal actions arising in the Grand Princedom of Finland were exempted from the rules of the Criminal Code.[27] The state, while maintaining its monopoly on defining the law of the whole land, ceded specific kinds of crimes to different legal jurisdictions and granted some subjects the right to judge certain kinds of criminality on their own terms.

The civil law expressed a similar inclusivity and particularity. For civil cases, the first principle was that "any conflict over civil rights is to be decided by a judicial institution."[28] This statute of the *Regulation on Civil Procedure* affirmed the supreme and unique authority of the law over subjects' rights. Disputes over rights had to be decided in a legal forum, and the law took it upon itself to resolve conflicts over jurisdiction.

The *Regulation on Civil Procedure* explicitly rejected uniformity as a prerequisite for justice. Statute 10 of the 1914 edition of the regulation forbade the refusal to decide a case on the grounds of "the incompleteness, lack of clarity, insufficiency or contradictions of the laws." Imperial law was to be universal in its coverage of the collectives of the empire, but it did not aspire to equivalency in legal processes or rules. Instead, imperial legalism incorporated custom into court practice in a capacious way. Custom was to be applied not only when "the law itself makes the application of custom obligatory," but also

> in making a decision, the court...may, citing one or both sides, be ruled by generally recognized local customs, when the application of local customs is allowed expressly by the law, or in cases that are not positively resolvable by laws. Litigants who in support of their claims cite local custom that is unknown to the court are obliged to demonstrate its existence.[29]

This regulation, based on 1912 and 1913 legislation, reiterated what we might call a fundament of imperial law. That is, custom, or a locally established rule, was the default law when no positive law was available.

The integration of custom into imperial law was enhanced by legislation permitting litigants to cite earlier custom-based decisions as evidence for the existence of a customary norm. Statute 10^2 established that "earlier decisions on similar matters and the attestations of appropriate institutions" could serve as evidence of the "existence of a custom" and thus as grounds for deciding a case.[30] This statute both displayed the state's respect for earlier legal decisions and acknowledged the courts as a realm of ongoing interpretation of social norms.[31] In this respect, the code-based legalism of the Russian empire opened a vast realm of precedent-based lawmaking.

The incorporation of prior decisions into jurisprudence completed a circle of interdependence of law and custom. Imperial law legitimated custom as a basis for legal decisions; legal decisions using custom became the evidence for the existence of established norms; these resolutions then entered into future judicial practice. The state's cautious treatment of uncodified normative practices, as well as its tolerance of a wide degree of judicial creativity in the definition of custom, empowered judges and litigants in local courts to engage and use the law in diversified yet legal ways.

Differentiated imperial jurisprudence was thus a domain where the imperial rights regime was activated by subjects. The local courts of imperial Russia—"rural oral courts" (*sel'skie slovesnye sudy*), *shariatskie* (sharia) courts, mullah's ordeal instances (*po proizvodstvu ispytanii na zvanie mulli*), township courts (with peasant judges), and "people's courts"[32]—were places where litigants, judges, clerks, and witnesses practiced and defined the social reach of imperial law in different languages, with different rules, with different social referents, and with the legitimation of official majesty.

Differentiation as a default practice of governance did not go unchallenged, particularly by administrators attracted to standardization as a seemingly more efficient and orderly way to rule. By the late nineteenth century, long-term efforts of imperial officials to manage the unwieldy but useful system of differentiated courts had produced some procedural similarities among the various instances of primary resort. First, litigants at local courts would bring their accusations, disputes, and hopes for justice before a college of judges from their region and usually of their religion. A basic principle for lower-level courts was the recruitment of respected members of local communities to serve as judges. At township courts in central Russia, judges were chosen for three-year terms from candidates elected by village assemblies. For example, at the rural oral courts in Dagestan, the judges would include a local specialist in Islamic law and a local specialist in *adat* (customary) law, both elected for three years, as well as elders from rural societies of the region, also elected for three-year terms.[33]

Regulations for elected judges stressed maturity, economic responsibility, probity, and various degrees and kinds of literacy. In the Russian township courts, township judges were to be "peasant householders [*domokhoziaeva*] who have reached the age of thirty-five, enjoy the respect of their co-villagers and [are], if possible, literate." Ineligible for election were men who had been convicted of property crimes or condemned to a severe punishment, sellers of alcoholic beverages, and officials occupying another post in the township or village administration.[34] These rules incorporated local patriarchs into imperial governance, legitimated choices made by local communities, and encouraged respect for court decisions.

A second common feature of jurisprudence at the empire's lower-level courts was the direct address of litigants to judges. Lawyers were not allowed at these lower-level instances; parties argued their cases themselves. Litigants and witnesses testified orally, although documents could be presented as evidence to the court. At the Russian township courts, participants in hearings signed their testimony, or had a representative sign for them, as an indicator of their truthfulness; in other areas, participants swore oaths appropriate to their circumstances.[35]

A third shared aspect of lower-level justice was a pragmatic concern for convenience. Instructions to hold hearings on established religious holidays meant that both litigants and judges would be free from their work and able to attend court sessions. The provision of a local court at the lowest level of administration meant that travel to court was not a major obstacle for rural people. In rural areas of central Russia, no place of settlement was to be farther than eight miles from the township court.[36] My study of distances traveled by litigants showed that both accusers and defendants came to court from villages distributed over entire townships.[37]

A fourth characteristic of lower-level courts throughout the empire was their connection to other, higher judicial institutions. Decisions of lower-level instances could be appealed. For courts connected to the civil or military administration, a three-tier hierarchy of legal instances in the provinces or territories emerged as a general pattern in the late nineteenth century. After 1889, litigants at township courts could appeal first to a district official, then to a countywide college of officials, then to a provincial board under the supervision of the governor. Litigants not satisfied with results of appeals could take their cases even further up the judicial ladder to the Senate—the empire's supreme court.[38]

These chains of connection were replicated in outlying regions. Decisions of the "people's courts" (*narodnye sudy*) of the steppe could be appealed to a township assembly of judges, and these decisions could be appealed to a yet higher "extraordinary" assembly. The rural oral courts of Dagestan were subordinated in appeals cases first to the district people's court and then further to an instance for all of Dagestan (*Dagestanskii narodnyi sud*). Some of these higher instances might also serve as courts of first resort for crimes or suits beyond the jurisdiction of lower-level courts. In a complication typical of the empire, other parallel judicial institutions might be empowered to hear cases concerning conflicts between litigants from different confessions or ethnicities.[39] For some kinds of cases, litigants had a choice between different instances, including custom-based courts, religious instances, and the courts based on civil and criminal codes.[40]

The empire's lowest-level courts were arenas not far from home where people from a particular locality came to engage in litigation conducted in their local language, validated by procedures familiar to them, and decided by judges from their own milieu. When litigants brought their small claims or accusations of small crimes to this kind of tribunal, they sought justice from a legal process fine-tuned to local practice and endowed with imperial authority. Police or other administrators had little interest in the kinds of disputes that litigants brought to lower-level instances—small debts, minor crimes, insults to dignity, family disputes—but the empire nonetheless provided institutions for subjects to settle such matters legally.[41] The habit of inclusionary legalism—the imperative to bring regulatory practices under the wing of empire—gave subjects rights in the enactment of the law.

The imperial rights regime was not a one-way street but a skein of connectivity. First, to subjects, imperial law provided rights assigned through collectives. Individuals, by belonging to one or another or the empire's collectives, were enabled by the law to marry, participate in various inheritance regimes, acquire and manipulate property, and engage in other social relations. Second, the law provided a framework of rules for the interactions of subjects as they exercised their rights. By insisting that all property transactions had to conform to the laws, however various, of the polity, imperial law enabled peaceful initiatives and liberated its subjects from violence and disorder. Third, imperial law offered a means to stigmatize and punish violators of legally established rights and locally defined morality. Because the law incorporated lower-level courts into the judicial system and gave local authorities a wide (and variable) range of powers to punish small crimes, subjects could participate in social discipline by prosecuting crimes defined and punished in accord with both statute law and local norms. Both judges, in their capacity as officials of the state, and litigants who defended their category-based rights in local courts, could imagine themselves connected to state power and see its workings in matters of immediate concern.

THE RIGHTS OF RULING

If imperial law granted subjects rights and enabled their use of these rights in localized ways, what did this inclusionary and differentiated rights regime mean for elites? A first consideration is that rulers and would-be rulers lived, like ordinary subjects, in a polity where rights derived from the state. Dependence on the lawgiver was, if anything, more apparent to elites than to lowly subjects. The state worked for centuries by granting rights (superior to those given to commoners)[42] to elites and displaying its capacity to take these rights away. The connections that bound elite servitors into the skein of rule and service were personal, but their ultimate reference was always to the state and its unmatchable ability to reward or punish.

Men who entered state service could see themselves as sharing in the power of the empire to grant or deny rights to other subjects. The weak development of administrative law—the legal regulation of relations between the state and subjects and of the administration itself[43] —meant that little stood in the way of functionaries' use of their powers in flexible and personal ways. Because ascribed rights, not natural ones, formed the essential link between individuals and the state, the persons who made this system work took their places among the ascribers. The manipulation of rights was the foundation of Russian administrative practice and a characteristic behavior of even humble bureaucrats.[44] Both lower and upper reaches of administration worked through responses to petitions, complaints, and pleas for justice expressed in the language of rightful claims that governors could satisfy or reject.

The people who could shape imperial policy most directly were the empire's high officials, including its ministers, military leaders, and governor-generals. As observed earlier, such people were not necessarily of Russian nationality; in this sense, they constituted, potentially, a "we" not of a nation but of the state. Collectivity, however, was not a quality easily come by for imperial officials. In stark contrast to the corporate reflex of professional, artistic, and laboring groups[45]—a reflex nourished by the long-term practices of collectivity encouraged by the imperial rights regime—insistent individuality was the hallmark behavior of powerful advisers, ministers, and bureaucrats. One explanation for the individualism of elite politics was that high officials did not have an institutional basis for seeing themselves as a group. After a false start in 1730, the traumatic history of official political institutions distinct from the emperor's administrative chain of command began only in 1906.[46] For most of the imperial period, the empire's officials served in ministries or other offices in administrative hierarchies leading up to the emperor.[47] In such a system, vertical and personal linkages were critical to making one's way within the state and to not falling off its ladders of command and reward.

For those elites who stayed within the state, the imperial regime of rights offered certain ways of doing politics and conceiving of it. First, the operative environment of government based on difference meant that an alternative principle of uniform administration was ever present as a proposition for reform. The aspiration to bring all the subjects of the empire into a uniformly ruled polity was not a product of nationalist imagination in the nineteenth century. Eighteenth-century rulers, including the empress Catherine the Great, shared the goal of an eventual "civilizing" of native populations according to Russian and European standards. Uniformity was also championed in the cause of national power. Russia would be strengthened, wrote one mid-nineteenth-century statist, by the "gradual merging of unlike elements into one whole, one unbounded state, where every one submits to the one Russian law, where the Russian language reigns supreme, and the Orthodox Church is triumphant."[48] The functioning regime of particularity provided reformers with a handy instrument of criticism: the ground was always prepared for ambitious administrators to propose systemwide rules, the extension of "Russian" law to all, and similar unifying projects.

But as the term "gradual merging" suggests, throughout the imperial period the project of unification was only minimally and sporadically engaged; legal and cultural likeness was a remote goal, not to be achieved in the short term. The ongoing tension between universalizing, homogenizing ends and pragmatic, differentiated practices was embodied in various "temporary" regulations produced during the reform period. The 1889 code introducing modifications to the township courts was issued as "Temporary Rules"; the 1868 statute on administration, including courts, in the steppe region was also described as "provisional."[49] Even in the early twentieth century, Russian officials shied away from policies that would force Russian Muslims out of confessional schools and into Orthodox, Russian-language institutions.[50] Only in the 1906 Fundamental Laws was the phrase "unified and indivisible" applied to the Russian state, a formula of rule borrowed from European models and drawn upon by law writers at a time of internal duress. Statute 3 of the new Fundamental Laws, which made Russian the "general language of state," allowed for "special laws" on the usage of other languages in state and public institutions.[51] To the end of the empire, and even after the bitter confrontation with ethnic, regional, and religious political formations in the Duma, differentiated governance remained the foundation of imperial rule.

This meant, for ruling elites, that projects directed toward the dreamworld of uniformity were always pushing up against practices of particularity. The pragmatic, plausible way to participate in governance was to accept the politics of difference and become a spokesman for "one's" people(s). Difference provided the foundation for recommending policies toward particular groups, for decisions about allocating resources, for exceptional statutes, and for special codifications. Arguments based on particularity provided both the language and substance of politics for imperial actors.

The "rights of difference" at work in imperial governance are visible in the odyssey of the Dukhobors, religious dissenters who gained an international reputation as anarchists thanks to Tolstoy's championing of their cause. But as a recent study by Nicholas Breyfogle reveals, the particularities of their claims and circumstances in imperial Russia were created through the politics of difference, a politics in which both rulers and subjects participated. In the first third of the nineteenth century, the government decided to sponsor resettlement of sectarians from central and southern Russia to the Caucasus. The origins of the policy lay in a request from Dukhobors living in Siberia for the creation of a "separate, mono-confessional colony." The Dukhobors' petition was communicated to the central administration by two high-ranking members of the Senate. In the mid-nineteenth century, Dukhobors and other sectarians moved to new villages in Transcaucasia, where they were allocated land and even provided with start-up provisions and houses built by Caucasian "native peoples" in anticipation of the settlers' arrival. After the trauma of relocation to an unfamiliar climate, the Dukhobors prospered and, for a time, were considered the empire's ideal "Russian" colonizers by central administrators.[52]

At every stage of the Dukhobors' journey, a politics of difference was at work, based in the imperial rights regime and mediated by administrators who spoke for their particular collectivities. Breyfogle's study describes the different positions taken by officials as they contemplated settling religious dissenters in the empire's borderlands. The greatest legislator of the early nineteenth century, author of the administrative code for governance of Siberia, and compiler of the empire's laws, Mikhail Speranskii opposed the resettlement terms as too generous compared to those applied in other areas and to other people. He feared that other groups, both peasants and nobles, might call out for similar deals. The minister of the interior, Lanskoi, wanted to put more distance between the contaminating sectarians and the majority Orthodox Russian population; he favored a generous settlement package. Both military leaders and the leaders of the Orthodox Church were hopeful that the sectarians could be used in combat on the front lines of engagement with Caucasian banditry.[53] General Paskevic wanted to enhance his armies with sectarian auxiliaries; the Orthodox Church, in the interests of "its" faithful, just wanted dissident Christians to die. Powerful members of the Georgian nobility living in the Caucasus had another idea: the sectarians could become indentured laborers on their huge estates, and to make matters even sweeter, the state could assign official administrators to ensure that the new laborers paid their bills.[54]

These discordant views on a single policy display assumptions, complications, and processes typical of Russian governance. First, everyone, including sectarians, made arguments based on particular interests, directly for themselves in the case of sectarians and Georgian nobles and for the people under their supervision in the case of senators, ministers, military men, and Orthodox churchmen. Second, all addressed the state as an allocator of alienable rights to groups. The state was recognized as having the power to decide which people could utilize which lands, where certain people had a right to live and where they were compelled to move, and what kinds of work they would perform, not to speak of whether they could practice their religion. The imperial rights regime, for those who manipulated it, explicitly acknowledged the administration's power to grant and to take away.

Consultation with the governed whose rights were in question was not part of this picture. Third, members of the ruling elite were divided in their views: the autocracy did have a politics beyond and around the emperor, a politics played by officials who voiced individual and conflicting opinions. At a very high level, the politics of difference was acrimonious and about getting one's way for particular interests. Fourth, the problem of sectarian settlers reveals dilemmas typical of imperial governance. The collectivities of the population did not line up in satisfying ways: Russians were not all Orthodox, even though they were supposed to be; the Caucasus were populated with many ethnic groups, including Russians, not neatly settled in separate spaces; Georgian nobles were more than willing to enserf Russian peasants; heretic and pacifist exiles made their fortunes by assisting the military in its wars against mostly Muslim enemies. But none of this was strange to people for whom the politics of difference was a given. The arguments for particular policies enjoyed a large playing field, full of exasperating contradictions, and thereby enabling a wide range of pleas.

The politics of difference put a premium on knowledge of the people who were being ruled. The question of which groups should receive which rights to resources, work, or religious practice—and who should be denied them—created an imperative to understand the distinctive ways the empire's peoples organized their lives. Beginning in the eighteenth century, scholars carried out ethnographic, cartographic, and statistical surveys in search of reliable information on the populations of the realm.[55] Respect for research on social groups presumed to be different in their fundamental being gives academics to this day an entrée into Russian governance, a claim upon the state's resources, and a salient place in the formation of policy.

"Knowing one's natives" was thus a strategy for Russia's ruling elites, but this knowledge was never secure. As the Dukhobor case illustrates, people could move around in their categories and undermine elemental ideas about how groups should be defined.[56] The assumption that each group had a singular way of life in which ethnicity, religion, and customs all cohered did not always work, perhaps especially for Russians. The confident positivism expressed in collections of facts about the peoples of the empire went hand in hand with the practical experience that categorical schemes could be challenged by other readings of the imperial map. Difference and groupness were the constants of imperial governance, but which differences and which groups would demand attention was not predictable. Governance took shape as a series of ad hoc and partial resolutions of claims to rights, which made perfect sense to people who understood that no solution was permanent and that new claims based on different differences could always arise.

Even in the late nineteenth century, when some reformers pushed harder for universal regulations, the principle of ruling through allocated and differentiated rights persisted. As Adeeb Khalid points out in this volume, newly conquered areas of Central Asia were incorporated as different types of units, as a province (Turkestan), as protectorates, and as part of adjacent regional territories. In the local courts, structural similarities were achieved in the composition of judicial colleges, but the judges themselves might be peasant elders, mullahs, other religious authorities, or other representatives of local communities, depending on particular arrangements in any region. The gradual enhancement of peasants' rights after the emancipation took place in a piecemeal and politically expedient way. Peasants in Polish areas received extensive land rights and freedom from all obligations to former owners in 1864,[57] while emancipated peasants in central Russia paid redemption dues for their land allotments over forty years.[58] The major legislation expanding peasants' rights to engage in financial activities, to change their places of residence, and to enter state service and educational establishments without the permission of the communities through which they paid taxes was issued in 1906. Typically of the imperial rights regime, this law did not abolish distinctions between peasants and other subjects. Nicholas II's *ukaz* ordered the provision

> to all subjects of Russia [*rossiiskie poddannye*] without regard to their descent, with the exception of native aliens [*inorodtsy*]...the same rights relating to state service, conforming to such rights of people of the noble estate, with the abolition of all special advantages dependent upon estate descent in appointment by the administration to certain posts.[59]

In other words, peasants' new rights to enter state service were defined by rights earlier allocated to nobles, and nobles were to lose their rights to preferential selection.

As the 1906 decree indicates, the rights described in this law were not applied to certain categories of subjects—the "native aliens." This generic term might seem to indicate a hardening of the divide between Russians and others in the empire. Paul Werth argues that the more frequent usage, dating from the mid-nineteenth century, of the untranslatable word *inorodets* (literally, a person of other origin) reflects a shift in imperial thinking from primarily religious to primarily ethnic and cultural kinds of identification systems. I use the translation "native aliens," suggesting comparisons with the term used in the United States in the same period for Native Americans: "resident foreign nations."[60]

In Russia, the distinctive treatment of *inorodtsy* through separate legal codes and regulations was fully in accord with the imperial rights regime and with the way that ethnic Russians were governed. To the end of the autocracy, and even after the reforms initiated by the revolutions of 1905 and 1906, imperial politics was based on the allocation, reallocation, and revocation of rights to different groups. Ruling through alienable rights allowed pragmatic solutions that were always subject to further change. The culture of imperial rule took shape in a distinctly nonbourgeois environment: rights to property could be given and taken away, people could be moved about, nobles could be deprived of or granted a labor force comprised of other members of the polity with their particular rights. For elites, the imperial rights regime enabled a wide range of arguments for or against a variety of particular measures, useful worries about setting examples that other groups might copy, and pragmatic propositions based on superior knowledge of one's terrain and peoples. Impermanence of rights meant that government was a flexible art, free from the constraints of universal principles and inherent equalities, free of democratic and consultative imperatives. If elites felt their personal vulnerability in the imperial scheme of things, they also knew the meaning of being of the state—the possibility of deciding rights for others, if not for oneself.

TENSIONS OF RUSSIAN EMPIRE: LIBERALS VERSUS PEASANTS

The political landscape I have described did not lend itself to imagining a single community, which may account for elites' lack of interest in institutionalizing democracy based on equal rights.[61] But in the last half of the nineteenth century and the beginning of the twentieth, Russian liberals were deeply concerned with the differentiated judicial system and in particular with what they saw as inferior (that is, unlettered, unprofessional, non-European) justice at the lower-level courts. The gradual introduction of "Russian" law to non-Russians was one unfulfilled civilizational concern of many liberal professionals and legal experts. Another area where unequal legalism came under attack was the township court system of the Russian provinces.

One irritant to liberal jurists was the subordination of township courts to administrative, rather than judicial, authorities. In 1889, the township courts had been placed under the immediate supervision of local noble officials: land captains. Liberal critics of the autocracy regarded these officials as retrograde nobles exercising their traditional prerogatives to rule the countryside. Equally repugnant to liberal reformists was the variability built into the legal system and exemplified by lower-level courts headed by different kinds of judges who made decisions on different kinds of cases according to different standards. The labels of "custom" and "customary law" were used to stigmatize the workings of local courts as inferior to "real"—that is, what was thought to be "Western"—law.[62]

It was not until the fall of the autocracy that the liberal reformers finally were able to write their own rules. After the abolition of estate distinctions in March 1917, the new government proceeded to create a nonestate administration at the township level (the township *zemstvo*) and to replace the township courts.[63] The essence of this reform was to destroy estate-based justice and to make all citizens of Russian townships, whatever their former estates, subject to the jurisdiction of a new local court. The judges at these courts would no longer be peasants elected by individual villages. Instead, cases would be decided by a college of judges: one justice of the peace elected by all voters, not peasants alone, in countywide elections, and two "members" of the court elected by all voters at a townshipwide assembly. The educational requirements for judges were substantially changed. A justice of the peace was to be at least twenty-five years old and had to have completed at least a secondary education, unless he (or she, in theory now) could demonstrate significant experience in legal practice.

The fate of the Provisional Government's attempt to institute a new kind of governance and a new kind of court at the township level in the first year of the revolution opens up another perspective on the imperial rights regime. In May 1917, the Provisional Government began to put its reforms in place. The new township zemstvo was established by decree to replace the former township administration; a local court was to replace the township court; the old township court was abolished.[64] In the liberal press, these initiatives were presented as unquestionably progressive and essential to the new democracy. A new pamphlet-size magazine called the *Township Zemstvo* (*Volostnoe zemstvo*) was produced in Petrograd to popularize these initiatives and to encourage rural people to vote in township elections to the new nonestate-based township administration. The elections to the township zemstvo began on July 30, 1917, and were completed by mid-September.[65]

The results were not what reformers had expected. The editors of the *Township Zemstvo* were forced to confess their disappointment. According to these enthusiasts of local power, almost everywhere peasants were indifferent to the elections—"busy with agricultural work and badly informed about what the township zemstvo is." One observer commented, "the general mass of the peasants is completely passive; it [the mass] is busy with the harvest and relates to the township zemstvo as if to something foisted on it, like a boss or a lord." Reporters to the journal wrote that peasants, if they voted, tried to send "useless, excess" people—those who could not work or those with little land—in the hope that the township zemstvo might give them new territory.[66]

The disappointing outcome of the Provisional Government's attempt to reform township governance displays the attractions that participatory local regulation held for lower-level subjects of the imperial rights regime. Peasants were right to see the township zemstvo as a usurpation of earlier administrative arrangements. According to the new regulations, representatives elected to the township zemstvo did not have to live in the same province of the zemstvo in question, let alone within the township they were to represent. It was hardly likely that peasants could outmaneuver better-educated people in the elections to the township zemstvo and to the bench of the new local court. Now not just one nobleman—the land captain—would supervise their township administrations and their courts. A raft of specialists, estate proprietors, teachers, and dacha owners would take over the local institutions that had been theirs to control. The ax hanging over the heads of township judges was clearly visible. For peasant users of the township courts, their right to administration and legal judgment by their peers was threatened by the abolition of their estate-based empowerment to elect their own judges and officials.

The fate of the township court was not determined by the Provisional Government's decrees. Contrary to what elite observers might have anticipated, rural people did not rush to shut down the township courts and did not wait for new people to come help them understand the laws. The township courts were in demand in the summer and fall of 1917. They provided a means for peasants to settle disputes and allocate property—when they could obtain the necessary documents—during the uncertainties of the revolutionary period. As authority in the capitals collapsed, at township courts in the countryside, judges continued to hear cases, and clerks entered their decisions in record books intended to become part of the empire's repository of law, law interpreted by peasant judges.[67]

THE IMPERIAL SOCIAL CONTRACT

The proposed replacement of peasant judges elected by their villages with judges unascribed to any estate and elected by all residents of a township was a violation of the imperial rights regime. Of course, legally the emperor could have at any time taken away peasants' rights to elect their own judges, but the experience and practicalities of administration meant that this kind of intervention in local affairs would have been unlikely. Experiments in shaping up peasant regulation through direct administration had failed miserably in the past.[68] More consistent with the ways the empire worked was the devolution of a great deal of power in the interpretation of rights to lowly, local people, at least when these rights did not impinge on those of other groups. For a half century, peasants had litigated before peasant men who had been chosen from villages in their townships and who were knowledgeable about local practices and problems. From a peasant perspective shaped by the imperial rights regime, the Provisional Government's proposal abolishing estate-based difference and instantiating a non-estate administration in the townships was a disenfranchisement.

It may be difficult for people whose political imaginaries—if not their practices—are shaped by the powerful idea of natural (human, in its recent variant) rights to step into the practices and assumptions of a fundamentally different rights regime. One way to cross this threshold is to juxtapose Rousseau's complex notion of a social contract (a political project) with the imperial rights regime (a social practice).

Rousseau's ideal version of the contract begins with people exercising their right to construct a government and to cede some of their individual rights to this formation in return for its protection of the expressed general will. Almost every element in this paradigm is incomprehensible from the perspective of Russian imperial practice. States spread their wings (and tentacles) over the widely distributed populations of the Eurasian plain; the project of making state law did not belong to the area's many peoples. The gathering of all would-be members of a would-be polity is not imaginable even as a conceit (as in Rousseau's text). Why would people want to make a government when their histories are of various kinds of socially ordered collectives, over which one or another conqueror claims superior authority, takes and gives, declares some kind of law, and adjusts to the realities of local arrangements? The long-term conquest arena of Eurasia has produced people who to this day see state power as properly and ideally emanating from a distant ruler, while at home they go about organizing their own affairs.[69]

The notion of ceding some of one's natural rights to the state is similarly alien to the imperial rights regime. What natural rights? Rights appear with the state and in relation to it, in gestures made by the distant ruler to appease, accommodate, and manipulate his or her subjects. Unless we want to impose the assertions of European theorists upon all humanity, there is, perhaps sadly, no reason to assume that people everywhere think they have natural rights. Rights are not necessarily "self-evident," nor do they necessarily reside in individuals. Rights are always relational, always expressions of claim outside the self, but in many historical and present-day contexts it is the state that makes the claim and asserts the rights. Under the imperial rights regime, a person obtains rights only when the state appears on the social scene and grants rights to its subjects. When a Soviet citizen, as was often the case, asserted in daily life, "I have the right to [buy this ticket, send this letter, etc.]," this person was wielding, or hoping to wield, the capacity to engage in an activity granted to her by the state.

The general will—a notion that bedevils liberal theory—would have been thinkable by some in the imperial rights regime. Liberated from institutions that might have formulated an empirewide will, Russian intellectuals certainly asserted their own notions of what "the people" wanted.[70] Elites' assignment of their—different—desires to the population was enabled by the empire's practice of differentiated governance and the absence of representative (anathema to Rousseau in any case) all-empire bodies until 1906.[71] As the case of the township courts suggests, the integument of justice and authority in the realm enhanced notions of segmentation (for example, our rights as peasants) rather than a sense of collectivity among all subjects. An assumption of nongeneral and nongeneralizable wills informed imperial government and was expressed in the diversity of institutions and standards included under the imperial legal umbrella.

If almost everything in the imperial rights regime turned Rousseau's ideal upside down and inside out, did Russian governance nonetheless express a social contract? An expansive notion of the social may be of help. Rousseau's project was a political one. He called his contract "social" because he rooted the authority to make law in society, not in already existing states. The Russian empire, in which the state made law, was always enacting a profoundly social kind of politics aimed at regulating and forming society. Both permanent rules that would freeze society in a single shape and foundational statements about legitimacy were avoided by a government that extended itself over already existing peoples and their recognized differences. Rights were assigned and alienable, which facilitated management of diverse collectivities. Unconstrained by imperatives of equality or universal good, rulers could fulfill their side of their kind of social contract: protection of those who were assigned rights. By defending the polity from external foes, by keeping the internal peace, and by providing superior legal authority, rulers provided the various peoples of a differentiated polity with the possibility to use their rights. Even the deprivation of rights or assertion of harsh regulatory practices over particularly recalcitrant or challenging groups could be seen as fulfilling the governors' properly imperial role. At the same time, of course, rulers filled their pockets and went to war and pursued their own self-defined goals in ways that benefited few and exploited many.

What did imperial subjects gain from this kind of social contract? For elites, the rewards were clear: they were positioned to play directly in the game of assigned rights and social manipulation. The state's legally unfettered ability to assign and reassign resources meant that elites situated in different locations could take part in regulation and exploitation of "their" people and others. But even ordinary subjects attained a share of social power through the differentiated rights regime. As individuals, subjects received their rights from the state; as members of collectivities, they participated in defining how these rights could be used. The existence of different kinds of ascribed boundaries allowed the empire's subjects to develop local, cultural, or confessional affiliations and to utilize these linkages for their various interests. On society's side, or better on the side of multiple societies, the social was allowed a good deal of self-shaping and self-regulating in the absence of an imperious and impossible general will.

Was there a contract at all between society and state in the imperial regime? At various moments in Russian history, the polity did come under threat, in ways that reveal the pragmatic bargains of the imperial rights regime. On the state's side, the contract was explicit. Groups that endangered the imperial order were punished collectively: moving the Dukhobors to Transcaucasia is a case in point. The disempowerment of dangerous or potentially dangerous elites was an obvious imperative. But subjects, too, shared a sense of an imperial social order. When groups of Cossacks, serfs, Bashkirs, and others joined the vast Pugachev revolt in the Volga–Ural region in the late eighteenth century, rebels' political imaginary reproduced imperial rule. A true tsar would grant better rights to different people.[72] When nobles assassinated emperors in the same period, the goal was a better break—for the nobility. Bolshevik slogans did not appeal for universal rights, but proletarian ones. An enduring politics of social particularity was one consequence of the imperial rights regime.

In conclusion, I return to questions of comparison. What difference does difference, as a premise of rule, make? Although all empires can be said to have universalizing aspects—in their attempts at extension in the universes they know—the Russian empire was not based on universalism within its borders. In 1813, Benjamin Constant bemoaned the homogenizing effects of empire:

> The conquerors of our times, peoples or princes, want their empire to possess a unified surface over which the arrogant eye of power can wander without encountering any inequality which hurts or limits its view. The same code of law, the same measures, the same rules, and if we could gradually get there, the same language; that is what is proclaimed as the perfection of the social organization.... The great slogan of the day is uniformity.[73]

Constant's reference and despair was Napoleon, and this generalization (a typical European's extension of his vision to all empires?) did not apply to Russian empire, then or now. Instead, the Russian empire made difference a part of government. There was no nationalized center, no single "we," but there were many, the more the better, "they's." There was also no sure "self," and all subjects—nobles, Muslims, sectarians, Bashkirs—were collectivized "others," defined by their differentiated and alienable assigned rights. The imperial rights regime, based on difference, was expressed in law, and imperial legalism empowered even lowly subjects in the enactment of justice in local settings. The politics of difference provided a flexible tool for rulers to use in administering, ordering, and trying to transform their polity.

Governance through social difference and through the imperial rights regime gave both rulers and subjects perspectives on politics that differ from those fortified by the ideal (and tensions) of natural and universal rights. There was no implicit standard of equality to work with, no declared rights of (all) men and citizens to be seized. For elites, the stakes of being in and of the state, where rights could be assigned and manipulated, were very high. Among imperial subjects, the practices of legalized and multiple differences allowed a certain flexibility as well—flexibility to use an array of localized institutions, to appeal on grounds of special needs, to address authorities who found power in speaking for a particular group. The petition and special pleading, political forms privileged by the politics of difference, enabled personalized connections to authority. Elite rule, a pragmatic politics of social inclusion, a citizenry that relates to itself in groups and to the state as petitioners and thinks that rulers should be distant, and a long-lived empire may be consequences of the rights of difference.

Notes

1. Dominic Lieven makes this point in his inspiring comparative study, *Empire: The Russian Empire and Its Rivals,* 224. On Siberia, see Anatolyi Remnev's comments in "Siberia and the Russian Far East in the Imperial Geography of Power."

2. On the Time of Troubles, see Torke, "From Muscovy towards St. Petersburg."

3. Bourdieu's category works well to describe the unrecognized self-reproducing and -adjusting field of practiced empire. For the classic statement, see Bourdieu, *Outline of a Theory of Practice,* 72–95.

4. On Russian expansion and geography, see LeDonne, *Russian Empire and the World,* especially pages 7–8 on a "forward policy." On the principles of Muscovite conquest, see Nol'de, *La formation de l'empire russe,* 63–76.

5. See Kollmann, *By Honor Bound,* and Kivelson, "Muscovite 'Citizenship.'"

6. Cited in Kappeler, *Russian Empire,* 70.

7. As in Dagestan in 1840, when the Russian authorities for a short time attempted to replace sharia and adat courts with Russian courts; see Bobrovnikov, "Sud po adatu v dorevoliutsionnom Dagestane," 31–32.

8. For an example, see Yuri Slezkine's discussion of Russian administration of northern natives in his *Arctic Mirrors,* 29–31.

9. On the superior claim of law, see Wirtschafter, "Legal Identity and the Possession of Serfs."

10. See the discussions by Dupret, Berger, and al-Zwaini, *Legal Pluralism in the Arab World,* esp. vii–xviii and 3–40.

11. Cited in Thomas, "Collecting the Fatherland," 97. The quotation is from a proposal drawn up by Burckhard von Wichmann and published in 1821.

12. On eighteenth-century views of peoples, see Slezkine, "Naturalists versus Nations."

13. On the multiplicity of imperial registers, see Burbank and von Hagen, "Coming into the Territory." On federalist projects for Russia, see in the same volume, von Hagen, "Federalisms and Pan-movements."

14. See Knight, "Science, Empire and Nationality," 124–29.

15. LeDonne, *Absolutism and Ruling Class;* Lieven, *Russian Rulers Under the Old Regime,* 1–26.

16. Lieven, *Russian Rulers under the Old Regime,* 48–49. By "non-Russian," Lieven means families that had not become Russian before 1600, a description that sees becoming Russian as a long-term process. Lieven emphasizes the domi-

nance of old landed families in the late ruling elite.

17. Age and sex were grounds for further specifications of rights, but these qualities were not usually addressed by separate legal rules (addressing all youths or all women, for example). Lawmakers seemed to see age and sex as inherent to every individual in every society, to be addressed by each social collectivity in its particular way.

18. "Svod Zakonov Grazhdanskikh" (Collection of Civil Laws; SZG), kn. 1, st. 1–99. SZG is volume 10, part 1, of *Svod Zakonov Rossiiskoi Imperii* (Collected Laws of the Russian Empire; SZRI). I am using an edition of the SZRI prepared for legal specialists. This version includes changes made according to the 1906 "continuation," including the Fundamental Laws declared that year.

19. In theory, an atheist might have found a way to marry legally, if he or she were part of an atheist "tribe" or "nation." But such a concept would have been outside the government's notion of historically established communities with cultural traditions, and establishing a new religious collectivity was a perilous endeavor in the late empire. See Werth, "Big Candles and 'Internal Conversion.'"

20. SZG, kn. 1, st. 25–33, 90.

21. SZG, kn. 1, st. 1.

22. SZG, kn. 1, st. 2–23.

23. SZG, kn. 1, st. 85, 61–78. On the question of "mixed marriages," see Shein, "Kistorii voprosa o smeshannykh brakakh."

24. SZG, kn. 2, st. 699.

25. SZG, kn. 2, st. 708, prim. 1, 4; SZG kn. 3, st. 961, 966, prim.

26. "Ulozhenie Ugolovnoe" (Criminal Code; UG), st. 1, 5. The UG is in volume 15 of the SZRI. I am using an edition of the SZRI, published in 1914, that incorporates the continuations of 1912 and 1913 into the 1909 edition of the code.

27. UG, st. 4–8.

28. *Ustav grazhdanskogo sudoproizvodsta* (Regulation on Civil Procedure; UGS), st. 1. The UGS is in volume 16, part 1, of the 1914 edition of the SZRI.

29. UGS, st. 10^1, p. 210.

30. UGS, st. 10^2, p. 227.

31. In other areas of Russian law, judicial revision took place at the higher level of cassation review. I argue here that for customary practices, law could in effect be made at a very local level. On judicial revision, see Wagner, *Marriage, Property, and Law,* 206–23.

32. For studies of these various kinds of courts, see on the Caucasus, Agishev

and Bushen, *Materialy po obozreniiu gorskikh i narodnykh sudov kavkazkogo kraia;* Bobrovnikov, *Musul'mane severnogo kavkaz,* 98–204; Jersild, *Orientalism and Empire,* 89–109; and Babich, *Evoliutsiia pravovoi kul'tury adygov,* 31–137; on nomad steppe courts, see Virginia Martin, "Barïmta"; on township courts, see Burbank, *Russian Peasants Go to Court.*

33. Bobrovnikov, *Musul'mane severnogo kavkaz,* 162. These were the terms of the Dagestan rural courts as reformed in the 1860s.

34. "Obshchee polozhenie o krest'ianakh" (General Regulation on Peasants; OPK), 1902, st. 115. The OPK is book 1 of *Polozhenie o sel'skom sostoianii: Svod Zakonov Rossiiskoi Imperii.*

35. On court procedures, see, for Russian township courts, OPK, st. 113–25, 132–39; for adat courts in the Caucasus, see Bobrovnikov, *Musul'mane,* 163–66; for lower level courts in the steppe region, see Martin, "Barïmta," 255–57.

36. OPK, st. 50–52. On the size of townships, see Latyshev, "Volost'."

37. See Burbank, *Russian Peasants Go to Court,* 57–58.

38. On appeals from township courts, see Popkins, "Peasant Experiences of the Late Tsarist State."

39. See, for example, the exemptions from the purview of the township courts for Jews and non-Russians of particular regions; OPK, st. 125, prim. 1, 2.

40. On the multiplicity of court systems and the tiers of appeals, see Martin, "Barïmta," 255–57, and Bobrovnikov, "Sud po adatu," 32–33; for the Russian township courts and their appeals ladder, see Eroshkin, *Istoriia gosudarstvennykh uchrezhdenii dorevoliutsionnoi Rossii,* 213–14, and Popkins, "Peasant Experiences."

41. On the content of cases at lower courts, see Burbank, *Russian Peasants Go to Court,* 77–91, 121–29.

42. I avoid the category "privilege" because of its grounding in the assumption of equality as the starting point. The point of assigning rights was to address and manipulate difference.

43. On the history of administrative law in imperial Russia, see Pravilova, *Zakonnost' i prava lichnosti.*

44. On law, personal power, and legal culture in Russia, see Burbank, "Legal Culture, Citizenship, and Peasant Jurisprudence," 82–85.

45. On corporate behavior among professionals, see Burbank, "Discipline and Punish in the Moscow Bar Association." For an intriguing analysis of group formation among intellectuals, see Barbara Walker, "Kruzhok Culture and the Meaning of Patronage."

46. In 1730 a proposal for a noble council that would set limits on the

autocrat was defeated, by other nobles; see Kivelson, "Kinship Politics, Autocratic Politics." The Duma, a parliamentary institution, was established in 1906 and continued until 1917.

47. For descriptions of the institutions of Russia's central government, see Eroshkin, *Istoriia gosudarstvennykh uchrezhdenii dorevoliutsionnoi Rossii,* 67–276.

48. Ustrialov, *Istoricheskoe obozrenie tsarstvovaniia gosudaria imperatora Nikolaia I,* 167.

49. OPK, st. 113–153; on the steppe statute and on hesitations concerning natives' ability to use "Russian" law, see Martin, "Barïmta," 255.

50. For a dramatic example of the autocracy's unwillingness to take a stand for Orthodoxy and against separate Muslim schools, see Geraci, "Russian Orientalism at an Impasse." On Russian policy toward natives in the Volga region, see Geraci, *Window on the East,* and Werth, *At the Margins of Orthodoxy.*

51. On the formula and its significance, see Nol'de, "Edinstvo i nerazdel'nost' Rossii." Even Nol'de acknowledged the complexities of statute 3; see page 226.

52. For a fascinating account of the Dukhobors as dissenting colonizers, see Breyfogle's monograph, *Heretics and Colonizers.* On the Dukhobors' request for resettlement, see pages 27–30.

53. *Banditry,* as applied to Caucasian people, is an old term, related to the long-term battle for control in this area; see Bobrovnikov, "Bandits and the State."

54. On policy makers' opinions, see Breyfogle, *Heretics and Colonizers,* 32–48; on Georgian nobles, see pages 183–86.

55. On eighteenth- and nineteenth-century ethnographic and geographic efforts, see Slezkine, "Naturalists versus Nations"; Knight, "Science, Empire and Nationality"; Geraci, *Window on the East,* 158–94; and Sunderland, "Imperial Space."

56. The idea that legal divisions of society provided everyone with a field to play on is developed by Wirtschafter, *Social Identity in Imperial Russia.*

57. *Ukaz ob ustroistve krest'ian,* February 19/March 2, 1864.

58. Redemption dues were finally abolished in 1907. On the emancipation's aftermath, see Macey, *Government and Peasant in Russia.*

59. *Polnoe sobranie zakonov Rossiiskoi imperii, Sobranie tretie,* vol. 26, 1906 (Saint Petersburg, 1909), 28392, I, October 5, 1906.

60. Werth, "Changing Conceptions of Difference." See also his discussion in *At the Margins of Orthodoxy,* 124–46. On "resident foreign nations," see Meinig, *Shaping of America,* 179.

61. For a Russian perspective on this issue, see Mark Vishniak's discussion of the weak interest in calling a constituent assembly to found a new political order; Vishniak, "Ideia uchreditel'nogo sobraniia."

62. On this issue, see Burbank, "Legal Culture, Citizenship, and Peasant Jurisprudence," 85–94, and Frierson, "Rural Justice in Public Opinion."

63. For the texts of civil rights and local court decrees, see Browder and Kerensky, *Russian Provisional Government,* 226–38.

64. *Sbornik ukazov i postanovlenii Vremennogo pravitel'stva,* II, 99; Browder and Kerensky, *Provisional Government,* 234–35.

65. *Volostnoe zemstvo,* 17–18, 1917, 343.

66. *Volostnoe zemstvo,* 17–18, 1917, 343–45.

67. On usage of the township courts in 1917, see Burbank, *Russian Peasants Go to Court,* 228–44.

68. One example was an early nineteenth-century attempt to organize Russian peasants in military colonies; see Yaney, *Systematization of Russian Government,* 164.

69. See the fascinating discussion of distant rulership in Liu, "Recognizing the Khan."

70. This was a theme of *Intelligentsia and Revolution,* my study of the Russian intelligentsia at the time of the Bolshevik revolution.

71. On the autocracy's attempts to undermine national representation in the Duma, see Tsiunchuk, "Peoples, Regions and Electoral Politics."

72. On a popular political imaginary, see Ingerflom, "Entre le mythe et la parole."

73. Cited in Alder, *Measure of Things,* 317.

4

The Soviet Union as an Imperial Formation

A View from Central Asia

Adeeb Khalid

The Soviet Union became an empire in its dotage, and its reputation as an empire has continued to grow since its demise. During its time as a superpower, the Soviet Union claimed to be a multiethnic federal state, a claim that most observers accepted, with only the political right in the West calling it an empire. However, during the crisis of legitimacy faced by the Soviet regime in its last years, its opponents (of all stripes) began describing it as an "empire." Since then, the designation of empire has been accepted across the political spectrum as a fact. In post-Soviet states (most notably Uzbekistan), a peculiarly post-Soviet postcolonial literature has emerged. This literature, although it pays scant attention to the cultural effects of empire and largely focuses on the economic and institutional structures, nevertheless takes for granted the imperial nature of the Soviet Union.[1] However, in Europe and North America, the research paradigm of Soviet history has shifted so that the notion of the Soviet Union as an empire has become commonplace.[2] Many scholars have grappled with the question of whether, or to what extent, the Soviet Union was an empire,[3] while a cohort of younger scholars has sought to apply insights from postcolonial studies to the Soviet case.[4]

In this article, I examine what the Soviet case can contribute to the study of imperial formations. I find the straightforward "application" of existing postcolonial theory to the Soviet case not very satisfactory. The Soviet Union was a sprawling, multiethnic entity characterized by inequalities and hierarchies of all sorts; its citizens were subject to political and economic decisions made far away, over which they had no control. However, while having certain similarities to various kinds of empire, the Soviet Union also differed in significant ways from the overseas colonial empires that have inspired much of postcolonial theory. I argue that the Soviet Union was far more similar to a different kind of modern polity—the activist, interventionist state that seeks to sculpt its citizenry in an ideal image. Confronting the Soviet case through the literature on empire suggests many fruitful questions: Where does empire end and other forms of nonrepresentative or authoritarian polities begin? When can empire be used in thinking about the forms of political inequality in the twentieth century? What are the specificities of colonial difference?

Two points should be noted at the outset. First, I am solely interested in the Soviet Union itself. The Soviet Union maintained unequal, exploitative relations that can quite easily be described as imperial with a number of other states, most clearly Mongolia and the Warsaw Pact countries of Eastern Europe. This "external empire" is, to my mind, not very problematic. It was a specifically twentieth-century form of empire in which the fiction of national sovereignty was maintained, and the colonized state remained de jure independent. The most relevant parallels are to be drawn with Japan's rule over Manchuria[5] or with US hegemony in the world at large. It is the actual Soviet polity itself—by self-designation a multinational federation—whose designation as empire is more problematic in my view. Second, my central concern in this paper is with Central Asia, a region that provides a particularly fruitful vantage point for my purposes. The region's marginal position to the Russian polity has made it particularly attractive to postcolonial analysis, and this very marginality means that the transformations wrought by the Soviet regime are visible in a much more highly accentuated form. Conquered in the second half of the nineteenth century (it was the last major territorial acquisition of the tsarist period), Central Asia was transformed in the Soviet period by a sustained campaign of cultural and economic change. Recent studies have interpreted this transformation as a form of colonialism.

I proceed via an examination of the Soviet transformation of Central Asia. To understand the nature of this transformation, we need to contrast the position Central Asia occupied in the Soviet state to the position the region occupied in the tsarist period. I argue that while tsarist Central Asia was quite straightforwardly a colonial possession, Soviet Central Asia was quite different. Soviet policies in Central Asia had far more in common with those of a host of other mid-century mobilizational states, but we can find few parallels for them in the history of colonial empires. My point is not to protect the Soviet Union from the posthumous odium of guilt by association with the very entities it set itself against, for the mobilizational states I compare it with were far *more* intrusive and oppressive than colonial empires. Rather, I hope to explore the specificities of empire in the twentieth century. Such specificities are important, I believe, for otherwise all exercise of political power can be construed as "colonialism," leaving little analytical utility in the term.

I am aware that my argument exists in some tension with most other contributions in this volume, which all seek to extend the definition of colonialism. I hope, however, that the tension is dynamic and that it helps us see both the scope and the limits of imperial formation as an analytical category.

CENTRAL ASIA UNDER TSARIST RULE

The Russian empire was built on the gradual accumulation of territory followed by the cooptation of existing elites into an empirewide nobility, whose ultimate loyalty was to the ruling dynasty. As Jane Burbank shows so well in this volume, the imperial state took difference to be normal, with a multiplicity of "we's" and "they's." The Russians as a nation enjoyed no particular privileges, while the state was run by a multiethnic service elite that included many non-Slavic and non-Orthodox members. Religious difference did not always matter: the state had arrived at all manner of accommodation with Muslim elites in the Volga basin, and even in the Crimea and Transcaucasia (present-day Azerbaijan), conquered in the late eighteenth and the early nineteenth centuries, respectively.

By the time Russian armies got around to conquering Central Asia, however, this vision of empire had changed substantially. Central Asia was conquered very much in the context of imperial competition with other European powers at a time when imperial rule over "uncivilized" peoples was clearly seen as a hallmark of civilization. As the tsarist foreign minister A. M. Gorchakov wrote in 1864, "The position of Russia in Central Asia is that of all civilized States which are brought into contact with half-savage, nomad populations, possessing no fixed social organization." "In such cases," he continued, "it always happens that the more civilized state is forced...to exercise a certain ascendancy over those whom their turbulent and unsettled character make most undesirable neighbours."[6] The Russian state imagined the conquest of Central Asia in a very different way than its previous territorial acquisitions.

The state made no attempt to co-opt existing elites into the Russian nobility, nor did it incorporate the indigenous population (referred to as *tuzemtsy,* natives) into empirewide systems of social classification based on ranks and standings (*sosloviia i sostoianiia*). The bulk of the Kazakh lands were consolidated into the steppe region of the empire, while large parts of Transoxiana were annexed outright and formed into the province of Turkestan. The two khanates of Bukhara and Khiva, however, continued to exist in greatly diminished territory as protectorates. This status was new to the Russian empire and again pointed to the colonial experience of western European powers. The direct models for the protectorates were the princely states of India. Turkestan was ruled by a governor-general answerable only to the tsar, and the region was under the jurisdiction of the Ministry of War, rather than Internal Affairs.

The Russian presence itself was thin, and to the end Russian administrators remained wary of this fact. The social and political distance between the rulers and the ruled remained greater than anywhere else in the empire, with the possible exceptions of Siberia and the Arctic north. Most significantly, both Russian administrators and the intelligentsia continued to see Central Asia in the manner of Gorchakov, as a colonial possession directly comparable to the colonies of other European powers.

The Russian conquest greatly affected the lives of Central Asians. They were incorporated into the broader imperial economy and made subject to new regimes of power. However, the Russian state had neither the desire nor the capability to assimilate the indigenous population or bring about radical cultural change. It had long been accustomed to particularistic arrangements of rule, whereby different social groups or provinces were governed by legislation specific to them. In Central Asia, that particularism was heightened by the much greater distance between the rulers and the ruled. Many administrative practices modeled on the colonial experience of other empires that tended to maintain—and heighten—colonial difference were put into effect. The two protectorates were left with internal autonomy, while in Turkestan a two-tier system of administration took shape. The lowest level of administration continued to be staffed by local functionaries who worked in local languages. Judicial affairs, too, remained largely in local hands and based on native laws (Islamic law or sharia, in sedentary areas and customary law, *adat,* among the nomads). Needless to say, these administrative practices crystallized the distinction between adat and shariat, just as they subtly altered their statuses. The main point here is that the state recognized the native population as different and institutionalized that difference in legal practice.[7]

This was empire on the cheap, typical of nineteenth-century empires. The state was primarily concerned with the maintenance of law and order, which would allow economic life to progress. It had no wish to intervene forcefully in local social or cultural life, especially when such intervention might meet substantial resistance. This was partly because of lack of resources. Empire was always built cheaply, but in tsarist Central Asia, fiscal restraint was particularly prominent in official discourse. Beyond that, however, like the colonial states on which it patterned its behavior, the state had little desire to micromanage society. The "old cities" were placed under the imperial administrative umbrella but did not feel the presence of the supervisory apparatus of the state; the indigenous population was exempt from conscription; and even the political police concerned themselves primarily with the settler population.

CENTRAL ASIA ACROSS THE REVOLUTIONARY DIVIDE

Central Asia's relationship to the imperial center was utterly transformed by the February Revolution of 1917. The Provisional Government declared all subjects of the Russian empire to be free and equal citizens, regardless of sex, race, creed, religion, and ethnicity, and all with an equal right to vote. The Bolsheviks who took over in October were motivated by an even more strident spirit of universalism. Theirs was an unabashedly evolutionary model of social change, one that brooked no exceptions. Yet the Bolsheviks were also intensely aware of the burden of Russia's imperial past, which they carried in the Russian borderlands, a past that made enlisting the toiling masses in the building of the Soviet state a complicated process. Nationalist movements, working on very different assumptions about politics and loyalty than the Bolsheviks, were very successful in the Russian empire during the political turmoil of the years that followed 1917. The Bolsheviks saw these nationalist movements as attempts by various local bourgeoisies to mark off "their" workers from each other and to inoculate them against the appeal of communism. Yet they also realized that previous policies of national oppression had sowed seeds of distrust in the minds of national minorities and that the political task at hand was to win over their trust. As Lenin wrote to A. A. Ioffe, a comrade sent to Turkestan on a tour of inspection, in October 1921: "For our entire Weltpolitik, it is devilishly important to *conquer* the trust of the natives; *to conquer* it three or four times; *to show* that we are *not* imperialists, that we will *not* tolerate deviations in this direction.... It is a global [*mirovoi*] question, without exaggeration global."[8] The Soviet nationalities policy that emerged as a result of these concerns had both ideological and tactical determinants. The non-Russian peoples of the new Soviet state had to be treated differently because they were non-Russians. They were to be allowed to use their languages and celebrate their identities, but primarily as a method of consolidating Soviet rule in those areas. The ends of Soviet rule, however—the building of socialism and achievement of a postcapitalist, classless utopia—were to be common to all Soviet citizens.

Yet as they set about building communism, the Bolsheviks were keenly aware of the fact (self-evident to them) of backwardness—of Russia vis-à-vis Europe and of Central Asia vis-à-vis the rest of the Soviet state. But nothing was beyond the voluntarism that Lenin had grafted onto Marxism. If a party of professional revolutionaries could do the work of the proletariat and, overcoming Russia's backwardness, lead it to revolution, then surely it could help other nations of the former empire overcome their backwardness vis-à-vis the center. Curiously for devoted materialists, the Bolsheviks construed the backwardness in cultural as much as economic terms. Lenin famously saw Russian workers' lack of "culture" as a major problem in the establishment of socialism in Russia. As far as "the East" was concerned, the problem was even more straightforward. As early as 1919, Stalin, then people's commissar for nationalities affairs, had pronounced that the tasks of Soviet power in "the East" were

> 1) In every way to raise the cultural level of the backward peoples, to build a broad system of schools and educational institutions, and to conduct our Soviet agitation, oral and printed, in the language which is native to and understood by the surrounding labouring population.
>
> 2) To enlist the labouring masses of the East in the building of the Soviet state and to render them the utmost assistance in forming their *volost* [county], *uyezd* [district] and other Soviets comprised of people who support the Soviet power and are closely connected with the local population.
>
> 3) To do away with all disabilities, formal and actual, whether inherited from the old regime or arisen in the atmosphere of civil war, which prevent the people of the East from displaying maximum independent activity in emancipating themselves from the survivals of medievalism and of the national oppression which has already been shattered.[9]

Much of the Soviet project was underpinned by a vision of the plasticity of human nature and of culture, which could be reshaped by that agent of world history, the Communist Party. The Party would do the work of History.

Soviet nationalities policy took the "objective" existence of nations or nationalities for granted. The task was not to abolish national identities but to co-opt them to the task of building the socialist utopia. Nations would flourish best, it was argued, under socialism, and socialism alone was the vehicle capable of bringing all nations and all peoples to the common final destination of humanity. In the 1920s, the Soviet state suffered from what Yuri Slezkine has called "chronic ethnophilia," coming to the aid of all nations in their struggle to advance through History, helping them skip stages at will.[10] Certain cultural features—language, costume, folklore—would continue to mark people as different, but the future that beckoned them all had a universal content. Stalin proclaimed that the cultures of the various Soviet nationalities were to be "national in form, socialist in content." In the name of this universalism, the Soviet project aimed at the *conquest* of difference.

It was precisely this aim that gave the Soviet project its legitimacy in the eyes of many in Central Asia as well as abroad, for the balancing of national authenticity (language, custom, folklore) with the demands of progress (and belonging to the modern world as full members of it) lies at the heart of all nationalist movements. In the early years of Soviet rule, moreover, anti-imperialism was constitutive of the Bolshevik worldview. The Tatar communist Mirsaid Sultangaliev articulated a "colonial" take on world revolution, arguing that world revolution could take place only through a colonial revolution, that the real division in the world was between "bourgeois nations" and "proletarian nations," and that a Colonial International would be a more likely agent of revolution than the Communist International. Sultangaliev's theoretical flamboyance led him to being purged, but his ideas clearly prefigure later formulations of Third Worldism.[11] At a more mundane level, the young Tajik member of the State Planning Commission quoted by Joshua Kunitz, an American communist who traveled in Central Asia in 1934, might have been uttering a cliché when he said:

> If you ever write about Tadjikistan, please don't fall into the error of most of the Europeans who visit us, don't descend to exoticism, don't become worked up over the magnificence of chaos....Please don't expatiate on the beauty of our apparel, the quaintness of our villages, the mystery hidden beneath our women's *paranjas,* the charm of sitting on rugs under shady plane trees and listening to the sweet monotones of our bards, of drinking green tea from a *piala*—and eating *pilaf* with our hands. Really, there is little that is charming about all that. Take any cultured Central Asian, cultured in the modern sense, that is, and to him most of the

> local customs mean simply backwardness, ignorance of the most elementary rules of sanitation and prophylactics.[12]

Nevertheless, the point was real and was made by many nationalists and many nation-states in the twentieth century. Langston Hughes, who had spent several months in Central Asia (for him, the Soviet Union's own "dusty, colored, cotton-growing South") in the winter of 1932–33 also found the new order inspiring for its abolition of difference:

> The gentlemen...who wrote lovely books about the defeat of the flesh and the triumph of the spirit...will kindly come forward and
> Speak about the Revolution—where flesh triumphs (as well as the spirit) ...and the young by the hundreds of thousands are free from hunger to grow and study and love and propagate, bodies and souls unchained without My Lord saying a commoner shall never marry my daughter or the Rabbi crying cursed be the mating of Jews and Gentiles or Kipling writing never the twain shall meet —
> For the twain have met....[13]

It is very easy, with hindsight, to scoff at such views of the Soviet experience, but they do remind us of the fascination of millions in the colonial world with notions of "revolution," "progress," and "culture," and with hopes of tossing out the old and doing away with inequality and difference. They also underscore the difference between the tsarist and Soviet regimes, a difference so vast from the vantage point of Central Asia that its elision in the label "Russian/Soviet" is truly inimical to analytical clarity. Any claim to continuity across the civil war must contend with the fact that the Soviet regime had vastly greater ambitions of transforming society and very little patience for tolerating difference.

THE SOVIET REMAKING OF CENTRAL ASIA

By the mid-1920s, as soon as it felt secure in power, the party-state unleashed what can only be described as a cultural revolution. Land and water reform was carried out in 1925–26. In 1926, Muslim courts, which had continued to adjudicate on personal matters, were finally abolished. The following year, the party turned its attention to tackling Islam in all its manifestations. Traditional schools were suppressed, a ruthless campaign was launched against the carriers of Islamic knowledge, and mosques, Sufi lodges, and madrassas (colleges) were closed.[14] This was part of a campaign against all forms of "superstition," which were considered to serve only as a cover of exploitation and which had no place in the rational society the party was building. If religion was a tool for the exploitation of the masses, then a society without exploitation would be atheistic. In the same year, 1927, the party launched a major assault (*hujum*) on the veil, which came to symbolize not just the oppression of women but the very backwardness of local society. Under the party's watchful eyes, thousands of women unveiled in public acts of defiance of tradition and patriarchal authority. The assault produced virulent reactions, as angry men, including relatives, assaulted, raped, or murdered hundreds of women. The campaign was called off in 1929, and veiling did not disappear for another two decades, but the state had staked its claim on women's liberation as a basic source of its legitimacy.[15]

The same period also witnessed a campaign for "liquidating" illiteracy among adults and establishing public education for children. In 1928, the Arabic script was replaced by Latin for writing all Central Asian languages (a decade later, it was replaced by Cyrillic). The conquest of backwardness also entailed the establishment of new norms of hygiene and public health, yet more technologies of power that allowed the state to establish its preeminence in indigenous society.[16] The biggest transformation was, of course, the collectivization of land and the rural economy between 1929 and 1932. The land and water reform had made a difference, but collectivization utterly transformed the context of people's lives, which became ever more dependent on the state. Collectivization was carried out with horrific violence, and in Kazakhstan its devastation acquired genocidal proportions. In the countryside, collectivization leveled economic hierarchies and devastated the power of older elites.

Does all of the above amount to colonialism? In the words of Paula Michaels, "the Russian and Soviet governments and other European imperial powers drew on similar methods to enforce colonial control."[17] Francine Hirsch points to continuities in ethnographic practice on either side of the revolution to argue that "Soviet nationality policy was indeed a variation on Western colonial policy."[18] Douglas Northrop, in perhaps the most sustained application of postcolonial criticism to Soviet Central Asia, has argued that "the USSR, like its tsarist predecessor, was a colonial empire. Power in the Soviet Union was expressed across lines of hierarchy and difference that created at least theoretically distinct centers (metropoles) and peripheries (colonies)."[19]

While the economy is the sphere where the colonial argument is the easiest to make, historians have long ignored it. Collectivization allowed state control over the agrarian sector. As landlord and monopoly buyer, the state could dictate what would be grown and what price would be paid. The federalism of the Soviet Union was largely a legal fiction (although in 1991 it became all important) and had no effect on economic practices or policies. The centrally planned economy came to function on the basis of regional specialization, in which each region contributed to a unitary, hypercentralized economy. Central Asia's role was to help the country achieve "cotton independence," a role that turned the entire region into a gigantic cotton plantation. No one could escape the despotism of cotton. Newly liberated women picked the cotton; urban schoolchildren were bused in to help with the harvest, all while cotton cultivation brought about environmental degradation on an appalling scale, as irrigation sucked rivers dry and pesticides generously coated fields throughout the entire region. By the 1970s, the cotton complex had come to determine the inner workings of local politics. The bulk of the cotton harvest was shipped to Russia for processing, with the finished goods sent back to Central Asia. The pattern of colonial dependence is unmistakable but was carried out in the context of a rigidly centralized state economy based on principles of regional specialization. Central Asia carried a very heavy burden, and local officials were constantly chided for "forgetting statewide interests in the face of local needs" if they demurred in the slightest.[20] Central Asia did receive infrastructural investments, and Uzbekistan and Kazakhstan acquired a base of heavy industry. But none of the republics, not even Russia itself, was meant to be economically self-sufficient. The interests that governed the economy were those of a single, unitary state, not that of a geographically separate colonial metropole.

In terms of cultural transformation, the situation is much more complicated. The decades before the revolution had seen the emergence of an indigenous movement for modernist reform in Central

Asia. Its proponents had tied new means of organization and communication to a rigorously modernist interpretation of Islam and called for a thorough reform of local social and cultural practices with the aim of saving "the nation" from degradation and destruction. When the revolution hurled the reformers into active politics, however, they found, much to their chagrin, that their enthusiasm for reform was not shared by the voters, who tended to favor social conservatives. The political defeats of 1917 radicalized the proponents of reform to a great extent, and beginning in 1918 many entered the Communist Party, which they saw as an agent capable of creating the revolutionary change they desired but had proven incapable of bringing about. The nation had to be dragged to the path of progress. Given that central authorities pushed for the inclusion and promotion of indigenous cadres, local elites saw themselves as partners in the reshaping of Central Asia, and indeed of the world as a whole. They too wanted to reshape ("modernize") the nation and to revolutionize its culture to make it fit for survival in the modern world that they very much aspired to join. Bolshevik notions of national self-determination and cultural revolution (and the two were intertwined, for the first was possible only through the second) appealed to them greatly. Central Asian societies in the 1920s were rife with conflict, and the side with the reformist social agenda found in the Bolsheviks a source of outside support that it desperately needed. The Bolshevik program overlapped to a great extent with preexisting reformist projects.[21]

The Bolsheviks were not interested, however, in helping indigenous reformers implement their own programs. From the very beginning, they had sought to incorporate members of the indigenous population into the new organs of power being built. They launched the policy of *korenizatsiia* ("indigenization") of Soviet power in the non-Russian borderlands through establishment of ethnically defined administrative units that would be staffed by members of the indigenous population. They also spent considerable effort in organizing the poor into trade unions that would function as channels for reaching into society. Trade unions existed for practically every craft in the cities. The regime also focused on political education, sending out teams equipped with posters, newspapers, films, and plays to propagate the new political message. The population had to be mobilized by the new institutions, but it also had to be taught new ways of thinking about politics. A network of Red Teahouses, Red Yurts, and Red Corners sprang up at many points in the region. These served as outlets for propaganda and showpieces for the new order the Bolsheviks hoped to establish. Propaganda campaigns utilizing film, music, theater, and the written word poured forth before every policy shift. Unlike that of the Jadids before the revolution, this form of exhortation was well funded by state resources. Youth organizations, such as the Young Pioneers (the Soviet equivalent of the Boy Scouts), the Komsomol (the youth branch of the Communist Party), and any number of "voluntary" organizations, brought people into the ambit of the new regime. Ultimately, a new political class emerged in the region. In the 1930s, it ousted Jadids of the prerevolutionary generation from Soviet institutions.[22]

Was this cultural revolution from above the same thing as a colonial civilizing mission? I would argue that the kind of cultural revolution the Soviets carried out would have indeed been inconceivable for a colonial empire. The tsarist state, with its fiscal conservatism and impulse to cordon off the realm of politics from civil society, was in general not interested in the kinds of mobilization and micromanagement of society that produce cultural revolutions. In Central Asia especially, the sense of the thinness of Russian rule and the ever-present fear of the "fanaticism" of the native placed further obstacles. But ultimately, it was the basic assumption that difference could not be transcended that made the tsarist state incapable of the wholesale assault on local culture on which the Soviet state embarked in the 1920s.

Colonial studies has highlighted the extent to which colonialism transformed the societies it conquered. The British Raj in India mapped out the country's geography and its natural resources; its classificatory apparatus reified caste and communal categories; and the economic relations it imposed vis-à-vis the metropole had a drastic effect on the lives of all the inhabitants of India.[23] Nevertheless, it did not aspire to the micromanagement of society, such as promising or enforcing universal education. It preferred dealing with "martial races" to conscription; it left agrarian power in the hands of notables rather than embarking on significant land reform; it brought in modern regimes of power, but it was not interested in modernizing the colonies. The wholesale uprooting of local life in the name of bringing the natives up to a universal standard, to force them to overcome their own backwardness, to bring them into the orbit of politics—these were not things colonial authorities concerned themselves with.[24] This tradition of nonintervention had paradoxical consequences. It partly explains why the states of South Asia today are among the weakest in the world (outside sub-Saharan Africa), unable to provide literacy or drinking water to the vast bulk of their populations, to collect taxes or garbage, to run public transport in the cities, or in many cases even to conduct an efficient and reliable census.

The Soviet assault on society, on the other hand, was possible only because the state looked upon the populace as citizens who, unlike colonial subjects, could and should be held to a higher standard. Central Asians faced the Soviet state as citizens, as did the Russians. The commonsense assumption that the Soviet Union was merely a Russian empire in an ideological guise is difficult to maintain. Recent writers have instead spoken of the colonialism of the Soviets, of communists, or of the party; others, recognizing that all three of these categories are multiethnic and coextensive with the purported colonial possessions, have spoken of the imperialism of the Central Committee of the Communist Party or the Kremlin.[25] All these points are important, but do they indicate anything other than the fact that the Soviet Union was an authoritarian regime where power was concentrated in specific hands? Does the fact that the Soviet Union had a rigidly centralized political and (especially) economic order qualify the polity as a colonial empire? It was this very centralization that destroyed "colonial difference" and created the idea of common Soviet *citizenship*, which denied *legal* differentiation along ethnic or racial lines. At the same time, it is myopic to see citizenship as synonymous only with rights—in far too many twentieth-century polities, citizenship has brought with it more obligations than rights, and so was the case with the Soviet Union. All citizens were equal in their right to be conscripted, enlightened, civilized, and dragged into utopia.

HIERARCHY AND DIFFERENCE IN THE SOVIET UNION

Even if official ideological proclamations claimed the equality of all Soviet citizens, what forms of hierarchy and difference operated in practice? To what extent and in which ways were Russians privileged in the Soviet Union? In short, did the rule of colonial difference operate in the Soviet Union?

The Soviet state's efforts to reshape society were exercised in the Russian countryside as drastically as they were in the non-Russian periphery. Literature generated in the mainstream Russian historiography clearly shows that the state saw its task as the same when it came to bringing culture and light to the Russian countryside. Russian peasants embodied Russian backwardness and an otherness that had been palpable for educated Russians since before the revolution. This backwardness had to be overcome too, and the assault on the peasant way of life (*byt*) was as merciless as the assault on Kazakh or Uzbek ways of life. The symbols of backwardness were different, but the idea was not.

Moreover, Russians did not enjoy any *legal* privileges that inhered to their ethnicity, as opposed to membership in the party or occupation of responsible posts. Nor did the Soviet state see itself as an instrument of the national interests of the Russian people.[26] Nevertheless, by the mid-1930s, the utopianism surrounding the nationalities policies of the 1920s had begun to be reined in. The 1930s saw a turn to conservative values in all spheres of life in the Soviet Union. As the need to build socialism in one country trumped world revolution and associated internationalism, Soviet patriotism came to the forefront of officially prescribed values. Stalin's original definition of the nation was tied to a particular point in the history of the development of capitalism, and a great deal of the actions of the 1920s and early 1930s had been premised on the assumption that nationhood was a passing phase. By the mid-1930s, however, national identities had acquired ever greater permanence, and official rhetoric endowed nationality with an objective essence that stretched far back into the past. The Soviet homeland (both fatherland, *otechestvo,* and motherland, *rodina*) was inhabited by many different peoples at different points along the long journey to utopia. Soviet political practice took "the East" to be an objective category and the division between "eastern" and "western" nationalities to be a matter of fact. The distinction between "cultured" and "backward" nationalities was routinely made throughout the 1920s; in 1932, this distinction was entrenched bureaucratically when the people's commissariat for education produced an authoritative list of "culturally backward" nationalities. The immediate context was official concern, emanating from Stalin himself, with providing universal elementary education in native languages. "Culturally backward" nationalities, which included all Central Asians, were to be "eligible for preferential assistance" in funding and in receiving allocations in institutions of higher education at the center.[27] Backwardness was something to be overcome. But like so many Soviet categories, the immediate evolutionary context gave way in the mid-1930s to primordial ones, and "cultural backwardness" became a permanent stain.

The Russians as a whole were deemed more advanced along the evolutionary path than others and therefore had a positive role to play in guiding other nationalities to the end of history. Russian high culture was rehabilitated; Russians became the "elder brother" of all Soviet peoples, while the Russian proletariat became the heroic bearer of light to other peoples still trapped in darkness. Russians were absolved of the sins of their empire, the sins of "tsarist officialdom" separated from the positive contribution of the "Russian vanguard intelligentsia" and the revolutionary proletariat. Indeed, by conquering all sorts of benighted peoples and incorporating them into the same polity as these wonderful groups, the tsarist empire had performed a historically important—and "objectively positive"—role. The very notion of conquest was consigned to the dustbin of historiography. Imperial Russia's borderlands had not been conquered at all, but united with or incorporated into the Russian empire; the common history of all the peoples living in the tsarist and now Soviet homeland was based on a "great friendship" that involved all "progressive" *natsionaly* seeing the objective goodness of conquest and the vanguard Russian intelligentsia taking a paternal interest in the historical fate of its wards. Russian culture became the default modern culture to which all Soviet nations aspired. The celebration of the "Great Russian people" reached its apogee in the war years, and at the moment of victory, Stalin could single out the Russian people as "the most outstanding of all the nations in the Soviet Union…not just because they are the leading people, but because they have a clear mind, hardy character, and patience."[28] While some of this rhetoric was scaled back after the death of Stalin in 1953, many features of the Stalin era—the great friendship, the elder brother role for the Russians, the historically positive nature of tsarist conquest, and the eschewing of the term *conquest*—became permanent features of nationalities discourse in the Soviet Union and remained so until glasnost loosened tongues in the late 1980s.

Not all non-Russian nationalities were equal, however. "Cultured" nationalities came after the Russians, with the Slavs (Ukrainians and Belarusians) leading the way. Those with union republics were ahead of those without that political status. The "small peoples" of the north came last. These hierarchies were made all too real in official spectacles, such as the numerous parades in Moscow to mark official holidays.[29] For a while, during World War II, the Ukrainian nation even bore the epithet of "great," something only the Russians normally deserved.[30] Moscow had railway and metro stations named after Kiev and Byelorussia, but none after any other republics or capitals. Georgians and Armenians were both classified as "western" nationalities and could celebrate their own histories more fully than could Central Asians, whose place in official parades was defined solely by their contribution to the Soviet economy.

This asymmetry also extended to the Communist Party's cadres policy. The country was ruled by the *nomenklatura,* the privileged elite of party and state officials who comprised the inner decision-making apparatus of the state. The one nonnegotiable prerequisite for entry into the nomenklatura was party membership; otherwise, the nomenklatura was directly reminiscent of the multiethnic service elite that had ruled the tsarist empire. Yet despite the juridical equality of all Soviet citizens (and all party members), the patterns of circulation of the ruling elite were hierarchical. Russians could be posted anywhere in the Soviet Union, a scope available to only a few other nationalities (mostly Jews and Ukrainians, but also Tatars and Armenians). However, it was exceedingly rare for Central Asians to be posted to high office outside of their own republic.

Yet all of this has to be set against yet other developments, especially during the Brezhnev period (1964–1982). As stability became a core political value, more and more power in the republics went into the hands of increasingly confident indigenous political elites, ensconced in the bosom of the party itself. As long as these party officials did not rock the boat politically—as long as they fulfilled the economic demands of the center, kept nationalism within Soviet bounds, and did not make egregious demands on the center—they could run the republics pretty much as they pleased. Affirmative action programs in favor of the "titular nationalities" of each republic existed quite legally (for jobs and admissions). But in addition, there were vast (quasi-legal and illegal) networks of patronage, headed ultimately by local political elites. Russians resident in the republics might dominate the technical professions (which they did), but they found themselves excluded from these networks. Without the ability to offer reciprocity in the exchange of connections and gifts, Russians found themselves able to offer only cash. To secure a seat in an institute, for instance, a Russian resident of Tashkent might have been expected to pay twice the sum paid by an Uzbek with connections.[31] The Russians also found themselves excluded from the lucrative "shadow" economy in Central Asia. Being Russian brought advantages in the Soviet Union, but by the late Soviet period, these advantages were never unadulterated.

The indigenous political elites were also powerful enough to provide protection to dissident national intellectuals. Major literary scandals in Brezhnev-era Central Asia concerned intellectuals who trespassed on the limits of the "great friendship" thesis and reinterpreted Central Asian–Russian relations in unauthorized ways. The most prominent of these scandals erupted in 1975, when the Kazakh author Olzhas Suleymenov published a maverick book that reexamined an iconic text of Russian identity. The bulk of the book is a philological reexamination of *The Tale of the Lay of Igor,* a story celebrating the battles waged by the Kievan prince Igor against his Turkic nomadic neighbors in the tenth century. Ever since the "discovery" of the text at the turn of the nineteenth century, the epic has remained a canonical text in the Russian pantheon, a marker of Russia's civilizational identity as the enemy of the steppe nomads. Suleymenov argued that far from proving the absolute opposition of Turk and Slav, nomad and sedentarist, the tale showed that relations between the two societies were quite porous and that cultural borrowing was commonplace.[32] Suleymenov's book was not a nationalist rant; in fact, quite the opposite, Suleymenov argued for tolerance and recognition of mutual influence. Nevertheless, his argument was subversive because it questioned various hierarchies that the Brezhnev era took for granted: the Russians as elder brother, the superiority of sedentary over nomadic societies, of the "West" over the "East." Perhaps most unforgivable of all was the liberty Suleymenov took in interpreting a national monument of the elder brother. The fact that the book was published in Russian (the only language in which Suleymenov has ever written) made the sin even graver.

A storm of criticism broke out, in Russia as well as in Kazakhstan, and the book was quietly withdrawn from circulation. Yet Suleymenov did not suffer personally for his misadventure. The Kazakh first secretary Dinmuhamed Kunaev afforded him protection and convinced Brezhnev of the inadvisability of persecuting the author. Suleymenov retained his position as secretary of the Central Committee of the Kazakhstan Writers' Union and was reelected to this position in 1977.[33]

One might also note that discourses of anticolonialism were used by nationalist elites in the Soviet Union only at the very end of perestroika, when the disintegration of the country was well advanced. Even given the fact of harsh (self-) censorship, it is striking that nationalist dissidence was seldom phrased in anticolonial terms in the Soviet period.

An "Imperialism of Benevolence"?

The Soviet transformation of Central Asia fits better into a different trajectory, which might be called the "imperialism of benevolence," an episode of which unfolded as this volume was being put together. The contemporary American neoconservative vision sees empire as a benevolent entity that can bestow the gift of law and order, justice, free markets, and democracy on those it seeks to bless with its attention. Benighted people have to be dragged, kicking and screaming, to their own salvation, through the use of "shock and awe" military tactics if necessary. The extreme case of this imperial mission has been provided by Iraq, although in less violent ways it has affected much of the rest of the world since the demise of the Soviet Union. In its universal applicability and in the implacable moral certainty that backs it, this vision of the remaking of the world is just as utopian as any social engineering the Bolsheviks ever contemplated. The parallels are worth investigating.

The contemporary neoconservative project seeks to remake the world by introducing "democracy" based on a regime of untrammeled private property, in which the state ceases to play any role in the economy. In many ways, privatization (of land, water, and everything else) is but the flip side of collectivization, with social and economic consequences just as drastic. The contours of this experiment are most clearly visible in Iraq, where the neoconservative economic experiment has been imposed by force of arms.[34] The rhetoric of "liberation" deployed on the eve of the invasion of Iraq was, of course, depressingly reminiscent of a whole host of Soviet interventions in its external empire or in proxy warfare in the "Third World" over the course of the Cold War, and we find traces of it during the civil war that led to the establishment of Soviet power in Central Asia. More striking is the eagerness to export "revolution" through armed force. The neoconservative eagerness to turn Iraq into a beacon of democracy through the armed overthrow of indigenous rule has plenty of precedent in Bolshevik practice. At key moments in the civil war, it was the Red Army and not the Communist Party, let alone the proletariat, that turned out to be the motor of revolution in the colonial world. A key role in the establishment of Soviet power in Central Asia was played by Mikhail Frunze, a Central Asian–born general of German extraction who headed the Red Army as it consolidated central control in the region. Frunze was averse to accommodating the universal mission of the party (and the Red Army) to any form of local difference. He opposed the formation of ethnically segregated indigenous units in the Red Army (which were seen by many as a way of showing the party's commitment to affirmative action on behalf of the local population), and he favored the export of the revolution. In the case of neighboring Bukhara, "revolution" was the only solution to the problem of the emir having consolidated his authority since 1917. "In order to form a revolutionary upsurge in Bukhara, it is necessary to wait not months, but years." Even then, "the [revolutionary] movement in Bukhara must be only a push; all the rest, approximately nine tenths, must be done by the Russian Red Army."[35] The emancipation of Muslim women has long been a cause dear to colonial officials, and in the autumn of 2001, the United States undertook its own hujum, when the bombing of Afghanistan was justified in terms of the liberation of its women. (The same rhetoric has been conspicuously absent from the assault on Iraq, where women's position in society has deteriorated substantially.)

Yet there remain substantial differences as well. If the Bolsheviks saw their mission as part of a universal human drama, in which they (or the Red Army) were doing the work of History, current American intervention is conceptualized more as a gift (of democracy and free markets) bestowed by the imperial power. The gift itself is seen as unique to the United States (or having a very specific lineage). In practice, the separation between "colony" and "metropole" is clear cut. Unlike the Soviet case, American empire does not seek annexation and inclusion in the body politic, and citizenship is not one of the benefits of empire, for the fiction of Iraq's national sovereignty is maintained. The parallels between the Soviet and the neoconservative cases cannot be pushed too far. Indeed, if there is a parallel in the American case with the experience of Central Asia, it is that of the inclusion into the union of places such as Hawai`i, New Mexico, and Minnesota, where annexation resulted in full incorporation into the "metropole." Even here, though, the parallels are imperfect, for annexation was followed by colonization by a racially distinct population that was very much the bearer of legal privileges. In any case, one can rest assured that the newfound respectability of empire in contemporary American discourse will not extend to non-Anglophone cases. The Soviets (and the Russians and the Ottomans) will continue to be cast as barbarians for having been empire holders.

MODERN MOBILIZATIONAL STATES

Might not the Soviet project be placed in a genealogy other than that of empire? I have argued that the intrusiveness of the Soviet project bears striking *dis*similarities with the conduct of previous colonial empires. I would now like to examine some of the similarities this project shares with the projects of many national states in the twentieth century to reshape or "sculpt" their citizenry. Twentieth-century history is replete with cases of states, equipped with modern means of mobilization and coercion, leading their populations on a forced march to progress and development. The Soviet project of overcoming backwardness, in Russia as well as in the borderlands, fits neatly into this history.

The Kemalist remaking of Anatolia, coeval with the Soviet transformation of Central Asia, underscores this point. Like its Soviet counterpart, the Kemalist regime originated from the flames of World War I. Both regimes emerged in a prolonged warfare that continued the devastation of World War I, and both were profoundly marked by it. Both regimes also pursued shock modernization programs that involved mass mobilization, nation and state building, and political centralization, as well as attempts at radical interventions in the realms of society and culture featuring state-led campaigns for the "emancipation" of women, spreading literacy, the elaboration of new literary languages, and, above all, secularization. The Turkish case is even more pertinent for Central Asia, for Central Asian intellectuals were connected to intellectual currents in late-Ottoman society. Some of them had been educated in Istanbul, and many more took the attempts by the Ottoman state to reshape itself as models to be followed.[36]

The Kemalist revolution reshaped the contours of local culture quite as thoroughly as the Soviets did in Central Asia. While there was no outright assault on Islam, the republic abolished the caliphate, religious courts, and Sufi lodges; it brought all religious expression under state control, effectively nationalizing Islam; it adopted the Latin script in the same year as the Soviet Union did. The status of women, too, figured prominently. The Kemalist state's ideal of a modern woman was one who was unveiled and clad in Western dress. Veiling, although not outlawed, was deeply frowned upon. A new civil code, modeled on that of Switzerland and introduced in 1926, began an assault on existing patterns of legitimation of law and authority through Islam.

The Kemalist project was the most thoroughgoing and successful in the Muslim world, but not the only one attempted. Reza Shah (who ruled from 1925 to 1941) laid the foundations of the modern state in Iran through a series of steps directly inspired by Turkey. He raised a conscripted army, created new systems of taxation and bureaucracy, and developed a system of secular public schools. He also introduced secular codes that curtailed the power of the *ulama* (Muslim scholars). A strident secular nationalism appealing to pre-Islamic Iranian history provided the legitimacy for his kingship. Unlike the Soviets or the Kemalists, Reza Shah actually banned the veil.[37] In Afghanistan, King Amanullah, with less success, pursued a similar course of action in which he tried to establish the machinery of a modern bureaucratic state, curbing the power of the tribes and the authority of the ulama. He too attempted to change the position of women and to establish a secular national basis for Afghan identity.[38]

The cases of Turkey, Iran, and Afghanistan are only the most directly comparable for Central Asia. In later decades of the twentieth century, Nasserist and Baathist variations on this theme wrought similar changes in several Arab states. Beyond the Muslim world, of course, there is no shortage of examples of national states that have reshaped "their" societies in very similar ways.[39] The crucial difference is that while all these states acted in the name of the nation, the Soviet Union was a multiethnic state. The ethnic differences between the core and periphery make the Soviet Union look like a colonial empire, where one people rule over another.

But this manner of posing the problem is premised on a rather uncritical view of identity and the role of modern states in identity production. The production of national identities was a major project for all national states in the twentieth century. The Turkish republic created the Turkish nation, not the other way around, in part through well-articulated policies of assimilation and the dispersal of groups that had suddenly become minorities and in part through the use of force in recalcitrant provinces.[40] Nor was Turkey unusual in this sense. Very few national states (Iceland might be the only one) are so homogenous as to be devoid of ethnically differentiated peripheries. The Soviet state, for its part, played an important role in the elaboration of national identities of its various nationalities, each of which it promised to escort to the final destination of History. Equally important, the Soviet state did have a parallel discourse of Soviet patriotism, a civic identity based on common citizenship (*grazhdanstvo*). Indeed, official Soviet discourse used the same term (*narod,* "people") for the community of all Soviet citizens as it did for the various ethnonational communities that inhabited it.[41] Soviet patriotism had real content based on common patterns of education and mobilization, participation in the Soviet economy and Soviet rituals, and, for men, conscription in the Soviet army.

The Soviet state, in common with the national states discussed above, dealt in varying degrees with the dialectic of the national and the universal and responded in ways that were not dissimilar. These responses all rested on the brutal exercise of *state* power, understood together under the rubrics "developmental dictatorship," "the gardening state," "the civilizing process," and "high modernism," at least as well as "empire."

THE SUBJECTIVE DIMENSIONS OF EMPIRE

There are similarities to be found in the Soviet case with various kinds of empire. The nomenklatura had much in common with the multiethnic service elite that helped govern the tsarist empire. The hierarchies of difference between "advanced" and "backward," "western" and "eastern," paralleled Western usages. But as I hope I have shown, few of the technologies of rule and of managing cultural difference used by the Soviet regime were unique to it or to colonial empires. They were part of a much bigger phenomenon of twentieth-century history, that of an activist, interventionist state that sought to sculpt its citizenry in an ideal image. The key concept here is, perhaps, that of citizen. Citizens might be considered primarily as bearers of rights, but all too often in the twentieth century, they were also bearers of *obligations*—obligations, moreover, that states extracted from them using vast machineries of coercion. What allowed states to do so was their willingness to intervene in society at a level that many colonial states would have found inconceivable. Much of this violence was done with the goal of exorcising difference from the (new) body politic, sometimes in explicit reaction to previously existing patterns of colonial difference.

Yet current wisdom holds the Soviet Union to have been an empire all along. In the last years of the Soviet Union, critics of the regime began using anticolonial discourses to denounce the Soviet Union. At the moment of the demise of the Soviet Union, during the drama of the failed coup of August 1991, protestors, predominantly Russians, carried placards that proclaimed, "Down with the Empire of the Red Fascists!" Since then, such anticolonial rhetoric has been institutionalized in some post-Soviet states. I would suggest that it is this evaluation of the polity as an empire that we have to analyze.[42] As Mark Beissinger reminds us, the use of the label "empire" was and is never neutral; it is "a claim and a stance" as much as a neutral descriptor.[43] In the normative structures of post–World War II international politics, empires are necessarily evil and illegitimate, and denunciation of a state as an empire adds rhetorical force to one's argument. Indeed, the lines connecting empires to mere states are not easy to discern. In other words, the distinction between state and empire is discursive. But is it only discursive?

Notes

Since its presentation at the SAR seminar in Santa Fe, this paper has benefited from comments from the editors of this volume as well as from two readers of the manuscript. In addition, I would like to thank Laura Adams, Peter Blitstein, and Adrienne Edgar for insightful comments.

1. Abdurakhimova and Rustamova, *Kolonial'naia sistema vlasti v Turkestane vo vtoroi polovine XIX-pervoi chetverti XX v.v.;* Abdurakhimova, "Colonial System of Power in Turkistan"; O'zbekistonning yangi tarixi.

2. Hirsch, *Empire of Nations,* 1-3.

3. For a sampling from this vast literature, see Suny, "Learning from Empire" and "Ambiguous Categories"; Terry Martin, *Affirmative Action Empire;* Beissinger, "Demise of the Empire-State"; Motyl, *Revolutions, Nations, Empires;* Crawford Young, *Imperial Ends;* Dawisha and Parrott, *End of Empire?;* Barkey and von Hagen, *After Empire;* and Slezkine, "Imperialism as the Highest Stage of Socialism."

4. See, most notably, Northrop, *Veiled Empire;* Michaels, *Curative Powers;* Cavanaugh, "Backwardness and Biology."

5. See Prasenjit Duara, this volume.

6. Quoted in Khalid, *Politics of Muslim Cultural Reform,* 50-51.

7. For recent work on the Russian empire in Central Asia, see Khalid, *Politics of Muslim Cultural Reform,* esp. ch. 2; Virginia Martin, *Law and Custom in the Steppe;* Brower, *Turkestan and the Fate of the Russian Empire;* Sahadeo, *Russian Colonial Society in Tashkent;* and Morrison, "Russian Rule in Samarkand."

8. Lenin, *Polnoe sobranie sochinenii,* 190; all emphases as in the original.

9. Stalin, "Our Tasks in the East," 246.

10. Slezkine, "USSR as a Communal Apartment."

11. Bennigsen and Lemercier-Quelquejay, *Sultan Galiev, le père de la révolution tiers-mondiste.*

12. Kunitz, *Dawn over Samarkand,* 13.

13. Hughes, "Letter to the Academy." Hughes also published a short book on his travels in Central Asia: *A Negro Looks at Soviet Central Asia.* On Hughes's Central Asian travels, see Moore, "Colored Dispatches from the Uzbek Border."

14. Keller, *To Moscow, not Mecca.*

15. The hujum has attracted considerable attention from Western scholars in recent years. Northrop, *Veiled Empire,* presents a relentlessly negative view of the hujum, which he sees as a case of imperial intervention into a pristine national community. He bases his account on much too clear a distinction between "Uzbek society" and "alien Bolsheviks." Northrop's account begins in 1927 and is thus oblivious to the conflicts that beset Uzbek society in the previous decade. His account gives no indication that different actors within Uzbek society had different goals, or that many Bolsheviks were also Uzbeks. Kamp, *New Woman in Central*

Asia, offers a more nuanced account of the hujum. It takes into account the longer-term development of Muslim attitudes on the question and the aspirations of women activists. For other excellent work, see Keller, "Trapped between State and Society," and Edgar, "Emancipation of the Unveiled." For an explicitly comparative perspective on the hujum, see Edgar, "Bolshevism, Patriarchy, and the Nation."

16. Michaels, *Curative Powers.*

17. Michaels, *Curative Powers,* 8.

18. Hirsch, "Toward an Empire of Nations." In her later work, Hirsch moderated her stance on this equation.

19. Northrop, *Veiled Empire,* 22.

20. Gitlin, *Natsional'nye otnosheniia v Uzbekistane,* 69.

21. I explore this point further in Khalid, "Nationalizing the Revolution."

22. This paragraph represents, in a very concentrated form, the results of an ongoing research project on the history of Central Asia in the early Soviet period. The existing literature is slim and laconic, and no useful overviews of the period exist, which explains the sparseness of citation here.

23. Prakash, *Another Reason;* Goswami, *Producing India;* Dirks, *Castes of Mind;* Edney, Mapping an Empire.

24. In the aftermath of World War II, faced with the need to reestablish their legitimacy and make their empires more productive, both the British and the French empires turned, for the first time, to "colonial development" as a policy. However, having finally arrived at "using colonization as a tool of social transformation, they very quickly backed off." See Cooper, "Modernizing Colonialism and the Limits of Empire," 64. The expense was too great, the political opposition in the metropole too massive to pull it off. Decolonization was the much better option.

25. Gitlin, *Natsional'nye otnosheniia v Uzbekistane;* Levitin, *Uzbekistan na istoricheskom povorote.*

26. Motyl, *Will the Non-Russians Rebel?;* Brandenberger, *National Bolshevism.*

27. Martin, *Affirmative Action Empire,* 163-67.

28. Quoted in Brandenberger, *National Bolshevism,* 130-31.

29. Petrone, *Life Has Become More Joyous, Comrades.*

30. Yekelchyk, *Stalin's Empire of Memory.*

31. Koroteyeva and Makarova, "Money and Social Connections in the Soviet and Post-Soviet Uzbek City"; Lubin, *Labour and Nationality in Soviet Central Asia.*

32. Suleimenov, *Az i Ia: kniga blagonamerennogo chitatelia.*

33. Ram, "Imagining Eurasia."

34. Klein, "Baghdad Year Zero"; Medani, "State Rebuilding in Reverse"; Chatterjee, *Iraq, Inc.*

35. Quoted in Genis, *"S Bukharoi nado konchat',"* 27, 21.

36. For a more sustained attempt at this comparison, see Khalid, "Backwardness and the Quest for Civilization."

37. Abrahamian, *Iran between Two Revolutions;* Cronin, *Making of Modern Iran.* For the contemporary comparative perspective, see Atabaki and Zürcher, *Men of Order.*

38. Gregorian, *Emergence of Modern Afghanistan;* Poullada, *Reform and Rebellion in Afghanistan;* Nawid, *Religious Response to Social Change in Afghanistan.*

39. See also Blitstein, "Cultural Diversity and the Interwar Conjuncture."

40. See, especially, Cagaptay, *Islam, Secularism, and Nationalism in Modern Turkey.*

41. Blitstein, "Nation and Empire in Soviet History."

42. See also the extremely valuable points made by Beissinger, "Soviet Empire as 'Family Resemblance,'" 302-03.

43. Mark Beissinger, *The Persisting Ambiguity of Empire* (Seattle: National Council for Soviet and East European Research, 1995), 155.

5

Erasing the Empire, Re-racing the Nation

Racialism and Culturalism in Imperial China

Peter C. Perdue

CHINA AND THE POLITICS OF IMPERIAL COMPARISON

Historical empires have long provided a source of contemporary political and social guidance. Just as the Roman empire informed the goals of the British and other Europeans in the early modern age, analysts today draw on the nineteenth-century British empire as a model for American policy. But a number of scholars realize that we must look beyond Europe for useful insight into imperial practice. This volume argues for the productive use of comparisons along a broad range of imperial formations, including those of Spain, Russia, China, and Japan.

The rise of imperial comparisons indicates dissatisfaction with the paradigms that defined nations as modern and empires as "traditional." These paradigms saw the transition "from empire to nation" as an index of modernity, supporting the decolonization movement.[1] Now the boundaries of nation and empire seem more blurred, and there is more interest in the achievements rather than the failures of empire. On one key point, the accommodation of difference, the looser structures of empires seem to have allowed for the coexistence of many peoples under a single authority much more effectively than the tight definitions of identity imposed by nations.

Imperial comparisons have indeed multiplied, but each comparison has its own political context.[2] Most analysts are far more interested in using their analogies to change government policy than in any responsible comparative historical analysis.

Imperial China has served as a reference point for European analysts ever since detailed evidence about the regime flowed back from Jesuit reports beginning in the seventeenth and eighteenth centuries. (Marco Polo, of course, had written his account of a fabulous empire five centuries earlier, but most readers dismissed him as a liar.) One of the key themes of the Enlightenment debate was the existence of private property rights in China. Baron de Montesquieu argued in *L'Esprit des Lois* that China was a pure case of despotism, in which no one held any secure title to land.[3] Voltaire, Quesnay, and other physiocrats argued that, by contrast, the rulers of China, restrained by a "natural law" that preserved property rights, took a genuine interest in the security and livelihood of their subjects. Although both sides invoked China, their real interest was France. Montesquieu used the Chinese example to support his claims for independent institutional authority for the nobility and exclusive control of property, while physiocrats argued for lighter taxation and greater promotion of the agrarian economy within the framework of the absolutist state. China served as an indirect mirror for European concerns over reconciling monarchical authority with noble claims.

Modern theorists who look at China have many similar concerns. Certain economic historians such as Douglass North, Eric Jones, and David Landes still view imperial China as a despotic "tribute pump" that only extracted a huge surplus from its peasantry with no concern for peasant welfare. They explain the "European miracle" in terms of European states' protection of private property regimes through contract law, laissez-faire policies toward the market, and encouragement of technological innovation and entrepreneurship. They have erected a factitious, simplified model of "Europe" in opposition to a despotic "China." Others, however, who look at empirical data instead of stylized descriptions, have found that imperial China up to 1800 displayed considerable economic vitality, that the state supported commerce and protected property rights, and that people wrote contracts that were enforced in court.[4] China in this view shares much with early modern Europe. Those who support this argument, of course, have their own political concerns: one may say that in general they are skeptical of the uniqueness of European institutions and of the need to follow only one track toward modernization. In both the eighteenth- and twentieth-century cases, the choices of comparison are driven both by new evidence and the modern political environment.

We can draw some lessons from this debate over China's economic dynamics when looking at other aspects of the imperial regime in comparative perspective. First, be aware that there are contradictory impulses in any two societies that we compare: singling out one side of a complex interaction only creates misleading binary oppositions. China was neither simply a "despotic" nor a "laissez-faire" state, and neither was any European state. As argued in the introduction, "modular comparisons" between component parts of imperial formations are more productive than static contrasts of one whole with another. Second, the practice of "symmetrical interpretation," as recommended by R. Bin Wong, helps to offset tendencies toward one-sidedness; that is, we should try to look at each society through the other's eyes. European proponents of unrestricted private property rights saw imperial China as excessively interventionist, but Chinese officials would have seen Europeans as neglecting the people's subsistence. In famine relief programs, for example, Europeans had mostly local parish relief, while imperial China had a network of "evernormal granaries" distributed around the empire to insure consumers against rapid price fluctuations. In this sense, China anticipated the social welfare states of the twentieth century. Similarly, instead of only looking at China's imperial past through nationalist eyes, we should also look at the nation-state through the eyes of past imperial officials, giving equal weight to both sides.

Here I apply these perspectives to an examination of imperial China's accommodation of difference: the way in which dynasties categorized the multiple peoples under their rule. Two contrasting principles governed views toward subjected peoples: a belief in "transformation" (*xianghua*), which allowed those not only within imperial boundaries but also within tributary states beyond those boundaries to approach "civilized" norms by submitting themselves to the orthodox classical tradition; and a belief in segregation, expulsion, or even extermination (*jiaomie*), which regarded those not at the core as irredeemably alien, closer to natural forces and wild animals than to human beings. Over time, these contradictory paradigms rose and fell depending on military, geopolitical, and cultural changes. Imperial China's classical tradition was neither simply "culturalist" nor "racialist," but an evolving dialectic.

From examining imperial management of difference, we can gain insight into the dilemmas of the modern Chinese nation-state. In brief, the "multinationality nation-state" of the People's Republic (*duo minzu guojia*) fuses both principles in an uneasy alloy: each of the "nationalities" (*minzu*) is defined by rigidly racialist criteria uniting territory, history, language, and genealogy in a single package; but the state as a whole embraces transformationalism, claiming to raise all the nationalities to a higher level of universal modernity. Both of these strategies run up against unavoidable theoretical and practical contradictions, leaving the tension still unresolved. In this sense, the imperial legacy continues to affect the conduct of modern China's relations with diverse peoples both within and beyond its borders.

SHANGHAI, 1903: RACISM AND NATIONALISM

> Sweep away millennia of despotism in all its forms, throw off millennia of slavishness, annihilate the five million and more of the furry and horned Manchu race, cleanse ourselves of 260 years of harsh and unremitting pain, so that the soil of the Chinese subcontinent is made immaculate, and the descendants of the Yellow Emperor will all become Washingtons. Then they will return from the dead to life again, they will emerge from the Eighteen Levels of hell and rise to the Thirty Three Mansions of heaven, in all their magnificence and richness to arrive at their zenith, the unique and comparable of goals—revolution.
>
> —Zou Rong[5]

In 1903, Zou Rong, a nineteen-year-old Chinese student living in Japan, published an inflammatory anti-Manchu tract in Shanghai. In this text, entitled *The Revolutionary Army* (*Gemingjun*), he attacked the Manchu rulers of China's Qing dynasty (1636–1911) for oppressing the Han majority, making them weak victims of foreign aggression. In Zou's view, China belonged to the Han Chinese, the descendants of the Yellow Emperor alone, and the Manchus were nothing but savages. Zou insisted that the Han people of the Yellow Earth and the Manchus and Mongols of the steppes were completely distinct races, which never did and never could mix. Zou was imprisoned and died under arrest the next year, but his tract soon reached a mass audience in China and Japan. Perhaps 100,000 copies eventually circulated. Zou was not the first to attack the Manchus, but his ferocious language and his virulent racial invective gave the radical nationalist movement unprecedented force. Sun Yat-sen, the founder of the modern Chinese Republic, incorporated much of this anti-Manchu rhetoric into his program when he created his own revolutionary nationalist organization, the Tongmenghui, in 1905.

These well-known events need a broader historical and discursive context. What were the sources of Zou's anti-Manchuism? Why did the passage from empire to nation produce such a violently racist ideology? To answer these questions, we must examine imperial Chinese discourse about peoples of the northwest frontier.

For nationalist historians, anti-Manchuism was an inevitable result of the atrocities committed by the Manchu elite at the time of the Qing conquest and the oppression of the Han people during the Manchus' two centuries of rule. Zou Rong regarded the Manchus as a completely alien race and hostility between Han Chinese and the barbarians of the north as eternal. He did not need to trace the history of Han/non-Han relations in detail because he viewed it as a static, permanent state of enmity.

Other historians, by contrast, have treated anti-Manchuism as only a brief transitional episode in nationalist ideology, soon to be replaced by Sun Yat-sen's concept of five nationalities. Soon after the formation of the Republic of China in 1911, Sun declared that the Chinese nation naturally consisted of five "nationalities" (minzu): the Han, Manchus, Mongols, Tibetans, and Muslims. Many Western scholars have viewed anti-Manchu mobilization as a factitious ideology because they believe the Manchu ruling elite had completely assimilated to Han Chinese ways by the end of the nineteenth century. If the Manchus were completely indistinguishable from Han, there could be no genuine anti-Manchu ideology based on racial difference. This interpretation reduced anti-Manchuism to a mere tactical maneuver of late nineteenth-century revolutionaries, without any social basis.

These older studies attempted to draw a sharp line between the empire and the nation in order to remove the disturbing influence of the past on the present. If Qing China's backwardness derived simply from Manchu atrocities, the new nation could begin with a clean slate, uncontaminated by racial prejudice and oppression. Likewise, if the Manchus had totally assimilated to the Han, the new nation could also make a fresh start. The ideology of the multinational state also distinguished itself from the "feudal," hierarchical distinctions of the empire by claiming to put all nationalities on an equal level. These techniques of erasure overlooked the lasting imprint left by Qing imperial classifications on the new constructions of the republican and communist nations.

Revisionist studies of the Manchus, however, have shown that the Manchus both objectively and subjectively remained distinct throughout the Qing. Even though most of them no longer spoke Manchu or carried on horse riding or shamanism, the banner system, an institution created by the Qing to ensure military, political, and economic privileges for the Manchus and their allies, still made them different in the eyes of the Han. Mark Elliott and Pamela Crossley have demonstrated how banner membership preserved a separate Manchu ideological and social identity. Zou Rong directed much of his fire at just those privileges that derived from banner membership. Edward Rhoads has argued that until the very end of the dynasty the Manchu court primarily protected the interests of its own house. Rhoads's view from inside the court accords well with Zou Rong's hostile attack from the outside.[6]

If we question Manchu assimilation, we must address more seriously the heritage that the Qing empire left to the builders of the nation-state. The Qing's two key characteristics were rule by a distinct elite with a central Eurasian background and the unprecedented expansion of the territory under imperial control. Both the People's Republic and the Nationalist government on Taiwan claimed legitimate authority over substantially the same territories encompassed by the Qing at its maximal extent, including Mongolia, Taiwan, Xinjiang, Manchuria, and Tibet. But these striking nationalist claims are not merely a question of size. By encompassing so many peoples under its imperial gaze, the Qing created the problem of incorporating difference, which required both ideological and institutional resolution. The imperial solution invoked universal claims to peace and order guaranteed by a heavenly mandate, but it never achieved total hegemony. Dissonant voices drew on definitions of racial difference that were deeply embedded in the classical Chinese tradition. I will address here how the Qing dealt with these dissenting voices.

There were at least three sources of anti-Manchu nationalism: a buried but latent tradition of racial discourse in the classical tradition; global ideologies of imperialism, scientism, and racism; and the particular contact points between Chinese students and the Western world, especially in Japan. During the 1900s, these three discourses joined together to form an explosive mixture of racial nationalism. The transition from empire to nation pivoted around this critical decade. Many of the components of Chinese nationalist ideology sprouted in this period and gained mass support. We can illuminate Chinese nationalism by examining concurrent developments in this decade elsewhere in the world in the light of comparative studies of racism and imperialism.

It so happens that W. E. B. Du Bois published *The Souls of Black Folk* in 1903, the same year as Zou Rong's manifesto. Du Bois's text contained the famous claim that "the problem of the twentieth century is the problem of the color line—the relation of the darker to the lighter races of men in Asia and Africa, in America and the islands of the sea."[7] Subsequent events fully bore out his grim prophecy. Racial ideologies of domination, exclusion, and extermination raged throughout the twentieth century around the world, contested by movements for decolonization, racial justice, and collective security. Although the Nazis were the most extreme example, Asians also experienced racial domination under imperial rule by Europeans and Japanese, as did African Americans in the United States. Du Bois did not write an anti-white tract, but he foresaw the coming salience of racial classification and the necessity to resolve social inequalities produced by it. He wrote, "now if one notices carefully one will see that between these two worlds, despite much physical contact and daily intermingling, there is almost no community of intellectual life or point of transference where the thoughts and feelings of one race can come into direct contact and sympathy with the thoughts and feelings of the other."[8]

Du Bois's book provides a counterpoint to Zou Rong's text by demonstrating that social analysis based on racial divisions flourished around the world in this decade. Nationalists and anticolonialists drew on this shared global discourse.[9] George Frederickson's recent short study also points the way to fruitful historical comparisons. Examining the evolution of European racial ideologies over the last five hundred years, he argues that anti-Semitism, white domination of African Americans, and South African apartheid share common features that justify comparative analysis. In his definition, "racism exists when one ethnic group or historical collectivity dominates, excludes, or seeks to eliminate another on the basis of differences that it believes are hereditary and unalterable."[10] For Frederickson, racism is neither a universal phenomenon of human prejudice, nor simply a specific product of one or two societies in the late nineteenth century, but instead a historical construction expressed in long-term institutional and ideological structures beginning in the sixteenth century. It is an extreme form of ethnic separation, distinguished from ethnicity by the refusal to allow mixed races or to accept conversion. Racism does not have to depend on any particular markers of difference such as skin color; its key feature is that these markers are seen as "innate, indelible, and unchangeable."[11] Hence, for Frederickson, true racial anti-Semitism, as distinguished from religious prejudice among Christians, begins only with the expulsion of converted Jews from the kingdoms of Spain in the late fifteenth century. During the Middle Ages, as long as Europeans accepted converted Jews as genuine Christians, they were guilty only of "culturalism," not racism.

The earliest racist ideologies of the Spanish did invoke familiar tropes of blood and bodily purity, but the classification of races of humankind in the eighteenth century added much greater pseudoscientific backing to these notions. Enlightenment philosophers not only ranked races in a hierarchy but also attached each of them to a particular climatic zone, putting Africans on the bottom because of their residence in the tropics. Jews were seen as "Asiatic" desert-dwelling people, parasites on the healthy European Christian community. Late nineteenth-century invocations of Darwinism to justify white racial superiority were only the last stage in a progressively developing European ideology that had begun in the sixteenth century.

Frederickson's approach has the advantage of placing racial ideologies in a long-term historical process, closely linked to European colonial expansion and the development of capitalism. His approach, however, contains several serious flaws, especially the persistent search for a single origin and coherent definition of racism found in so many comparative studies.[12] Frederickson still focuses only on the minds of European white elites, excludes consideration of British colonialism, which had a strong racial component, and does not discuss Asian racial perceptions at all. But his basic distinction between *racism,* which excludes all possibility of bridging the gap between peoples, and *culturalism,* which endorses a hierarchy of power and civilization but allows for "transformation" or assimilation, helps us look at China's views of "barbarians" comparatively.

Expanding Frederickson's analysis to Asia by looking at the theme of conversion or assimilation, we can investigate how closely ideologies of difference in China approached racial exclusiveness. Discussions of cultural differences in classical Chinese texts constantly addressed the question of the nature of "barbarians" (*yi*), particularly the nomads of the northwestern frontier. Some scholars contrast classical Chinese "culturalism" with Western "racialism" by emphasizing that Chinese writers allowed for all barbarians to civilize themselves if they studied the classical texts and adopted Chinese customs. In this view, Chinese elites maintained a distinction between civilized and uncivilized peoples but allowed for substantial mobility or "transformation" (*xianghua*) by barbarian inferiors.

This was, however, only one possible interpretation of the classical tradition. Another view held that barbarians were radically different from Chinese and could never become civilized. One or the other perspective could dominate, depending on the character of the ruling elite, relations of Han with non-Han peoples, military and political exigencies, and development of religious and scholarly traditions. Rather than trace all the ups and downs of these two contrasting perspectives, I will give only a few examples, emphasizing the contingent characteristics of this debate. Neither perspective excluded the alternative voice.

The prominence of ideas of racial exclusivism depended on both the composition of the ruling elites and the dynasty's success in war. Non-Han conquest dynasties that encompassed large territories endorsed the most incorporative definitions of peoples, without promoting assimilation. They divided the people they ruled into separate categories but regarded each of them as legitimate subjects. Their classifications did not correspond to modern ethnic divisions: the Mongol Yuan Dynasty (1279–1368 CE), for example, separated the Han Chinese of the north (*hanren*) from those of the south (*nanren*). The dynasty gave special political privileges to northern Chinese to divide them from those in the south. The Manchu incorporation of some northern Chinese into the banner system as *hanjun,* or "Chinese martial," followed this practice.

Those non-Han conquest dynasties that brought the core areas of Han China under their rule divided the Han population to prevent the emergence of a unified Han nationality. Non-Han regimes with more limited scope, which did not conquer all of modern Chinese national space, distinguished different groups but also had purification movements or struggles between those in favor of assimilation of some Chinese ways and those promoting reaction to older nativist elements.

Han-ruled regimes, when they expanded successfully, constantly faced choices between assimilating the northwest tribes and driving them away. After the second century BCE, with the rise of the Xiongnu nomadic confederation, dynastic rulers debated frontier policy in terms that divided between culturalist and racialist approaches. Those who saw the Xiongnu as irredeemably alien argued for aggressive military expansion, claiming that barbarians could not be trusted; they understood only force. But other policy makers responded that expensive military campaigns excessively burdened the people; it was better to sign treaties and trade agreements with the Xiongnu than to fight them. They recommended use of the "five baits" to lure the Xiongnu into becoming softer, thus "transforming" them into civilized people (that is, dependent on China).[13] The nomads on their side had similar debates: some favored engagement with China (which was usually very profitable for the nomadic regime); others rejected engagement as a Chinese policy to soften them up. Ironically, sometimes Chinese advisers who defected to the nomadic side made the strongest anti-Chinese arguments. In each case, political and military strategies were based on underlying conceptions of the degree to which the enemy was alien and irredeemably uncivilized.

Han-ruled regimes that did not conquer the steppe, such as the Song (960–1279 CE) and Ming (1368–1644 CE) dynasties, had the most purist, antibarbarian stances. Ming Dynasty views of the Mongols indicate a form of separatism, based not on conquest but on a defensive stance toward the steppe. By the sixteenth century, when the full-fledged Great Wall strategy had developed, most Mongol tribes were beyond Ming control. The Ming viewed Mongols as a force of nature that could not be directed by human motivations but only deflected by physical barriers. Zeng Xian, for example, argued in the mid-sixteenth century for an aggressive campaign to drive the Mongols out of the Ordos region of the northwest, stating

> I compare it [defense] to building a dike to stop flood waters. If one morning the dike breaks, a huge flood cannot be stopped. If we recover the Ordos by brandishing our military might, drive out the exterior cause of calamity, and create a barrier along the Yellow River...the enemy's courage will be shattered, their wolfish glances will turn into a timid hush, and they will not dare to plunder for several hundred years. It will be like Great Yu controlling the flood using the sea as a ditch so that the water returns to its proper place, and does not flood...it will be an achievement that Han and Tang cannot equal.[14]

Zeng Xian's statement completely equates the Mongols with forces of nature, bestial or physical. Nowhere is there any recognition of them as having human qualities or of being subject to persuasion. They do not obey any moral codes, and their only desire is to plunder and destroy. Force is the only consideration, and the only constraints are the great costs of mounting a military expedition. The assumptions underlying Zeng's argument clearly reflect the inability of Ming officials to establish any sustained commercial or diplomatic contact with the Mongolian tribes. But it was the prior classification of Mongols as nonhuman, not a general Chinese assumption that all outsiders responded only to force, that justified the use of force against them.

The great expansion of the empire in the seventeenth century allowed the Manchus to form alliances and negotiate with the Mongols, as well as to use military force. The "Manchu" conquest of the Ming was not really done solely by Manchus but by a triple coalition of newly united tribes of the northeast region (who had only recently created the name Manchu for themselves), Han Chinese settlers on the northeastern Ming border, and Mongol horsemen. From its origins, the Manchu state was inclusive and multiethnic. Mongols, in particular, married into the Manchu royal clan and provided key support in major battles, especially with their cavalry detachments. Only some Mongols, however, aided the conquest. Others fought against the Manchus in an effort to preserve their autonomy. The Chahars under Ligdan Khan were the first major group to resist the Manchu military machine; they held one of Chinggis Khan's royal seals, giving them the right to claim legitimate descent from the Yuan Dynasty. By defeating Ligdan Khan and capturing the seal in 1632, the Manchus could claim to have legitimately taken over the right to call themselves khans of the Mongols. All Mongols were invited to join with the Manchus as part of the same family. Hong Taiji, the second great Manchu ruler (who ruled from 1627 to 1643), appealed to Manchu–Mongol unity, claiming that both peoples shared the same customs and origins. He married twelve of his daughters to Mongolian chieftains. Most eastern, or Khalkha, Mongols eventually joined the Qing side. In this early phase, Manchu–Mongol relations were modeled on familial ties, and both in effect viewed each other as part of the same racial group. Both sides had reasons to blur the boundaries between them: the Manchus needed allies to complete the conquest, and the eastern Mongols saw the advantage of cooperation with the new power moving into the wealthy regions of China.

Western Mongols, however, descendants of the Oirat confederation that resisted the Ming, rejected Manchu claims to hegemony. The Zunghar Mongol Galdan returned from his seminary in Tibet in 1670 to create a powerful state that challenged the Manchu bid for dominion. Galdan invoked the protection of the Dalai Lama, who had named him Khan with a Heavenly Mandate (Boshoktu Khan), giving him equal status with the Qing emperor. The Kangxi Emperor (ruling from 1662 to 1722) at first tried to win Galdan over, stating the common interests they shared in bringing peace to the Mongols and appealing to principles of Buddhist compassion to urge Galdan to stop his attacks on the northwest frontier. Galdan was reported to have sworn an oath before a Buddhist figure, "asking forgiveness for his crimes, promising to go far away to a place with good water and grass, and no [settled agricultural] people." The emperor stated:

> My fundamental goal is to ensure peace and security for all people, even those on remote frontiers.... I regard all of the people under Heaven as under my protection. To nurture them and relieve their sufferings is my constant obligation.... When will the enmity between you Ölöd (Zunghars) and the Khalkha cease? It will end only in dust and ashes. The Dalai Lama and I have hearts of love and compassion. We especially want your two countries to stop fighting and make peace.... You violated the Dalai Lama's teachings and my edicts, under pretext of pursuing the Khalkha.... If you accept the honest desire for harmony of the Dalai Lama and myself, our troops will not pursue and kill you; you may lead your troops beyond our borders and live at peace.... If you suffer hardship please tell me, and I will help you, despite your previous enmity. If you violate your oath again, I have troops and horses ready, and we will thoroughly destroy you."[15]

In the emperor's public statements, Galdan's oath to Buddha obliged him to refrain from attacking the Qing, and the emperor and Dalai Lama shared common goals of peace among the Mongols. Galdan, and all Mongols, could attain the benefits of civilized nations if they would follow Buddhist precepts, which the Qing endorsed. Mongols were included within the human sphere, even though their cultural norms were recognized to be different. If, however, Galdan violated these norms, the Qing would use ruthless military force to destroy him. In 1696, the emperor decided on a military campaign to exterminate Galdan. Although he defeated Galdan in battle, he never captured or killed Galdan himself. Galdan died (probably poisoned by one of his allies) in 1697.

Kangxi's rhetoric of extermination marked a radical shift in tone and ideology toward the Mongols, but it was consistent with his earlier threats. The demand to wipe the Zunghars out and "pull them out by the roots" indicated that they were no longer human, and not just a rival power but a force of evil whose existence was intolerable. Qing exterminationism, however, was different from the hostility of Ming officials who uttered similar words. Hard-line Ming officials classed all Mongols together as uniformly barbarian and violent, all deserving elimination. In practice, the Ming could do nothing about them, but in principle they wished them all to disappear. The Kangxi Emperor's rage, by contrast, was directed only at Galdan, and only because he had betrayed his oath to submit to the Qing. This reaction was closer to the vengeance of a betrayed khan than to all-out racial warfare against a people.

Kangxi's campaigns against Galdan went well beyond the bounds of strategic necessity. This "small tribe in the northwest corner of Asia," as he contemptuously called them, did not deserve four major campaigns led by the emperor himself. The campaigns were based on the emperor's sharp division between those who kept their oaths and those who did not. Kangxi personalized the contest between himself and Galdan because his central Eurasian roots broke through the Confucian facade and because he did not embrace a systematic ideology of ethnic classification. Each Mongol tribal leader could decide to join or fight the Qing, and the emperor held each leader responsible for his decision. Mongols, for the Qing, were human, while for Ming officials they were only animals. Being human, they could respond to moral and self-interested appeals, but likewise, they deserved punishment if they violated their commitments.

The Yongzheng reign (1723–35) marked a significant military and ideological shift in Qing relations with the frontier. The Yongzheng Emperor was not interested in leading military campaigns. His own efforts to move against the Zunghar state ended in failure. In 1731, Furdan, his loyal but incompetent general, suffered an embarrassing defeat in western Mongolia when he was lured into an ambush by Zunghar troops. After this defeat, the anguished emperor concluded that heaven had turned against him. The Zunghar state had survived and even grown in power since the death of the Kangxi Emperor, and the Qing had no choice but to settle for a truce on the frontier.

At the same time, Zeng Jing (1679–1736), an obscure schoolteacher from Hunan, attempted to inflame anti-Manchu sentiment among the Han literati elite. The emperor's fierce reaction to Zeng Jing's criticism revealed serious fissures in the Qing regime.

Chinese literati, of course, certified by examinations that the Qing had restored, made up the vast majority of the local administration and local elites. Nearly all of them accepted the legitimacy of Manchu rule since it preserved their status and brought them peace and order. But some literati still privately argued that the Manchus could never become civilized like the Han.

In 1728 a poverty-stricken scholar named Zeng Jing, in a remote county of Hunan, wrote an appeal to one of the most powerful Chinese generals to overthrow the Manchu government. Zeng Jing argued that the people were starving because of Manchu rule, and it was the duty of Han officials to rebel against Manchu oppression to relieve the people. The general immediately reported Zeng to the emperor, and Zeng and his few followers were subjected to interrogation and torture. This was never a serious military threat to the Qing; what is remarkable is how seriously the emperor took it. Instead of just executing Zeng Jing, he launched an extensive search to find out where Zeng got his ideas, and the trail led back to the writings of a seventeenth-century scholar in Zhejiang who had been loyal to the Ming Dynasty until his death in 1683.

Zhejiang was one of the richest and most cultivated regions of the country; what really worried the emperor was that the sophisticated Han literati and officials, beneath the veneer of acceptance of Manchu rule, secretly had contempt for his people. And he found some evidence for his suspicions. Also, the emperor himself had come to power in a mysterious way, and there was constant suspicion that he had usurped the throne. Zeng Jing not only called the emperor a usurper, he also claimed that all the Manchus were illegitimate rulers of China. The upshot was that Zeng Jing was forced to write a confession ("self-criticism") repudiating his views, and the emperor wrote a long text refuting the idea that the Manchus were uncultured barbarians. He published his edicts, the record of Zeng's interrogation, and Zeng's confession together in a fascinating text called *How Great Righteousness Awakens One from Delusion* (*Dayi Juemilu*), which he made mandatory reading in all schools.[16]

This text explicitly lays out the contrast between racialist and culturalist ideologies of rule. Like his European counterparts in the eighteenth century, Zeng saw a close correspondence between land, environment, heredity, and racial character. Zeng and the Ming loyalist writings, supported by citations to classical texts, argued that the relationship between the Han Chinese (*Hua*) and the northern barbarians (*Di*) was like that of humans and animals, not like ruler and subject. Because the Chinese were born in the "central lands" (the Yellow River valley), they were civilized; but the barbarians came from the periphery (the northeast and northwest), so they had a totally different character, incompatible with that of the Chinese. They could not coexist, and it was proper to drive them out. According to Zeng, Confucius himself had said that the purpose of establishing a state in China was to protect civilization against destruction.

The emperor argued just the opposite: that the differences between peoples depended on their culture, not on their territory or lineage. Therefore, those from outside the central plains (*zhongyuan*) could become civilized. The key relationship that preserved social order was that of ruler and subject. The Ming Dynasty had fallen apart because the Chinese rebelled against their ruler; the Manchus had actually saved the Chinese from disorder, inheriting the Mandate of Heaven. So they took power legitimately, just as the Mongols and other conquest dynasties had done in the past. Yongzheng did not say that the Manchus had turned into Han. He believed in cultural difference and hierarchy, not assimilation. The Manchus were separate, but equally civilized, and they deserved to rule over the Chinese because they maintained order and made the people prosperous.

For Yongzheng, then, it was not ancestry or territory that made a people civilized but the values they held. Zeng Jing, by contrast, claimed that Manchus could never be civilized because they came from a barbarous territory and lineage: this essential difference could not be overcome. On the surface, Yongzheng won the argument, but the Manchu elite could never be fully confident that they had eradicated dissent. It was easy for them to repress open criticism, but harder to control rumors, the language of the streets, or private conversation. Zeng's public confession, extracted by threat of torture, might not have persuaded the literati that he had genuinely changed his mind. This undercurrent of awareness of the Manchus as ineradicably different, including contempt toward their culture, remained during the empire. Outside Qing boundaries, in Korea, scholars carried on a stance of loyalty to Ming customs and contempt for "degenerate" Manchu practices. They performed sacrifices to Ming emperors and continued to use the Ming Dynasty calendar. Even when they visited China on tributary missions, Korean scholars recorded in their diaries striking criticisms by lower-ranking Chinese literati of the unjust privileges assumed by the Manchu elite.[17]

Yongzheng's anxiety in the face of criticism suggests that he had less confidence in the appeal of Manchu achievements to his Chinese subjects than his father had shown. He had few military victories to his credit, and what victories he did gain were due to his generals, not to him personally. Yongzheng did complete the negotiations of a trade treaty with Russia in 1727, but the major rival to Qing power, the Zunghar state, remained beyond his reach. In his refutation of Zeng Jing, Yongzheng rested the legitimacy of Manchu rule on the enforcement of domestic political order by an autocratic regime, while in practice negotiating with rival states, using trade more than military means. This contradiction left latent tensions between Manchu and Han that could only be resolved by further expansion and pacification.

The Qianlong Emperor (who ruled from 1736 to 1795) destroyed the Zunghar state in the 1750s and had expanded Qing rule into the oases of modern Xinjiang by 1760. Although he was only a desk general who never went out to war, he completed the project that Kangxi had begun. The Qing state now had firmly defined boundaries and no rival states to challenge it. At the same time, Qianlong rewrote the history of the frontier campaigns to make them seem like a smooth, heaven-sent fulfillment of an irresistible mandate. He confiscated all the indigenous Mongolian genealogies (which no longer survive) and had his loyal scholars write definitive histories of the Zunghar campaigns. Qianlong also redefined Manchu identity by rewriting the genealogies of the Manchu tribes, restricting marriage with Han Chinese, and expelling many of the anomalous Chinese soldiers (hanjun) from the banner system. He also attempted to shore up the Manchu bannermen against the infiltration of seductive Chinese practices. His great Southern Tours, for example, were planned as mock military campaigns, designed to train the banners in military organization and to display to the Han literati the massive, expansive power of the Qing ruling elite.[18] Qianlong also promoted the compilation of ethnographic atlases of the many peoples within the empire, defining them as distinct groups with their own "customs" (*fengsu*) and colorful rituals. These practices shifted Qing ruling ideology and social practice toward systematized classification, purer and more distinct ethnic definitions, and closer connection of lineage with collective identity.[19]

In sum, each of the high Qing rulers, despite his intentions, fashioned elements that could later be used in a racial definition of the state and the people it ruled. Kangxi contributed a militant demand to exterminate those who betrayed him, Yongzheng an insistence on political order as the primary basis of legitimacy, and Qianlong a project of detailed classification of peoples by history, territory, and genealogy. The dominant, orthodox ideology proclaimed universal culturalism: all peoples under the Qing enjoyed the benefits of peace, prosperity, and "civil" (*wen*) order. However, dissenters could reassemble elements within the official ideology to support very different conclusions.

LATE NINETEENTH-CENTURY REVIVAL OF RACIAL IDEOLOGY

The spores of racial ideology could lie dormant as long as the empire prospered, but by the end of the nineteenth century, as the empire suffered repeated defeats by Western powers and especially by Japan in 1895, they had sprouted into a new racial ideology blaming the Manchus for making China weak in the face of imperialist pressure. Three new global developments—the perception of China's weakness, humiliation, and failure; the spread of social Darwinism; and the concept of minzu, or nationality, imported from Japan—consolidated the new ideology.

As Frederickson and others note, a perception of relative weakness in international competition fuels feelings of *ressentiment:* the envy of superior powers and self-hatred, leading to a search for internal enemies. For example, Jews were blamed for causing Germany's loss in World War I; blacks in the southern United States were blamed for deserting to the Union side, causing the loss of the South; and blacks in South Africa were blamed for holding back their country's progress.

Radical Chinese nationalists made the Manchus their scapegoat to explain how China, despite its long history of cultural greatness, was so weak in facing the modern West.[20]

Second, the enthusiastic adoption of social Darwinism in Asia, both as a racial categorization and as a mobilizing ideology, reinforced anti-Manchu ressentiment. As a global ideology, believed to be a scientific explanation of social change, social Darwinism implied that the Chinese were weak because they were disunited. China, a nation for the Han race alone, the Sons of the Yellow Emperor, thus had to expel its alien conquerors.

Third, the idea of minzu, derived from Japan via Germany as a synonym for *volk*, supported essentialist definitions, splitting different peoples from each other and uniting each minzu around common territory, language, history, and genealogy. Adopting the minzu perspective meant rejecting the classical Mandate of Heaven theory. The foreign conquest dynasties could not be accepted as legitimate: they were eras of barbarian oppression of the Han Chinese people.

Reality was quite different: some of the active reformers in the nineteenth century were Manchu princes; many of the reactionaries were ethnically Chinese. But the ideology provided a simple explanation for China's failures. Furthermore, the new internationalization of Qing China after 1895 allowed students to freely debate minzu and social Darwinist ideas in Japan.

Racial anti-Manchuism allied to revolutionary nationalism grew particularly intense after 1900. Zhang Binglin (1869–1936), the father of modern Chinese nationalism, was its most vociferous advocate.[21] In 1900 he became well known for audaciously cutting off his queue and for publishing articles attacking the Manchus as barbarians who had no right to rule China. (The Manchus had forced all Han Chinese to wear this long pigtail and had imposed the death penalty for cutting it off.) He argued that historically the Chinese (Hua or Han) had always been radically different from the barbarians of the north, whom he called "monkeys and tigers" with no right to rule over Han. For Zhang Binglin, the difference between Han and barbarians was one of race (*zhongzu*), not culture. Zhang attacked well-known reformer Kang Youwei's proposals to create a constitutional monarchy that preserved Manchu rule. He agreed with Kang on the primary goal—to unite the

Chinese people against foreign invasion. However, Kang thought it possible to overcome Manchu–Han divisions to unite all the people of China, while Zhang argued that only by expelling the Manchus could China become strong. Invoking the humiliation, slaughter, and rape committed by Manchus against the Han population during their conquest of the empire in the seventeenth century, he called for the Han people to awake from their slumber, rise up, and take revenge. Revenge on the Manchus became the core of nationalism and freedom for Zhang.

Zhang called himself a Confucian, but he endorsed a republican government without an emperor. Like Kang Youwei and Liang Qichao, the leading reformers, Zhang advocated popular participation in government but called for directing revolutionary energy internally at the Chinese political structure first as means of strengthening the nation. Kang and Liang held the opposite position; they advocated preservation of the imperial structure, while reforming it, to strengthen the nation's ability to resist the West. Kang and Zhang displayed a clear opposition of culturalist and racialist ideologies, each invoked as a means of strengthening national unity. Significantly, this debate took place in Japan among the exiled reformers, and the main audience was overseas Chinese students in Japan, sent there by the reform program begun by the Manchu court itself.

RETURNING TO ZOU RONG

Zou Rong was one of the students in Japan who followed eagerly the debates over the racial character of the empire and the nation. Zou, a product of Qing classical learning, had studied classical texts intensively in his hometown of Sichuan. He did not use the abstruse philosophical reasoning of Zhang Binglin, but he responded eagerly to Zhang's message. Although Zhang was one of the most esoteric and difficult of late Qing writers, Zou absorbed the basic elements of his reasoning. No one could accuse Zou of logical coherence, but he put Zhang's subtle reasoning into passionate language, making it accessible to a much wider audience. Zhang likewise supported Zou Rong, including his letter refuting Kang Youwei's reformism in the same volume as Zou's *Revolutionary Army*.[22]

Even though Zou invoked many Western thinkers and actors, from

Rousseau to Mazzini and Napoleon, his argument relied on a fundamental reinterpretation of Chinese history and drew primarily on Chinese examples. Zou defended Qing territorial expansion, domination of frontiers, and ethnic incorporation but attacked the Manchus for failing to fulfill the historical mission of the Chinese people.

Zou and Zhang exploited the tensions within Qing imperial ideology to reconstitute a new nationalist ideology. Kangxi had rested Qing success on territorial expansion, the elimination of rival powers, and the restoration of social order. Qianlong had incorporated the conquests into a historical narrative representing them as inevitable outcomes of a heavenly mandate. By the mid-eighteenth century, the defense of borders, not of moral principles, had become a key test of imperial authority. If these were the essential elements of a successful empire, then the late Qing had failed in its fundamental mission. Zou Rong, just like many of the Qing rulers, agreed that Manchuria was an inseparable part of China. The fact that Manchuria had never been part of the Ming Dynasty did not matter:

> Outside Shanhaikuan there are certain districts known as Manchuria, Heilongjiang, Jilin, and Shengjing. Are they not what the Manchu scoundrels call an auspicious land, the country of nomads which they ought to make every effort to defend? Now they are bowing and kowtowing and presenting it to the Russians.[23]

Not only had the Manchus stolen land from the Han Chinese, but they could not even defend their own homeland from foreign incursion. This weakness made the Han Chinese doubly enslaved, to the Manchu despots and to the foreign powers that extracted concessions from them. Zou took over from the Qing the idea that China's national territory had to correspond with the maximal boundaries of the Qing state, a time of unprecedented expansion. With these claims, the nationalists imported into their ideology new contradictions. If China was the land of the Han Chinese only, how could its territorial claims embrace so many lands with non-Han residents? If each race deserved its own nation, and the races (minzu) were radically separate from each other, shouldn't the Manchus have their own country and the Mongols, Uighurs, and Tibetans likewise?

Zhang Binglin drew the logical conclusion that each minzu was entitled to its own nation. Kang Youwei argued that one of the Qing's great contributions had been to unify Mongolia, Xinjiang, Tibet, and Manchuria under one state; he evoked the cosmopolitan vision of the coexistence of the nationalities and their eventual transformation into a single modern people. Zhang, by contrast, declared openly, "if the chieftains of Xinjiang, because their hatred of the Manchus pierces their bones, generate such resentment against the Han people that they want to separate from us and restore the Turkish lands, we must allow them to do so. We can see that our relation to the Manchus is like that of Xinjiang toward us." Although he did not support independence for Muslims under Chinese rule, he did propose that China and Xinjiang could form an "alliance" against Russia if it suited Muslim interests. If not, Muslims in Xinjiang could go their way separately from the Chinese state.[24]

Zou, on the other hand, resolved this contradiction by outrageous claims of Han superiority. His racial classification included Japanese and Koreans as part of the "Han race" and Tibetans, eastern Siberians, and even the Siamese as part of the "Races of China." Mongols, Manchus, Turks, Hungarians, and others all belonged to the "Yellow Race," which was engaged in a life-or-death struggle with the "White Race":

> The yellow and white races which are to be found on the globe have been endowed by nature with intelligence and fighting capacity. They are fundamentally incapable of giving way to each other.…When men love their race, solidarity will arise internally, and what is outside will be repelled. Hence, to begin with, clans were united and other clans repelled; next clans of villages were united and clans of other villages repelled; next tribes were united and other tribes were repelled; finally, the people of a country became united, and people of other countries were repelled. This is the general principle of the races of the world, and also a major reason why races engender history."[25]

Countries grew from racial solidarity, and races must struggle with each other. The Han race was the greatest on earth because of its enormous numbers. Besides the 400 million in China, emigration also proved Han superiority: Zou claimed that ten million Chinese had gone into Qinghai and Tibet, three or four million into Japan, and many others into Southeast Asia and across the Pacific. The transnational ties of the Han Chinese in Zou's eyes did not generate cultural interaction or mixed identities; they only testified to the vast potential power of a united single culture. Zou inverted the "Yellow Peril" rhetoric of the West, which warned against the threat of vast hordes of indistinguishable Chinese, to create a new discourse of power.

Zou agreed with modern revisionist scholars of the Manchus that no true assimilation had occurred. Zou argued that "for over two hundred years Manchus have kept themselves to themselves, and Han have kept themselves to themselves, and have not assimilated."[26] The Qing emperors had been greatly concerned about the Manchus losing their identity as a separate ruling elite. Zou took the Qing reinforcement of boundaries at face value and turned it against them. He mobilized the rigidified "color line" of the Qing to mobilize the Han majority against a tiny elite, repeatedly asserting the injustice of having a mere five million Manchus rule over 400 million Chinese. Zou defined this numerical logic, dividing peoples into majorities and minorities, which shaped nationality policy after the fall of the Qing.

Zou passionately expressed the humiliation of seeing the Han people subjugated by barbarian inferiors. He constantly equated the Han people with slaves and even invoked Harriet Beecher Stowe to indicate the potential for liberation of slaves by enlightened leaders.[27] With the slavery metaphor, Zou ingeniously linked the struggle for African American civil rights with the attack on servitude under the Manchus, since the same word (*nu*) stood for both "slave" and "bond servant."[28] But, he insisted, the Chinese people must liberate themselves. The nation was "sick" and needed a strong cure. Rousseau and revolutionary ideology could supply the "elixir of immortality" that would resurrect the Chinese people.

Humiliation was particularly painful for the Chinese scholars who served the Manchu regime. Zou attacked the emasculation and servility of the Chinese literati:

> Chinese scholars certainly have hardly a breath of life in them. Why is this so? The people are stupid because they do

> not learn. The literati are stupid, then they learn things they should not learn, and are the more stupid for it. Moreover, the Manchu scoundrels harass them in every possible way, they humiliate them in every possible way, they confuse them in every possible way, they hobble them in every possible way, and they injure them in every possible way; and when they become old and worn out, their bodies are lifeless husks and the whip points the way.[29]

Beaten down by eight-legged essays, literary inquisitions, poverty, and discrimination, the Chinese literati only supported Manchu despotism by accepting the classical education system that supported the state. Zou's arguments linked the Confucian reformism of Kang Youwei and Liang Qichao and the radical reforms of 1905, which abolished the examination system. Zou attacked the Manchus for giving away Shandong, the homeland of Confucius, to Germany: "A people never having possessed the sacred and inviolable home of Confucius will make the 400 million inhabitants of this ancient land lose their civilization and degenerate into barbarism." But by proclaiming "we Chinese have no history. The so-called Twenty-Four Histories are in fact a huge history of slaves," he opened the troubling line of thought that not just Manchu oppression but the entire classical heritage might be responsible for China's weakness.[30]

We should not regard Zou Rong's text, then, as merely a bizarre outburst of extremism or as a simple adaptation of Western revolutionary theory to Chinese conditions. The text gathered mass support among students abroad and in Shanghai because it exposed the hidden tensions of Qing imperial ideology and pointed the way to an ideology that promised to revive China's international position in a world filled with racist practices. Empire, transnational cultural contact, and new scientistic and racialist ideologies joined in the first decade of the twentieth century to create the combustible mixture of modern Chinese nationalism.

TENSIONS OF MULTINATIONALITY: SEXUAL POLITICS AND ECONOMIC DEVELOPMENT

I will close by briefly illustrating how the nationality policy of the People's Republic of China (PRC) retains contradictions that derive from China's imperial past. China describes itself today as a "multinationality nation-state" (*duo minzu guojia*) consisting of fifty-six nationalities. Han Chinese, who constitute some 92 percent of the population, are the majority nationality, and the other fifty-five are "minority nationalities" (*xiaoshu minzu*). The minority nationalities have their own Nationality Research Institute, a Nationalities Palace in Beijing, publications in their native languages, and representation in the People's Congress and the Communist Party. General histories written in China trace the "unity of China's nationalities" (*minzu tuanjie*) back to the origins of civilization itself. These histories, in effect, erase the *imperial* character of empire, that is, those aspects of rule that created difference, in favor of the unifying force of autocratic rule from a single center.

Closer examination of individual cases, particularly the relationships between imperial China and the peoples of the northwestern frontier, reveals great tension between the surface proclamations of unity and recalcitrant facts. Historians have to do a lot of massaging to fit China's extremely long and diverse ethnic relationships into the narrow straitjacket of the "unity of peoples." Mongolian anthropologist Uradyn Bulag's recent book brilliantly links the writing of history with contemporary China's concern for unity.[31] He shows, for example, how both imperial regimes and the PRC mobilize sexual politics to construct discourses of unity, but also how these discourses are riven with contradictions along the lines of racialism and culturalism.

Wang Zhaojun, for example, a Chinese princess sent in the first century BCE to marry the chieftain of the nomadic Xiongnu confederation, has long served as an exemplar of a woman who tied empires and nations together. Bulag argues that "China's contemporary imagination of its *minzu tuanjie* [national unity/amity between nationalities] is largely derived from the symbolic and institutional logic of its historical relations with Inner Asians...the Chinese discourse of national unity is gendered," based on the institution of "peace marriage" (*heqin*).[32] By sending court women and princesses to marry barbarian chieftains and bear them children, the dynasties planned to tame and transform the chieftains, as with the five baits, but also to use kinship connections as the underpinning for legitimation. There are now more than a dozen "tombs" of Wang Zhaojun scattered across Inner Mongolia to bolster the claim that China has always held sovereignty over this region. The culturalist argument for unity of Han and Mongols today relies on this invocation of kinship ties between the two peoples.

Claims for sovereignty based on kinship, however, cannot paper over all difference. The Han and Tang dynasties did use heqin as an effective diplomatic tool, but these marriages connected only a small number of elites, not whole peoples. The Qing rulers indeed expanded linkages between Manchus and Mongols, systematically marrying literally thousands of Mongol nobles into Qing royal families. They did not, however, marry civilian Han Chinese with Mongols or Manchus; in fact, they strictly forbade most intermarriage between Manchus and Han in order to keep the Manchus a separate ruling elite. Furthermore, the image of Wang Zhaojun changed over time depending on dynastic relations with the frontier. Later Han officials (third century CE) who opposed peace treaties with barbarians wrote her story a different way: they claimed that she lived among the Xiongnu homesick and miserable and committed suicide there, longing for "home." In this view, the Xiongnu were alien to Chinese ways, and anyone who went to their territory went into exile in a wasteland. In the Song Dynasty, literati bitterly hostile to northerners even claimed that Wang Zhaojun drowned herself in a river to avoid exile to the Xiongnu. Popular novels in the Ming and Qing dynasties rehearsed the tragedy of the chaste woman forced to leave her true "husband," the emperor, for the savage northwest. But this rhetoric of alienation did not suit the twentieth-century need to assert historical control over the frontier. In 1929, a scholar praised the heqin policy for helping promote the "fusion of races," meaning the assimilation of Mongols, Manchus, and other minorities into the master Han race. During the Cultural Revolution, however, writers denounced Wang Zhaojun and the heqin policy as instruments of class oppression by the Han ruling class. In the 1980s, Wang returned as the emblem of "love" between the nationalities, and the message of unity in the guise of sexual romance was broadcast in a ten-part TV drama and inscribed on stone monuments in Mongolia.[33]

The alterations in this story demonstrate, in Ann Stoler's words, "the discursive bricolage whereby an older discourse of race is 'recovered,' modified, 'encased' and 'encrusted' in new forms."[34] Changing political contexts pushed the interpretations back and forth between the two poles of racial alienation and cultural assimilation.

As one other example of the continuing polarities of nationality discourse, we may cite the new "Develop the West" economic policy. Today, China has launched a program designed to integrate the impoverished interior regions of the country with the prosperous eastern coast. This "Develop the West" program aims to redress the severe regional income inequalities produced by the reform decades, but it also has consequences for ethnic unity since most of China's minority nationalities live in the interior provinces. Official endorsements of the program once again carry the strong ring of cultural assimilation, as they claim to be raising the cultural level of the minorities by bringing to them the economic benefits attained by the Han people.

The PRC thus counters the arguments of ethnic separatists with the claim that economic progress depends on social stability. Legqog, chairman of the regional government of Tibet, for example, "blamed the Dalai Lama Clique and hostile forces in the West for their interference and disruptions which deprived Tibet of development opportunities in the 1950s and 1980s. Between 1987 and 1989, riots and protests occurred in Lhasa, the regional capital, resulting in economic setbacks." Likewise, deputies from Xinjiang to the National People's Congress argued that "social stability has created a sound social environment for economic development."[35]

On the other hand, the primary vehicles in practice for developing the West are the building of transportation and communication infrastructures for military security and the encouragement of large-scale Han immigration to the interior. In many ways, the new western development program repeats the integration policies of the Qing Dynasty when it first conquered the western regions of Mongolia and Xinjiang. As in the Qing, the promotion of Han immigration in particular has exacerbated tensions between local peoples, such as the Muslim Uighurs, and the new immigrants. After bombings in cities in Xinjiang, the Chinese authorities characterized Uighur political activists as terrorists (a label the United States has supported), and they continue to attack those who resist Han immigration as "splittists" who are trying to undermine national unity. The Chinese government applies the same label of "splittist" to the Dalai Lama when he asserts Tibetan rights to autonomy, or to advocates of the independence of Taiwan.

In modern terminology, the label of "splittist" recapitulates the exclusionist racialism of the imperial era and the early twentieth century by putting beyond the bounds of acceptability anyone who advocates any moves toward greater regional or ethnic autonomy. The ideology of cultural assimilation driven by economic progress carries on the "transformation" rhetoric, while the attacks on "splittism" continue the pattern of excluding those whose values are alien to those of the ruling elite. Today, the core elite values are not Confucian classical values but loyalty to a Leninist one-party state. Yet imperial rhetoric still persists: new wine in old bottles.

Notes

I presented versions of this paper at the seminar series of the African-American Studies Center at Boston University; the graduate workshop Asia in the World, the World in Asia, University of Chicago, March 2003; and the workshop Race, Science, and Culture in 20th-Century East Asia and America, MIT, April 25–26, 2003. I am grateful to all those present at both workshops for their comments.

1. Emerson, *From Empire to Nation.*

2. Stoler, "Tense and Tender Ties."

3. Perdue, "Constructing Chinese Property Rights."

4. Eric L. Jones, *European Miracle;* Landes, *Wealth and Poverty of Nations;* Myers, "Customary Law, Markets, and Resource Transactions"; North, "Paradox of the West"; Pomeranz, *Great Divergence;* Wong, *China Transformed.*

5. Tsou, *Revolutionary Army,* 58.

6. Crossley, *Translucent Mirror;* Mark C. Elliott, *Manchu Way;* Rhoads, *Manchus and Han.*

7. Du Bois, *Souls of Black Folk,* 11.

8. Du Bois, *Souls of Black Folk,* 149.

9. For a fascinating discussion of literary expressions of racial nationalism in this period, see Tsu, *Failure, Nationalism, and Literature.* Rebecca Karl also describes how "through a recognition of the uneven global space of modernity, problems of state-people relations were identified in China's turn-of-the-century moment." Karl, *Staging the World,* 29.

10. Frederickson, *Racism,* 170.

11. Frederickson, *Racism,* 5.

12. Stoler, "Racial Histories and Their Regimes of Truth,"

13. Barfield, *Perilous Frontier,* 51.

14. Zeng Xian, *Mingchen Zouyi,* 18b–19a. Cited in Perdue, "Culture, History, and Imperial Chinese Strategy," 268.

15. Zhang Yushu, *Qinzheng Pingding Shuomo Fanglue,* juan 8.16b–18b.

16. Min Tu-ki, "Ch'ôngcho ûi hwangche sasang t'ongche ûi silche"; Perdue, *China Marches West;* 470–76; Spence, *Treason by the Book.*

17. Haboush, "Contesting Chinese Time, Nationalizing Temporal Space"; Min Tu-ki, *National Polity and Local Power,* 1–19.

18. Chang, "Court on Horseback."

19. Crossley, *Translucent Mirror;* Hostetler, *Qing Colonial Enterprise.*

20. Ansart, *Le ressentiment;* Tsu, *Failure, Nationalism, and Literature.*

21. Shimada, *Pioneer of the Chinese Revolution;* Zhang Binglin, "Letter Opposing Kang Youwei's Views on Revolution."

22. Tsou, *Revolutionary Army.*

23. Tsou, *Revolutionary Army,* 78.

24. Gasster, *Chinese Intellectuals and the Revolution of 1911,* 206; Onogawa Hidemi, "Cho heilin no haiman shisô"; Zhang Binglin and Zhang Taiyan, "Shehui tongquan shangdui," 18.

25. Tsou, *Revolutionary Army,* 106.

26. Tsou, *Revolutionary Army,* 68.

27. Tsou, *Revolutionary Army,* 60.

28. For other uses of the global slavery discourse in China, see Karl, "'Slavery,' Citizenship, and Gender," and the discussion of the Chinese translation of *Uncle Tom's Cabin* in Tsu, *Failure, Nationalism, and Literature,* 56–65.

29. Tsou, *Revolutionary Army,* 69.

30. Tsou, *Revolutionary Army,* 77, 115.

31. Bulag, *Mongols at China's Edge.*

32. Bulag, *Mongols at China's Edge,* 64–65.

33. Bulag, *Mongols at China's Edge,* 99.

34. Stoler, *Race and the Education of Desire,* 61.

35. Xinhua News Agency, March 14, 2001; Perdue, "Identifying China's Northwest."

Part 2
Rethinking Boundaries, Imaginaries, Empires

6

Empire Out of Bounds

Tibet in the Era of Decolonization

Carole McGranahan

Tibetan discourses on empire have always had an edge to them. From nationalist alternatives to aristocratic Anglophilia in the 1940s to impassioned charges of Chinese colonialism in the 1990s, the twentieth-century Tibetan imperial experience is best described as slightly off center. Never colonized by a European power, Tibet instead had imperial relations with both Great Britain and Qing China prior to 1950 and with the People's Republic of China (PRC) and the United States of America following 1950. Each of these imperial polities sought—and in the latter two cases, continue to seek—to put their imprint on Tibet through an educating of sensibilities, a cultivating of political affiliation, a delineating of favorable borders, and/or a disciplining of the population.[1] Their relationships with Tibet were unique yet simultaneously recognizable as imperial in a broad sense. Tibetan imperial stories, however, are not composed of familiar categories of empire. Instead, they depart from colonialism, capitalism, and European moorings, and thus from the primary foci of colonial studies and postcolonial theory.[2] In this essay, I suggest that exploring empire through the lived realities of people in polities and relationships not always considered imperial offers unexpected but invaluable insights for theorizing empire. Specifically, I focus on the period of and after decolonization, roughly the 1940s to the present, and on Tibetan imperial experiences that may be best thought of as "out of bounds," a category not as marginal to empire as it might appear at first glance.

Thinking empires out of bounds provides a means for addressing extraperipheral spaces and the roles they play in imperial imaginations. No empire ends at its geographic boundaries. Indeed, imperial boundaries may mark sites of transgression or centrality as much as they denote limits for action and analysis. Yet if empire is a contradictory and complex project within its boundaries, then what sort of project is it beyond its boundaries? Boundaries, of course, are not only geographic.[3] They are conceptual and cultural, academic and analytical. They order social worlds and cultural representations as much as they do trade relations and political statuses.[4] These orderings and claims to fixity operate in part through ambiguity: boundaries are often ambiguous and arbitrary despite claims to the contrary. The "spatial malleability" of boundaries is also constitutive of imperial formations in underappreciated ways.[5] Indeed, as Carl Schmitt argues, "every true empire around the world has claimed such a sphere of spatial sovereignty beyond its borders."[6] Boundaries are deployed as strategy in service to empire, establishing modes and spatial representations in which empires are visible or not, legible or not, responsible or not. In the case of Tibet alone we see this in the "forward" policy of the British empire, the anti-imperialism of the Chinese socialist state, and the long-standing haziness surrounding US "empires."

Yet if Tibet's imperial turn has been particularly multifaceted over the last century, the "imperial turn" in scholarship has not made a substantial impact in Tibetan studies.[7] Our ability to think critically about empire as a Tibetan reality or about Tibetan experiences as distinctly imperial remains underdeveloped. Peter Hansen contends that the absence of a subaltern studies—that is, the absence of a critical, theoretical, and subaltern engagement with empire and nation—for Tibet is due to the general persistence of "Tibetan exceptionalism" as both a politics of knowledge and a politics of the present.[8] Especially enduring is the vision of Tibet as an isolated Shangri-la, or paradise on earth, remote and forbidding yet enticing and seductive.[9] The idea of Shangri-la simultaneously positions Tibet as offering and needing salvation, as offering spiritual advancement alongside its own socioeconomic disadvantages. This hegemonic vision combines with newly polemical and rigid histories of Tibet under Chinese rule to discourage complexity, contradiction, and critique.[10] For Tibet's displaced government in exile as much as for the PRC government, questions of Chinese empire in the present pose new and often unwanted attention on issues of sovereignty and subjectivity. In this chapter, I use the specific case of Tibet to question our analytics of empire in the present.

In the era of decolonization, empire is a story of imperialism denied and disguised. If decolonization discouraged colonialism as a specific form of imperialism, it ironically opened the world to other forms of similar domination.[11] Evolutionary languages of development and progress transformed former colonies into developing countries dependent on external powers in familiar but new arrangements; multilateral institutions and corporations joined powerful nation-states to replace past empires in name if not in content.[12] However, not all decolonized forms of political and economic domination were or are imperial.[13] Frederick Cooper argues that "the contemporary use of the word 'empire' as a metaphor for unbounded power sits uneasily with scholarship on actual historical empires."[14] In this essay, I understand empire in general as an expansionist polity oriented toward or rooted in a combination of the following: cultural influence, economic gain, hierarchical relations, political domination, and/or territorial acquisition. *Imperialism* connotes the direct or indirect external influence, control, or domination by one polity and people over another; *colonialism* is the system of direct rule and domination by one polity and people over another in the latter's home territory.[15] With this in mind, what is imperial about contemporary empires?

Postcolonial empires do not possess a one-to-one correspondence to earlier forms of empire. Nor, however, as the essays in this volume attest, do earlier empires follow a singular model. In advocating for "imperial formations" as an analytic of empire, rather than as a descriptive synonym for it, we directly reference the in-process state of being of all empires.[16] This instability does not mean that there is not also consistency within and across empires. In the twentieth century at least, as Partha Chatterjee has argued, an inseparability from the nation-state and a "rule of difference" (that is, hierarchical relations and inequitable treatment across socially constructed categories such as race) are consistent imperial features.[17] In practice, difference becomes a civilizing imperative, that is, either a "pedagogy of violence or a pedagogy of culture."[18] Territorial or nonterritorial, by direct rule or indirect control, contemporary empires are in service to such civilizing missions and the nation-state.[19] The rules under which the nation-state is hitched to and compels empire, however, have changed. Disavowal of imperial status is now de rigueur, such that imperial practice and policy are embedded in national languages of defense, development, and global responsibility. These changes are themselves historical, linked as much to the efficacy of any given imperial strategy as to new political categories and moments. Contemporary imperial formations respond anew to issues of sovereignty, citizenship, and human rights, and to periods and programs of the Cold War, late capitalism, postsocialism, neoliberalism, and so on. Opening our analytical frameworks to imperial formations outside Europe and in the time of decolonization is not to forfeit historical particularisms but to acknowledge that empire can no longer be a static story solely about Europe.[20]

In the present, we have not just empires by other names but also colonialisms by other names. As the case of Tibet demonstrates, the political rhetoric and practices that sustained colonialism are still with us today. Yet at the same time that certain peoples and polities have been linked so closely to empire, others have been dissociated from it. What politics and histories, academic tendencies, and imperial strategies support these associations and dissociations? In this essay, I contend that the stories that dissociated peoples and polities have to tell about empire deserve our attention.[21] The twentieth-century transition to more diffuse and less visible forms of imperialism in the name of decolonization is one of these stories, a story I tell from the perspective of Tibetan subjects rather than from that of architects and agents of empire.

The story of Tibet's experiences with three different empires—British, Chinese, and American—grounds my analysis in this chapter. Imperial and colonial priorities never solely directed Tibetan politics or popular life, nor defined Tibet as some have argued.[22] Nonetheless, there is an important imperial imprint on modern Tibetan history. A century of off-center imperial relations has produced a strong sense of international ambiguity regarding Tibet's political status prior to and during current Chinese rule. Derived primarily from imperial-designated political statuses such as suzerain or autonomous, this ambiguity shortchanges Tibetan pasts and futures. Thinking empire out of bounds opens new spaces for theorizing such colonial and imperial experiences, for acknowledging the transgressive reach of imperial formations (such as their appearance in unexpected locales), and for assessing how imperial categories continue to impact people's individual and collective lives. I present here a view from the inside out, from the Tibetan side of the equation, one specifically designed to allow a detailed yet broad view of these three disparate empires.

ONE COUNTRY, THREE EMPIRES

The twentieth century was not kind to Tibet. It began with the "great game" among the British, Qing, and Russian empires and ended with the severe Strike Hard campaign in the People's Republic of China. While Tibet was an independent state for centuries, its economic, military, political, and religious relations with neighbors China, India, Mongolia, and Nepal shifted over the years. During the period of this study, Tibet was an independent state until it became a part of China in 1951. Although the People's Republic of China continues to proclaim that itsincorporation of Tibet was a "peaceful liberation," the exiled Tibetan government considers it a military occupation and forced colonization. Since 1959, Tibet has existed in dual spheres: as Tibetan "autonomous" units within the People's Republic of China and as a "government in exile" located in India with a refugee community centered in South Asia but increasingly spread around the world.

British efforts to court Tibetan allegiance began in the late eighteenth century but took full force in 1904 when Lord Curzon, viceroy of India, dispatched a mission to Lhasa. The "Younghusband Expedition" (whose time in Tibet is remembered by Tibetans as the Anglo-Tibetan War) successfully fought its way to Lhasa, forced the Dalai Lama into temporary exile in Mongolia, and secured favorable trade and political agreements with the Tibetan government. With the 1911 fall of the Qing Dynasty, British officials of both British India and the British Consular Service in China ensured that their "good offices" were involved in all negotiations and governmental interactions between the Tibetans and Chinese.[23] Key to British interests at the time was transforming Tibet into a friendly buffer state between India and China. Tibet was an example of the British "forward" policy in which the literal boundaries of empire were bypassed in favor of gaining influence with and power over those on the other side of the border.[24] As British India became independent India, and Republican China became the People's Republic of China, change came also to Tibet. However, while the thirteenth Dalai Lama had predicted in 1933 that the communist Chinese would threaten Tibet, no one was quite prepared for the changes that were about to take place.

In 1949, two years after the British quit India, the communist People's Republic of China was formed from the ruins of Chiang Kai-shek's Republican China. One of Chairman Mao Zedong's first publicly stated goals was the "liberation" of Tibet. People's Liberation Army (PLA) troops arrived first in eastern and northeastern Tibet, and on October 19, 1950, the Tibetan governor of Chamdo surrendered to the Chinese. One month later, at the age of sixteen, the fourteenth Dalai Lama was fully vested with spiritual and temporal powers as the head of the Tibetan state. The Tibetan government unsuccessfully appealed to the United Nations for assistance and eventually began negotiations with the Chinese in Beijing. On May 23, 1951, Chinese and Tibetan officials signed the "Agreement of the Central People's Government and the Local Government of Tibet on Measures for the Peaceful Liberation of Tibet," commonly known as the Seventeen-Point Agreement. Tibetan officials, however, had not sent the terms of the agreement to the Dalai Lama or Tibetan cabinet for approval before signing. Although the Tibetan government felt that the agreement was signed under duress,[25] it ultimately decided not to renounce it for a number of reasons, including its inability to secure the international support necessary for diplomatic or military defense. The agreement called for the "local government" of Tibet to remain in place.[26] However, it was soon clear that the Chinese did not intend for joint governance of Tibet but for power to rest solely in the hands of the Chinese Communist Party. It was not long before ordinary Tibetans began to protest Chinese rule, including by an organized armed rebellion in eastern Tibet. By 1959, the situation had deteriorated to the point where the Dalai Lama fled Lhasa for India, where he and the Tibetan government in exile remain today. The regeneration of Chinese empire had begun.

Great Britain and China argued over Tibet for decades, yet Tibet's imperial history is a triple one. Thus joining this examination of twentieth-century Tibet is the United States of America, whose imperial shepherding of Tibet—and the globe at large—increased following European decolonization.[27] In late 1949, with communist troops massing in eastern Tibet, the Tibetan government asked the United States for support if it were to apply for UN membership. The United States turned Tibet down, as did Great Britain, whose new policy was that Tibet was no longer a British issue but one for the independent government of India. Whereas Indian leaders chose not to intervene on Tibet's behalf with the leaders of the People's Republic of China, the United States did intervene to a limited extent and in a mostly quiet manner. Cold War discourses of the United States as a global but not imperial power kept the United States from full investment in the Tibetan situation, as did events in Korea. On October 7, 1950, US troops crossed the thirty-eighth parallel in South Korea on their way to recapturing Seoul, drawing China into the war on the side of North Korea. On the very same day, forty thousand Chinese troops marched into Tibetan territory directly controlled by the Tibetan government.[28] With the subsequent arrival of the Chinese People's Liberation Army in Lhasa, the United States offered assistance to the Tibetan government, but it was not until 1955 that the Tibetans accepted US military aid.

Hesitation in US policy is also attributable to the external ambiguity in the status of Tibet. For the most part, the United States and many other world powers have evaded serious questions of Tibet's political status by treating Tibet as a humanitarian issue rather than an issue of political sovereignty. Humanitarianism enables new imperial moves, both continuing with an imperial "politics of sympathy"[29] and adding a new sense of individual agency to the imperial equation. The diplomatic and analytical ability to slip from national sovereignty to individual rights is a Tibetan imperial effect established by the British that continues in the present day (surely but not only in US imperial endeavors). This is not solely Tibet's imperial past but also its imperial present.

OUT OF BOUNDS: EMPIRE AFTER DECOLONIZATION

In the advent of movements for independence and self-determination following World War II, anti-imperialist sentiment spread around the world.[30] Once global reality, the concept, practice, and semantics of empire turned quickly and overwhelmingly negative. Decolonization involved an evacuation of global tolerance for empire with or without colonialism. Imperialism and colonialism could no longer be known as such. Decolonization did not mean that empires went away but that they went underground, surfacing in guises ranging from socialist empire in the Soviet Union and China to various forms of neoimperialist aggressive democracy as in the case of the United States. Yet each of these polities fiercely guarded itself against any accusations of empire or imperialism. Strategies for so doing varied widely. In the case of Tibet, the Americans and the British both feared Chinese charges of imperialism should they intervene. As a result, American intervention was solely covert or behind the scenes (for example, at the United Nations), while the British declared that Tibet was now the responsibility of India. China, on the other hand, used imperialism, or more specifically socialist-style "anti-imperialism," as one of its primary justifcations for its intervention in Tibet. As a socialist state, China's anti-imperialism was specifically anticapitalist.

Political maneuvering during (and after) the Cold War raises the question of whether there can be empire without capitalism. If earlier Chinese dynasties are unproblematically labeled "imperial," what would it mean to analyze the People's Republic of China as an empire? Using Tibet as an example, and the concept of "imperial formations" as an analytic term, characteristics of contemporary Chinese imperialism include accumulation, territorial expansion, direct rule, military intervention, and the simultaneous cultivation of inclusive and exclusive categories of national belonging. This list of features is as particular to imperial formations as it might be to China.[31] In the absence of capitalism, it is not sufficient to label these practices "nationalist" or "expansionist" or even "Chinese" without also seriously considering how they might also be imperial.[32] China's socialist economy exists in tandem with—and is increasingly a direct part of—the global capitalist economy.

While Lenin may have been right that the highest form of imperialism is capitalism,[33] we should not interpret this to mean that the *only* form of imperialism is capitalism. Economic exploitation for imperial gain is certainly a key feature of all empires over the last several centuries—it is not solely a feature of capitalism or capitalist empires. Yet the fact that all empires involve economic gain does not cancel out other facets of empire, namely that economic forms of exploitation are not the sole determinant of empire or, more controversially perhaps, that not all empires operate solely within a capitalist political-economic system. Indeed, the historical trajectory of the People's Republic of China directly challenges this interpretation.

From the perspective of Tibet, the PRC can and should be understood as an imperial power. Writing from within the PRC, Chinese intellectual Wang Lixiong argues that Chinese rule in Tibet is a form of imperialism in which "the Tibetan nation's consciousness of self" is denied: "No matter how much [Chinese rule] has tried to achieve other benefits, it has categorically suppressed Tibetan self-expression. The empire wants to control expressiveness of any kind; any breakthrough invites punishment."[34] State efforts to shape Tibetan identities and histories are just as central to PRC projects in Tibet as they were for European colonial projects elsewhere in Asia.[35] Such experiences are basic components of the history of empire in Tibet. The lived experience of foreign rule and the cruel hopes sustained by unequal imperial relationships are felt deeply in everyday life, not just in state and intellectual levels of discourse and action. For the generations of Tibetans who "came of age colonized" inside and outside Tibet[36] it matters little whether or not China is a capitalist or communist state. This is not to say that it does not matter to all Tibetans; for those Tibetans with deep commitments to socialism,[37] Chinese policy in Tibet is a sad example of the failures of state socialism. The statewide persistence of Han chauvinism and the recent move to a modified capitalist system are but two examples of decades of deviation from the strict Marxist and Leninist teachings upon which the People's Republic of China was created.[38]

The Cold War provided thick cover for new imperial formations after (and throughout) the process of European decolonization. By positioning themselves against empire, the PRC and the United States each used the political moment of decolonization as a safe space from which to launch new forms of empire.[39] Their anti-imperial discourses—also anticapitalist for the PRC and anticolonial for the United States—served to preclude the inclusion of these two states on a possible roster of contemporary empires. Chinese and American anti-imperialisms were not abstract but were specifically directed at European (capitalist) states. As both political moment and political ideology, the Cold War was effective in thwarting charges of imperialism against China, including international criticism of China's expansion into Tibet. Time and again, in private offices in Washington, DC, and New Delhi and in public sessions of the United Nations, politicians and diplomats refrained from truly acting on charges of imperialism brought before them.[40] Much as Chinese protests against imperialism laid the ground for the Chinese takeover of Tibet (and for the absence of serious global critique), American critiques of colonialism underwrote America's new empire. As Engseng Ho argues, "US anticolonialism is not simply a cloak for US empire, but rather a language that informs the very representation of its imperial authority."[41] If the cover of decolonization made this denial of empire possible, invisibility made its practice feasible. The strategic ambiguity of boundaries surrounding imperial projects made even overt imperial practices appear invisible.

US empire, be it in the American West, Puerto Rico, the Philippines, or beyond, was rarely considered in the same imperial realm as European empires of the same period, and this analytic of political difference continued with decolonization.[42] The postcolonial period was marked by domination without colonization (although incorporated territories or new domestic states were allowed) and with the cultivation of the sort of influence and action that could no longer be either politely or publicly called imperial. The covert military intervention that repeatedly characterized US actions around the globe is a relatively little-known part of Tibetan history as well. US–Tibetan relations began only in 1942, when the United States wanted to transit war supplies to troops in China through Tibet. Relations quickly strengthened in the 1950s as the United States took over the British role as Tibet's closest ally (vis-à-vis China), and this position continues to define US–Tibetan relations today. Although American empire is by no means solely a twentieth-century phenomenon, at present US imperialism involves a combination of military action, economic power, and political influence specifically developed in the vacuum left by European decolonization.[43] Even at its most blunt, however, American empire relies on invisibility as its strategy.[44] The CIA provides the most obvious example. American operations in Tibet were not only run by the CIA and considered top secret at the time, but they remain classified today.

Tibetan imperial experiences are not easily categorized or neatly summarized. I turn now to case studies of each empire involved—the British, the Chinese, and the American. These are not parallel or consecutive stories, nor are they commensurate or even comparative; instead, I see these stories as complementary. While they do present a cumulative narrative about contemporary empire, this is not the only labor I ask of these histories. Instead, I present a different sort of story for each empire with the goal of illuminating the multiple ways—the stark, the subtle, the intimate, the impersonal—that empire is experienced in everyday life. These are histories, therefore, that move from the state to the individual and back again, that are told in distinct tones and distinct times. I start with the story of Rapga Pangdatsang and British archival debates over out-of-place Tibetans in India, move next to a discussion of a communist propaganda text as a pedagogy of imperialism, and conclude with a presentation of Tibetan guerrilla histories that highlight the intimacy and invisibility of US empire and CIA operations.

NOT COLONIZED: TIBET AND BRITISH INDIA

What did it mean to live in somebody else's empire? If we no longer accept a rigid separation of colonizer and colonized,[45] what space and subject positions do we recognize for noncolonized peoples? Agents of empire did not stop at colonial boundaries in terms of political intervention, cultural concerns, or the disciplining of populations. Outside empire, projects of knowledge and rule were even more incomplete than within colonial territories and yet had enormous implications for other states and peoples. As Thongchai Winichakul has convincingly shown in the case of Thailand, European notions of citizenship, geography, and sovereignty introduced via neighboring British and French polities altered concepts and practices of both nation and state in Thailand.[46] Elsewhere the incorporation of noncolonized peoples into empire involves repercussions that persist in the present day. Nepali Gurkha soldiers, for example, still fight today in not just the Indian army but also the British army.[47] As I will argue here, Tibetans resident in British India presented a series of categorical problems to colonial officials that highlight the troubled importance of the "not-colonized" category for Tibetans and British officials alike.

Like many Tibetan intellectuals in the 1940s, Rapga Pangdastang was drawn to intellectual currents in China and India and spent time in both countries developing progressive political and social ideas intended to be implemented in Tibet.[48] Earlier efforts by the thirteenth Dalai Lama to modernize Tibet were mostly unsuccessful due to the unrelenting opposition of conservative monastic officials who comprised over half of the Tibetan government.[49] Envisioning, if not implementing, progressive, modern change was thus in itself radical. Rapga's vision for Tibet included educational and monastic reform, literacy programs, and reform of the conservative political system.[50] The vehicle for these ideas was the Tibetan Improvement Party, which Rapga headed and operated out of Kalimpong, India. At the time, there were no political parties in Tibet, and opposition to the government was not well tolerated. In India, however, the British allowed for opposition political parties, and Rapga therefore based his party there. The Tibetan Improvement Party, however, was not solely a Tibetan party. As a member of an elite family, albeit a nouveau riche one, Pangda Rapga was a product of the Tibetan patronage system in which both vertical and horizontal social networks provided financial and other necessities to those born to such privilege. These networks were not limited to Tibetans but were part of a broader (and often politically strategic) system incorporating neighboring peoples such as the Bhutanese, the Sikkimese, and the Chinese.

As empires compared strategies between themselves, so too did peoples within the imperial realm. Comparison, competition, and cooperation were strategies against empire, not just of it. Rapga was particularly fond of the writings of Sun Yat-sen and translated his *Three Principles of the People* into Tibetan. He based his political party in part on the Kuomintang and accepted financial support from them. In his view, this affiliation enabled the organization of his party but did not subsume the interests of Tibet under those of China.[51] In 1946, Rapga was living in Kalimpong, working to recruit members to the party. He worked openly on the Tibetan Improvement Party such that eventually colonial officials learned about it. They decided they could not allow such "hostile" activities against a "friendly government," for if change was to come in Tibet, it would come with British influence rather than from within (or worse, from the influence of another country).[52] As they set about to disband the party, a serious problem was immediately apparent: Pangda Rapga had not broken any laws of British India.

Upon learning about Rapga's political party, the Tibetan government requested that the government of India extradite him to Tibet. Officials of British India turned down this request because plotting against a friendly government was not a chargeable offense, nor was there an extradition treaty between India and Tibet. The categorical nonstatus of Tibetans in India was an immediate problem for colonial officials. Under British rule, noncitizens were legally categorized as "foreigners," yet Tibetans were not subject to this categorization and thus lived in India as neither citizens nor foreigners. This in-between status was a position of both power and vulnerability, enabling Tibetans to live mostly free from the regulation of the Foreigners Act but also leaving them without the security of any state-awarded rights (or the burden of accompanying obligations).[53] Yet in not classifying Tibetans as foreigners, the British were also left without grounds for disciplining Tibetans who transgressed colonial law or sensibilities. This categorical dilemma offers insight into the colonial disciplining of those who were not colonized, those who were not subject to the law because they were categorized as residing outside of it.[54]

The case stalled for a bit until officials discovered that Rapga held a Chinese passport. This immediately provided them with an opening, because as a Chinese citizen, Rapga was liable to Indian laws that did not apply to Tibetans. British and Indian colonial officials debated Rapga's nationality and decided they could legitimately categorize him as Chinese rather than Tibetan. This categorization was a bureaucratic convenience for the colonial state rather than an instance of prepostmodern flexible nationality or citizenship on Rapga's behalf.[55] His political affinity with Republican China was genuine, as was his affiliation with the Kuomintang through the Office of Mongolian and Tibetan Affairs. In the context of the times, however, his possession of a Chinese passport did not forfeit his Tibetan nationality, heritage, or subject-citizen position. In 1946, the Tibetan government did not have a passport system. For Tibetans who traveled abroad, possession of a Chinese passport might have signaled a travel convenience or a political affinity or perhaps both, but it was not necessarily a cancellation of Tibetan nationality or citizenship. While change was dangerously imminent in Tibet and its borderlands, this was one part of the world in which geopolitical borders and identities remained locally defined (and contested) rather than internationally assigned.

In his dealings with officials of British India, Rapga claimed both identities—Chinese and Tibetan. He consulted with a lawyer on how to avoid deportation, and the following document written by Rapga gives a sense of his relationship to these identities:

> I have considered over the matter and I believe that the Government of India has been placing much stress on my departure as I am the holder of an Official Passport and under the employment of the Chinese government. The Consul General might now clarify from Government whether they are prepared to allow me to stay in India if I give up employment under the Chinese Government. My opinion is that as I am a natural Tibetan born and brought up in Tibet, I have not given up the Tibetan nationality, I do not come under the Foreigner's Act. It is the question of my employment under the Chinese government which is causing all this difficulty. I shall consider over the desirability of propriety of giving up the job if that will prevent my departure from India.[56]

His efforts to be recategorized as Tibetan were futile. As a Chinese citizen, Rapga was charged with routine violations of the Foreigners Act of 1940 and the Registration of Foreigners Act of 1939. He was deported on July 3, 1946.[57] While disciplinary authority rested with colonial officials in that Tibetans could be recast as "foreigners" and deported, such categorical disciplinarity was both fictive and fleeting. In the early 1950s, distraught over the Chinese takeover of Tibet, Rapga Pangdatsang returned to Kalimpong, to an India no longer British, and lived there until his death in 1976. Not all identities authored by the colonial state continued in the postcolonial period. Rapga's state enemy status disintegrated with the advent of an independent India, but other aspects of his story and his remembered identity and place in history remain indebted to colonial archives. Of the many ways he is remembered, the colonial version of Rapga as Chinese spy is perhaps the most persistent.

Although not composed of the usual colonized–colonizer dialectic, this tale of empire involves familiar issues of authority, discipline, and imposed subject positions while also raising new ones such as extra colonial spaces within empire and the "noncolonized" category. The residence (and not just temporary presence) of noncolonized individuals such as Tibetans poses new questions for our understandings of British empire. We already know that empire is an ad hoc, uneven, and imprecise project at times, and a smug, self-assured, and flexible one at others;[58] our understanding of imperial practices and processes, however, is almost exclusively based on colonial relations. British–Tibetan relations allow us to explore the confidences and shortcomings of a colonial empire outside of the colonial domain, in an imperial zone fraught with uncertainties definitive of the imperial imagination. Thinking outside assumed or claimed boundaries is to open for analysis the unacknowledged and understated aspects of empires.

This story is also, however, important for Tibet. At stake is nothing less than the political status of Tibet. For a country never colonized by the British empire, Tibet's history and current political status are heavily impacted by the British.[59] Thus, although Rapga's personal problems with colonial terminology might have been resolved with the advent of Indian independence, those of Tibet writ large continue. The out-of-bounds nature of British relations with Tibet both created and crystallized a politically ambiguous status for Tibet. With the British out of India, the new People's Republic of China took immediate advantage of this political ambiguity by moving into Tibet and calling it an anti-imperial act of benevolence.

EMPIRE AND ANTI-IMPERIALISM: TIBET AND THE PEOPLE'S REPUBLIC OF CHINA

Chinese rule in Tibet directly challenges claims that colonialism is "over." It is colonialism, however, with a twist: direct foreign rule accompanied by the claim that the colonized peoples have the same rights as all citizens of the home state. Tibetans are, after all, citizens of the PRC. Yet just as socialism does not preclude capitalism or imperialism, citizenship does not rule out colonization. If modern imperialism and colonialism both operate under the pretenses of civilizational superiority, then Chinese rule in Tibet works in a similar fashion. In the PRC, the story first told about Tibet was one of socialist difference, an evolutionary tale of needing to bring the backward Tibetans forward into a socialist modernity. Folded next into the story was a timelessness, the assertion-turned-truism that Tibet has "always" been a part of China. Neither narrative is cast in colonial or imperial language; yet each labors to justify Chinese rule in Tibet. Different emphases, forms, and strategies mark such justification attempts over the last five decades, with one constant factor being the "civilizing mission" quality of the socialist project in Tibet.[60]

From its inception, Chinese socialism was a didactic project, involving educating the masses on their deficiencies and providing instruction for remedying these faults.[61] In Tibet as elsewhere, the most egregious deficiencies were reserved for the elite (for landowners, intellectuals, chieftains, and religious leaders). As the elite were targeted for criticism, the lower classes were projected as collaborators in the socialist project. Through a combination of disciplinary and discursive projects, agents of the state—mostly Han Chinese but also some Tibetans—sought to reeducate Tibetan peasants and nomads and to reorder Tibetan society. This required disavowals of Tibetan political history, religious practice, and cultural sensibilities. While generally and enthusiastically overt, unapologetic, and paternalistic, Chinese legitimization strategies reflect their respective eras. Initially, a main focus was on introducing Tibetans to socialism. This project had both retrospective and prospective aspects and in general was distinctly communal, class-oriented, and formulaic in language, strategy, and tone. The predominant message was blunt and intended to be clear to all Tibetans: Tibetan society was backward and oppressive, but Chinese-style socialism was modern and liberating. Tibetan identity was not to be entirely eliminated, just aligned with Chinese socialist principles. Propaganda thus reinforced a Tibetan ethnic identity while forging a PRC citizen identity, and denigrated upper-class identities while celebrating lower-class identities. While propaganda took many forms, texts played an important role in encouraging Tibetan consent to Chinese rule.

Rebirth of the Tibetan People (*Bod mi dmangs gsar skye thob pa)* is a classic example of Chinese justification strategies. It was published by the Beijing Nationalities Publishing House in 1960, a time of crisis. Just the year before, the Dalai Lama had escaped into exile in India, and thus there was a heightened urgency to Chinese efforts to legitimate and celebrate their presence in Tibet. Bilingual in both Chinese and Tibetan, *Rebirth of the Tibetan People* works to legitimate Chinese rule in Tibet to both colonizers and colonized alike. The book is organized into three sections: (1) class-based oppression in traditional Tibetan society, (2) Tibetan rebellion against the Chinese liberation, and (3) the glorious new life of Tibetans under the PRC. In contrast to later propaganda, the book is noticeably restrained on certain topics. The Dalai Lama is not criticized at all but is said to have been kidnapped; the term *zhing 'grin* (peasant or serf) is used rather than *tshe gyog* (slave); in reference to the Tibetan rebellion, the term *lhing 'jags bzos* (pacify or subdue) is used instead of *phams* (defeat); and the book includes some positive comments about traditional Tibetan society rather than just negative ones. Other topics covered remain standard fare—for example, China and Tibet have a long history of relations, Tibet is an inalienable part of China, and Tibet has been "reborn" into a Chinese socialist paradise.

Asserting sovereignty is one means of fixing political subjectivities. Creating and re-creating subjectivities involve the reining in of unruly boundaries, populations, and ideas (at the same time that state-authorized ambiguities are maintained).[62] Pedagogies of violence and of culture may both be at work in educating a people such as the Tibetans to the very new project of Chinese state socialism. If socialism and its prescriptive system were new to Tibet, Chinese imperialism was not.[63] Tibet was a part of the Qing imperial sphere, albeit to different degrees under different emperors, and always with its own interpretation of this relationship.[64] Earlier imperial and expansionist periods—Han Chinese, Manchu, Mongolian (or even that of the Tibetan empire)—certainly left traces that resonate in the PRC but had different histories, practices, and rhetorics. In assessing the imperial nature of Chinese rule in

Tibet, we need to be mindful of this past but also bold enough to assess the present in analytical spheres beyond those of "the Tibet Question" or any sort of Asian, Chinese, or Tibetan exceptionalism.

The opening pages of *Rebirth of the Tibetan People* make blunt links between sovereignty and subjectivity, pedagogy and politics. Two vastly different yet equally iconic images comprise its opening pages, aligning the reader immediately with the state in its various manifestations—socialist, imperial, national, multiethnic. The cover page depicts smiling Tibetan women expressing their gratitude to the Chinese, while inside the book, following the title page, is a portrait of Mao. Whereas the first image is iconic for its generic message of "minority" gratitude,[65] the second is iconic for its ubiquity throughout the People's Republic of China, including Tibet.[66] Images of Mao played a major role in legitimating socialism in Tibet and, along with his spoken words, marked landscapes both literal and figurative throughout Tibet. The lead marcher in choreographed political parades always carried Mao's portrait high, and Mao's images hung in all public spaces and in many private ones. Under his watchful eye, Tibetans would be instructed on proper thinking via phrases of his they were made to memorize. Literacy was not required for fluency in Mao Zedong thought, as Mao's phrases were repeated time and again on loudspeaker systems in villages, as well as in communal education meetings. They were also were pasted on walls and literally written into the land with stones. Even if you could not read, you knew their message. While such projects are no longer central to Chinese socialism in Tibet, Mao's words remain on walls and on hillsides in many Tibetan villages. These icons and their accompanying artifacts may now be familiar, but the fear associated with them does not solely reside in the past. Such fears reveal successful strategies for cultivating consent and the insecurities upon which such projects often rest.

Familiarity and fear, intimacy and intimidation have long been recognized as twin components of the European colonial project.[67] The impulse to rein in or act upon insecurities surrounding boundaries and sovereignties might indeed be a pan-imperial characteristic. Evident in the British archival debates on Rapga Pangdatsang's case, such insecurities are perhaps a better representation of imperial reality on the ground than is any sort of monolithic view of empire as a singularly coherent or consistent project. Anxieties present in imperial projects reveal the sites where empire is perhaps not as secure as some would like to believe.[68] Chinese anxieties of rule are easily recognizable in mechanical expressions of Tibetan gratitude to the Chinese.

The first thing a Tibetan reading or listening to *Rebirth of the Tibetan People* in the 1960s might have noticed is that it is highly formulaic. Stock messages included criticism of "old" Tibetan society, praise for Chinese socialism, and multiple examples of cooperation between Chinese and Tibetans. These messages were constantly reinforced through repetition and thus were familiar to all Tibetans. They were also, however, understood as a specific sort of truth.[69] As Chinese rule progressed throughout the 1950s and 1960s, many Tibetans learned to assume that Chinese propaganda was false. It was bluntly evident that there was no space for public dissent and increasingly little space for private dissent. The lack of a civil sphere for discourse and action meant that the Chinese Communist Party enjoyed passive acceptance rather than active support, and that dissent against the party was primarily underground in the form of a guerrilla resistance army and locally based acts of protest.[70] While some Tibetans subscribed to socialist principles (if not the discursive fictions and disciplinary threats associated with the incorporation of Tibet into the PRC), overall there was a massive cultural disconnect between the socialist project and Tibetan society. Response to this disconnect took multiple forms, the most important of which was rebellion. The discussion—and containment—of the rebellion in *Rebirth of the Tibetan People* reveals particular anxieties of an imperial project in its early stages.

From 1951 to 1959, Tibetan resistance to Chinese rule varied widely throughout the country. In Lhasa in 1954, for example, a People's Party (*mi dmangs tshogs pa*) formed to publicly protest the Chinese. In eastern Tibet in 1956, villagers, nomads, and monks took up arms in response to increasingly harsh Chinese reforms; these eastern Tibetan uprisings turned into an organized but independent movement to "defend country and religion" (*bstan srung dang blangs dmag*, later consolidated as *chu bzhi gangs drug dmag*) that fought against the PLA through 1974 from a base in Nepal.[71] Finally, in March 1959, there was a mass popular revolt in Lhasa during which the Dalai Lama fled to exile in India. Chinese propaganda collapsed all these acts into one category—acts by "high class separatists."[72] Singling out the upper classes was an effort to create new divides among the Tibetan population (or to give new meaning to existing divides). Labeling the resistance as upper class allowed for the fiction that other Tibetans did not participate in or support it.

Graphic images and descriptions in *Rebirth of the Tibetan People* detail peasant suffering under the elite in the "old Tibetan system." These same elite, it is claimed, continue to disrupt new life under socialism as high-class separatists. Rebellion is treated as a bourgeois aberration, a collaboration with "imperialist and foreign separatists," and a continuation of the feudal oppression of the Tibetan people. Photos that accompany the text reinforce these messages through heroic images of PLA soldiers arresting "rebel bandits," working with Tibetans in the fields, and dancing with Tibetans after "pacifying" the rebellion. While Tibetan resistance was to continue in ways that we are still learning about today, its members did not fit the "high-class" profile claimed for them in Chinese propaganda materials. Instead, as a movement drawn from all socioeconomic strata, the resistance contradicted the message of national unity and local gratitude cultivated by *Rebirth of the Tibetan People*. With few exceptions, the happy, smiling Tibetans who animate the pages of such texts have yet to tell their stories outside of state-sponsored media. In exile, however, the "rebel bandits" have begun to tell their stories, tackling head-on Chinese imperial narratives, negotiating the national pretensions of the Tibetan government in exile, and departing in key ways from the projects and preferences of their "imperialist" counterparts, the US government officials involved in supporting the Tibetan resistance.

IMPERIAL DEFAULT: TIBET AND THE UNITED STATES OF AMERICA

Intervention and invitation, intimacy and invisibility define the Tibetan story of US imperialism. As a story of Cold War intervention, this case fits a classic pattern. Anticommunism and the evangelization of democracy fueled US action on Tibet, while Tibetan reasons for working with the Americans similarly fit a decolonization-era pattern of seeking external assistance for internal political goals. The new Pax Americana grew through a combination of imperial default and involvement in nationalist independence projects.[73] Historically and politically specific, as all empires are, the new American imperial formation looked quite different from its European predecessors, being highly militarized, covert, indirect, and propelled (in Asia at least) by new, period-specific ideas of integration and interdependence.[74] As we know so well, however, empire is never only a story of the imperialists and their intentions; imperial subjects have their own interpretations, agendas, and perspectives. For Tibetans, US assistance was not a denial of their own agency and autonomy but an acknowledgment of it. This is not (solely) a naïveté regarding international or imperial politics, but a window into the type of imperial experience some Tibetans had with the United States.

A story of masculine intimacy, relationships between CIA agents and Tibetan soldiers are an example of empire on a very human scale: a homosocial history best told through the joys and pains of personal involvement and commitment; a history that is not abstract but lived. For Tibetan veterans, empire is a biographical tale, a sense of accomplishment, a feeling of betrayal, and a perpetual and lingering hope as much as it is a story of geopolitics and governments. The Tibetan men who served in the resistance army were supported not by a faceless "America" but by real people, by men with names, men who became their friends. For the American CIA officers who trained the Tibetans, this appreciation and respect was mutual. Bonds of friendship, commitment, and expectation persist between these two groups of men in ways highly unusual for CIA officers. In a perhaps unexpected appearance of Tibetan exceptionalism, officers' ties to Tibetans were rarely replicated in their work with other groups around the world. The legendary late Tony Poe, for example, who spent much of his career and personal life invested in Laos and with Laotian communities in the United States, repeatedly told me that "the [Tibetans] were the best men I worked with."[75] As far as Tibetan soldiers were concerned, US involvement in the Tibetan struggle was not an abstract diplomatic endeavor. Although they recognized the anticommunist politics guiding US action, empire in this instance was for them a very personalized, joint, and face-to-face endeavor.

Partnership is how many Tibetan soldiers viewed their relationship with their American "teachers."[76] The Tibetan resistance army considered CIA support to be an American endorsement of the righteousness of the Tibetan cause and, importantly, to be a collaboration between Tibet and the United States. From 1956 through 1969, the CIA covertly supported resistance activities: military excursions against the PLA, a military headquarters in Nepal, intelligence-gathering operations, the parachuting of troops into Tibet from unmarked CIA planes, provisioning of supplies, weapons, and funds, and education campaigns among Tibetans in Tibet.[77] The CIA also trained Tibetan soldiers in secret locations throughout Asia and the United States. At the US Army's Camp Hale in Leadville, Colorado, CIA officers taught classes in paramilitary operations, bomb building, mapmaking, photography, radio operation techniques, intelligence collecting, and world history and politics.

At the ground level, the Americans and the Tibetans saw each other as providing the assistance needed to accomplish their own goals, be they the securing of rare intelligence on the PRC or the securing of one's country.[78] Notions of working together on these goals involved acknowledged differential access to information and resources. At higher levels, US interest in Tibet never went as far as the Tibetans wanted, as evidenced in a January 9, 1964, memorandum: "The CIA Tibetan Activity consists of political action, propaganda, and paramilitary activity. The purpose of the program at this stage is to keep the political concept of an autonomous Tibet alive within Tibet and among foreign nations, principally India, and to build a capability for resistance against possible political developments inside Communist China."[79] The degree to which Tibetan exile political projects have been influenced and shaped by US interests remains underappreciated by both Tibetans and their foreign supporters.[80] However, despite the limits of high-level US support for Tibet, the intimate cooperation between the men on the ground enabled a very particular and potentially disappointing interpretation—a sense of imperialism as opportunity, as a chance for agency, action, national participation, and independence.[81]

The Tibetans in the resistance army were not career soldiers. Farmers, nomads, traders, and monks, they possessed among them a range of skills including literacy. One of their self-initiated projects at Camp Hale (known to the Tibetans as Camp Dumra, from *ldum ra,* or "garden"), was the writing of short books for distribution in Tibet, responses to communist propaganda such as *Rebirth of the Tibetan People.*

Written in colloquial Tibetan with accompanying narrative illustrations, the books beautifully demonstrate the convergence of Tibetan political projects and American imperial guidance. One example is *A Pleasure Garden for Blossoming the Tibetan People's Wisdom to Reestablish an Independent Republic of Tibet* (hereafter *A Pleasure Garden*).[82] Authored in 1960 "by the people of Camp Dumra," this twenty-six-page book is a combination of handwritten text and line drawings that together compose a primer on Tibetan history and world politics. The book has five text sections—reasons for the rebellion, regaining independence, today's world, global independence struggles, friends of Tibet—and a sixth "history" section composed solely of illustrations. Written in the same year and for the same Tibetan audience as *Rebirth of the Tibetan People,* the soldier-authored *A Pleasure Garden* tells a very different story of Tibet under communist rule.

A Pleasure Garden immediately lays out the reasons for the Tibetan rebellion, contending that the Chinese not only invaded independent Tibet but also intend to destroy the Tibetan people and their culture:

> They redistributed monastic estates and cut the revenues so that it made it impossible to have a monastic community. Aiming to take away Tibetan identity completely, they forcefully sent young Tibetans to China to study communism. Older Tibetans, monks, nuns, and lay people, both male and female, are continuously forced to engage in unbearable hard labor.[83]

After laying out these facts, the book then takes a pedagogical tone, explaining the need for an organized and united rebellion force and an accompanying nonviolent aspect to the struggle. They will succeed, they contend, because world history is on their side. "Except for us Tibetans," the authors instruct, revolution has swept the world such that old governments are transformed into one of two new forms—democracy "based on peace and justice" or communism "based on violence and deception."[84] They explain that the primary difference between the two systems is that under democracy, language and religion are left unchanged, but "negative aspects of the old system" are changed only with the consent of the people of the country, not through interference from other countries.[85] Communism, on the other hand, seeks to turn all peoples into communists and to destroy traditional languages and religion and despite professing to make changes with the consent of the people, "in reality does not give any power to the people."[86] While thus far *A Pleasure Garden* is a direct response to Chinese propaganda, its next two sections introduce new information about colonial revolution to its Tibetan audience.

Tibetans trafficking in critiques of European empire at this time were mostly intellectuals in exile—Rapga Pangdatsang, Gedun Chophel, and other Tibetans in India, China, and Japan, some of whom left documentary traces, others of whom did not—and their audiences were not necessarily the Tibetan villagers of *Rebirth of the Tibetan People* and *A Pleasure Garden.* Through lectures on world history at Camp Hale/Dumra, Tibetan soldiers developed a new approach for explaining Chinese rule in Tibet to their fellow Tibetans via analogies to specific examples of colonialism:

> A country called Algeria was occupied by France one hundred years ago. Algeria was very much like today's Tibet. For example, because they did not have good leadership, the people of the country were not unified, and therefore the country was defeated by the French. After six years of French occupation, an educated Algerian man living in a neighboring country started the Algerian Freedom Movement. He planned for five years how best to unify the people and revolt. Through the dual violent/non-violent method, the country regained its independence. Today, Algeria is a developed and democratic nation.[87]

The story of Ethiopia is told with similar themes: Ethiopia was independent but with poor leadership and without a unified population; Italy was able to defeat the Ethiopians; the revolt was planned in exile by Haile Selassie; an Ethiopian people's guerrilla army formed and was able to defeat the Italians, thereby regaining independence for the country.[88] The narrative structure of these mini-histories parallels that presented for Tibet, thereby legitimating the Tibetan rebellion against the Chinese. Paired with a discussion of Tibet's "friend countries" around the world, some of which were formerly colonized and all of which are now democracies that "love world peace and freedom," the Tibetan revolt is effectively globalized as an anticolonial, anticommunist struggle.[89] This narrative places Tibet squarely within an imperial circuit of knowledge production emanating from the United States over the course of the twentieth century.[90]

In a telling example of US imperial invisibility, the United States is not mentioned in *A Pleasure Garden.* Empire recedes on behalf of a national liberation struggle. While the United States could be included among the "sixty countries" that support Tibet, the specific nature of US assistance was neither acknowledged nor equated with empire. US support for the resistance was a public, but not printable, secret among Tibetans.[91] The absent presence of American influence in *A Pleasure Garden* is attributable to Tibetan soldiers' notions of partnership with their American counterparts and to more general US anticommunist strategies in which overt policies are paired with ongoing covert activities. This intimate intervention is not singular on any side of the equation—the Tibetan veterans were not the Dalai Lama's exile government, nor were the CIA officers simply carrying through dictates they received from Washington, DC, or Langley. Multiple interests and multiple strategies were (and remain) at work to achieve parallel goals: the expansion of US influence and the regaining of Tibet.

As with empires past, this new imperialism is frequently defended as benevolent, as "empire-building for noble ends rather than for such base motives as profit and influence."[92] This is a story imperialists tell themselves. For the majority of Tibetan refugees, however—and perhaps for Tibetans within Tibet as well—a critique of the shadows underlying benevolence is not the issue: discomfort with American empire building on the back of the Tibetan struggle pales in comparison to the gratitude for the support. Intervention by the United States provided (and continues to provide) external legitimation of the threat that China posed to Tibet. Nonterritorial and noncolonial, US imperial involvement in Tibet is a hybrid of earlier and new US and other forms of empire, neither simply replicating past forms nor abandoning them entirely. It is out of bounds only in the sense that US empire itself seems at times to have no boundaries but also in that the term *empire* is still only uneasily and unevenly applied to the United States. CIA operations in Tibet are thus part of a "larger phenomenon of imperialism in all of its historical complexity [and of] the US role as the hegemonic power of the capitalist world."[93] Simply put, the contemporary United States is not an exception to the category of empire. Sometimes public, sometimes invisible, this is an imperial formation that has more than its fair shares of corners, shadows, and secrets. Tibet is one of them, an example of the painful inequalities of empire and its unflagging persistence in the present.

CONCLUSIONS

> We are often told "Colonialism is dead." Let us not be deceived or even soothed by that. I say to you, colonialism is not yet dead. I beg of you, do not think of colonialism only in the classic form which we of Indonesia, and our brothers in different parts of Asia and Africa, knew. Colonialism has also its modern dress, in the form of economic control, intellectual control, actual physical control by a small but alien community within a nation. It is a skilful and determined enemy, and it appears in many guises. It does not give up its loot easily. Wherever, whenever, and however it appears, colonialism is an evil thing, and one which must be eradicated from the earth.
>
> —President Achmed Sukarno, Bandung, 1955 [94]

Thinking empire out of bounds casts new light on the sovereignties each empire has claimed beyond its boundaries (to return to Carl Schmitt's observation). These sovereignties, these entitlements of power, are so often couched in other names, hidden from public debate, and never as stable or singular as they are thought to be. If we are to accept Sukarno's challenge to continue the battle against colonialism in the present day, we must open our analyses to empire in the era of decolonization. I suggest that thinking out of bounds, for both classic European empires and the ones that followed them, will open our understandings of empire to microscopic and wide-angle perspectives at the same time.[95] This approach is microscopic in terms of getting inside the minutiae or even the marginalia of empire, the centrality of people's everyday lives and experiences,[96] but wide-angled in terms of assessing the unexpected, the not allowed, the renounced on the larger scales of nations, empires, and their respective histories.

In the supposed absence of empire, the importance of Tibetan imperial experience is undeniable. Rapga Pangdatsang and British India, Tibetan peasants under the People's Republic of China, Tibetan soldiers and CIA agents—each of these individual examples reveals the deep impact of empire on Tibetan communities. Together we see how these different imperial formations attempted to shape experience, to shape historic and political subjectivities that have had lasting effects for individual Tibetans as well as for the Tibetan state as it currently exists in exile and as part of the PRC. In terms of this volume, I suggest that our collective efforts to think more broadly about empire must be in dialogue with peoples in a range of relations to empire. Living in someone else's empire was similar to, but not the same as, being colonized. To be an imperial subject was not necessarily to be a colonial one. Key here, however, is unraveling the similarities, not just the differences. What historical lessons do we learn from an analysis of the category of the noncolonized? Or from the condition of lived empire in cases of imperialism denied?

Empire is as cultural and social as it is economic, military, or political. Building on William Appleman Williams's idea of "empire as a way of life,"[97] Amy Kaplan advocates attention to the cultural zones of empire as a means of gaining insight into empire at home as well as abroad:

> To understand the multiple ways in which empire becomes a way of life means to focus on those areas of culture traditionally ignored as long as imperialism was treated as a matter of foreign policy conducted by diplomatic elites or as a matter of economic necessity driven by market forces. Not only about foreign diplomacy or international relations, imperialism is also about consolidating domestic cultures and negotiating intranational relations.[98]

I turn again to Wang Lixiong for a perspective from China that is similar to Kaplan's. Wang states that present-day imperialism operates in disguise and in the realm of culture, albeit with the same notions of civilizational superiority and benevolence of earlier imperial formations:

> Imperialism in its contemporary state is neither only about military force and politics, not only regarding the acts of a

> handful of colonizers. It is also about culture and involved with the participation of ordinary people in empire.... [In China, with regard to Tibet, cultural imperialism] has taken root in the mind of every member of the ruling nation. Since it has become a collective consciousness, to change it is de facto a difficult task.[99]

Empire folds into the national consciousness. How and why this takes place is often consonant across imperial formations.

As Shangri-la, for example, Tibet has an important spot in the imperial imaginaries of Great Britain, the United States of America, and the People's Republic of China. Utopian, exceptional, mysterious, Shangri-la is now perhaps not so much a religious idea, an unreachable place, or even a state of mind as it is a state-sponsored tourist destination in the PRC: Shangri-la County in Yunnan Province, formerly known as Zhongdian County.[100] Putting Shangri-la on the map was a joint British–American–Chinese endeavor: British writer James Hilton penned the novel *Lost Horizon* in 1933, American director Frank Capra made the film *Lost Horizon* in 1937, and seven decades later the Chinese state made Shangri-la not just a county but a premier domestic and international tourist destination. Tibetans, of course, have been both intimately involved in and absent from each of these projects. Each is imperial in its own way, each involves representations of the Other, and each pushes civilization up against salvation.

If these three imperial formations are all out of bounds in some ways, be it in relation to Tibet, to other empires, or to academic or popular discourses on empire, then I suggest we consider this extraperipheral space as an opening to be further explored. In terms of Tibet alone, an out-of-bounds approach raises new questions for empires we thought we knew well in addition to those we still need to understand. This is, undoubtedly, part of a larger critique of the transformation of particular regional or historical versions of empire and experience into universal forms of knowledge.[101] Arguing that "colonial differences" are "the house where border epistemology dwells," Walter Mignolo suggests that the hegemonic transformation of such differences into values theoretically downgrades the experiences of some imperial formations and colonized peoples as derivative.[102] In this formulation, we lose the ability to "create new possibilities for thinking from and about the exterior borders of the system," about cosmological as well as temporal and structural differences between imperial formations.[103] In the era of decolonization, empire is not limited to one state model. Thus, while China is more commonly said to have "occupied" Tibet than to have "colonized" it, and while Tibet fell within British imperial realms and still falls within the realm of the new US "empire" without being colonized by either power, the imprints of all three of these states—these imperial formations—resonate in people's individual and collective everyday lives.

Tibetans' relationships with British India, the United States, and the PRC are not neatly commensurate with each other. Instead, they point to the difficulty of translating empire across time and state form. They also direct us to the necessity of specifying the differences and analyzing the similarities between such "empires" and the political projects that accompany them. Analyzing empire through the twentieth century requires attention to imperial spheres in which colonialism is but one model for imperial powers. In the wake of decolonization, therefore, critical approaches to empire must involve a reconfiguration of places and players, of our conceptual and geographic maps, and of how we understand a "decolonial" but still profoundly imperial world.

Notes

My thanks to the Tibetan men and women who not only made these histories come alive but also taught me that they were imperial and ongoing. For helping me put them to paper and theorize them beyond Tibet, my gratitude to Tenzin Bhagen, David Bond, Carla Jones, Charlene Makley, Mithi Mukherjee, seminar participants in Santa Fe, two anonymous press reviewers, and, for over a decade of encouragement and support with this project and much more, Ann Stoler.

1. For histories of these periods, see Goldstein, *History of Modern Tibet;* McKay, *Tibet and the British Raj;* Norbu, *China's Tibet Policy;* Shakabpa, *Tibet;* Shakya, *Dragon in the Land of Snows;* Sperling, "Awe and Submission"; and Tuttle, *Tibetan Buddhists in the Making of Modern China.*

2. For work in colonial studies, see Comaroff and Comaroff, *Ethnography and the Historical Imagination;* Dirks, *Colonialism and Culture;* Cooper, *Colonialism*

in Question; and Cooper and Stoler, *Tensions of Empire.* On postcolonial studies, see McClintock, "Angel of Progress"; Said, *Orientalism;* Shohat, "Notes on the Postcolonial"; and Spivak, *Critique of Postcolonial Reason.*

3. As Inderpal Grewal argues in the case of the contemporary United States, "as a superpower, America produced subjects outside its territorial boundaries through its ability to disseminate neoliberal technologies through multiple channels." Grewal, *Transnational America,* 2–3.

4. An eclectic sampling of influential thinking on borders and boundaries in anthropology and history includes Barth, *Ethnic Groups and Boundaries;* Donnan and Wilson, *Borders;* Gupta and Ferguson, "Beyond 'Culture'"; Rosaldo, *Culture and Truth;* Sahlins, *Boundaries;* and Winichakul, *Siam Mapped.*

5. The term "spatial malleability" is Ian Lustick's. He argues that state borders are always "products of war and other processes of territorial aggrandizement, contraction, or consolidation...contingent as well as constitutive of political, technological, economic, cultural, and social processes." Lustick, *Unsettled States, Disputed Lands,* 43–44.

6. Schmitt, *Nomos of the Earth,* 281.

7. On the imperial turn, see the collected essays in Burton, *After the Imperial Turn.*

8. Peter Hansen, "Why Is There No Subaltern Studies for Tibet?" The Subaltern Studies Collective, originally headed by Indian historian Ranajit Guha, rewrote and retheorized Indian experiences under British rule from the perspective of the "subalterns" of society; see *Subaltern Studies,* vols. 1–11. For critiques of and engagements with subaltern studies, see Chaturvedi, *Mapping Subaltern Studies and the Postcolonial,* and Ludden, *Reading Subaltern Studies.*

9. On the myth of Tibet as Shangri-la, see Bishop, *Myth of Shangri-la;* Dodin and Rather, *Imagining Tibet;* Lopez, *Prisoners of Shangri-la;* Norbu, "Dances with Yaks"; and Shakya, "Tibet and the Occident."

10. See Hansen, "Why Is There No Subaltern Studies for Tibet?"; McGranahan, "Truth, Fear, and Lies"; Powers, *History as Propaganda;* and Shakya, *Dragon in the Land of Snows.*

11. See Brennan, "From Development to Globalization"; Coronil, "Beyond Occidentalism"; Duara, *Decolonization;* Kelly and Kaplan, *Represented Communities;* Le Sueur, *Decolonization Reader;* and Louis and Robinson, "Imperialism of Decolonization."

12. On development as imperial practice, see Escobar, *Encountering Development.*

13. See Adeeb Khalid, this volume, for a consideration of "where empire ends and other forms of nonrepresentative or authoritarian policy begin."

14. Cooper, "Empire Multiplied: A Review Essay," 247.

15. For one effort to establish working definitions of imperialism and colonialism, see Osterhammel, *Colonialism.*

16. Stoler and McGranahan, this volume.

17. Partha Chatterjee, *Nationalist Thought and the Colonial World, Nation and Its Fragments,* and "Empire and Nation Revisited."

18. Partha Chatterjee, "Empire and Nation Revisited," 495–96: "There have been in history only two forms of imperial pedagogy—a pedagogy of violence and a pedagogy of culture. The colony must either be disciplined by force or educated ('civilized') by culture."

19. See Hardt and Negri, *Empire,* for a counterargument, specifically that empire is now in service to a global, hybrid, democratic network dissociated from singular nations or territories.

20. Stoler and McGranahan, this volume.

21. On dissociated histories of empire, see also Coronil, this volume, and Stoler and McGranahan, this volume.

22. Richards, *Imperial Archive.*

23. On this period, see McGranahan, "Empire and the Status of Tibet."

24. See G. N. Curzon's outlining of the "forward" policy in his *Frontiers.* For a history of this British policy in the Tibetan context, see McKay, *Tibet and the British Raj.*

25. The Chinese government, however, vociferously claimed that this was a legally binding document. For a discussion of these competing claims, see Shakya, *Dragon in the Land of Snows.*

26. "Local government" is a Chinese communist term used to refer to the Tibetan government in Lhasa. Prefacing *government* with *local* is intended to displace other possible (and less desirable) modifiers, such as *national* or *state,* which might imply a Tibetan polity distinct from that of China.

27. The United States did not start a global campaign to win Tibetan hearts and minds until relatively late. The two countries first had diplomatic contact in 1942, when President Roosevelt dispatched two Office of Strategic Services (OSS) officers on a covert mission to Tibet. Strong US relations with China (i.e., Chiang Kai-shek's Republican China) meant an acknowledgement of Chinese proprietary sentiment toward Tibet but also an awareness that (1) Chinese officials held multiple opinions on Tibet, and (2) Tibet was an independently functioning government

at the time. As President Y. P. Mei of Yengching University (and also Tibetology professor Li An-che) explained to US consular officials in Chengdu, "any attempt to extend Chinese control over Tibet by force would be bitterly resented by the Tibetans"; see "The Charge in China (Atcheson) to the Secretary of State, September 20, 1943," in *Foreign Relations of the United States,* 639. Thus, while Roosevelt addressed the Dalai Lama as a religious rather than secular leader, OSS officers Ilya Tolstoy and Brooke Dolan traveled to Lhasa via India with no mediation by or discussion with the Chinese. This first contact set the tone for all future US–Tibetan relations as secretive and cautious.

28. For a discussion of the simultaneity of these events, see Shakya, *The Dragon in the Land of Snows,* 43

29. Rai, *Rule of Sympathy.*

30. On post–World War II decolonization, see Chamberlain, *Longman Companion to European Decolonization;* Duara, *Decolonization;* Le Sueur, *Decolonization Reader;* Louis, *Imperialism at Bay;* Louis and Robinson, "Imperialism of Decolonization"; and Springhall, *Decolonization since 1945.*

31. On China's imperial and expansionist histories (especially the Qing), see Bulag, *Mongols at China's Edge;* Cohen, *Discovering History in China;* Hostetler, *Qing Colonial Enterprise;* Millward, *Beyond the Pass;* Perdue, this volume, and *China Marches West;* and Teng, *Taiwan's Imagined Geography.*

32. We would also do well to consider that capitalism has never been entirely absent from socialism; elements of capitalism flow through the socialist system, even if only in the recoil of a response in earlier decades or in a more direct current postsocialist form. Nonetheless, for both periods, we need to consider how the socialist state might also be colonial and imperial in certain places and times.

33. In Marxist–Leninist thought, the "briefest possible definition of imperialism... is the monopoly stage of capitalism," or more specifically, "imperialism is that stage of capitalism at which the dominance of monopolies and finance capital is established; in which the export of capital has acquired pronounced importance; in which the division of the world among the international trusts has begun, in which the divisions of the territories of the world among the biggest capitalist powers has been completed." Lenin, *Imperialism.*

34. Wang, "Tibet Facing Imperialism of Two Kinds."

35. Cohn, *Colonialism and Its Forms of Knowledge;* Dirks, *Colonialism and Culture.*

36. I take my inspiration here from Ulysse, "I Came of Age Colonized Now My Soul Is Tired and I Am Feeling All This Rage."

37. Goldstein, Sherap, and Siebenschub, *Tibetan Revolutionary.*

38. On Han chauvinism, see Gladney, *Dislocating China;* Harrell, *Cultural Encounters on China's Ethnic Frontiers;* and Louisa Schein, "Gender and Internal Orientalism in China."

39. Indeed, categorizing either the People's Republic of China or the United States as an empire in the present remains subject to debate. While the issues animating these debates are different, I submit that the reasons for the debates are similar, specifically issues of category and strategy. For a counterperspective on the United States as empire, see Kelly, "U.S. Power, after 9/11 and before It."

40. See US Department of State documents pertaining to Tibet in the 1960s (e.g., the Foreign Relations of the United States series).

41. Ho, "Empire through Diasporic Eyes," 228.

42. See Burnett and Marshall, *Foreign in a Domestic Sense;* Dunbar-Ortiz, "Grid of History"; Gill, *School of the Americas;* Go and Foster, *American Colonial State in the Philippines;* Joseph, Legrand, and Salvatore, *Close Encounters of Empire;* Kaplan and Pease, *Cultures of United States Imperialism;* Ryan and Pungong, *United States and Decolonization;* and Stoler, "Tense and Tender Ties," and *Haunted by Empire.*

43. Brennan, "From Development to Globalization"; Louis and Robinson, "Imperialism of Decolonization"; Lutz, "Empire Is in the Details" and *Homefront;* Steinmetz, "Return to Empire."

44. Ho, "Empire through Diasporic Eyes." On the invisibility *and* visibility of empires, see Stoler, "Imperial Formations and the Opacity of Rule" and "On Degrees of Imperial Sovereignty."

45. Stoler, "Rethinking Colonial Categories."

46. Thongchai, *Siam Mapped.*

47. On Nepali Gurkha soldiers in the British and Indian armies, see Caplan, *Warrior Gentleman;* Mary DesChene, "Relics of Empire."

48. In keeping with Tibetan convention, I reserve the singular name Pangdatsang for Rapga's older brother, Yamphel, the family head. I refer to Rapga Pangdatsang as he was and is referred to by his contemporaries, as either Pangda Rapga or simply Rapga.

49. Goldstein, *History of Modern Tibet.*

50. In 1975 scholars Samten Karmay and Heather Stoddard interviewed Rapga at his home in Kalimpong; see Stoddard's *Le Mendiant d'Amdo.* See also McGranahan, "In Rapga's Library."

51. Stoddard *Le Mendiant d'Amdo.*

52. India Office Record, London, British Library: L/P+S/12/4211 No. 36, File 39(1) Tibet: Chinese Intrigues (Rapga), Hopkinson to Foreign New Delhi, April 29, 1946.

53. In an interesting but perhaps not surprising parallel, this in-between status under the Raj has remained the same for Tibetan refugees in India since 1959. As India has not signed any UN conventions on refugees, the status of the Tibetan community in India has remained individually negotiated between the Dalai Lama's exile government and the government of India, from the rule of Jawaharlal Nehru up to the present day. At present, the overwhelming majority of Tibetans in India are not citizens but have Indian-designated refugee status.

54. On dilemmas of residing outside the law, see Agamben, *Homo Sacer,* and Das and Poole, "State and Its Margins."

55. Ong, *Flexible Citizenship.* See also Inda, "Flexible World," for an extension of Ong's argument to nonelite or "everyday" communities.

56. India Office Records, London, British Library: L/P+S/12/4211 No. 36, File 39(1), document 41, "Pleader's advice re: my departure from India."

57. India Office Records, London, British Library: L/P+S/12/4211 no. 36, file 39(1), "G. C. L. Crichton, Joint Secretary to the Government of India to the Chinese commissioner, New Delhi."

58. See Stoler, "In Cold Blood."

59. Sources for this period in Tibetan history are erratic. Tibetan-language sources (inside and outside Tibet) are still surfacing or being approved for release, although many remain inaccessible for political reasons. Chinese-language sources are highly restricted, as are Indian archival sources (given that any documents having to do with India's borders are censored). In contrast, British colonial archives offer easy access and have thus been well trodden by scholars of Tibet.

60. On China's "civilizing mission" among non-Han Chinese peoples across time, see the collected essays in Harrell, *Cultural Encounters on China's Ethnic Frontiers.*

61. On this period in China and the continuing evolution of Chinese-style socialism, see MacFarquhar, *Politics of China, 1949–1989.*

62. On these points, see Borneman, "State, Anthropological Aspects"; Hansen and Stepputat, "Introduction: States of Imagination"; Trouillot, "Anthropology of the State in the Age of Globalization"; and Weldes and others, *Cultures of Insecurity.*

63. On the prescriptive nature of power under the Chinese communist state, see Anagnost, "Constructing the Civilized Community," 354.

64. On Tibet–Qing relations, see Hevia, "Lamas, Emperors, and Rituals"; Kolmas, *Tibet and Imperial China;* Petech, *China and Tibet in the Early XVIIIth Century;* and Sperling, "Awe and Submission."

65. Diamond, "Miao and Poison"; Makley, "On the Edge of Respectability"; Schein, *Minority Rules.*

66. On Mao as icon, see Hubbert, "(Re)Collecting Mao."

67. These questions have long animated colonial studies, from the early work of Taussig, "Culture of Terror," to the recent essays in Stoler's *Haunted by Empire.*

68. On this point, see the collected essays in Cooper and Stoler, *Tensions of Empire.*

69. For a skillful analysis of Tibetan interpretations of Chinese truths, see Makley, "'Speaking Bitterness.'"

70. Three first-person exile narratives of this period are Jamyang Norbu, *Warriors of Tibet;* Pachen and Donnelly, *Sorrow Mountain;* and Tapontsang, *Ama Adhe.*

71. For a history of the founding of the Tibetan guerrilla army, see McGranahan, "Tibet's Cold War."

72. *Rebirth of the Tibetan People* does not have page numbers, but this stock phrase is found throughout the text. For one representative example, see the "Editor's Comment" at the beginning of the text.

73. Louis and Robinson, "Empire Preserv'd," 161.

74. Klein, *Cold War Orientalism,* 16.

75. Interview with Tony Poe, San Francisco, December 17, 1999.

76. Indeed, as many veterans have explained to me, some resistance members considered the resistance army, the Tibetan government in exile, and the US government to be equal partners in the struggle for Tibet in the 1960s.

77. Histories of the CIA and Tibetan resistance army include Conboy and Morrison, *CIA's Secret War in Tibet;* Knaus, *Orphans of the Cold War;* McGranahan, "Truth, Fear, and Lies" and "Tibet's Cold War"; and Tsering, *bsTan rgol rgyal skyob.*

78. In 1961 a Tibetan resistance team captured a PLA commander's pouch. It contained invaluable and otherwise unavailable classified information about the successes and failures of the Chinese Communist Party in Tibet and throughout the PRC. I tell the story of the documents in McGranahan, *Tibet's Cold War.*

79. *Questions Pertaining to Tibet,* 337. Memorandum for the Special Group

(January 9, 1964), 731 (from Department of State, INR Historical Files, Special Group Files, S.G. 112, February 20, 1964. Secret; Eyes Only).

80. One scholar who has repeatedly directed attention to this connection is A. Tom Grunfeld in, for example, *Making of Modern Tibet.* Grunfeld's argument, however, is not congruent with mine: where he contends that the US–Tibetan connection reveals the compromised position of the Tibetan exile government, my argument is that we must understand this relationship as part of broader US geopolitical imperial policies that complicate and influence but do not necessarily compromise Tibetan governmental decision making.

81. To be clear, the issue for the soldiers at the time (and for many of them at present) was independence from China, not genuine autonomy within China. While the Dalai Lama currently supports autonomy rather than independence, many (if not most) Tibetans in exile continue to desire independence.

82. I am unaware if any of these texts are extant (or perhaps, more accurately, remain hidden) in Tibet or in the veterans' community in India and Nepal. At present, none of the texts are in the public domain. For access to these texts, I am grateful to a retired CIA officer.

83. "A Pleasure Garden," 1.

84. "A Pleasure Garden," 6–7.

85. "A Pleasure Garden," 7–8.

86. "A Pleasure Garden," 8.

87. "A Pleasure Garden," 9–11.

88. "A Pleasure Garden," 11–12.

89. "A Pleasure Garden," 13–14.

90. On the United States and "circuits of knowledge production" in its imperial domains, see the collected essays in Stoler, *Haunted by Empire.*

91. On public secrets, see Taussig, *Defacement.* See also McGranahan, "Truth, Fear, and Lies."

92. Steel, *Pax Americana,* quoted in Foster and McChesney, *Pox Americana,* 7.

93. Foster, "New Age of Imperialism," 165.

94. From President Sukarno's opening address at the Asian-African Conference in Bandung in 1955, as cited in Chatterjee, "Empire and Nation Revisited," 487.

95. I borrow the term "wide-angle view of empire" from Morillo-Alicea, "Uncharted Landscapes of 'Latin America,'" 27.

96. For similar approaches that also extend beyond European empires, see the collected essays in Stoler's *Haunted by Empire,* and Ballantyne and Burton, *Bodies in Contact.*

97. William Appleman Williams, *Empire as a Way of Life.*

98. Kaplan, "'Left Alone with America,'" 14. See also Lutz, *Homefront,* for an excellent treatment of the domestic side of US military imperialism.

99. Wang, "Tibet Facing Imperialism of Two Kinds."

100. Hillman, "Paradise under Construction."

101. For a range of arguments on this point, see Barlow, "Colonialism's Career in Postwar China Studies"; Coronil, "Beyond Occidentalism"; Hevia, *English Lessons;* and Mignolo, *Local Histories/Global Designs.*

102. Mignolo, *Local Histories/Global Designs,* 37. See also Chatterjee, *Nationalist Thought and the Colonial World* and *Nation and Its Fragments.*

103. Mignolo, *Local Histories/Global Designs,* 44.

7

The Imperialism of "Free Nations"

Japan, Manchukuo, and the History of the Present

Prasenjit Duara

As the editors of this volume stress, we would be hard-pressed to find an imperialism or empire that operated in a historical vacuum without reference to other imperial practices and ideas circulating since at least the early modern era. Meiji (1868–1912) Japanese imperialism was shaped by two historical forces: modern Western imperialist nationalism and the historical circumstances, models, and ideas of the East Asian region. These two currents produced a schizoid Japanese self-perception. Anxious nationalists eager to gain recognition from the Western powers by creating an empire in the contiguous region, the Japanese leadership also felt victimized by these very powers and identified with its weaker "Asiatic brethren." This generated a highly contradictory imperialism that shaped the fate of the East Asian region in the early twentieth century.

Interestingly, this contradiction spurred Japanese imperialists to experiment with new forms of empire drawn from diverse global and regional sources; such experimentation crystallized in Manchukuo, the Japanese puppet state established in northeast China from 1932 until 1945. I argue that Manchukuo was the first full-blown instance of what

I call the "new imperialism"—an imperialism rooted in the historical circumstances of the United States, the Soviet Union, and Japan, rather than in those of the older European colonial powers. I have also called this new imperialism the imperialism of "free nations" after the well-known "imperialism of free trade" coined by Ronald Robinson and John Gallagher to describe the British empire over fifty years ago.

According to Robinson and Gallagher, while formal colonial empires tended to dominate the world and our understandings of imperialism after the late nineteenth century, the broader and older tendency was represented by the imperialism of free trade. British policy applied formal controls only when it was not possible to safeguard and extend British interest through informal control. Eventually, it was the foreign challenge to British dominance in tropical Africa in the late nineteeth century and the inability to create strong and supportive indigenous political organizations there that made it impossible for the British to conduct "imperialism on the cheap" and led them to switch to modes of direct control and formal rule.[1]

The new imperialism (the imperialism of "free nations") that evolved through much of the twentieth century is to be distinguished both from the earlier European colonial imperialism and free trade imperialism in several ways. While the new imperialists maintained ultimate control of their dependencies or clients through military subordination, they often created or maintained legally sovereign nation-states with political and economic structures that resembled their own. The new imperialists espoused anticolonial ideologies and emphasized cultural or ideological similarities; they made considerable economic investments, even while exploiting these regions, and attended to the modernization of institutions and identities. In other words, these imperialist formations were not founded in principle upon the sustained differentiation between rulers and ruled characteristic of most colonial formations; nor were they founded upon a general indifference toward political forms—as long as they were pliable—so characteristic of free trade imperialism.

The new imperialism reflected a strategic conception of the periphery as part of an organic formation designed to attain global supremacy for the imperial power. Although subordinate states were militarily dependent on the metropole, it was not necessarily in the latter's interest to have them economically or institutionally backward. Thus this imperialism occasionally entailed a separation of economic and military/political dimensions. In some situations, as in the Soviet Union–Eastern Europe and the Japan–Manchukuo relationships, massive investments and resources flowed into the client states, thereby breaching the classical dualism between an industrialized metropole and a colony focused on the primary sector. In this way, too, my conception of the new imperialism differs from theories of neocolonialism, which continue to emphasize underdevelopment and traditional forms of exploitation.

Another aspect of this new imperialism, and one that distinguished it still more from the imperialism of free trade, was its tendency to form a regional or (geographically dispersed) bloc formation promoting economic autarky as a means for the imperial power to gain global supremacy or advantage. In this formation, while benefit to the metropole continues to be the rationale for domination, benefit does not necessarily derive from transferring primary wealth to it but often entails the industrialization of the puppet or client state. Thus the new imperialism was related to the principle of nationalism that extends the benefits and pains of creating an integrated, globally competitive entity but extends them *unevenly* over the whole. By the same token, the imperial formation is often ripped apart by enduring nationalist prejudices fostered in earlier times and simultaneous processes of nation building, especially within the imperial metropole.

ANTI-IMPERIALISM AND IMPERIALISM IN THE INTERWAR PERIOD

The emergence of anti-imperialist *nationalism* represented, of course, one of the most important conditions for the transformation of imperialism. The end of World War I, as is well known, introduced epochal changes that made the world the stage of history in the twentieth century. No longer could the world be made to appear, in the words of Oswald Spengler, to "revolve around the pole of this little part-world" that is Europe.[2]

Anti-imperialist nationalism, sanctioned by the still emergent global powers, the United States and the Soviet Union, grew out of a brew of two new global ideologies: socialistic egalitarianism and the discourse of multiple civilizations. Virtually all the significant thinkers of the new nationalisms espoused some combination of these ideals to create nationalisms that could claim to be fundamentally different from the prewar social Darwinist ideology of imperialist nationalism. Socialistic ideas provided both a critique of imperialism and a powerful model of social justice and resource redistribution. At the same time, they also entailed, through the model of a party-state, new structures of mobilization and surveillance that were continuous with the competitive nationalisms of central Europe and the older nation-states.

Socialistic ideas came to be intertwined in many cases with a new conception of civilization. The nineteenth-century imperialistic idea that Civilization was a singular phenomenon closely associated with the European Enlightenment had served to colonize the non-European world by denying rights and sovereignty to people without Civilization (and/or History). The unequal treaties contracted in East Asia, for instance, were based on this premise. The Japanese and Chinese spent considerable energy revamping their societies and institutions in order to renegotiate these treaties as "civilized" societies. Nonetheless, an alternative discourse of civilization as multiple, spiritual, and moral—as opposed to materialistic and legalist—that had survived in the penumbra of the singular Civilization received an important fillip toward the end of the war. The rise of this alternative conception accompanied the global critique of the "civilizing mission," which was seen by the colonized and many Western intellectuals—such as Arnold Toynbee—to be a fig leaf for the barbarism of European civilization demonstrated by the war. Western Civilization had forfeited the right to represent the highest goals of humanity, and the new national movements sought to turn toward their own civilizational traditions—often reconstructed in the image of Civilization—to found the ideals of the new nations and the right to sovereignty.[3]

Anti-imperialist nationalism attained a new height in East Asia with the March 1919 protest against colonialism in Korea and the May Fourth Movement in China in the same year.[4] While both movements were directed against Japanese imperialism, ironically, the Japanese also began to develop an anti-(Western) imperialist civilization discourse of pan-Asianism. Japanese nationalism originated under the threat of Western imperialism and racism; events such as US immigration laws denying naturalization to Japanese and other Asians in 1922 and leading to final exclusion in 1924, and the denial of naval parity to Japan by the United States and Britain in the Washington Conference hardened this self-perception. Thus Japanese nationalists tended to see themselves as victims of Western imperialism and racism even while building their own empire and brand of racist nationalism.

Sensitive to the scrutiny of the West, at certain historical moments Japanese empire builders tended to take the rhetoric of new empire seriously. At another level, they were bound by the pan-Asian rhetoric of common victimhood that became intertwined with the development of a contiguous empire (in part because of security concerns) in a region occupied by people whom the Japanese perceived as culturally or racially continuous with themselves. Thus while Japanese imperialism targeted East Asian societies, ideologically it sought to incorporate them through ideas of pan-Asian brotherhood. It is, I believe, less fruitful to view this ideology simply as a smoke screen than as a highly contradictory ideology of the new imperialism in which domination and exploitation coexisted with development and modernization.

Of course, historically, modern imperialism had always been closely identified with nation-states. From a world-systems perspective, capitalism was a product of competition between states for global resources: the more sophisticated versions of this theory eschew simple economic arguments. According to Giovanni Arrighi, the creation and maintenance of global capitalism was made possible by the fusion of "two logics," territorial and capitalist. Competition among states in the early modern period entailed the capture of mobile capital for territorial and population control, and the control of territories and people for the purposes of mobile capital. Beginning in the seventeenth century, the territorial state (possessing absolute jurisdiction within its boundaries and growing military and organizational capabilities) became necessary to control the social and political environment of capital accumulation on a world scale. In Arrighi's scheme, the hegemonic power in the competitive system of European states—Dutch power in the seventeenth and eighteenth centuries, British power in the nineteenth—was successively challenged by latecomer territorial states that sought, in the drive to become globally competitive, to first mobilize the economic and human resources within their own jurisdictions, thus producing some aspects of nationalism. Immanuel Wallerstein was more explicit, declaring that nationalism became the means whereby a state or social formation sought to leverage itself out of the periphery of the world system and into the core.[5]

From the late nineteenth century, the mobilization of human resources for competition in the name of the nation became very significant. Nationalism was deployed to rally the population and resources for war preparation and for the war itself. State-administered mass organizations to mobilize civilian support for war were first developed by states such as Japan, the Soviet Union, and Italy, which were not principals in World War I but observed the insufficiency of civilian support during the war. Japanese planners saw the need to prepare for a long-term economic war by mobilizing resources over an area that went beyond the Japanese empire. Mass organizations in competitor nation-states were developed along the model of a conscript army and were elevated rhetorically to represent the will of the people. In this way they would call on the people to transcend immediate and particular interests, such as forgoing personal consumption or delegitimizing striking workers within the nation.

To be sure, one can hardly explain the rise of nationalism during this period by global competition alone. Several other factors, having to do with the emergence of industrial society and its needs, competitive democratic politics, and the spread of mass communications, featured significantly in the emergence of nationalism. These factors appeared to have combined with the drive for global competition to shift the balance in the functional relationship between imperialism and nationalism in the world. If during the nineteenth century, as Eric Hobsbawm and Hannah Arendt have argued, imperialism was largely the business of competitive nation-states and nationalism was mobilized to further their interests, by the twentieth century *nationalism had become the driving force behind imperialism.* Arendt commented that imperialists appeared as the best nationalists because they claimed to stand above the reality of national divisiveness and represent the glory of the nation. While nationalism represented the incentive of glorious recognition to drive global competition, it also entailed the granting of the rights of citizenship and the obligations of discipline to enable the nation-state to transform itself into a sleek competitive body. In the process, imperialism not only became an important goal for some nationalisms, it also became an important means of the formation of this nationalism.[6]

Nationalist principles became still more deeply implicated with imperialism in the intensifying competitive environment. Responding to this heightened—including military—competition, several imperial formations sought to organize colonies into relatively autarchic regional structures or economic blocs. In Britain and France, the value of empire for military competitive purposes was not fully recognized until World War I, when colonial troops and resources played a vital role. In Britain, Joseph Chamberlain's neomercantilist ideas of colonial development (which had been largely ignored before the war) and "imperial preference" began to be taken more seriously. But as a consequence of entrenched ideas of colonial self-sufficiency, postwar capital needs at home, and, not least, demands for protection by British industry, only once before 1940 did expenditure on colonial development creep above 0.1 percent of British gross national product.[7]

The post–World War I transformation of French attitudes toward the colonies is summed up in Albert Lebrun's words that the goal was now to "unite France to all those distant Frances in order to permit them to combine their efforts to draw from one another reciprocal advantages."[8] But while the French government extended imperial preference and implemented reforms, particularly with reference to legal and political rights in Africa during the 1930s, investments in economic and social development projects were insignificant until the creation of the Investment Fund for Economic and Social Development in 1946. Both evolutionist ideas of backward races (and their incapacity for modernity) and protectionist pressures from agrarian society served as impediments to development.[9]

To compete with Britain and France, Germany had sought to develop a regional bloc in central and eastern Europe since the end of the nineteenth century.[10] This trend accelerated during the interwar years, and German commercial influence before the war peaked in 1938, when Austria was incorporated into the Reich and Hitler annexed the Sudeten region of Czechoslovakia. Hannah Arendt regarded the German (and Russian pan-Slav) movement as an expression of "continental imperialism" whereby latecomer nationalists sought to develop their empires through the nationalistic pan-German movement.[11] This racist ideology seemingly authorized the Germans to annex or dominate territories belonging to other states. At the same time, Nazi racism excluded such large numbers of people that even the rhetoric of anti-imperialism or solidarity of cultures was made impossible.

The German economic New Order in Europe, built upon states that were essentially German puppets or had German military governors, was designed to supply the German war effort. However, there were also plans to build an economic region around a prosperous Germany linked to new industrial complexes in central Europe and captured areas of the western USSR. This unitary European market, however, remained a nationalistic German vision—and we should be wary of seeing it as a predecessor of the European Union. The German plan represented in several ways no more than an aborted version of the new imperialism.[12]

The Japanese economic bloc, built throughout the 1930s and intensified during the Pacific war, resembled the German New Order in that the entire occupied zone became subordinated to Japanese war needs, and Japan's defeat represented a failure of the new imperialism. Still, Japan's initial experience with Manchukuo reveals the lineaments of a more functional version of the new imperialism, not entirely driven by wartime needs though often representing a preparation for war. Moreover, beginning especially in the 1930s, after the establishment of Manchukuo, the Japanese exploitation of colonies such as Korea was accompanied by increases in productive capacity. As the Korean economist Sub Park has demonstrated, while Indian growth between 1900 and 1946 was under 1 percent annually, the yearly mean growth rate of gross domestic production in Korea was 3 percent from 1915 to 1940.[13] The accumulated per-capita British investment in India and Japanese investment in Korea were eight dollars and thirty-eight dollars, respectively, in 1938.[14]

Given the common global climate, how and why did Japanese colonial policy become more oriented toward economic development than European colonial policy did? Pan-Asianism had emerged as an ideology incorporating Japan's curious role as both victim and victimizer in the imperialist game, and that ideology permitted the Japanese the conceit that Japan was obliged to lead the Asian nations against the

West. Such claims were, however, belied by the vigorous nationalism of Asian peoples against the Japanese. In response to this complicated scenario, Japanese colonial bureaucrats, military officers, and intellectuals began to experiment with modes of association and alliance that would reinvent empire and nation.

MANCHURIA AND JAPANESE IMPERIALISM

Manchuria, or what the Chinese refer to now simply as the northeast, was rapidly settled by Han Chinese from northern China from the latter half of the nineteenth century. This settlement represented the reversal of the ruling Manchu regime's earlier policy of keeping Han Chinese out of their ancestral homeland and was in response to Russian and Japanese imperialist penetration of the region. The Lytton Commission, which was assigned the responsibility of investigating the Japanese puppet state in this region, declared that Manchuria was "unalterably Chinese." It should be noted that this was largely a consequence of the demographic and cultural integration that took place in the first half of the twentieth century, when 80 percent of the population came to be Chinese, and not because of some primordial or age-old Chinese claim to this region. However, despite this settlement, Manchuria remained a contested borderland; whereas in earlier periods Chinese dominance was challenged by Manchus, Mongols, and others, the challenge in the modern period came first from the Russians and then from the Japanese.

From early in the Meiji period, Japanese imperialism was justified by nationalism, and mainland northeast Asia was characterized as the outer zone of national defense against the advancing Euro-American powers. Japanese expansionism in northeast Asia during the first three decades of the twentieth century was accompanied by the rhetoric that Korea, Manchuria, and Mongolia represented the "lifeline" of the Japanese nation. The Treaty of Portsmouth that concluded the Russo–Japanese War of 1904–1905, while acknowledging in theory China's sovereignty in Manchuria, granted Japan the Russian lease on the Kwantung Peninsula and the South Manchurian Railroad. From this time, Japanese interests and influence grew, particularly after the annexation of Korea in 1910 and during the imperialist power vacuum in East Asia during World War I.[15]

The economic and political affairs of the Japanese-leased territories were managed by the Kwantung government and the South Manchurian Railway Company, a quasi-governmental corporation with many subsidiary enterprises and one of the largest research organizations in the world until 1945. Japanese investment in the South Manchurian Railway Company in 1920 alone was 440 million yen. By 1927, 85 percent of Japanese foreign investment was in China, and of its Chinese investments, 80 percent was in Manchuria. In 1932, Japan's share of the total industrial capital in Manchuria was 64 percent, while the Chinese share was 28 percent.[16]

As early as the 1920s, the Japanese controlled Manchuria economically and militarily by means of an unstable alliance with the warlord of the region, Zhang Zuolin. Each party had its own reasons for the alliance. Zhang's desire to control Beijing increasingly militated against Japanese interests in Manchuria, whereupon the Japanese murdered Zhang. Zhang's son and successor, Zhang Xueliang, was, however, even more China-directed and declared his allegiance to the Kuomintang. It was under these circumstances that elements in the Kwantung army overthrew the Zhang regime on September 18, 1931, and established the puppet state of Manchukuo in 1932.

Until recently, Manchukuo was thought to represent a break in Japanese imperial policy. In this scenario, the Japanese government in the 1920s sought through diplomacy to secure concessions from imperial powers and subject nations such as China. The September 18 Manchurian Incident was considered a new turn because onsite army officers took the initiative and presented the Japanese government with a fait accompli.[17] This event may be seen as the first in a sequence of faits accomplis in the 1930s, enabling the military to take over the civilian government in Japan and ultimately leading Japan into the China war (1937), the Pacific war (1941), and ignominious defeat.

But recent scholarship has changed this account of events in several ways. First, while military officers, with or without the tacit approval of higher authorities, did present the Japanese government with imperialist faits accomplis, there was enormous popular support mobilized for their actions. After fifty years of steady and forceful nation building, by the 1920s Japanese nationalism had developed a life of its own, not fully within state control. The emergent mass media and various social and political organizations such as labor unions, political parties, and social associations were infused with high nationalist—and imperialist—sentiments that military officers could and did easily mobilize.[18] By the late 1920s, with the onset of the Depression, which affected Japanese farmers acutely, agrarian radicals, together with young disgruntled military officers—the Showa restorationists, who felt that capitalists, politicians, and bureaucrats had abandoned the true Bushido ("way of the warrior") spirit of Japan—catalyzed this popular nationalism and laid the conditions for support for imperial expansion.

Second, as Yoshihisa Matsusaka and others have pointed out, new imperialist ideas had been incubating, especially among members of the military stationed in the colonies and Manchuria since the last years of World War I. The primacy of diplomatic and multilateralist approaches of party governments during the 1920s kept these ideas out of the limelight, but several advocates of the new imperialism were busy experimenting with them in the 1920s, especially in Manchuria. The scale and duration of World War I convinced the Japanese military that the competition for global resources would be a long, drawn-out war for which Japan would need to be economically self-sufficient. Thus was born the idea of "strategic autarky," which entailed an entirely new conception of imperialism: the colony or dominated region was to be made structurally and organizationally amenable to imperialist intent by utilizing the principle of the nation-state and nationalism. Military analysts such as Major Koiso Kuniaki, who would later become chief of staff of the Kwantung army, conceived of resource mobilization within a regional rather than merely national framework. For Koiso, the idea of autarky implied an alliance: the Chinese would supply land, resources, and labor, and the Japanese would furnish technology and capital. He was mindful that a genuine autarky would involve some sacrifice of Japanese interests for the sake of the whole.[19]

With the growth of nationalism in these territories and the spread of pan-Asianist ideas among various Japanese groups in the 1920s, the conditions for regional control came to be seen, increasingly, to involve cooperation (or forced cooperation) with potential allies. Matsuoka Yosuke, who argued the Japanese case for the independence of Manchukuo from China at the League of Nations in 1933, best exemplified the strategy of the new imperialism. In the 1920s, when he served on the board of directors of the South Manchurian Railroad Company, he developed the idea of autarky by creating a relationship of dependent alliance with Zhang Zuolin; the Kwantung army at the time embraced Matsuoka's ideas. Through a series of loans for railroad construction and other projects, Matsuoka sought to transform Zhang's administration into a client state. At the same time, according to Tak Matsusaka, Matsuoka's vision transcended the old imperialist game of dealing with native allies merely to gain concessions and privileges. Rather, Matsuoka's goal was first to bring the regional government, principally through financial ties, firmly under Japanese control, and subsequently to pursue economic policies for developing Manchuria as a whole. Development was to take place not by excluding Chinese and others but by encouraging them to contribute to the prosperity of the region. The Japanese (who were presumed to be the principal actors and natural leaders of this effort), could only benefit from this general development.[20]

While the new imperialism was being tested in Manchuria, experimentation with strategies of colonial development also characterized the 1920s in Korea. The shock, to the Japanese, of the March 1919 nationalist uprisings in Korea was processed originally by academics, journalists, and colonial bureaucrats, and emerged as a policy called Cultural Rule. Cultural Rule was designed to produce cooperation between colonizer and colonized in economic and political matters. Characterized by slogans of "Japanese Korean joint rule" (*Nissen dōchi*) and doctrines of "coexistence and coprosperity" (*kyōson kyōei*), Cultural Rule was in many respects a failure: the Japanese would have had to give more autonomy to the Koreans than they were prepared to do. The new thinking in Japanese colonial discourse was driven, according to Michael Schneider, by middle-class professional and managerial classes keen to align Japanese colonialism with the norms of international modernization, respond to the rising nationalism of the colonized, and develop the colony within a wider program of regional integration and management under Japanese leadership. The policy of Cultural Rule was, as Schneider has said, "an attempt to fit Japanese colonialism into the new internationalism of the 1920s."[21]

In the aftermath of World War I, Japanese imperialism came to be rethought radically in the context of pan-Asianism, the new discourse of civilization that began at the time to burgeon in Japan and many other parts of the continent. Pan-Asianism also had a special meaning for Japanese nationalists and thinkers during the 1920s because of the growing perception that, despite Japan's effort to become a world-class nation-state (with colonies to boot), the Japanese continued to encounter racism and discrimination. Discrimination was perceived at the international conferences in Washington (1922) and at the London Naval Conference (1930), when Japan was allotted a lower quota of ships than the British and Americans. But most of all, it was the buildup of exclusionary policies in the United States and the final exclusion laws prohibiting Japanese immigration in 1924 that galled Japanese nationalists. In their view, Asian civilization did not exhibit inhuman racist attitudes and policies of this kind, and for militants such as Okawa Shūmei and his followers in the Kwantung army, these ingrained civilizational differences would have to be fought out in a final, righteous war of East against West.

In providing a moral explanation for wrongs inflicted upon Japan, pan-Asianist discourse also demanded empathy for the other exploited peoples of Asia, including those that Japan itself colonized. The ideas behind the cultural policy in Korea reflected, in theory, some of this empathy. During the 1920s, many intellectuals argued that Japanese and Koreans had the same ancestors, and this idea grew together with a theory of the mixed origins of the Japanese. Note that this expression of pan-Asianism led ultimately to the policies of assimilation of the Koreans (and Taiwanese) into the Japanese nation.[22] In Manchuria, pan-Asianism was expressed in a strategy not of assimilation and homogenization but of independence and alliance. Not only would it have stretched the contemporary imagination outrageously to argue that the Chinese and Japanese had the same origins, but the national movement and international opinion regarding the status of China was much too strong for the Japanese to seek to assimilate the Chinese in Manchuria, whom they insisted on calling Manchurians. Here pan-Asianism, expressed as shared Asian ideals and common history (especially against Western imperialism), spoke to the newconceptualization of global domination through regional autarky.

To achieve an industrial resource base in Manchuria, the Japanese military had to develop an alliance with key groups in this society, among the Chinese but also among the Japanese settler community on the Kwantung Peninsula. Accordingly, the military was compelled to champion the rhetoric of these allies, which included talk of a sovereign state. Ishiwara Kanji and his associates in the Kwantung army, Itagaki Seishiro and Doihara Kenji, recognized that they could ignore the new discourse of rights and autonomy only at their peril.[23] Pan-Asianism thus necessarily served as the basis of this alliance and "economic bloc."

Ishiwara Kanji (1889–1949) was perhaps most representative of the young radicals in the Japanese army who were fired by Japanese nationalist ideals and distrustful of the contemporary military and civilian leadership's commitment to achieve greatness at home and abroad. Ishiwara's nationalism was itself framed by an image of the inevitable confrontation between East and West. His nationalism also drew from a vision of militant Nichiren Buddhism, a protonationalistic millennialism that first developed in response to Mongol threats to the Japanese islands in the thirteenth century. In this vision, Japan was the center of the faith, and it was the duty of Japanese to propagate the faith in the world. Over time, this millennial vision in Ishiwara was overlain by a pan-Asianist view of the ultimate clash between East and West. The most articulate exponent of this view was Okawa Shūmei, a scholar of Hindu philosophy and a translator of the Koran who used the Hegelian dialectic to predict an ultimate battle of the civilizations of East and West. Under Okawa's influence, Ishiwara sought to blend his nationalism with this pan-Asian civilizational vision and proclaimed the necessity of cooperation with China and Manchuria under Japanese leadership for success in this holy war or righteous duty (*zhengyi, seigi*).[24]

Ishiwara and his colleagues who precipitated the Manchurian incident became committed to the formal equality of Asian nations and advocated the concord of nationalities in Manchukuo. Ishiwara found no contradiction between viewing the alliance as representing the supposed opposition between Asian ideals and Western imperialism and viewing it as a means in a final war for global dominance. He was among the few Japanese officers to oppose the military expansion into China in 1937. But Ishiwara's concern for more genuine partnership with the Chinese was pushed aside by higher levels of the military government, and he was put under surveillance by the military police after 1938.[25]

The idea of an autarkic Japan–Manchuria bloc was influenced by models of autarky in fascist Europe but was understood within the civilization discourse of pan-Asianism. By the mid-1930s, the bloc idea had helped to produce the East Asian League (*Tōa renmei*) and the East Asian Community (*Tōakyō dōtai*), and still later the Greater East Asian Co-prosperity Sphere (*Dai-Tōa Kyōeiken*). Indeed, figures associated with the propagation of these institutions were critical of Nazi theories of racial superiority and emphasized cooperation with the Chinese in a regional alliance under Japanese leadership.[26] To be sure, commitment to the idea of an alliance—and even to the notion that Japan should renounce extraterritoriality in Asian countries—was premised on a belief in intrinsic Japanese superiority and the need for Asian nations to accept Japanese leadership. Yet it is impossible to fully understand why the military encouraged the rapid modernization and industrial buildup in Manchuria without grasping the framework of pan-Asianism.

MANCHUKUO

In an earlier period, Manchukuo might have become a colony. But the new conceptualization of imperialism entailed that the might-have-been colony become more like a subordinate ally or client-state in global competition. The status of the dependent state under the new imperialism was quite fluid, in part because the rapidly changing demands of global competition could, depending on the circumstances, give it more leverage (as in the case of the relationship between postwar Hong Kong and Britain) or generate more resistance and further subordination. The status of Manchukuo over its fifteen-year history gradually shifted in official rhetoric from that of an independent nation-state—with Japan conceived as a friendly country (*youbang*) and ally (*mengbang*)—to that of a dependent kinsman, even a child or younger brother. In the end, the rhetoric used was Confucian: the language of the "family state" model of imperial Japan. By the time of the Pacific war, Manchukuo had become, in the words of its ambassador to Japan, Li Shaogeng, "the eldest son of the Greater East Asian Co-prosperity Sphere."

Pu Yi, the last Manchu emperor—who became first president and then emperor of Manchukuo—underwent a rebirthing ritual in 1940. He emerged from the womb of Amaterasu, the Shinto sun goddess and ancestor of the Japanese royal family, as the younger half brother of Hirohito, the Japanese emperor.[27] Ridiculous as this may sound to us (and as it did to the Chinese), it is fruitful to think of this ritual relationship as an innovation made possible by the theory of the mixed origins of the Japanese nation, a theory studied closely by Oguma Eiji. According to Oguma, a leading sociologist and historian of Japanese nationalism, the imperial family state ideology was able to incorporate this theory because it privileged the (modern) Japanese ideal of the *ie* or household, which unlike the lineage model could accept outsiders by adoption into the family: "In this system," Oguma writes, "as long as ancestors of the *ie* are linked to the current membership, blood is of secondary importance."[28] Becoming the younger brother of the emperor entailed, of course, a strictly dependent and subordinate status. Brotherhood in the Confucian understanding reflected a hierarchical relationship. In more modern rhetoric, brotherhood was often invoked instead to characterize egalitarian relationships: Sun Yat-sen used the slippage in this trope to rally secret fraternal societies (of the inegalitarian kind) while entering them in the historical record as at the core of revolutionary brotherhood (of the egalitarian kind).[29] The same slippage in the idea of brotherhood was also very important in pan-Asianism, and we might even say that brotherhood was the pivot that joined the hierarchical family state ideology with pan-Asianism.

Brotherhood, or more broadly the family relationship among East Asian peoples, implied sharing a mission regardless of one's preferences. It was the obligation of the patriarch or the older, dominant brother to create the ethos of the family, to form its enterprise, and to deliver the goods it promised. Japanese rhetoric did not fully develop this metaphor to embrace the relationship between Japan and Manchukuo, and the rhetoric always appeared somewhat contradictory, perhaps because of the continued lip service to the independence of Manchukuo. Nonetheless, by 1940 the family state model was utilized to characterize the relationship of citizen to state within Manchukuo: "National citizenship is the expanded version of family membership. Just as the family member has an obligation to obey the family unconditionally, so does the citizen have to obey the state."[30] Manchukuo was developed as an East Asian brother or son who set up a house modeled closely upon, but subordinate to, that of the Japanese patriarch. Practically, this structure meant using Chinese officials at all levels, including in the top administrative and political positions, but having their activities supervised by Japanese officials responsible ultimately to the Kwantung army.

Developing the family enterprise and delivering the goods amounted to creating the modern developmental state in Manchukuo, which emerged as the most industrialized part of Asia outside Japan. The Manchukuo banking system was reformed, and for the first time the currency of the region was unified. The new currency was made equivalent in value to the Japanese yen, which facilitated its integration into the yen bloc. There was a dramatic rise of Japanese investments, which, according to Louise Young, grew to almost six billion yen between 1932 and 1941 (in 1941 exchange rates)—a figure far greater than any other transfer from a metropole to a colony. By 1945, Japanese investment in Manchukuo exceeded the combined total of its investments in Korea, Taiwan, and the rest of China.[31] Industrial production tripled between 1933 and 1942, and producer goods output grew the fastest.[32] Considerable attention was also paid to the social infrastructure, at least in urban areas, including public health and education systems.[33] The new regime always touted these achievements as having reversed the decades of warfare and economic chaos perpetuated by the previous warlord government.

The rapid increase in industrial employment meant that despite some early efforts of the government to restrict immigration from China, Chinese continued to pour in and amounted to roughly 90 percent of the population of 40 million in the 1940s. Koreans came into Manchuria in large numbers from the 1920s, and their numbers reached almost 800,000 by 1935. The Japanese had a plan to bring five million Japanese settlers into Manchukuo, but the rural settler population never exceeded 250,000. In the mid-1930s, the total Japanese population was under 600,000.[34]

The other side of this development state was the brutality of an occupying army. The massacres of the resistance, the notorious human experiments with bacteriological toxins developed by Unit 731 in

Harbin, the dispossession of agricultural land from Chinese farmers, and other brutal crimes have been well recorded.[35] Manchukuo presents us, on the one hand, with a record of cruel violence and, on the other hand, with the record of a developmental state.

There is perhaps no better symbol of the antithetical structure of the modern state in Manchukuo than its police. Manchukuo's huge police force conducted punctiliously detailed censuses and surveys; made extensive and complex plans for settlements; paid close attention to hygiene and welfare; made available education, drinkable water, and shelters; and mobilized the population for inoculations—sometimes at gunpoint.[36] But there were many modern states characterized by this duality. What made Manchukuo different from Italy, Germany, the Soviet Union, or Japan was that it lacked the legitimacy of a nation. In a time when nation-states allegedly represented the "will of the people," the Manchukuo regime claimed instead to represent the essence of Asian culture.

The "kingly way" was presented as the ancient Chinese ideal of the just and moral ruler, a trope that Sun Yat-sen—widely regarded as the father of modern China and provisional president of the Republic of China in 1912—extended beyond Chinese civilization in a lecture on pan-Asianism delivered in Kobe, Japan.[37] In Manchukuo, the kingly way, related notions, and the example of the Manchu emperor were deployed as symbols of pan-Asian civilization, bringing together diverse groups who, whether by choice, opportunism, or necessity, came to support the new regime. These included many of the warlords and political leaders of the old society, dyed-in-the-wool Confucian monarchists, and, most numerously, the deeply religious and universalist redemptive societies. The followers of the redemptive societies in China and Manchuria included many millions, and while some were closely associated with sectarian traditions including the worship of Buddhist and folk deities, they mostly represented the late imperial syncretic tradition (*sanjiaoheyi*), which combined the three religions of Confucianism, Buddhism, and Daoism into a single universal faith. These societies had historically been persecuted by the Chinese state (both imperial and modern), and the Japanese in Manchuria sought to reach out to them. Tachibana Shiraki, architect of Manchukuo ideology, said that the redemptive societies exemplified the essence of Asiatic civilization and were amenable to mobilization as civic organizations.[38] Less easy to manipulate than the Japanese had hoped, these societies seized the opportunity to pursue their own goals: by the late 1930s, the Morality Society of Manchukuo claimed a membership of eight million out of a total population of forty million.[39]

The second legitimacy claim made by the puppet regime was that it represented the "concord of nationalities" (*minzoku kyōwa*), a conceit that was supposed to represent two advances over older colonial ideas. Not only was the concord supposed to reject exploitation and the reproduction of difference between ruler and ruled, but it was also designed to counter the homogenization of differences that nationalism had produced and that had led to nearly insoluble conflicts. By allegedly granting different peoples or nationalities their rights and self-respect under a state structure, Manchukuo presented itself as a nation-state in the mode of the Soviet "union of nationalities." Among others, Tominaga Tadashi, the author of *Manshūno minzoku* (*Nationalities of Manchuria*), wrote copiously about the early Soviet policy toward national self-determination. It was a policy that fulfilled the goals of federalism and protected minority rights while at the same time strengthening Soviet state and military power, particularly with regard to "separatists" in the old tsarist empire. Writing in the early 1940s, after the war machine was in full throttle and riding roughshod over niceties of nationality policy, Tominaga, like many others committed to Manchukuo, continued to warn and plead against repressing Asian nationalist movements. Recalling Soviet policy, he believed that these nationalities could be utilized positively for the goals of the state and were, indeed, the only hope for the Japanese empire.[40]

These constituencies of potential support were managed, maintained, and mobilized by the Concordia Association (Chinese: *xiehehui*, Japanese: *kyōwakai*), which was effectively the Manchukuo regime's party. But whereas in theory the association was to represent the will of the people and was ultimately destined to replace the Kwantung army, by mid-decade it was purged of its original leadership and made into an instrument of the army and government.[41] Less a means of ethnic, cultural, and occupational representation than of mobilization and surveillance, the Concordia Association closely resembled contemporary "totalitarian parties" in Europe. The leaders refrained from calling it a party precisely because the appellation smacked too much of partisanship. The association enrolled all officials and government functionaries, including teachers, as well as important figures in society. All youth between the ages of sixteen and nineteen were compulsorily enrolled beginning in 1937, and by 1943 the association included about 10 percent of the population (as compared to 5 percent for the Chinese Communist Party in the PRC today).

Like its fascist counterparts, the Concordia Association was corporatist, anticommunist, and anticapitalist and sought to overcome class divisions by organizing people through their communities, both occupational and ethnic, while promoting a dirigiste economy. But the association was distinctive in representing Asian communities—Mongols, Manchus, Hui Muslims, Koreans, Japanese, and white Russians (accounting for about 10 percent of the population), as well as the majority Chinese—and their traditions. This commitment often meant supporting the religious leadership among these peoples: Mongol lamas, Manchu and Daur shamans, Muslim *ahongs,* Buddhist monks, and Confucian moralists. The regime's control of local society was enhanced by the work of association units established within, for example, Manchu villages, Hui mosques, and the Chinese community self-surveillance system (*baojia*). Thus pan-Asianism came to play an important role in maintaining both the corporatist, fascistic character of the regime and its claim to legitimacy based upon adherence to the "kingly way."

At the same time, the Concordia Association had been founded to realize the modern goals of nation-state building (Chinese: *jianguo;* Japanese: *kenkoku*). Japanese ideologists like Tachibana saw no contradiction between the goals of republicanism, equality, and modernization, on the one hand, and the "Eastern" values of community, solidarity, and the moral state, on the other. After all, did not Japan exemplify a synthesis of the best of both worlds? In practice, however, the very different programs and interests pursued by modernizers and pan-Asianists led to many tensions and conflicts that leave us with a view of Manchukuo as a polarized rather than harmonious society. Mongol youth demanded modern education and the elimination of the power of the lamas; Chinese supporters were fiercely divided between those who favored the restoration of the emperor and those who opposed it. Propaganda activists were frustrated by their inability to mobilize redemptive societies for wartime work. The contradiction reflected in particular the tensions of an artificial nation-state dominated by an imperial power in an age of nationalism. The inability to construct a truly independent nation-state led Manchukuo to cling to constituencies that would have to be gradually overcome in the process of national modernization. As it was, the wildly ambitious Japanese imperialist military leadership derailed the entire process by plunging this carefully constructed state into a mad and destructive war.

CONCLUSION: TRAJECTORIES AND AFFINITIES

The Japanese domination of Manchukuo represented a new form of imperialism. As nationalism, rights consciousness, and social mobilization developed in the colonized and semicolonial world, the costs of direct colonial rule increased while the conditions for indirect rule were enhanced. With the creation of modern institutions in the military dependencies, it became possible to control these areas more economically by dominating their institutions of resource and social mobilization (such as banks, the transportation infrastructure, and the Concordia or redemptive societies). Japan, like the later Soviet Union and the United States, sought to bring its client-states into a structure of governance that not only permitted dominance but also integrated them into a regional, and ultimately global, game plan.[42]

As alluded to above, the Soviet Union's internal nationality policy, both through perception and influence, served as an instrument of control in Manchukuo. During the post–World War II era, the Soviet Union's creation of a regional system of militarily dependent states in eastern Europe reflected many features of the new imperialism. A shared anti-imperialist and anticapitalist ideology sanctioned a centralized economic and political system. The Soviet Union combined economic leverage and military threat to integrate states that were often more economically developed than itself into a regional economy. In some ways, the imperialism of the Soviet Union revealed the countereconomic consequences of this logic of empire. Not only were the client-states of the Soviet Union in Europe often more developed, the USSR may have been subsidizing their economies by supplying them with cheap oil and raw materials while importing finished products from their economies. This was the price paid by the imperial power to create and maintain dependence upon it and ensure its security.[43]

In part because of the consciousness of its own colonial past, and with the exception of a few places (most notably the Philippines), the United States had long practiced imperialism without colonialism. After the Spanish-American War in 1898, the United States created a system of client-states around the Caribbean basin in Central America. These nominally independent states became increasingly dependent on the United States, which accounted for more than three-fourths of the region's foreign trade as well as the bulk of foreign investment.[44] During the 1920s, when Japan was experimenting with indirect imperialism in Manchuria, the United States too was seeking to develop and refine informal control over Central American countries, especially as it faced anti-Yankee, and frequently revolutionary, nationalism in the region. Officials, diplomats, and business groups stressed means such as US control of banking and communication facilities, investments in natural resources, and the development of education—particularly the training of elites in American-style constitutions, "free elections," and orthodox business ideas. But the threat and reality of military intervention remained close at hand.[45]

Of course, American imperialism was characterized not only by the Monroe Doctrine but also by the Open Door Policy. Although there were contradictions and tensions between the two approaches, there were also continuities, most importantly in the practice of using sovereign or nominally sovereign polities to advance American interests. In 1917, Woodrow Wilson pointed to the continuities when he declared that the nations of the world should "with one accord adopt the doctrine of President Monroe as the doctrine of the world...no nation should seek to extend its polity over any other nation or people." But just two weeks before, Wilson had sent troops to the Dominican Republic and committed US military forces in Haiti and Mexico as well.[46] The United States sought to foster an ideological and economic hegemony among its client-states by creating them as reliable emulators subject to external economic and military constraints. Note, however, that this imperialism did not become developmentally oriented until the 1950s, when it sought to respond to the Cuban revolution.[47]

The tensions between American interests and global enlightenment were to be contained not only by military power but perhaps more importantly by the notion of a *limited* self-determination, the idea of tutelage. As Secretary of Interior Franklin Lane wrote in 1922, "what

a people hold they hold as trustees for the world. . . . It is good American practice. The Monroe Doctrine is an expression of it. . . . That is why we are talking of backward peoples and recognizing for them another law than that of self-determination, a limited law of self-determination, a leading-string law."[48] Little wonder then that the Japanese representative at the League of Nations hearings on Manchukuo repeatedly insisted on the Asiatic Monroe Doctrine as Japan's prerogative in Asia. Indeed, the tension between enlightenment and self-interest paralleled the same tension in Japanese pan-Asianism.

In the post–World War II period, this combination of interest, enlightenment, and military violence has developed into what Carl Parrini has called "ultraimperialism." The latter refers to US efforts to maintain cooperation and reduce conflict among imperialist nations who were busily scrambling to create monopolistic or exclusive market conditions in various parts of the world during the first half of the century.[49] Ultraimperialism is secured by a chain of military bases around the globe—and structures such as the International Monetary Fund, the General Agreement on Tariffs and Trade, and the World Bank—to enable the conditions of cooperation among advanced capitalist powers and to facilitate the new (developmental or modernizing) imperialism in the decolonized world.[50] Although the United States is hardly a regional power any longer, as a global empire it employs, in the words of Arrighi, Hui, Hung, and Selden, a vast system of "political and military vassalage" and fosters a "functional specialization between the imperial and vassal (*nation*) states." In this respect, the postwar United States represents the apogee of the imperialism of "free nations."[51]

Looking at Manchukuo comparatively, it is clear that its creators were influenced by both the United States and the Soviet Union and by German ideas of the economic bloc. But by an eclectic and adaptive mixing, Manchukuo also synthesized these ideas into the prototype of the developmental client-state within a new imperialist formation that could be found after World War II in eastern Europe, French Africa, the British sterling zone, and the US empire. The United States in particular favored the model of modernizing client nation-states centered on royal identity in Asia—witness Japan, Vietnam, Iran, Saudi Arabia, and others.

Despite the differences between this form of imperialism and the "classical" nineteenth-century forms, nationalists have emphasized the continuities between the "classical" and the clientelistic or dependent forms, and they have been right to note the lack of autonomy in both.[52] But does the ability of power holders to influence and manipulate institutions and rhetoric overwhelm the effects of new institutions and policies in changed domestic and international circumstances?

To be sure, Manchukuo remained a highly exploited society. For instance, rural society remained stagnant, largely because the landowning classes represented an important base of support for the regime. Chinese workers received less than a third of the wages paid to Japanese workers in state factories. The Manchukuo government and Japanese enterprises, which controlled 72 percent of total invested capital, made it hard for Chinese capital to penetrate the modern sector.[53] At the same time, the idea of strategic autarky necessitated the development of Manchukuo as a developmental state, with advanced technologies of economic growth, generating higher standards of urban life until the Pacific war.

In general, the state in Manchukuo was able to deploy modern technologies of control, surveillance, discipline, and mobilization among the populace. The regime and its affiliated organizations—such as the Concordia Association and the redemptive societies—penetrated people's lives to keep a stricter watch on them but also to generate new consciousness regarding, for instance, the proper nuclear family, consumer spending, engagement in afforestation programs, and other projects prioritized by the mobilizing state. If some of these projects were driven by the immediate needs of the metropole, others were driven by the logic of a modernizing state. Is it possible to think of Manchukuo as the beginning of an imperialism that culminates with Hong Kong in the sterling area? Or in Iraq?

The immediate factors behind the failure of Manchukuo had to do with its growing dependence on Japan and the role that it was forced to fill in the Japanese wartime empire. Indeed, the Manchukuo model of client-states was partially extended to regimes in occupied China and in Southeast Asia during the Pacific war. This regional imperial formation bent upon global domination was characterized by a set of interdependencies within an imperially dictated enterprise. A simple model of economic exploitation, utilizing existing modes of production and colonial difference, was to be supplemented (if not replaced) by high levels of investment, the development of new modes of mobilization and identity production, and a rhetoric of brotherhood and regional federalism. All of this came to naught with defeat.

Recently, some scholars have suggested that modern imperialism was tending to transform itself into a form of federalism. Anthony Pagden, who provides the most cogent version of this argument, believes that "it would be far wiser to look upon both the United States and the European Union as, in their very different ways, attempts to revive a federalist rather than an imperial object." Pagden traces his ideas to thinkers such as Joseph Schumpeter and Jean Monnet (credited with the idea of a "United States of Europe"). According to Pagden, the ages of conquest and commerce were, by the twentieth century, being replaced by a global order in which the eighteenth-century European idea of sovereignty was transferred from the nation-state to "something more amorphous: a modern, or postmodern, global society." At the base of this development was the idea of empire, which survived the competitive nationalisms of the nineteenth century, as an "extended protectorate" and in the words of Edmund Burke, a "sacred trust."[54]

Yet I think Pagden is far more sanguine about nationalism having basically been overcome, especially on the part of the imperial or "federating" power, than the historical record shows. Ultimately, the case of Manchukuo reveals the fault lines of the new imperialism. By pointing to the wartime emphasis on the fact that the Japanese were of mixed origins, Oguma Eiji has stressed the importance of assimilation over nationalist-racist elements within Japanese imperial ideology. Others, such as Komagome Takeshi, an expert on Japanese colonial education at Kyoto University, have persuasively argued that while Japanese imperialism reflected the extension of the principles underlying national integration, Japanese nationalism was a contradictory affair composed not only of the principle of common language and culture (or civilization) but also of "blood descent." Whereas language and culture created possibilities of integrating the colonized based on assimilation or alliance, historically the exclusionary principle of blood descent invented new ways—institutional, legal, or attitudinal—to circumvent the incorporation of non-Japanese in the empire as equal citizens.[55]

Imperialist competition in the first half of the twentieth century was catalyzed by a particular configuration of capitalism and nationalism. Although novel formations and ideals—then and now—have sought to transcend both capitalism and nationalism, the force of nationalist identity and interests from the earlier period have proved remarkably tenacious, particularly as they develop new linkages with competitive capitalism.[56] The globalization, cooperative economic blocs, and regional formations of our own time are not unprecedented developments—and the precedents are not encouraging.

Notes

1. Gallagher and Robinson, "Imperialism of Free Trade." The way I use "new imperialism" should be distinguished from the older historiographical term "new imperialism," which refers to the late nineteenth-century scramble for Africa and efforts to "slice the Chinese melon" that destabilized the imperialism of free trade. Creating nominally sovereign modern nation-states was not part of that imperialism or the imperialism of free trade.

2. Spengler, *Decline of the West,* 12.

3. Adas, "Great War and the Decline of the Civilizing Mission"; Duara, "Discourse of Civilization and Pan-Asianism."

4. The March 1, 1919, movement in Korea was a major nationalist demonstration against Japanese colonial rule and was inspired by Woodrow Wilson's ideal of the rights of self-determination by weak nations. Japanese authorities brutally crushed the movement. The same year in China, the May Fourth Movement was also an anti-imperialist demonstration. In that case, youthful students and workers responded to the failure of the signatories to the Treaty of Versailles to return German territories seized by Japan during World War I to China.

5. Arrighi, *Long Twentieth Century,* 34–58; Wallerstein, "Construction of Peoplehood," 81–82.

6. See Hobsbawm, *Nations and Nationalism since 1780,* 102, and Arendt, *Origins of Totalitarianism,* 152–53.

7. Constantine, *Making of British Colonial Development Policy,* 25, 276; Havinden and Meredith, *Colonialism and Development,* 148–59.

8. Quoted in Marshall, *French Colonial Myth,* 44.

9. Marshall, *French Colonial Myth,* 48, 224–26.

10. Eichengreen and Frankel, "Economic Regionalism," 97.

11. Arendt, *Origins of Totalitarianism,* 222–23.

12. See Overy, "World Trade and World Economy."

13. Park, "Exploitation and Development," 5.

14. Park, "Exploitation and Development," 19.

15. C. Walter Young, *International Relations of Manchuria,* 136–52.

16. McCormack, *Chang Tso-lin in Northeast China,* 7–8.

17. On September 18, 1931, the Japanese Kwantung army used the pretext of a bombing of the Japanese-controlled South Manchurian Railroad line near Mukden (now Shenyang) to militarily occupy Manchuria. In February 1932, Japan proclaimed the puppet state of Manchukuo.

18. Louise Young, *Japan's Total Empire,* 112.

19. Matsusaka, *Making of Japanese Manchuria,* 214–23.

20. Matsusaka, *Making of Japanese Manchuria,* 285.

21. Schneider, "Limits of Cultural Rule," 122.

22. Oguma, *Genealogy of "Japanese" Self-images,* 125–42.

23. Komagome, *Shokuminchi Teikoku Nihon no Bunka Tōgō,* 236–37.

24. Yamamuro, *Kimera: Manshūkoku no Shōzō,* 42–48.

25. Peattie, *Ishiwara Kanji and Japan's Confrontation with the West,* 167, 281, 335.

26. Morris-Suzuki, *Reinventing Japan,* 97–101.

27. Yamamuro's Kimera emphasizes the parent-child relationship between the Japanese emperor and Pu Yi, but the image of brotherhood was also current, even in the passages that Yamamuro himself cites: 261–64.

28. Oguma, *Genealogy of "Japanese" Self-images,* 337.

29. See Duara, *Rescuing History from the Nation,* ch. 4.

30. Kōmin, *Chianbu keisatsushi,* 41.

31. Louise Young, *Japan's Total Empire,* 183–84, 213–15; Francis Clifford Jones, *Manchuria Since 1931,* 139.

32. Sun, *Economic Development of Manchuria,* 101–02.

33. Han, "Puppet Sovereignty," chs. 3–4.

34. Han, "Puppet Sovereignty," 233; Matsusaka, *Making of Japanese Manchuria,* 414.

35. See, for instance, Harris, *Factories of Death.*

36. Han, "Puppet Sovereignty," chs. 3–4.

37. Sun, "Da Yaxiyazhuyi."

38. Komagome, *Shokuminchi Teikoku no Bunka Tōgō,* 265.

39. Yong, *Zhongguo Huidaomen,* 321.

40. Tominaga, *Manshūkoku no Minzoku Mondai,* 43–45.

41. Peattie, *Ishiwara Kanji,* 171, 174.

42. Further, creating similar institutions fostered a similarity of interests and goals between elites in metropolitan and dependent societies. Thus Latin American societies have found it difficult to sustain socialist states or even large-scale public expenditures without incurring the disfavor of the United States, and the Soviet Union would not tolerate "market-happy" bourgeoisies. Manchukuo too began to resemble (and in several instances led) the military-dominated dirigiste economy and centralized political system that developed in Japan beginning in the 1930s. See also Jane Burbank, this volume.

43. See Marer and Poznanski, "Costs of Domination, Benefits of Subordination."

44. Coatsworth, *Central America and the United States,* 18–19, 52–53.

45. Robert Freeman Smith, "Republican Policy and the Pax Americana," 273–75.

46. Bacevich, *American Empire,* 115–16; Woodrow Wilson quoted on page 115.

47. Coatsworth, *Central America and the United States,* 90–91.

48. Quoted in Smith, "Republican Policy and the Pax Americana," 271.

49. Parrini, "Age of Ultraimperialism," 7–9.

50. Parrini, "Age of Ultraimperialism," 8–11; Cumings, "Global Realm with No Limit," 53–54.

51. Arrighi and others, "Historical Capitalism, East and West," 301.

52. To be sure, even within the power structure in Manchukuo there were forces working for autonomy. On several occasions, the Kwantung army attacked special Japanese rights, most notably in 1936, when extraterritorial rights for Japanese citizens were abolished and a series of significant privileges began to unravel. The Japanese government also raised tariffs against the overwhelming exports from Manchukuo. In general, more recent research takes seriously the Kwantung army's autonomy from the despised civilian governments at home—at least until the war in Asia. Han, "Puppet Sovereignty," 257-58; Louise Young, *Japan's Total Empire,* 205, 211.

53. Duara, *Sovereignty and Authenticity,* 67-70.

54. Pagden, "Empire's New Clothes." The present essay appeared in a rather different form (Duara, "Nationalism, Imperialism, Federalism and the Example of Manchukuo") as a response to Pagden in the same volume. For another expansive and revisionist view of empire, see also Cooper, *Colonialism in Question.*

55. Komagome, *Shokuminchi Teikoku Nippon no Bunka Tōgō,* 356-70.

56. We need only glance at the record of atrocities and killings committed in Iraq and Afghanistan by the US-led coalition forces under the name of national security, or the growing nationalist rivalry between China and Japan in an economically highly interdependent East Asian region, to be persuaded of this.

8

After Empire

Reflections on Imperialism from the Américas

Fernando Coronil

> Imperialism, like any word which refers to fundamental social and political conflicts, cannot be reduced, semantically, to a single proper meaning. Its important historical variations of meaning point to real processes which have to be studied in their own terms.
>
> —*Raymond Williams*

The subject of empire, an old-fashioned and respected scholarly issue usually confined to erudite rumination in ivory towers, has recently become a public concern in the United States as well as abroad. Tossed around and accented with new meanings by competing parties at the onset of this new millennium, "empire" has been brought from its seclusion as a relic of the past and turned into a hot term of current political discourse. No doubt, its present salience as a word and as an issue is largely due to the more explicit and forceful role the US state has assumed as the self-proclaimed defender of "civilization" after September 11, 2001. Although it may not always be clear what is meant by this expression, the United States is now increasingly addressed as an empire —whether a "lite," "reluctant," "benevolent," or simply less-concealed one. Now that empire looms large before our eyes, how are we to look at this dusty relic? How useful is it as an analytical category for understanding not only colonialism or postcolonialism but also noncolonial geopolitical dominance, past or present?

This essay is a response to a timely invitation to look at empire beyond its usual European location, to explore its varied historical expressions, and to discern its usefulness as an analytical construct for engaging contemporary politics. Recognizing that "from the literal to the metaphorical to the contemporary, empire and anthropology have long and entwined careers," I welcome the call "to take the anthropological study of empire to the next level, specifically to look beyond the European empires upon which we have overwhelmingly focused."[1] I also take this call as an invitation to counter the complicity between imperial histories and anthropology, history, and other social sciences.

My turn to "other" empires entails a shift not just of place but also in time. Situating "empire" within an expanded spatial and temporal landscape makes it easier to overview its varied historical forms. This larger frame places the study of European colonial empires, which have been the prominent objects of colonial and postcolonial scholarship in the modern era, alongside that of empires without colonies, whose diverse forms have been commonly seen as belonging to the past and yet, in my view, are of singular relevance for considering the present. Some of these forms were already highlighted in the 1950s by Kohn, who considered colonialism as only one of five modalities of imperial control. Focusing on past empires, his other four modalities of "imperial but non-colonial solutions" are, at opposite extremes, political formations that accord subjects full autonomy within an imperial framework (Hungary under Austria), those that annihilate or expel original inhabitants (Native Americans under US settlers), and, in between, "solutions" that keep indigenes on their land but as inferior subjects (India or South Africa under British rule) or grant citizenship to natives but submerge their nation within a larger nation (the Kurds under Turkey).[2]

This expanded landscape also allows exploration of the connection between new and old imperialisms, a distinction made by Halavi in a pioneering article, written over forty years ago, in which he argued that in the "new imperialism," informal economic control is as effective as the direct political control of old imperialism.[3] One of the earliest and potentially most productive uses of a distinction between the formal and informal dimensions of imperialism was proposed by Gallagher and Robinson in 1953 and taken up by scholars of the British empire.[4] While it does not build on the formal/informal distinction, the concept of "imperialism without colonies" also recognizes that imperial control can be predominantly exerted by economic influence rather than by direct political control.[5]

This expanded temporal and spatial frame facilitates, more significantly, a shift in viewpoint. Rather than being confined to given imperial genealogies, so intimately linked both to the self-images of empires and to sharp distinctions between "the market" and the "state," the "political" and the "economic," or the "formal" and the "informal," which have been so central in their self-representation as well as in academic discussions, I wish to observe what may be termed "imperial effects." While a focus on effects is associated with postmodern critiques of unitary subjects and grand narratives, I intend here to develop a subalternist perspective to tackle the consequences of domination for those who are subjected to it. By observing these consequences, I seek to bring into view particular power formations within general processes, without assuming, but also without assuming away, their systemic structures, inner logics, or identifying boundaries. My attention to effects is at once conceptual and practical; the aim is to recognize systems of domination by their significance for subjected populations rather than solely by their institutional forms or self-definitions.

Since dominance—however one understands this elusive concept—is a rather regular dimension of interregional or international life, specifying the criteria used to define its specific character is a condition for analysis. Lest we let these criteria be established by convention—so often the expression of dominant perspectives—they ought to specify the object of our analysis only by becoming its object. For my purposes here, I argue for the usefulness of the concept of empire to engage relatively large geopolitical formations that establish dominion by hierarchically differentiating populations across transregional boundaries. (For other purposes, one may find this notion either too boundless or too bounded.) Always concerned with the lived experiences of those at the margins, Edward Said insisted that "the historical experience of imperialism for the imperialized entailed subservience and subjection."[6] I seek to develop a perspective that pluralizes empires and provincializes their European forms but most importantly, counters the effacing of those subjected to imperializing powers, regardless of their apparent forms.

EMPIRES "BEYOND EUROPE"

I will "move beyond Europe" not by leaving Europe behind but by moving toward other literal and metaphorical "Europes." One of my most vivid childhood memories concerns my first trip to Spain. I remember that when we crossed the Pyrenees by car, as we left France and entered Spain, my relatives remarked, as if these mountains stood as an invisible sign that identified and contained a "real" Europe: "*Dicen* [they say] that Europe ends at the Pyrenees; we are leaving it now." I did not understand then who was the "they" who said this, but it was clear to me that this phrase did not express the views of either my relatives or Spaniards. As a Latin American in Spain, it was impossible for me not to feel that I was in Europe, at the heart of what had been a vast empire, whose allegedly superior civilization had legitimated the conquest and colonization of the Americas. I have since learned that from the vantage point of the dominant centers of Europe, Spain appeared then as "non-Europe," or at least as "not Europe yet," a region that, like my home country and the rest of Latin America, needed to "catch up" in order to become fully modern. Now I see that "Europe" means the shifting apex of modernity.

It is ironic that southern Europe, seen then as marginal to Europe, was the birthplace of the modern empires of Portugal and Spain and the crucible of modern colonialism. During the early modern period, Portugal and Spain established not only model empires but also the conditions for the emergence of the empires that stand now as canonical in colonial studies: those of England and France. Such shifts in the location of imperial centers have become familiar in Latin America, a region whose populations have been subjected to various regimes of control by many political centers. Before the Iberian conquest, the Aztec and Inca empires subjected and integrated large regions and populations; these empires provided persisting structures of rule upon which Spain built its own empire in the Americas. After the conquest, the area of the Americas under Iberian control became colonies of Spain and Portugal, until independence in the nineteenth century. As independent nations, Latin American countries were subjected to the informal imperial control of England and France until well into the twentieth century, and their ethnic minorities to various forms of internal colonialism by local elites. Of course, from its emergence as the hemispheric power at the end of the nineteenth century until its position now as a global hegemon, the United States has been the fundamental imperial force in the region.

The recognition that it is now common to exclude Spain and Portugal from Europe and to place the United States at Europe's center makes evident that "Europe" is an imaginary construct that blurs the boundaries between literal and metaphorical frontiers. As a hyper-real construct, "Europe"—or its more general embodiment, "the West"—is a geohistorical sign that points to the apex of modernity and contains it within limits no less constraining for being shifting and imaginary.

The view from the apex obscures what lies below, the larger whole of which it is but a part, particularly since the apex's self-fashioning as such involves disavowing its connections to the rest. As a fetish that embodies powers not of its own, the West is construed as superior through occidentalist modalities of representation that associate it with the rest of the world through dissociations—by separating relational histories, reifying cultural difference, and turning difference into hierarchy. It is by looking at this apex from the perspective of the obscured transcultural histories that sustain it atop that I seek to explore European empires beyond Europe.

SEPTEMBER 11: NAMING HISTORY

It is a privilege of empires to make their histories appear as History. September 11 has become an evocative sign that points not just to a singular instance when the United States was deeply wounded within its borders by foreign attack, but to an open-ended historical phase construed by the United States as an endless global war against terror; this date names a bounded moment as well as a momentous era. I will use September 11 as a "clue" (à la Ginzburg) to examine the imperial character of this era.

It is generally assumed that 9/11 names this event, and not any other time in any other place. Not unlike naming famous people by only their first names, "9/11" identifies *its* September 11. Its "surname," 2001, is assumed. Yet if one moves South and gives this date a year, 9/11 names a different history. In 1973, on another September 11, an elected socialist president and many of his supporters died defending a democratically established government in a coup organized by the local opposition with the support of the US government and US-based transnational corporations. As a result of the coup, which included the bombing of La Moneda, the presidential palace in which Dr. Salvador Allende died defending his government, a regime of terror, also supported by the United States, was established. The regime was responsible for the deaths of over three thousand and torture of more than 28,000 Chileans, and the exile of many more over many years.

A brief look at the historical arc that joins these two dates, pieces of a much longer historical process, offers a different view of the significance of each event and of the common history that forged them. While the US September 11 has brought into the open the subject of empire, I will use the memory of Chile's September 11 to resurrect the subject of imperialism, a topic buried in the global North for over a quarter century but whose specter has always hovered around the global South. From the vantage point of this historical arc, I ask the following: How useful is it to think of the present not just in terms of empire but in terms of imperialism? Are there significant continuities between both dates, or are we facing an altogether new configuration of power that makes these concepts irrelevant?

ENTWINING EMPIRE AND IMPERIALISM

The attack against Salvador Allende on 1973's September 11 must be placed within a long tradition of US interventions in the hemisphere —ranging from the direct use of force to various forms of influence— that began with the conquest of native territories before the United States became an independent nation. While after its independence the United States used force of arms many times in Latin America during the nineteenth century, one intervention stands as a major landmark: US participation in the Spanish–Cuban–American war in 1898. This intervention was followed by the US occupation of Puerto Rico and Cuba in the Caribbean and of Guam and the Philippines in the Pacific. A major turning point in global relations, 1898 signified a transfer of imperial control over the hemisphere from England and Spain to the United States. While Puerto Rico acquired an ambiguous colonial status, Cuba, whose long struggle against Spain (1868–1898) made it more resistant to direct imperial control, first became a protectorate (1901) and then an independent republic (1902). As an independent republic, Cuba remained subjected to various forms of US control and influence, including several direct armed interventions. It was not the direct possession of territories and populations, however, but the indirect control over Cuba that came to define US relations with Latin America during the twentieth century.

The Monroe Doctrine, proclaimed in 1823 to defend the Americas from foreign intervention, came to be interpreted after 1898 as a charter to justify US influence over the region. The mechanism for this change was the 1905 Roosevelt Corollary to the Monroe Doctrine, signed in the aftermath of the Spanish–Cuban–American war, through which the United States authorized itself to intervene in Latin America whenever it considered intervention necessary. According to Lafeber, with the ascendance of the United States as the hegemonic power in the region, "the Doctrine itself shifted to mean that Latin Americans should now be controlled by outside (that is, North American) intervention if necessary."[7] The Roosevelt Corollary became the principal political device to justify the new role of the United States as an agent of "order" in the region.

After 1898, the United States became a Janus-faced entity for Latin America, a dominant empire but also a model postcolonial nation. As Mexican novelist Carlos Fuentes notes, "Spain, our old empire, was defeated and dismantled by the United States, our new empire, in 1898; the Philippines and Puerto Rico became North American colonies, Cuba a subject state. Our sympathies shifted to the defeated empire: the United States desatanized Spain while satanizing itself." This satanization, however, came together with the idealization of its republican democracy. Fuentes aptly expresses the double character the United States came to have in Latin America, particularly among its political and intellectual elites: "the United States became the Jekyll and Hyde of our wildest continental dreams: a democracy inside, an empire outside."[8] Although it was not clear in 1898 what kind of empire it was going to be, it became evident that the United States would exert control following not the Puerto Rican but the Cuban model. Indirect control, however, did not preclude the direct exercise of force.

The US empire became the invention of Latin America, just as Europe, as Fanon famously put it, was the invention of America.[9] Latin America "invented" the US empire as its primordial imperialized subject similar to its earlier invention of European empires as their major colony. Given their mutual formation, the reverse of course is also true—Europe also invented America, but under asymmetrical conditions that require reversing mainstream currents that efface their mutual engagement. As the region became not only the object of imperial policies but also an active agent of responses to them, it became a crucible of empire that often produced imperial policies or "modular" reactions transportable to other imperial contexts.

The heterogeneity of the region made it necessary for the United States to develop different forms of control. In areas geographically closer, the United States would be more inclined to use open military might, while in those farther away, the United States would rely more on economic pressure, diplomatic influence, and concealed force. For example, the United States took half of Mexico in the mid-nineteenth century (it acquired the territories and populations of the current states of Texas, New Mexico, Arizona, Colorado, Nevada, California, and parts of Oregon and Utah); under US influence, Colombia lost its northern region of Panama in 1903, and Panama as an independent nation gained control over the canal built in 1914 (a project that had given birth to Panama as a nation) only at the end of the twentieth century. While as the "backyard" of the United States Central America and the Caribbean became the main field of its armed interventions in the region, the rest of South America became its favored ground for dominion through a vast network of alliances and economic investments in ever-expanding and more diversified areas of the economy. In all cases, the United States sought to protect its interests in the area by actively supporting, or helping place, suitable rulers, including ruthless dictators, whether in Central America, the Caribbean, or South America.

Needless to say, there were differences between the aggressive expansionism of Theodore Roosevelt's Big Stick policy and Tafts's Dollar Diplomacy, at the outset of the twentieth century, and the quiet imperialism of Franklin D. Roosevelt's Good Neighbor Policy during the 1930s, or between the outwardly progressive Democratic policies of John F. Kennedy's Alliance for Progress and Jimmy Carter's Human Rights and the more overtly aggressive stance of the Republican administrations of Richard Nixon, Ronald Reagan, or George Bush, father and son. Despite the differences among these different administrations, they established a consistent position in Latin America characterized by the establishment of strategic alliances with local allies, cemented by common economic interests and ultimately backed by armed force.

Most direct armed US interventions in Latin America and the Caribbean took place during the first half of the twentieth century; these interventions were generally brief and intended to achieve specific political or economic outcomes, not direct and permanent political dominion. Yet there were also a number of lengthier occupations: Cuba (1906–09), Nicaragua (1912–25), Haiti (1915–34), Santo Domingo (1916–24), Cuba (1917–22), Mexico (1918–19), Panama (1918–20), Nicaragua (1926–33). These examples are only the tip of the iceberg. Between 1898 and 1920, US armed forces intervened twenty times in the Caribbean.[10] A report of the Foreign Affairs Division of the Congressional Research Service lists seventy-three instances of use of the US armed forces in Latin America between 1798 and 1945, over half after 1898.[11] According to Harvard historian John Coatsworth, between 1898 and 1994, the US government "intervened successfully to change governments in Latin America a total of at least 41 times. That amounts to once every 28 months for an entire century."[12]

As a leader of the free world during the post–World War II Cold War (in reality a hot war carried out in many areas of the Third World), the United States increasingly exerted force indirectly through alliances with local actors. A paradigmatic example is the US-orchestrated coup against Guatemalan president Jacobo Arbenz in 1954, which involved a gamut of activities, from diplomatic influence to cultural warfare and military intervention. A wide range of actors, including the State Department, the CIA, United Fruit Company, the US Information Agency (which led a propaganda war), local and US-based churches, the Guatemalan armed forces, and the neighboring governments of Nicaragua, Panama, and Honduras, took part in the coup. From Honduras, Castillo de Armas led the CIA-supported army invasion that eventually toppled Arbenz. "Success" in Guatemala served to model another invasion that turned out to be what Fidel Castro has often called the "first defeat of US imperialism" in Latin America: the Bay of Pigs fiasco of 1961. President Eisenhower's plan to overthrow Fidel Castro through a CIA-organized invasion carried out by an army of exiles failed, partly because of determined resistance in Cuba but also because of President Kennedy's concern to avoid identifying the invasion with the United States and his decision to suspend the use of US airplanes to support it. What had become "formal" in Latin America was for the United States to act "informally."

Still, even after World War II there were several instances of outright US military intervention in the area, such as the 1965 invasion of Santo Domingo, involving an extraordinary force of 22,000 marines, ostensibly to prevent the return to power of Juan Bosh,[13] and the invasion of Grenada (1983), intended to control forces sympathetic to Maurice Bishop's People's Revolutionary Government, despite the fact that Grenada was a member of the Commonwealth. But in most cases, as in the overthrow of Chile's Allende, US participation was covert. While there is evidence that major US corporations and the US government endorsed a regime change in Chile, it took years to obtain declassified materials that demonstrate more conclusively their complicity in supporting the advent and consolidation of the Pinochet regime.[14] It may also take years to determine how deeply the United States was involved in the April 11, 2002, coup that toppled Venezuela's president Hugo Chávez for the span of forty-eight hours.[15]

Although not always a last resort, the deployment of military forces has certainly not been the favored US option. Indeed, US policy toward Latin America seems to have been guided by the principle of extending control through domestic forces whenever possible and by external force whenever necessary. With this notion I am paraphrasing Gallagher and Robinson's argument that British policy in the nineteenth century "followed the principle of extending control informally if possible and formally if necessary."[16] Their larger argument about the need to relate the formal and informal aspects of empire has particular relevance for understanding US involvement in Latin America in the twentieth century.

According to Gallagher and Robinson, "the usual summing up of the policy of the free trade empire as 'trade, not rule' should read 'trade with informal control if possible; trade with rule when necessary.'"[17] But rather than separate free trade from imperial trade, or informal from formal empire, they argue for the need to see these as part of a unitary process, marked not by fundamental differences of kind but by shifting degrees of control. They ask to approach history through the "concept of the totality of British expansion." As they put it, "a concept of informal empire which fails to bring out the underlying unity between it and the formal empire is sterile. Only within the total framework of expansion is nineteenth-century empire intelligible."[18] While critical of totalizing narratives that assume the character and direction of historical change, my argument here also seeks to develop a holistic framework for the study of empire.

The scholarship on imperial relations in Latin America, mostly concerned with US influence in the region, has only occasionally employed the notion of informal empire to explore US expansion in the region. This may seem puzzling, since it makes sense to treat US involvement in the region as mostly "informal." Yet perhaps the recognition that US influence was mostly "indirect" or "informal" made the distinction less useful; in the US case, the "informal" *was* indeed the "formal." With a few exceptions, the concept of "informal imperialism" has been largely confined to studies that examine specific aspects of the British "informal empire" in the region, which contrasted with its large formal empire elsewhere.[19]

In Latin America the presence of imperialism has often been assumed as part of a commonsense understanding of reality, often not even named as such. Scholars writing not just about but from Latin America have developed structuralist perspectives to examine processes of uneven development, emphasizing skewed patterns of accumulation and foreign control over key economic sectors in the domains of production, finance, and commerce, in conjunction with associated forms of class relations, state formation, and political culture.[20]

This structuralist perspective views imperial domination as a two-way process rather than a one-sided external imposition. Working within the *dependentista* perspective, Gunder Frank's notion of the "development of underdevelopment," even as it emphasizes the movement in one direction, calls attention to the reciprocal formation of centers and peripheries.[21] Similarly, Cardoso and Faletto's notion of "associated dependent development" shows that US influence does not involve an external imposition but a triple alliance among foreign, domestic, and state capital within national formations.[22] As with Gallagher and Robinson's concern with developing a "total framework" for examining imperial expansion, these structuralist perspectives argue for a holistic view of historical transformations in Latin America in the context of imperial relations.

These works make evident shifts in modes of US influence in the region. From a focus on controlling productive enclaves through direct investment in mining and agriculture during the first half of the twentieth century, the United States diversified investments in all areas of the economy, often participating as a "domiciliated" corporate citizen in joint ventures in industry, banking, services, and commerce.[23] While US influence in its various modalities is more dominant in countries closer to its borders (Mexico, Central America, and the Caribbean), the US presence as an industrial investor, trading partner, and financial center is strong in all countries, including Brazil, despite diversified trading partnerships. Heavy debt burdens, slow economic growth, and the need for foreign capital have made most countries in the region heavily dependent on US industrial and financial capital, as well as on institutions over which the United States exerts dominant control, such as the IMF. After 1973, with US support and the guidance of the "Chicago Boys" (economists following the University of Chicago's liberal economic doctrine), Chile's free market program was imposed and hailed as a model of development for Latin America and the rest of the world.

In retrospect, then, Chile's September 11 stands as a landmark of three facets and phases of the US imperial role: its long-standing economic and political involvement in the hemisphere, its political leadership in the struggle against socialism during the Cold War, and its emerging hegemonic role as the center of a globalized market organized around neoliberal principles.

Yet several decades after its initial "exemplary" implementation in Chile, even advocates of the free market are concerned with its disruptive effects, both globally and in Latin America. International organizations such as the World Bank and the International Labor Organization (ILO) have singled out growing worldwide poverty as a central problem of the global economy. According to the latest report of the ILO, half of the world's 2.8 billion workers earn less than two dollars per day, leaving them and their families with "few prospects to escape from grinding poverty." Metropolitan centers, with 21 percent of the world population, consume 78 percent of global goods and services and 75 percent of the world's energy. Wages for equivalent work are twenty times higher in the North. Today there are probably three times as many slaves as the approximately 12 million people who worked as slaves in the Americas for over three centuries; the claim that "an overseas woman can be bought for about the same price as a kitchen blender—$40" seems hard to believe in a world accustomed to the idea that slavery is matter of the past—or that the value of slaves today would be higher.[24] The unrestrained expansion of the market is undermining not just its own material foundations but the natural conditions of life for everyone. As rampant deforestation continues, it will be a pyrrhic market victory when water becomes, as predicted by many, a precious commodity.

In Latin America the social and ecological effects of market reforms are particularly pronounced. The implementation of free market policies (including the dismantling of the welfare state, privatization and denationalization of key economic sectors, deregulation of the financial sector, and exploitation of forests and mines) has intensified fractures in already divided societies, further polarizing income inequalities (the highest in the world), expanding the informal sector (which now employs the majority of the population), undermining already weak public services, intensifying quotidian personal and criminal violence, eroding their natural foundations, and developing new forms of racism, ethnic discrimination, and class conflict.

While formal equality before the market creates a universalistic framework that can serve to uphold egalitarian claims beyond the market, market practices are creating deep inequalities that undermine their realization. In highly polarized societies with limited prospects of collective improvement, social and economic boundaries are becoming also moral and cultural frontiers. Amid the promise of equality among different peoples promoted by the market, these cleavages are naturalizing difference within hierarchical structures and conjuring up images of superior and inferior peoples, as in colonial empires.

THE SUBJECT OF EMPIRE

A creative promiscuity of criteria has made it possible to bring together under the rubric of "empire" such vastly different geohistorical formations as the Roman, the Aztec, the Incan, the Russian, and the "American." In the modern period, in part because of the association between empires and overseas expansion, the treatment of both the Russian and US political systems as empires has been marked by deep ambivalence. Russia, despite its huge land conquests in Asia, has not been recognized as an empire like the maritime empires of the Spanish or the British. The United States did see itself as an empire in the eighteenth century, but the more it expanded across land and seas, the more it presented itself as a leading democratic republic and the less inclined it was to see itself as an empire.

Empire as a category has a long history, yet its meaning shifted significantly when it was used to refer to modern political systems.[25] When used in relation to premodern social formations, "empire" refers to a variety of centralized forms of rule involving differing degrees and forms of political control over populations typically spread over adjacent territories. The Latin *imperium* was used to refer to systems of authority of strong political centers over peoples generally located in contiguous territories. In the modern period, "empire" came to be associated with European political systems based on strong states that exerted control over distant populations, propelled in part by the expansion of trade and industry.

The scholarship on modern colonial empires makes evident that their fundamental political problem has been the differential incorporation of colonizers and colonized into a common and yet exclusionary system. The extensive racialization of difference after the eighteenth century, so commonly associated with northern European colonialism, was built upon previous classifications of American people in terms of variable combinations of natural and cultural factors (which in turn drew from biocultural classifications of Christians, Moors, and Jews during the Spanish *Reconquista*). Racial formations entail the making of identities through the fusion and confusion of visible and invisible markers. Certain sensorial facets, such as skin color or facial features, signifying descent, serve to define social identities, naturalizing what is social. As a form of fetishism, racial thinking turns the social into the natural, wholes into parts, faces into facets, and attributes to these elements powers and significance that lie elsewhere.

The essential analytical premise is that imperial formations, whether colonial or not, involve variable systems of difference between dominant and subaltern subjects; discerning *what* these differences are and *how* they are constituted under specific imperial situations serves to establish a comparative reference rather than exclusive standards for the study of imperial formations. What makes a difference is not specific differences but the systematic production of unequal difference. Since the differences that imperial powers claim as foundational are historical rather than inherent, what seems constant is constantly made, the object of ongoing and conflictual social making, whose object is their re-creation or transformation.

Empires encompass distinct populations, whether contiguous or not, of the same or different ethnic or racial identification. Whatever their particular form, empires involve hierarchical relations that do not just rank but differentiate subjects, making differences of degree into differences in kind, whether in principle, as in colonial empires, or in practice, as in postcolonial empires. They are structures of domination that bring different populations under one encompassing formation as different and unequal subjects. Whether subjects are exploited economically, exterminated or segregated racially or ethnically, granted partial autonomy, offered equality of rights, or assimilated, they are subjected and turned into "Others" by making the different unequal, the unequal different. In Latin America, the current crisis has created a cultural chasm between social classes that has often led to the racialization of class differences and social spaces, turning the poor, from dominant perspectives, into an internal "other." Otherness is a universal human condition only if one forgets the particular conditions that make some selves inferior others. Empires are thus embodiments of the tension between the incorporation of subjects and their subjection.

THE SUBJECT OF IMPERIALISM

"Imperialism" as a category emerged in northern Europe in contests over its colonial rule; in contrast to "empire," imperialism thus has a recent history. It was first used in France as a critical term (*imperialiste*) to refer to a partisan of the Napoleonic empire; it was later employed to criticize the Caesarist ambitions of Louis Napoleon. From this rather domestic origin in critiques of the French imperial policies of uncle and nephew, it evolved during British expansionism in the second half of the nineteenth century, first as an invective to criticize

Disraeli's policies and then as a positive term to refer to the project of establishing a "Greater Britain" through the expansion of England into an "imperial federation" that would include Britain, its overseas settlements, and India. Although increasingly associated with British colonialism, the term came to refer to the expansionist drives of any European state.

Imperialism gained theoretical status when it was used to explain the underlying factors that cause European expansionism. This critical use characterized its deployment in debates over the Boer War and Europe's further entanglements in Asia and Africa. During this period, imperialism developed as a category to explain the political and economic dimensions of European colonialism.[26] In *Imperialism: A Study* (1902), Hobson argued that imperialism was driven by the need of states to find external markets because of the limits of consumption at home.[27] Building on this argument, a number of Marxist writers developed a more systemic theory of the links between capitalism and imperialism.[28] While Luxemburg developed Hobson's notion of underconsumption into a theory of the necessary limits of capitalist accumulation within one country, and Kautsky developed the concept of ultra-imperialism to argue that the exploitation of poorer nations led to the alliance of imperial powers, Lenin's classical analysis of imperialism as the highest phase of capitalism emphasized the necessity of interimperial rivalry during a phase of capitalist expansion based on the monopolization of production, the merger of financial and industrial capital, and the export of capital.

While I recognize limitations of the concept and its association with stale debates and teleological narratives, I think imperialism is out in the streets as an indispensable political term. Despite its shortcomings, it continues to have currency in political discourse among peoples subjected to the devastating effects of global powers, evoking memories and affects and making sense of current experiences of inequality, exploitation, and domination. Particularly after September 11, 2001, some scholars have offered strong arguments for considering its ongoing relevance.[29] In my view, if we want to engage contemporary politics beyond the high walls of academia, the question is not so much whether to use this term or not but how to recast it to make it useful.

RECASTING IMPERIALISM

Most discussions of imperialism tend to reproduce the provincial Eurocentric focus that marked it original framing. Ironically, although the scope of imperialism is global, Europe has been its main if not only active subject. As non-Europe, the rest of the world participates in these discussions as the object of imperial subjection, not as an agent in imperial formations. On the basis of the Latin American historical experience, I seek to decenter this concept and reconsider its validity in light of different assumptions.

Three interrelated premises have framed discussions of imperialism. First, capitalism is seen as a European phenomenon. Second, European capitalist nations are viewed as the basic agents of imperialist expansion, even if it is recognized that these nations interact in a global market. Third, imperialism has been seen as following capitalism, even if it is not always regarded as caused by capitalism or as its higher phase. Rather than entering the discussion on imperialism in these terms, I wish to recast them by looking at "empires beyond Europe" on the basis of different premises, building on work that has already questioned them.

Dependency, world-systems, and a number of colonial and postcolonial scholars have argued for the need to view capitalism as a global rather than a national or regional process. Debates on the origins of capitalism tend to focus on specific relations within Europe itself. A global perspective redefines the discussion of its origins by framing it within a different scale. This perspective does not deny the role of local relations; rather, it places them within global interactions. The issue is not to choose to locate the origins of capitalism, as in a famous debate, in class relations of the European countryside[30] or in urban trade[31] but to place Europe itself in the context of global relations. Through a discussion of just one commodity, Mintz offers a glimpse into this worldwide process, showing how Caribbean sugar came to sustain not just the British state and ruling sectors but also Britain's laboring classes, transforming eating habits, desires, and individual and collective identities and possibilities.[32] As other scholars have shown, Caribbean slaves did not just give sugar to Europe or provide a major source of earnings to states, traders, and industrialists, but contributed to changing global understandings of humanity and citizenship. For example, slaves in Saint Domingue forced French revolutionaries to abolish slavery and make more universal their provincial universalism.[33] The abolition of slavery in Haiti also created conditions for the generalization of "free labor" everywhere, which has always been supported by forms of "unfree" and poorly remunerated labor, such as highly gendered housework or work in subsistence agriculture.

If labor, capital, and land are the "trinity form" that "holds all the mysteries of the social production process,"[34] this trinity form helps explain the mystery of its historical development. Not just capital and labor but also land (as the socially mediated powers of nature) has been engaged in the worldwide production of capitalism. The Iberian colonial experience in the Americas provided Europe with immense wealth in the form of riches extracted from American soil as well as surplus value exploited through many forms of coerced labor. It also provided other European powers with models of rule and production. Spanish jurisprudence, largely developed on the basis of debates resulting from the colonial encounter, established the foundation for international law.[35] Caribbean and Brazilian plantations, integrating agriculture and industry in large-scale productive structures, were early forms of agribusiness that served as templates for industrial production in Europe.[36] As Ortiz shows through his evocative "counterpoint" of American tobacco and European sugar, the modern world is best seen not as originating in one isolated European region but as the result of "transcultural" engagements among metropolitan and colonial societies and cultures.[37]

From this perspective, capitalism did not originate in Manchester, Liverpool, or the British countryside and then spread to the tropics. It developed between colonial and metropolitan regions in the expanding world economy of the sixteenth century. Its origins thus lie not *in* one region but *between* regions in the processes that formed them. Free labor is the dominant as well as the most disguised form of coerced labor under capitalism, not its defining criterion. Capitalist development is not just uneven but unequal, its multiple regional forms reflecting its polarizing dynamics and the shifting worldwide power relations within which it unfolds. Increasingly defined by networks of capital and labor that transcend national boundaries, the capitalist division of both labor and nature continues now to divide humanity, separating it between zones that concentrate knowledge and skilled labor and areas that produce labor-intensive and nature-intensive commodities.

The formation of nation-states has been intimately linked to the worldwide development of capitalism. As political centers, empires promoted the expansion of capitalist trade and industry even before nations were constituted as independent states. Spain as a nation was formed in the long *durée* that included both the constitution and dissolution of its empire. During the colonial period, Spain was composed of separate principalities ruled by the Castillian king. "Spain" represented a unitary ideal that encompassed the peninsula but also extended to the colonial relation. As Silverblatt has argued, "Spain's two referents—national ideal and colonial power—developed in tandem."[38] Latin American independence struggles, Anderson has insisted, pioneered modern nationalism. The dissolution of the Spanish empire led not only to the formation of independent nations in the Americas but also to the formation of Spain itself as a nation-state. As Fred Cooper shows in this volume, the entity called France, referring to an empire-state and also to a nation-state, became strictly "national" after the dissolution of its empire in the second half of the twentieth century. Nations have been formed in tandem with empires through different forms of defining, incorporating, and differentiating their distinct subject populations.

From this perspective, imperialism does not result from the expansive dynamics of advanced capitalist nations. Rather, imperialism is capitalism's coeval condition of possibility. Capitalism and imperialism developed together as twin forces in the creation of a world market beginning in the sixteenth century; they are the cause and effect of the interactions between imperial centers and colonial peripheries. The export of capital, the search for markets, the interaction between financial and productive capital, and interstate rivalries and alliances —factors highlighted by theorists of imperialism as taking place at a particular phase of metropolitan national capitalisms—have been at work in different forms from the colonization of the Americas to the present; their specific configuration at any specific moment (as in Lenin's classical formulation) defines a modality of imperialism, not its defining manifestation. Just as imperialism makes evident the political dimension of capitalism, capitalism makes visible the economic dimension of imperialism, revealing "states" and "markets" as dual facets of a unitary process. Without capitalism there would be no modern imperialism, but equally, without modern imperialism there would be no capitalism.

Writing during the first half of the twentieth century (1936), the Peruvian political leader Haya de la Torre argued that in Latin America imperialism is not the highest stage of capitalism but the first phase of its capitalist development (Nkrumah made a related argument in *Neo-colonialism: The Last Stage of Imperialism*).[39] Here I extend Haya de la Torre's argument. What he says about Latin America is true of all capitalist development. Yet I do not mean to reverse Lenin's dictum and say that capitalism follows imperialism in the periphery or elsewhere, but to argue that in the modern world capitalism and imperialism are coeval processes that mutually condition each other in historically variable contexts. Just as there were empires before there was capitalism, there were (and there might be) forms of imperialism without capitalism, but modern imperialism is intimately bound up with capitalism (including imperial socialist states that are integrated into the capitalist world economy and control rather directly their domestic capital and markets).

Based on this broad conception of modern imperialism, I wish to distinguish three of its dominant modalities. At the risk of reducing complex processes to flat distinctions, I define "colonial imperialism" as the formal dominion of a political center over its colonies; "national imperialism" as the informal dominion of a nation-state over independent nations; and "global imperialism" as the informal dominion by a network of capital and states over an increasingly integrated worldwide system. Each of these modalities may involve different forms of "internal colonialism," a category developed to analyze the subjection of marginalized populations within a territory by domestic elites. Needless to say, any form of imperialism also articulates with related forms of subjection based on other principles of difference, such as gender, age, and religion.

This scheme of modes and phases of domination allows for historically variable expressions of their relation to each other in specific contexts, without assuming that they are linked in a teleological progression of universal stages. Thus, while colonial imperialism preceded and made possible national and global imperialisms, it may coexist with them. For instance, the British empire combined colonial and national imperialist modalities; it involved a formal empire in Africa and Asia as well as an informal empire in Latin America. The current period encompasses the three modalities of imperialism, but it is defined by the articulation of its national and global forms. Since World War II, the United States has been the major national imperial power, but in the last two decades it has also increasingly been at the center of an emerging system of internationalized capital, states, and culture, leading some thinkers, such as Negri and Hardt, to argue for the emergence of a "global empire."[40] To the extent that globalization has led to the appearance of a unified world despite its internal fractures, Eurocentrism gives way to globalcentrism as a mode of constructing difference, creating a common ground for potential equality but also redefining the spaces and meanings of different forms of alterity and subalternity. Yet the US reaction to the attacks of September 11, 2001, has made evident the persistent national foundation of transnational networks and alliances. Rather than consolidating global networks, the current crisis seems to be stimulating the more open development of the dual character of the United States as a nation-state and an empire-state. This development has also intensified the deployment of cultural and religious factors as markers of hierarchical difference between the United States and its opponents.

This scheme may help us observe features and changes of imperial formations. The movement from national to global imperialism seems to be related to a generalization and growing abstraction of the main forms of capital (land/ground-rent, labor/wages, and capital/profits, and its derived mode, money/interest). Financial markets have expanded dramatically, impacting a "real economy" that involves the commodification of ever more domains across space and time (by 1997 derivatives were exchanged for $360 trillion, twelve times the value of world economic production). Labor has become more globally integrated and specialized, giving tangible support to Marx's notions of "abstract" labor, the collective "social worker," and expanded units of production beyond traditional factories. Since wealth derives from the union of value produced by labor and riches gifted by nature, the relentless pursuit of wealth under global imperialism propels the international division of both labor and nature into ever wider domains, dividing time and space ever more minutely and fragmenting nations and markets ever more mindlessly.[41]

These transformations are inseparable from the changing articulation of states and markets. Current modes of global capital accumulation place new strains upon the reproduction of state legitimacy at the national level. States and capitals vary in their capacity to negotiate this tension. While metropolitan nations orchestrate this process through such institutions as the IMF, WTO, GATT, and G7, nations from the "South" find themselves increasingly subjected to directives from international organizations and to the pressures of transnational capital (including their own transnationalized capital). The widening gap among and within nations affects more severely populations of nations in the South. The joint unfolding of capitalism and imperialism, in tandem with the formation of nations and empires, has always entailed not just the articulation but also the construction of "economics" and "politics" as separate domains or functions. For Gallagher and Robinson, imperialism is a process "of integrating new regions into an expanding economy"; its "sufficient" function is political; its "necessary function" is economic.[42] Yet under current forms of "national" and "global imperialism," it becomes increasingly difficult to separate politics and economics and argue that one or the other is the "sufficient" or the "necessary" function of integrating new regions into an imperial domain. As the "economic" becomes ever more evidently "political" in its effects, analysis should make increasingly clear what was opaque before: the unity of the formal and informal, the political and the economic within the open-ended and ever-changing totality of imperial formations.

NATION-STATE AND EMPIRE-STATE: THE UNITED STATES AND NATIONAL AND GLOBAL IMPERIALISM

In the 1950s, William Appleman Williams noted that while a dominant theme of US historiography is that the United States is not an empire, historians, if pressed, would admit that the United States once had an empire and speak persistently of the United States as a "world power."[43] Building on Williams's work, cultural critic Amy Kaplan four decades later treated the "absence of empire in the study of American culture" as a central aspect of its imperial culture.[44]

Current debate about the international role of the United States reenacts the old ambivalence about casting it as imperial, yet it also exhibits a growing inclination to recognize it as such. For example, a recent *The New York Times Book Review* features several reviews on the subject of empire, including an article reporting a dialogue between two Yale historians, revealingly titled "Kill the Empire! (Or Not)." While the title dramatically captures the entrenched ambivalence about identifying the United States as an empire, the dialogue shows that empire, however unpalatable, must now be accepted as common sense, a fact about America. As John Lewis Gaddis puts it, the notion of empire has been present from the birth of the United States as a nation: "We've always had an empire. The thinking of the founding fathers was we were going to be an empire. Empire is as American as apple pie, in that sense. The question is, what kind of an empire do we have?"[45]

Before September 11, the significance of imperialism for the present was debated within very restricted scholarly circles. Scholars were divided. Some asserted imperialism's persisting centrality, others were ambivalent about it, and still others affirmed that imperialism has ceased to be a relevant category, as it has been replaced by the notion of a global empire.[46] Yet after September 11, 2001, many radical critics have argued more insistently that imperialism has validity as a concept for the present. For Jonathan Schell, imperialism is even a more fundamental category than empire; for him, we now face "imperialism without empire," since the United States is unable to exert sufficient worldwide control.[47] Others prefer to recognize novel forms of empires and imperialism that involve fundamental changes in the forms and spaces of imperial domination.[48]

In his incisive critique of Negri and Hardt's *Empire*, George Steinmetz offers a forceful argument for the relevance of imperialism today. According to him, after September 11, 2001, imperialism became an explicit element of US politics. Integrating insights from regulation and world-system theories, he argues that a "structural" change took place after September 11, 2001. This involved continuity at the level of the core framework for regulating post-Fordist imperial globalization but discontinuity at the level of its ideological legitimation, characterized by a "more imperialistic politics and a more authoritarian interior order."[49] For Steinmetz, "September 11th was the shock that allowed an explicitly imperialist and authoritarian rethinking of the model of regulation to come to the fore.... This emergent framework is still post-Fordist with respect to the core model of industrial production, but the state model is domestically authoritarian and geopolitically imperialistic."[50]

While for Steinmetz September 11 turned imperialism into an explicit state ideology, for Panitch and Gindin it revealed what had until then been hidden: "the American empire is no longer concealed."[51] Building on Poulantzas's argument that the US state is the center of an "imperialist chain" that has established hegemony over other societies by "generalizing its relations of production and domination inside other metropolises" (Poulantzas), Panitch argues that US dominance involves a new type of "non-territorial imperialism maintained not through direct rule by the metropolis, nor even through political subordination of a neo-colonial type, but rather through the 'induced reproduction of the form of the dominant imperialist power within each national formation and its state.'"[52] What is needed, according to Panitch and Gindin, is not to dismiss the relevance of imperialism because the market is now globalized, but to

> transcend the limitations of the old Marxist "stagist" theory of inter-imperial rivalry, and allow for a full appreciation of the historical factors that have led to the formation of a unique American informal empire. This will involve understanding how the American state developed the capacity to eventually incorporate its capitalist rivals, and oversee and police "globalization"—i.e., the spread of capitalist social relations to every corner of the world.[53]

This need becomes even more urgent now that the United States encounters increasing difficulties in ruling a "truly global informal empire" in alliance with states subjected to ever more intense domestic pressures.[54]

IMPERIAL EFFECTS

If a focus on imperial effects may serve to recognize empires, it may also be used to endorse them. Thus, for Niall Ferguson, since the United States functions like an empire, it should more fully behave like one. According to him, "if you do not recognize that you are essentially performing the functions of an empire, you are incapable of learning from the mistakes of past empires." Asked why he calls the United States an empire despite the fact that "most Americans don't think of their country that way," Ferguson offers a revealing answer:

> Well, it functions like an empire, in the sense that it projects its military power globally, its economic interests are global, its cultural reach is global. In many ways, it's a more impressive empire than any empire has ever been. The only strange thing about it is that its citizens don't recognize the fact. That's odd, because the Founding Fathers quite openly called the United States an empire. Jefferson, Hamilton, Madison, Washington all used the e-word to describe the United States.[55]

Even before September 11 there were calls for the United States to assume an imperial role, but based on the extension of informal influence. In 2000, Richard Haass, as director of Foreign Policy Studies and chair in International Security at the Brookings Institution, proposed that Americans "re-conceive their role from one of a traditional nation-state to an imperial power." As he explains: "An imperial foreign policy is not to be confused with imperialism. The latter is a concept that connotes exploitation, normally for commercial ends, often requiring territorial control. It is grounded in a world that no longer exists."

Revealingly, Haass proposes an imperial (but not imperialist) role for the United States through a misreading of Gallagher and Robinson. Arguing for the relevance for the United States of their axiom that "the British followed the principle of extending control informally if possible, and formally if necessary," he proposes that the United States should be an informal empire so as not to be an imperialistic one: "[I]ndeed, an American empire would have to be informal if it were to succeed if only because American democracy could not underwrite an imperial order that required constant, costly applications of military power."[56] How are we to interpret the extraordinary US military presence throughout the world—which includes over seven hundred conventional military bases, not to mention those under leaseholds, concealed, or under other arrangements[57]—and its costs to democracy at home and abroad? Was Haass asking for the dismantling of this huge military establishment? Should we believe, like Haass, that by becoming an informal empire—by avoiding "the constant, costly applications of military power"—the United States can avoid being an imperialist one?

Haass wrote this before September 11, 2001, when post-1989 globalization had made war seem unnecessary. As Bacevich has noted, "before September 11, the conventional wisdom had been that globalization was fast making war obsolete; after September 11, the conventional wisdom was that globalization was making war an all but permanent and inescapable part of life in the 21st century."[58] Since September 11, 2001, terror has been presented as an enemy without national boundaries or centers, a diffuse force that blurs the boundaries between military and civilian agents, between armies and "the people." The elusiveness of terror makes it increasingly untenable for the United States to separate central from collateral damage, political from military targets, external from internal enemies, severely restricting civil rights at home. Now that an endless war against terror defines US domestic and foreign policy, how are we to think of its imperial role?

According to Gallagher and Robinson, Britain's informal empire was no less imperialistic than its formal empire; rather, the informal imperialism of free trade was Britain's preferable modality of imperialism. Their main argument is that imperialism is a total process that includes formal and informal dimensions; these dimensions do not entail essential differences but rather varying degrees and modes of control. More than the term "empire," "imperialism" helps show that imperial control is achieved through the joining and transformation of distinct communities brought together by the force of the market as well as by armed force—whether actively deployed or kept as threat.

AFTER EMPIRE

The war against terror has forcefully brought "home" the imperial problem of rule over "Others." In a remarkable article in the *New York Times* titled "What does the Pentagon see in the 'Battle of Algiers,'" strangely presented under "film studies," the author reports on a screening in the Pentagon of Pontecorvo's classical anticolonial film *The Battle of Algiers*.[59] The idea of showing and discussing the movie came from the Directorate for Special Operations and Low-Intensity

Conflict, a civilian-led group entrusted with the responsibility "for thinking aggressively and creatively" on issues of guerrilla warfare. Forty officers and civilians were invited to consider "the problematic but alluring efficacy of brutal and repressive means in fighting clandestine terrorists."

The *New York Times* article gives us an unusual glimpse into an intraelite debate about the war occurring not just in the Pentagon but, evidently, through the US media. The flier inviting the selected guests to the Pentagon screening framed their viewing of the film in the following terms:

> How to win a battle against terrorism and lose the war of ideas. Children shoot soldiers at point-blank range. Women plant bombs in cafes. Soon the entire Arab population builds to a mad fervor. Sound familiar? The French have a plan. It succeeds tactically, but fails strategically. To understand why, come to a rare showing of the film.

This article on "film studies" concludes as follows:

> If indeed the government is currently analyzing or even weighing the tactical choices reflected in the "Battle of Algiers," presumably that is being done at a higher level of secrecy than an open discussion following a screening of the Pontecorvo film. Still, by showing the movie within the Pentagon and by announcing that publicly, somebody seems to be raising issues that have remained obscured throughout the war against terror.

What are these issues? Is there a link between the Pentagon's screening and the *New York Times*'s reporting? If tactics following the French victory in the Battle of Algiers in 1957 led to France's loss of Algeria in 1962, what is the danger to be avoided now? What strategic victory should follow the US tactical victory in Iraq in 2003? Clearly, somebody is trying to tell somebody else something, but we—the general readers of the *New York Times*—do not really know who is speaking to whom or what is being said. What has happened since this article was published—public revelation of widespread torture and growing resistance in Iraq—make this exchange about tactics at elite circles all the more significant. This exchange reveals—even without knowing more about it—that for people with the power to stand at the apex of the world and to make decisions that affect the lives of people below, the battle over Iraq is not unlike the battle over colonial Algeria. For them, the US republican state, whatever we call it, has much to learn from the French imperial state.

In effect, as Macmaster has shown in his analysis of torture from Algiers to Abu Ghraib, French colonial officials involved in Algiers taught the United States practices of torture it has used in Iraq.[60] But then the United States has deployed globally a gamut of imperial practices—from torture to subtle forms of cultural influence—which it either learned from other imperial experiences or developed on its own, and which in most instances it first practiced in Latin America. From the vantage point of Latin American history it is difficult not to see the presence of the United States in the region as imperial. But whether we call the United States an empire, an imperialist state, or a republic, in the end what matters is how the concepts we use help us understand and counter formations of domination. Attending to these effects, this essay has sought to make domination in the modern world—whether in Algeria or in Iraq, in the name of the French empire or the US republic—at once more intelligible and more intolerable.

Notes

This paper has benefited from the advice of many. I would like to thank my SAR colleagues and friends, my Harvard students from a seminar on globalization and imperialism (fall 2004), and Genese Sodikoff, Eduard Murphy, and David Pedersen for their invaluable comments.

1. McGranahan and Stoler, "Empires: Thinking Colonial Studies beyond Europe."

2. Kohn, "Reflections on Colonialism," 3–4.

3. Hamza, "Imperialism Old and New."

4. Gallagher and Robinson, "Imperialism of Free Trade."

5. See, for example, Magdoff, *Imperialism,* and Prasenjit Duara, this volume.

6. Said, *Reflections on Exile and Other Essays,* xxviii.

7. Lafeber, *Inevitable Revolutions,* 38.

8. Fuentes, "Prologue," 16.

9. See Fanon, *Wretched of the Earth,* 102.

10. See Robert Freeman Smith, *United States and the Latin American Sphere of Influence,* 152, as well as Wood, *Making of the Good Neighbor Policy,* 5, and DeConde, *History of American Foreign Policy,* 536.

11. Blum, *Killing Hope,* 444–51.

12. Coatsworth, "United States Interventions."

13. In an illuminating discussion of the causes of US intervention in Latin America, Coatsworth argues that the Santo Domingo invasion was the result of domestic politics, not of external threats: President Johnson "felt threatened by Republicans in Congress." Coatsworth, "United States Interventions," 8.

14. Kornbluth, *Pinochet File;* Maxwell, "Case of the Missing Letter in Foreign Affairs."

15. For a discussion of US involvement in the coup based on declassified US government documents, see Golinger, *El Código Chávez.* The United States immediately endorsed the interim government of Pedro Carmona and blamed president Chávez for his downturn. While the US government denies it was involved in the coup, Chávez's government claims it was carried out with US support. I am presently writing a book on the coup. For a discussion of other aspects of the coup, see Coronil, "Nación y Estado durante el golpe contra Hugo Chávez."

16. Gallagher and Robinson, "Imperialism of Free Trade," 13.

17. Gallagher and Robinson, "Imperialism of Free Trade," 13.

18. Gallagher and Robinson, "Imperialism of Free Trade," 7.

19. One exception is Salvatore, who uses the notion of "informal empire" to examine the "representational machinery" of empire. Yet in his work this term does not really build on the work of Gallagher and Robinson but rather serves to address mostly cultural productions in the area. See Salvatore, "Enterprise of Knowledge." Following Gallagher and Robinson more closely are works that examine the British empire in Latin America, for example, Graham, *Britain and the Onset of Modernization in Brazil;* Monteón, "British in the Atacama Desert"; Winn, "Britain's Informal Empire in Uruguay"; Carl, "First Among Equals"; and Gravil, *Anglo-Argentine Connection.*

20. For a discussion of the place of Latin American scholarship within the field of postcolonial studies that highlights the significance of the deep temporal experience of colonialism and imperialism in Latin America, see Coronil, "Latin American Postcolonial Studies and Global Decolonisation."

21. Andre Gunder Frank's concept is developed in his pamphlet *The Development of Underdevelopment.*

22. See their classical book *Dependency and Development in Latin America;* Peter Evans developed this idea in his work on Brazil, *Dependent Development.*

23. On the basis of Richard L. Sklar's "doctrine of domicile," I use the notion of "domiciliated corporate citizen" to refer to the sector of foreign capital that becomes rooted socially and politically in dependent nations. Sklar, *Corporate Power in an African State,* 186.

24. Weyrich, "Contemporary Slavery." The United Nations defines slavery as a variety of human rights violations. In addition to traditional slavery and the slave trade, these abuses include the sale of children, child prostitution, child pornography, the exploitation of child labor, the sexual mutilation of female children, the use of children in armed conflicts, debt bondage, traffic in persons and the sale of human organs, the exploitation of prostitution, and certain practices under apartheid and colonial regimes.

25. In "Empire," Eisenstadt offers a useful discussion of the problem of incorporating subject populations in premodern and modern empires. Of course, the "modern/premodern" distinction is problematic. While aware of its pitfalls, here I follow those who roughly place its temporal divide around the sixteenth century and associate modernity with the colonization of the Americas and the rise of capitalism as a global social and cultural formation.

26. Daalder "Imperialism."

27. Hobson, *Imperialism: A Study.*

28. See, for instance, Hilferding, *Finance Capital;* Luxemburg, *Accumulation of Capital;* Kautsky, *Die Internationalitat und der Krieg;* Lenin, *Imperialism;* Bukharin, *Imperialism and World Economy;* Leonard Woolf, *Economic Imperialism;* Dobb, *Studies in the Development of Capitalism;* Sweezy, *Theory of Capitalist Development;* and Sweezy and Baran, *Monopoly Capital.*

29. For example, the Cuban journal *Temas* 33–34 (April–September 2003) and the *Socialist Register* (2004).

30. Dobb, *Studies in the Development of Capitalism,* and Brenner, "Origins of Capitalist Development."

31. Sweezy, *Theory of Capitalist Development.*

32. Mintz, *Sweetness and Power.*

33. James, *Black Jacobins;* Dubois, *Colony of Citizens.*

34. Marx, *Capital,* vol. 3, 953.

35. Schmitt, *Nomos of the Earth.*

36. Williams, *Capitalism and Slavery;* Mintz, *Sweetness and Power.*

37. Ortiz, *Cuban Counterpoint;* Coronil, "Transculturation and the Politics of

Theory" and *The Magical State.*

38. Silverblatt, *Modern Inquisitions,* 137.

39. Haya de la Torre, *El imperialismo y el Apra;* Nkrumah, *Neo-colonialism.*

40. Hardt and Negri, *Empire.*

41. See Coronil, "Towards a Critique of Globalcentrism."

42. Gallagher and Robinson, "Imperialism of Free Trade," 5–6.

43. William Appleman Williams, *Empire as a Way of Life.*

44. Kaplan, "Left Alone with America."

45. Gaddis and Kennedy, "Kill the Empire! (Or Not)."

46. See, respectively, Magdoff, *Imperialism;* Hobsbawm, "Addressing the Questions"; and Hardt and Negri, *Empire.*

47. Schell, "Imperialism without Empire."

48. Neil Smith, *American Empire.*

49. Steinmetz, "State of Emergency," 327.

50. Steinmetz, "State of Emergency," 341.

51. Panitch and Gindin, "Global Capitalism and American Empire," 1.

52. Panitch, "New Imperial State," 9.

53. Panitch and Gindin, "Global Capitalism and American Empire," 4.

54. Panitch and Gindin, "Global Capitalism and American Empire," 30.

55. Gorilovskaya, "Imperial Denial."

56. Haass, "Imperial America."

57. Chalmers Johnson, *Sorrows of Empire.*

58. Bacevich, *American Empire,* 225.

59. Kaufman, "What Does the Pentagon See in 'Battle of Algiers'?" 3.

60. See Macmaster, "Torture: From Algiers to Abu Ghraib." I am grateful to an anonymous reviewer of this article for this reference.

Part 3

New Genealogies of the Imperial State

9

Modern Inquisitions

Irene Silverblatt

> We can no longer afford to take that which was good in the past and simply call it our heritage, to discard the bad and simply think of it as a dead load which by itself time will bury in oblivion. The subterranean stream of Western history has finally come to the surface.
>
> —*Hannah Arendt*[1]

Hannah Arendt, puzzling over the rise of fascism, searched for a precedent in Western history—a form of government supporting the worldwide dominance of a master race—that would have eased the way for "civilized" peoples to embrace barbarity. She found it in nineteenth-century imperialism, when northern European nations, such as England, were putting machinery in place to rule colonies around the globe. That machinery included an organization for absolute political control and an ideology of social superiority: nineteenth-century imperial powers governed colonies as despotic bureaucrats, argued Arendt, and racial ideologies turned bureaucrats into members of a superior caste. Her fear was this: intertwined, race thinking and bureaucratic rule could unleash "extraordinary power and destruction," destruction all the more terrible since it was bathed in the aura of "rationality" and civilization.[2]

Hannah Arendt demanded that the "civilizing" side of European colonialism be placed under scrutiny, and several essays in this collection also question enduring assumptions about European colonialism and its "civilizing" practices.[3] Her articles are skeptical of the righteous claims made by northern European powers and explicitly challenge the prevailing model of modernity that delineates northern Europe as the civilizing core that then incorporates peripheral, noncivilized polities.

In "Modern Inquisitions," I dispute this classical colonial paradigm in several ways. Like other authors in this collection, I question both the "civilizing" nature of colonial endeavors and the attendant assumption that Europe spread modernity to the world's backward and marginal peoples. However, unlike other essays, "Modern Inquisitions" explores "civilized" colonialism as a phenomenon emerging in the sixteenth and seventeenth centuries and thus sheds light, in different ways, on the colonial processes. I argue that the Spanish empire was at the forefront of European global expansion and that Spanish colonialism established a tone for subsequent imperial endeavors. By arguing that civilized colonial politics did not begin in England or France, this essay engages one of this volume's dominant goals: to recenter the study of imperial formations within a wider frame than the British imperial model. But, more keenly, this essay serves, as the editors intended, as a kind of gadfly: a counterpoint to the accepted wisdom regarding modernity's origins and a critic, therefore, of the "modernist cast" of the volume as a whole.[4]

This essay also argues that the Spanish empire must be understood in its global dimensions—meaning both in relation to rival powers such as the British, Dutch, and Ottomans and in relation to subjugated peoples. This perspective suggests that imperial projects must be about the politics of comparison and be explored in relation to the ways that regional rivalries spurred colonial politics as well. Looking at imperial rivalries also suggests how empires developed propaganda tactics to vaunt their particular brands of "civilizing" and "extracting" as superior to that of their competitors. (Here I am thinking of the "Black Legend," first developed by England in the sixteenth and seventeenth centuries to distinguish itself from Spain.)

This paper is in conversation with other essays in this volume that address questions about imperial legitimacy and the elaborate institutional and ideological processes through which social difference has been constructed. Along with them, it explores the cultural and social means through which states and empires have gained legitimacy by obscuring the political origins of exploitation.[5] It clarifies, moreover, some of the dilemmas surrounding seemingly global concepts of social (or "racialized") difference by emphasizing that in Europe, colonialism and state making were entwined: colonialism was an integral part of European state making, just as the emerging ideologies of nation, nationhood, and national belonging were born from colonial processes. An inquiry into Europe's first wave of colonialism clarifies the ways that a sense of "nationhood" could be rooted in colonial processes—processes that simultaneously made "rulers" into both "national" representatives and privileged, colonizing subjects.[6]

Like other authors in this volume, I emphasize the importance of placing colonial processes in history. Highlighting the historical construction of imperial difference forces us to explore variations, which can then be analyzed comparatively to reach broader abstractions about empire. But only history can explain some of the confusions and contradictions that imperial systems can produce. Only history can clarify the means by which different processes—of politics, economy, and culture—overlap in state making and colony making. In the Spanish case we see how nation, ethnicity, economic privilege, religion, and race thinking can merge, fuse, and divide and how these confusions can open spaces for political contestation. We can also get a flavor of how political and cultural distinctions can harden, ossify, and be converted into something like race.

In sum, contrary to our persistent assumptions, I argue that in Europe, colonialism's governing principles were not launched by nineteenth-century imperialism; rather, that honor goes to Europe's first wave of colonial expansion, spearheaded not by northern Europe but by Portugal and Spain. From the sixteenth century through the mid-seventeenth century, Spain was in the vanguard of the modern world, installing cutting-edge bureaucracies and race-thinking designs—along with civilizing missions—in its widely dispersed colonies. Life in the seventeenth century was very different from life in the nineteenth, of course; but it was Spain's colonial efforts, not northern Europe's, that initiated the mix of "civilizing," bureaucracy, and race thinking at the heart of modern experience.

What happens to our sense of modernity once we trace its elementary forms from the nineteenth century back to the seventeenth?[7] If we take the first wave of European empire as the origin of modernity and what Arendt called the civilized world's "subterranean stream," we have a better grasp, I think, of its inherent disorder, irrationality, and illusions. Apprehending why and how this conceptual blindness—or ignorance—of modernity's seventeenth-century roots has been sustained might illuminate our blindness to the "civilized world's" terrible, and conjoined, underside. Colonial Peru and particularly the Lima office of the Spanish Inquisition will serve as our case in point.

BUREAUCRACY, THE STATE, AND MODERN LIFE

First, we should examine some theoretical considerations regarding modern life, bureaucracy, and the state. Bureaucracy has stood for modernity in the eyes of Western social theorists, who have believed it crucial for shaping modern experience and sensibilities. This argument's most famous proponent, Max Weber, held bureaucracy to be the most fully rationalized organization—and therefore the most modern—in the contemporary world. Two contemporary theorists of the state and bureaucracy, Michel Foucault and Pierre Bourdieu, also connected bureaucracies to modern ways, but their interest was in the advent of the modern state; for them, bureaucracies were significant because they helped fashion the state as an autonomous entity, with a rationale apart from the sovereignty of kings. Unlike Weber, Foucault's and Bourdieu's concerns with the erosion of dynastic power took them to the sixteenth and seventeenth centuries. Like Weber, neither talked about Spain's contributions to state making.[8]

Foucault, exploring the evolution of what he called the "arts of government," believed the seventeenth century marked a watershed in European state formation and the history of the West. The seventeenth century not only witnessed the birth of large-scale administrative units that would come to challenge dynastic sovereignty; it also witnessed radical transformations in political vision.[9]

In the seventeenth century the "state" was, for the first time, something to talk about.[10] "State" was a meaningful concept, understood as an independent entity, born out of dynastic rule but significantly different from it. Seventeenth-century philosophers and political scientists wrote about the state, describing what a good state should do and be, the obligations subjects owed the state, the obligations the state owed subjects, and the essentials of proper state comportment. This new thing, with its own logic, its own way of being, its own conceptual expression, was "governed according to...principles...intrinsic to it," according to "its own form of rationality."[11] State rationality, Foucault pointed out, was practiced and structured through administrative bureaucracies—the bureaucracies of the absolutist state. Schools, "manufactories," armies—these were the institutional forms, the techniques of government that for Foucault constituted the seventeenth century's emerging "society of regulation and discipline."[12]

Like Foucault, Bourdieu centered on processes making the state into an autonomous entity, emphasizing its structures of existence, rationale of being, and patterns of classifying the world—its imposing epistemology. Bourdieu untangled the dialectic between bureaucracy and state, arguing that while the state constructed bureaucracies to administer populations, bureaucracies constructed the state by ordaining its format, its categories of order. Bourdieu's concerns were at once cognitive and structural: his intention was to chart the dynamic making these two facets of social experience inseparable, to focus on the emerging ideologies and institutions that jointly opened the political spaces known as the state. Bureaucracies were key to Bourdieu's scheme, with their capacity to at once frame institutions while monop-olizing information, knowledge, and even moral sensibilities.

Bourdieu called bureaucrats a "state nobility," the state-era equivalent to an aristocracy. They formed a charmed circle, argued Bourdieu, with monopoly over productive means, here knowledge rather than land; they even acquired a cloak of divine mystery, having powers to bestow identity cards (credentials), and determine admission into their elite ranks.[13]

Bureaucratic claims jostled with dynastic privilege during state making's early stages, and Bourdieu suggested that this conflict accounted for ideological changes both accompanying and spurring the autonomy of state institutions. The state nobility, working against the hegemony of dynastic power, developed a special vocabulary to frame its version of political morality and of political imagination. The emerging idiom was that of universalism and rationality—a new theory of special interests but employing the language of "the public." Public good, public will, and public order were, in Bourdieu's words, "working to autonomize reason of state from dynastic reason." Bourdieu understood the growing legitimacy of state institutions to be part of an emerging "habitus," implicit knowledge framing a societal common sense. And as the reach of bureaucracies grew, a growing number of human beings would share a sensibility toward the world defined by common categories produced by—and producing—state bureaucracies.[14]

Would these, our great theorists of modernity (or even us Anglophones), have considered Spain's administrative bureaucracies, and its Inquisition in particular, modern? I will argue this case below.

THE STATE AND ITS ILLUSIONS

Other theorists, arguing that "the state" is at heart an illusion, help us think about how aspects of modern power are not only misrepresented but disappear from public awareness. For Philip Abrams, "the state" is an ideology, a mask, and not a tangible being; it is, rather, a misrepresentation of what states are: "politically organized subjection." The state, he contended, is a figure in an ideology that presents political institutions as if they acted in the common interest, as if they were morally legitimate, as if the violence committed for reasons of state were inherently justified.[15] Abrams, like Foucault and Bourdieu, focused on the state as it came into being, but unlike them challenged the very concept of the state by exploring the "state-idea" as it emerged during the restructuring of European power relations.[16] The state-idea, according to Abrams, is "an illusory account of practice," a "mask" that cloaks a reality of political subjection. Or we could say, bringing Arendt into the dialogue, that it camouflages the West's "subterranean stream." The records of the Spanish Inquisition in Peru are both witness to and part of the process, making the state an entity we have come to take for granted.

Michael Taussig also refused to ignore Hannah Arendt's terrible realization that violence is as much a part of our Western legacy as the most uplifting of civilization's values; at his best, Taussig presented the West's hidden violence with a frightening sense of immediacy. He traveled to the Amazon basin to reveal the horrors carried out in the name of civilization. There, during the turn-of-the-century rubber boom, the British savagely tortured (dismembered, hung, burned) Indian laborers in the Putumayo. For Taussig, modernity's dark, infernal core, capable of unleashing enormous cruelty, was violence begotten by power, by the ability of some Western men to command the very being of others.[17] Like Arendt, Taussig also understood that Western rationality could perfume violence in the colonies as well as violence at home.

By conceptualizing the state as a modern fetish, Taussig went beyond Abram's metaphor of state as mask: although the state's fetishized power might be illusory, it is, Taussig discerned, preeminently and materially real. It is no less than the means through which we apprehend, grasp, and make sense of our political world. Our belief in the essential rationality of the modern state is, Taussig continues, what stops us from seeing the sectarian, all-too-human interests behind official deference to the public good. Our faith in "reasons of state," in our "rational, legal state," is a faith we will not admit.[18]

THE ILLUSION OF THE BOUNDED STATE

State fetishism—transforming an illusion, "the state," into an entity with a life and powers of its own—cast a wide net, one that obscured the subjection of people as well as the subjection of nations. State fetishism created a remarkable historical illusion that European nations were closed off, bounded, with pasts that were independent of the larger world community. It encouraged the fiction that European countries (make that northern European countries) were self-made; that successes enjoyed since the time of the conquest were rooted in their preferred position on civilization's highway, apart from any integral relationship with peoples outside their borders. Put another way, this version of state fetishism denies any intrinsic, relational hierarchy among nations, economies, or peoples; it denies that states and colonies were party to each other's creation, including the re-creation of structured inequities; it denies that Western state making, including its basic mechanics of rule, was honed in the colonizing process. State fetishism denies history.

Fernando Coronil has described this Western mythology as "occidentalism."[19] State fetishism, in its occidentalized format, wrested Western nation building from its roots in global politics—a fictional divorce as characteristic of the first round of fetishism as of the more commonly discussed nineteenth-century version. The modern world, from its inception, was transnational in scope and hierarchical in structure. And perhaps nowhere are these characteristics more evident than in the sixteenth-century categories that were to order the newly globalized humanity: the categories of race thinking.

RACE THINKING, NATIONALISM, AND THEIR COLONIAL FOUNDATIONS

Tracing the modern world back to the sixteenth century, when Iberia was simultaneously building a state and an empire, lets us better grasp another of the modern world's deceits. State fetishism—veiling our origins in a globalizing, hierarchical world—has veiled our origins in race thinking as well; it has made us lose sight of our colonial foundations and of the antagonistic and racialized social relationships at its core.

Hannah Arendt, choosing her words carefully, did not so much talk about "racism" as about "race thinking." Race thinking cuts a wider swath than race because it moves us behind and beyond racism's narrow, nineteenth-century roots. Race thinking lets us place social processes that we tend to analytically separate into the same framework: that is, instead of studying ethnicity and race, or caste and race, or nationalism and race as autonomous social forms, we can, under the rubric of race thinking, better grasp how these processes have interpenetrated and shaped one another over time.

According to almost every major historical text, Latin America was a society of castes. Spain divided conquered peoples into corporate groups—Spanish, Indian, black—each with associated rights, privileges, and obligations. Ideally, castes were endogamous, and since caste-mates were to marry one another, membership was, in principle, determined by descent. The caste system was patently a device of colonial political order, and even though descent played a part and even though color (black or *negro*) named one constituent, caste is understood to be a legal or social (as opposed to biological) construct at heart. Unlike caste, race is understood to be principally a question of ancestry and phenotype, a biological phenomenon (or so goes the ideology), and as a consequence, independent of social or political regimes. Race emerged as a dominant account of social differentiation in the West's "modern," liberal age, and the nineteenth-century revolutions in the natural and human sciences provided its explanatory frame. Race was inherited, and, since human capabilities were linked to race, human capabilities, according to racist doctrine, were also inherited.[20]

Race thinking does not negate the colonial caste system, nor does it deny that caste and race systems represent two different modes of organizing and explaining inequality. Race thinking does help us see, however, what the race–caste division hides: that race and caste were not separate systems but interpenetrating. Race thinking helps us understand how race and caste might, chameleonlike, slip in and out of one another;[21] how a relatively innocent category (like color) could become virulent; how politically defined differences (like nationality) could so easily become inheritable traits.

Race thinking, then, broadly refers to any mode of construing and engaging social hierarchies through the lens of descent. It represents a potential way of sensing, understanding, and being in the world, a cultural possibility that can become part of social identities and social practices. Its most significant property, however, is its most difficult lesson: race thinking is invariably tied to other expressions of power, other forms of social antagonism, and is best interpreted in dialectic with those relations.[22] Arendt was especially concerned with how race thinking could become embedded in the bureaucracies of state and colonial governments. Like her, I center on this dynamic, while trying to understand how these relations have been so difficult to grasp.

THE PERUVIAN SETTING OF COLONIALISM AND STATE MAKING

Academic blindnesses have tended to overlook the fact that history wedded state making in Europe to European colonialism. Spain is, perhaps, the prototype of this double-edged politics: Castilian monarchs were vying to increase their authority over the Iberian Peninsula when they triumphed in the Americas; struggling to control Iberian principalities when they worked out details of colonial government; battling the English when they established Indian courts; skirmishing with the Dutch when they defended colonial borders. The Spanish experience, fashioned out of colonial efforts and European conflicts, colored all of Europe's state-building projects.

To make a Spanish colony out of what had been the Inca empire was an extended process. Although begun in the 1530s when Spanish conquistadors, led by Pizarro, overwhelmed Cuzco's native forces, it was not until the century's end that royal authorities—having confronted civil wars, rebellions, and settlers' raw ambitions—could successfully root institutions of government. The Crown quickly learned that colony building pivoted on control over immigrant colonists in equal measure to control over native peoples, and it instituted bureaucracies to curb and "administer" both. Learning from pitfalls on the peninsula, the Crown consolidated colonial state power in ways impossible in Europe: strengthening bureaucracies, it gave royal authorities (as opposed to Spanish settlers) jurisdiction over Indian commoners and turned royal bureaucrats into brokers between Peru's colonizers and colonized natives. The Crown appointed magistrates to supervise Spanish–Indian relations, designated local headmen to represent native communities to royal authorities, and established courts, armies, and district governors to oversee the rest. It fell to the Crown's ally, the Church, however, to instruct Indians, as well as colonials, in the ways and necessities of civilization.[23]

Like all bureaucratic administrations, colonial Peru's functioned through a cultural matrix, and race thinking was its scaffold. Royal authorities, grounded in the experiences of a developing absolutist state, imposed broad, racialized classifications on their imperial subjects. They created two unequal "republics" as the foundation for colonial rule: Native Americans and their descendants, regardless of origin or ethnicity, were classed as Indians; descendants of Iberia, regardless of origin, ethnicity, or social rank, were classed as privileged Spanish colonists. With the exception of the native nobility, all Indians owed tribute and labor to the Crown; unlike their lower-status kin in Europe, however, Spaniards in the colonies had no such obligations. When Indian populations, decimated by disease and upheaval, could no longer meet labor demands, the Crown turned to slavery, spurring the creation of a third abstract category of government: Africans brought to Peru and their descendants—regardless of origin, ethnicity, or social rank—were classed as *negros*, or blacks. Ancestry determined the official categories of colonial order. But as authorities were to soon realize, colonial realities could not be contained within colonial categories, and "hybrid" racial classes (such as *mestizo, mulato,* and *sambo*) entered the Spanish political ken. This was Spanish legal theory's flat presentation of colonial order—a caste trio of *español, indio,* and *negro* along with mixtures.[24] Like most categorical descriptions, it concealed the historical processes—and the contradictions—at its heart.

THE MODERN INQUISITION

Most Anglophones regard the Spanish Inquisition as an implacable, premodern institution, manned by greedy fanatics, who gleefully and brutally defended Spain's religious purity.[25] This stereotype, with roots going back to Queen Elizabeth's propaganda wars against King Felipe II, has blinded us to the fact that the Spanish Inquisition was one of the most modern bureaucracies of its time.[26] It has also blinded us to the fact that the tribunal's function as defender of the faith and nation was inseparable from its bureaucratic structure.[27]

The Inquisition was one structure of many that were involved in the colony's moral regulation, but it was nevertheless responsible for the empire's rawest displays of cultural force. In the great theater of power, the auto-da-fé (a public ceremony manifesting tribunal judgment), and in smaller, daily theaters of reputation and fear, the Peruvian Inquisition clarified cultural blame: presenting those among the colony's non-Indian populace[28] who held beliefs or engaged in life practices that were considered threats to its moral and civic well-being. These threats included a range of heretical crimes—from blasphemy to sexual misconduct (including the solicitation of sexual favors by priests) to witchcraft to the capital offense of practicing non-Catholic religions, whether Islam, Protestantism, or Judaism.[29]

The Spanish Inquisition was established at the end of the fifteenth century to meet a perceived threat to national security, namely, the undermining of Spanish dominions, first by Judaizers and then by all manner of heretics. Nonetheless, in spite of its religious demeanor, the Inquisition was an institution of state, under the jurisdiction of the Crown (and not the pope).[30] As an institution of the Spanish empire, it was enmeshed in its national mission to impose Catholicism and expand political dominion. Linked to its role as defender of national security, the Inquisition was responsible for enforcing "purity of blood" statutes—measures that restricted political offices and professions to men of pure "Spanish" stock. It was also the only institution of government with jurisdiction throughout the Spanish realm; and it was an institution that proudly held a reputation for pursuing heretics regardless of their social standing.[31]

Spain brought this renowned institution to the Americas, establishing branch offices in Lima (1569–71), Mexico (1569–71), and

Cartagena (1610).[32] The Lima Inquisition was launched under Viceroy Francisco de Toledo, a prepotent administrator often credited with solidifying Spain's presence in the viceroyalty. His attitude toward the tribunal, like that of many royal authorities who followed, was one of studied ambivalence. On the one hand, Toledo never doubted the colony's serious religious needs and took great delight in the tribunal's arrival;[33] on the other, he was wary of the tribunal's incursions into the domain of royal power, even warning Madrid of difficulties arising "because the [inquisitors] were extending their jurisdiction much more than they should."[34]

Like any bureaucracy, the Inquisition was run according to procedures and rules, and its workings were overseen by bureaucrats, the credentialed *letrados* (learned men, university graduates). The ideal Lima inquisitor was to be "circumspect, judicious...not greedy or covetous, understanding, very charitable...and experienced and informed about life in the Americas"; he was *pacífico*—tranquil, unperturbed, and not a hothead, unlike a swashbuckling conquistador.[35] The ideal inquisitor, bureaucratically disposed, was immersed in rules, and the tribunal seemed to have rules for everything: officeholders (each local tribunal had twenty—inquisitor, attorney general, defense attorney, notary, constable, office manager, accountant, pharmacist, and porter, among others); job descriptions and requirements (inquisitors had to be university graduates, preferably with a degree in law and extensive professional experience). There was even an ecclesiastic career ladder (inquisitor was higher than prosecuting attorney), and most believed that an American posting was a rung on the stairway to bureaucratic success (through 1635, seven of nine Lima magistrates graduated to positions of higher authority; the other two ruined their chances because of, shall we say, irregularities on the job).[36]

While not precisely a court of law (the Inquisition was established to "meet a perceived national threat"),[37] the Inquisition had much in common with the secular and ecclesiastical courts of the day. In principle, its practices were guided by regulations designed to promote equity and justice as well as limit the powers of officeholders according to an established hierarchy of command.[38] Inquisition manuals gave specific instructions about evidence needed for arrest and conviction, methods for conducting interrogations, and criteria for determining sentences. And, as if to doubly check for fairness, tribunal decisions were reached with the input of external consultants at every stage in the trial process—from indictment to penance.[39]

Like most European courts, the tribunal assumed that the accused were guilty unless shown otherwise. And although the burden of proof remained squarely on their shoulders, defendants were supported by a number of statutes: they were entitled to a lawyer (appointed by the tribunal), to name corroborating witnesses, and to provide a list of enemies who might testify out of spite.[40] Procedures notwithstanding, however, assumptions of guilt, coupled with the (also regulated) use of torture, seemed to make the fight for innocence almost hopeless.

Lima's inquisitors thus depended on and contributed to a growing transatlantic paper trail. Because of their considerable record keeping, inquisitors were able to investigate religious activities over time and across continents, and they frequently turned to archives to either verify testimony or ferret out unsavory characters for further investigation. Accused heretics found that once captured in writing, earlier convictions could turn into a decades-long plague. For example, the archived transcript of Manuel Bautista Perez's 1624 arrest for Judaizing was to play a critical role in his 1635 conviction. And in a scenario worthy of Kafka, Joan Vicente was forced to languish in jail for eight years while the tribunal waited for copies of his Evora (Portugal) trial to reach Peru.[41]

Many of us presume that the inquisitors always got their man or woman, that the verdict was fixed, that the tribunals were, if anything, mere show trials. Indeed, the accused were severely handicapped. Presumptions of guilt, the character of testimony, the use of torture, and the nature of evidence all worked to the prisoner's disadvantage. Disadvantaged, however, is not the same as preordained. Inquisitors did not act as a concerted group, executing the will of their superiors; verdicts did not catapult themselves forward. Lima inquisitors, mid-level bureaucrats, were a quarrelsome bunch: they quarreled among themselves, and they quarreled with their superiors. Magistrates, albeit rarely, had to publicly admit to errors of judgment and publicly concede mistaken arrests. Men and women accused of heresy and imprisoned—sometimes for years—while waiting their cases to run their course could, in the end, be "suspended" or even exonerated.[42] These exceptions help us see the obvious: the Inquisition, like all state institutions, was not a monolithic, coherent body; the Inquisition, like all state institutions, was structured by bureaucratic exigencies; the Inquisition, like all state institutions, was only, or all too, human.[43]

No act painted the Spanish Inquisition with greater infamy than torture. Like its peer institutions throughout Europe, the Spanish Inquisition believed torture was a means to the truth—albeit, in the Spanish case, a reluctant one. Contrary to stereotype, torture was subject to a goodly number of rules and was more supervised and less often practiced in Spain than in other nations we associate with Western civilization.[44]

It is a devastating irony that inquisitors employed torture to get to the truth while at the same time doubting the truth of confessions obtained by torture. Magistrates believed "voluntary" confessions were more reliable than coerced ones, and trial transcripts nearly always indicated if confessions were freely given or not.[45] Across the board and throughout the empire, torture was employed in a minority of cases reaching the bench; most detainees, accused of relatively insignificant heresies (such as bigamy or cursing the name of God), did not suffer this anguish. But torture's weight cannot be judged by these statistics alone, because while not resorted to frequently, torture was applied selectively and fiercely: the bulk of its victims were Judaizers, Protestants, and *moriscos* (converted, of Moorish ancestry). In Peru, most victims were Judaizers. According to Henry Kamen's estimates, over three-quarters of all accused Judaizers were tortured in late seventeenth-century Spain. The Viceroyalty of Peru bears this figure out.[46]

THE INQUISITION AND STATE MAGIC

With jurisdiction over pivotal aspects of religious life—in a country in which Catholicism was akin to a nationalist ideology—Spanish inquisitors, along with their episcopal counterpart, were commanding figures in colonial life. More than commanding figures, they became godlike, as the state, surreptitiously, took on a life of its own.

Inquisitors and their targets participated in the making of state illusions, making the state appear to be what it was not: autonomous, unified, and even sacred; making bureaucrats appear to be what they were not: a godlike aristocracy; and, making state subjects appear to be what they were not: abstract ciphers in a dossier of statistics.[47]

The political rituals of baroque statecraft were lessons in spectacle writ large, and the Inquisition's notorious autos-da-fé, the public celebrations of final judgments and punishments—when some were whipped and humiliated, others burned at the stake—were formidable examples. Inquisitors understood these religious theaters as pedagogical displays on a mammoth scale and said as much: the autos would school the public in civic values, morality, and the implacability of Spanish Catholicism. As indelible reminders of the tribunal's command over life and death, however, autos would also serve to propagate the mysteries of the state, transforming magistrates into gods and the Inquisition into a force—a being—of its own.

The auto-da-fé celebrated in 1639 was the most grandiose, and perhaps most infamous, auto-da-fé Lima ever witnessed. The procession winding its way from the tribunal to the scaffolding must have been an extraordinary sight. It began with clergy carrying crosses—draped in black cloth as a sign of mourning—from every one of Lima's churches, followed by nearly seventy penitents, lined up in order of the severity of their crimes. The eleven to be executed were found at the very end, "wearing crowns and tunics, embossed with flames and devils in various guises as serpents and dragons."[48] Lima's many dignitaries, dressed in the opulence of their class, accompanied the procession, while two royal squadrons stood guard—one in the Inquisition's plaza and the other in Lima's principal square.

The autos-da-fé performed the tribunal's illusions of unity and transcendence on a grand scale; but there were also less spectacular rites that projected the state on a smaller scale, but no less effectively. For example, magistrates were careful that accused heretics never see beyond a facade of perfect agreement, never guess that officials disputed among themselves about the justification of arrests and the solidity of evidence. When Manuel Henriquez, accused of Judaizing in 1635, claimed not to know the reason for his arrest, the inquisitors, in one voice, replied that "they were not in the habit of arresting anyone without sufficient evidence."[49] Inquisitors thundered the same response when anyone dared protest his or her innocence.[50]

The cultural routines of rule—the government technologies (to coin Foucault) that habituate subjects to a particular political order —are not as obvious as the grand rites of state and perhaps for that reason are much more pernicious. They have similar effects but, enacted in the day-to-day of state activities (such as repeatedly providing information about birth, marital status, and race), appear unexceptional, commonplace. Through modest rites of state as well as the more dazzling, inquisitors were promoting an institutional persona: the Inquisition as a unified, autonomous, rational, and just political being. Taken together, sensational rites and mundane routines are the cultural practices that urge us to imagine power in certain ways: making state categories (such as race thinking) and the classifications used to make sense of the world one and the same; making state history disappear from social awareness.

Inquisitors were bureaucrats with a mission. Their job was to safeguard God's new chosen people—Spaniards and their empire—from heretical incursions. Magistrates must have drawn the force and pretension to make inordinate decisions over others from what they believed to be their divine charge. Tribunal work, however, was carried out by means of bureaucratic practices, and bureaucratic practices also provided a semi-divine grounding to the commission of otherwise unthinkable acts.

Standards, rules, and protocols were the stuff of statedom and bureaucracy; and tribunal members, like their counterparts around the globe, were immersed in them. Peru's inquisitors took a vow to follow the rules seriously: they maintained steady contact with Madrid despite what would seem to be preposterous obstacles (thousands of miles and months of travel), and they made a show of abiding by protocol, even when they sidestepped their superiors. But nowhere were the inquisitors' attachment to procedure more evident than in the fervor to find (and make) the truth. When Antonio de Acuna, arrested early in 1635, begged for an audience to confess his (and others') heresies, an inquisitor, forgoing sleep, remained at Acuna's side from dusk until dawn.[51] Inquisitors took pride in their efforts, even when these efforts were for naught (such as spending hours writing down what was later discovered to be perjured testimony).[52] For inquisitors, the prize was not just the outcome or the evidence but the social practices themselves.

In the dialectics of state making, godlike inquisitor bureaucrats transformed human beings into "its"—the fragments of humanity reworked by "state science" into statistics. Neither bureaucracies nor statistics are inherently evil; they are necessary (how else to administer polities of such size and complexity?). But regardless of the end to which they are put, statistics, like the bureaucratic institutions in which they thrive, mold human understandings. They shape our sense of the makeup of society, the structure of the political world, the significance and morality of human practices, the rights of state managers and state subjects—and the appropriate way to represent and investigate them.

The inquisitors collected all kinds of information about the men and women under their purview. Interrogations read like a modern census form: age, place of birth, education, residence, family, "race." Inquisitors were nowhere more godlike, however, than when they used violence in the name of state reason; and the most disturbing use of state-talk was in the documentation of torture.

In the seventeenth century, state torture was neither formally illegal nor a source of shame or scandal; and, never doubting its legitimacy, inquisitors made records in abundance. Their very existence documents a significant modern practice of state making: the objectification of experience, the transformation of social relations into recordable—or legible—form.[53] This set of "statistics" is particularly egregious, mutating as it does relations of power and pain into a digestible flatness. Yes, we find elaborate descriptions in the archives. But no set of words can translate the defilement of a human being's very humanness.

In the bureaucratization of torture, records expose what can be unleashed in the name of public welfare—not only the physical terror, but structures of thinking and feeling built on the abstraction of life. State abstractions seem to remove these acts from the realm of accountability, and they do so by dismembering humanness; abuse is splintered into columns of an account ledger, torture is fragmented into events and responses, horror is objectified into smaller and smaller components, and then acts are legitimized by following the rules. Perhaps intentionally—but most probably not—the breakdown of human existence into fractures make a whole life easier to discard. This is the pornography of bureaucratic rendering, deafening the perpetrator—and us readers—to torture's cries and distracting us from the web of social relations, the power, behind what the bureaucrat registers as truth.

The tribunal, like other bureaucracies, projected a twinned vision: on the one hand, it was an independent, irrefutable force of state; on the other, it was a human organization made up of magistrates who could be upright but also despicable. The tribunal was seen as a legitimate institution, an unquestionable institution—and a sham. It inspired dynamic, ambivalent, and incompatible sentiments: deep faith and trust, gratitude and hope, skepticism and hatred, terror and awe.

In the dialectic of perceptions about the tribunal's character, presumptions of suprahumanity were never far from the most vulgar of human attributes. It was not uncommon to hear the Inquisition called an unconscionable institution, whose magistrates were no more than greedy hypocrites. Lima's magistrates heard themselves named "cruel" and "barbaric" for their savage executions or "just thieves" for their selfishness and false sanctimony.[54] Others were shamed for being womanizers or drunkards.[55] The Inquisition spewed fear: you can feel it in the testimonies, the despair after the arrest of friends, family members, or business partners. "Here is the [Lima] Inquisition, so detested and feared by all of the peoples [living there]," wrote an anonymous chronicler.[56] Menacing, threatening, prompting dread and hopelessness, the tribunal compelled submission.[57] Intimidation had snowballing effects: eroding bonds of trust, sabotaging social relations, augmenting isolation and feelings of vulnerability. And as fear wore down social relations, it must have enhanced the Inquisition's image as a force in its own right. The Inquisition seemed to be everywhere and see everything: Pedro Baez, a witness in Manuel Henriquez's trial, supposedly said in wonderment, "he did not know how the inquisitors could possibly know about all these things."[58] This aura was no doubt nurtured by the tribunal's magisterial autos-da-fe. But it was also inflamed by rumors: the stories about the Inquisition's attainments, about its reach, and, ultimately, about its irrationality.

Yet in spite of these suspicions and stabs of cynicism, the Inquisition undoubtedly enjoyed the support of the public at large.[59] Most Spanish subjects living in the viceroyalty—or in the empire for that matter—believed that the tribunal served the general good, even if it did act excessively at times or on occasion punish the innocent. The great majority of colonials saw the Inquisition as a bulwark of civic order.

The crowds provide evidence of the Inquisition's popularity. During the dragnet of 1635, when nearly one hundred were brought to Lima on charges of illicit Judaizing, swarms of young men stood by the tribunal's doors to cheer on the noblemen bringing in suspects.[60] Throngs also attended the autos-da-fé. Bystanders might have been there for a host of reasons—because they were supposed to be or because it was a form of local entertainment; nonetheless, they expressed a sturdy desire for the tribunal to carry out its duties.[61] This is how one observer described the audience at a seventeenth-century auto: "an infinite number of onlookers" from all parts of Lima and beyond, crammed into available windows, terraces, balconies, and scaffolds, jostling for space, spending the night in bleachers (the elite got reserved cushions with tickets from the deputy inquisitor), and overwhelming guards with their numbers and enthusiasm.[62]

One of the most extraordinary statements of tribunal support was penned by Felipe Guaman Poma de Ayala, a descendant of the indigenous nobility, who authored a thousand-page critique of colonial society. Although Guaman Poma severely faulted colonial rule, he was a loyal subject and devote Christian. Poma spared no one for shunting the moral promise of Christianity and famously took priests to task for their hypocrisy. Nonetheless, Poma understood the Inquisition to be an ally in his mission, one that was willing to defend Christian ideals and punish the wicked regardless of their social standing. Poma judged the tribunal as the one Spanish institution with the integrity, power, and interest to rein in colonial officials, whether sinning priests or transgressing governors. He praised it as a fierce standard of public order in a colonial world run amok.[63]

The Inquisition represented itself as the defender of the colony's religious and civic order. Its job was to protect the viceroyalty from enemies within, from the heretics—fraudulent *beatas,* witches, blasphemers, bigamists, adulterers, and hidden Jews—who would undermine the Spanish empire and civilization (one and the same). Its purview was religious crimes, but as the Inquisition explained to everyone, including the Supreme Council, the viceroy, the king, and "the people," its mission was unmistakably political. When challenged by their superiors for executing accused Judaizers in the 1639 auto-da-fé without first getting headquarter's permission (a regulation), Lima inquisitors justified their breach of protocol by turning to reasons of state:

they claimed to have uncovered, in the course of their investigations, that the men burned at the stake, together with the Dutch, were behind a plot to blow up the port city of Callao. The Inquisition was a centurion of national security.[64]

A vision of the Inquisition as an irreproachable institution of government was, by the seventeenth century, appearing to dominate the viceroyalty's cultural politics; and, the Inquisition's inescapable presence surely contributed to making the state an intimate part of a colonial "modern" self. State ideologies made the Inquisition into an entity larger than life, and its institutional being appeared increasingly anchored in the viceregal way of living in and imaging the world. Tribunal records, opening bureaucracy to inspection, suggest how inquisitors, immersed in their bureaucratic practices, might have contributed to that dawning, modern concept that the state was an entity apart—separate from dynastic history—with its own logic, its own needs, and its own "reason." They help us imagine how the state could be perceived as if it were a concrete, material thing in and of itself, how the state could become a fetish. Further, these records help us imagine how the state could become a part of our social beings and, as a concept through which we apprehend the world, could impede our ability to envision power in any other way.

NATIONAL ILLUSIONS

The Inquisition held a special place in Spanish statecraft, as an arbiter of religious orthodoxy in a country that defined religion as nationalism and a bureaucracy responsible for the empire's cultural (that is, national) security. It was an institution of state that defined what nationhood meant by fixing internal cultural boundaries in tandem with Spain's position in an increasingly global world. As such, the Inquisition held an advantaged position in one of state magic's most prodigious feats: constructing a "nation" as if it were autonomous and self-directing when, in fact, it was neither.

The Inquisition's mission would appear to be only an internal affair. But in fact, concerns about Catholic preeminence had everything to do with political and ideological battles that crossed state borders: The history of Islam on the Iberian Peninsula was tied to victories of North African caliphates over Spain's Gothic lords; Spain's thriving

Jewish communities of the fifteenth century were made up not only of victims of the Roman diaspora but also of Jews expelled from medieval England and France. But most significant, the Spanish Inquisition was consolidated as an institution during a period of extended warfare on two fronts: war with the Muslim Ottomans and war with Protestant Europe—political conflicts that were also religious wars.

Throughout the seventeenth century, the Inquisition contributed mightily to defining the boundaries of political and religious orthodoxy within Spain, boundaries it feared were being permeated by the ideas and ships of Spain's Protestant and Muslim enemies. Vigilance, the tribunal declared, was required both at home and in the vast stretch of territories—in the Americas, Asia, and Africa—forming Spain's colonial possessions. Threats internal to Catholic Spain were inseparable, then, from the broader theater of European hostilities, an arena now global in scope. The Inquisition, that most Spanish of institutions, was produced in the cauldron of modern global politics.

The very notion of a closed, bounded, autonomous state—Abram's reified state, Coronil's occidentalist state, the state of modern times—was a sham. And, state making's own cultural work was such that it shrouded the state's international, colonial, and race-thinking make-up from view. Working for the benefit of the state, bureaucratic practices put blinders on officeholders, clients, and subjects alike. These blinders focused attention on the state as an independent being, with its own autonomous rationale divorced from global politics.

What knowledge have we lost by detaching the nation-state from its more than five-centuries-deep global roots? We have lost our origins in colonialism—which means we have lost our origins in race thinking. The sleights of hand fashioning "the state" and "race" have been colleagues for years—together partners in building the West's "subterranean stream." State making's mysteries not only institutionalized race thinking and gave it legitimacy; these mysteries also made race thinking part of the body politic.

THE INQUISITION AND RACE THINKING

The modern state, following Foucault, took "government in the name of truth" as its charge; and one of the most profound social truths for state officials to judge was the nature of human personhood.

Inquisitors' day-to-day activities included specifying various aspects of that "truth": determining if someone constituted a threat to God and empire was one; determining, like other viceregal authorities, the official colonial race category of persons appearing before the bench was another.[65] Inquisitors, working through and in state structures, secured racialized ways of defining the world, judging the world, and being in the world.

Peru's inquisitors (as little gods) were inscribing race thinking into institutional practice at the same time they were producing the state. By the seventeenth century, magistrates (and other functionaries) were officially dividing people into Spanish, Indian, and black boxes as a matter of course; and "Indian," "black," and "Spaniard" were taking on the appearance of things—of self-evident qualities of human being. Like "state," "race" was a phantasm, and part its mystique was to appear as if it were a category of individuals and not a social relation produced in the political and economic turmoil of modern, colonial state making.

Bureaucrats control knowledge, and as social analysts have pointed out, therein lies a source of their power.[66] But inquisitors dominated a special kind of knowledge. Inquisitors could determine the most profound of societal truths—membership in a human community. Inquisitors, after all, determined the "blood purity" of those appearing before them, just as they determined if behavior was heretical and therefore outside the Catholic–Spanish pale. Seventeenth-century inquisitors inherited a world whose humanity was increasingly understood in racialized terms, and magistrates played a significant (if unwitting) role in deepening and consolidating race thinking as a way of life. In their bureaucratic practices, inquisitors were delineating the very terms of social experience: the terms by which the world was to be judged and the terms framing any individual's social truth.

It was the fusion of bureaucratic rule and race that Arendt found so dangerous, and it was "state magic" that helped make race thinking so powerful, ubiquitous, and illusory.

SPAIN, SPANIARD, SPANISHNESS

Nationalism and race thinking, in concert, propelled the modern world's most destructive beliefs; yet we have trouble visualizing the depth of that connection because our historical sensibilities rarely put colonialism at the core of modern life. Debates about the meaning of "Spaniard" and an incipient "Spain"—their spiritual and biological core—suggest we do otherwise.

There was no Spain (as a government and nation) in the seventeenth century; what we now call Spain was composed of regional principalities, including the New World colonies, under the dominion of the Hapsburg Dynasty of Castile. But in spite of governmental forms, a sense of "Spanishness" was permeating Iberia. When the concept of "state" was coming into being, the peninsula's philosophers and policy specialists were also writing about a Spanish character and a Spanish people.[67] And most significantly, that sense of "Spanishness" was emerging as modern colonialism took form. In 1532, Peru's *conquistadores* did not call themselves Spaniards but called themselves Christians—armed to fight the infidels; however, within several decades, the Iberian immigrants who were establishing the viceregal government and the structures of the colonial state were referring to one another as Spaniards.[68]

What our state theorists—Foucault and Bourdieu—do not put in the picture is that philosophers were talking about a Spanish character as Castile was conquering and colonizing around the globe. Investigations into "Spanishness" in Europe were taking place at the same time that colonizers were civilizing Indians, enslaving Africans, and distinguishing themselves from the lower orders of Indians and blacks by calling one another Spanish. The historical meeting of state making and colony (race) making meant that the two senses of "Spanishness"—as incipient nation and as category of colonial rule—penetrated each other. Something of the nation must have been made with every use of *español* in the colonies. Reciprocally, Madrid's discussions of the Spanish character must have drawn on a vision of the colonial español. Moreover, not only was Spanish—as a colonial category—racialized, so was its hidden partner, the potential Spanish nation. By the seventeenth century, learned and popular opinion held that a Spaniard's spiritual core was, in fact, biological and that an authentic Spaniard could be defined by his purity of blood.

Hannah Arendt's analysis of nineteenth-century British colonialism as fascist precedent points a finger at singular tensions within its race-framed categories of rule. Colonialism required that its superior caste of administrators and functionaries be able to find peers wherever the Union Jack flew. English, she argued, had to be a global phenomenon. Yet Englishmen were not all equal; they did not share the same possibilities in life. Race thinking had to obscure these internal divisions; yet at the same time, race thinking had to leave these divisions in place.

The category "Spaniard" filled similar shoes: it defined a unifying experience for all colonizers (*españoles* did not owe tribute or labor service), gave that experience substance as an "unmixed race," and portrayed the kingdom/race as God's chosen. But as Lima's authorities —who, like their English counterparts, harbored elite expectations and pretensions—were to discover, "unmixed race" stretched precariously over the internal hierarchies it was supposed to mute. Peruvian Spaniards, as viceroys and inquisitors bemoaned, had forgotten their place. Tensions within español—between metropolitan-born and creole, between nobility and commoner, and, significantly, between aristocrat and merchant—were unbearable for many peninsulars at work civilizing Peruvians. Some of the Inquisition's most grievous tragedies, particularly the persecutions of New Christians of Jewish ancestry, were the result.[69] Rules of blood purity were an impossible attempt to stanch the brewing threats of the modern colonial world.

Administrators in Spain and Spain's colonies used a particular race-thinking notion to shape and calibrate the "natural order" of political life. They argued that blood carried stains and that stains could determine character traits, intelligence, political rights, and economic possibilities. The notion of blood purity was first elaborated in Europe, where it was used to separate Old Christians from Spain's New Christians—women and men of Jewish and Muslim origins whose ancestors had converted to Christianity. New Christians carried stained blood and consequently were perceived as a potential danger to official life; New Christians were by statute, if not always in practice, prohibited from holding political positions, going to university, or entering professions. Reigning learned and popular opinion, by the sixteenth century, held that a Spaniard's spiritual core was, in fact, biological in origin and that a true and legitimate Spaniard could have only pure blood coursing through his veins.[70]

Conquistadores brought the curse of New Christians, the concept of stained blood (*mancha*), to the Americas. Inquisitors, the bureaucrats responsible for certifying blood type, were obliged to indicate the "race" and blood purity of everyone brought before them; their records give us a ringside view of the New Christian dilemma in the New World. With debates spinning about the nature of blood stains (Were they indelible? Could baptism override them? Could New Christians of Jewish descent ever lose their stain?), authorities in the Americas were also vexed by blood-related questions. Were all New Christians alike? Was the blood stain of Europe's New Christians the same as the blood stain of Indians or blacks? Were all stains equal? When inquisitors and their colleagues responded to these issues in their daily chores of statecraft, they were helping make race into a calculable thing. They were also imbuing "race" with very modern, often state-related, confusions—of nation and religion, culture and genes, color and ability.[71]

When inquisitors condemned the newly converted on both sides of the Atlantic, when they declared that not only the blood of Europe's New Christians but also the blood of Indians, blacks, mestizos, and mulattos carried stains, they provided "Spanishness" with another common ground. Spanish blood, whether in the context of colony or "nation," was pure blood. Not only was the Spanish caste racialized, so also was its contemporary partner: the potential Spanish nation. There are benefits to exploring modernity's elementary forms, and one is a more transparent—and stunning—view of this process.

PROBLEMS AND CONFUSIONS

In the Andes, the confusions and contradictions of race thinking could often come out as breathtaking conspiracies involving New Christian merchants, witches, Indians, and blacks. Inquisitors, at different times, lumped together various members of the above categories as colluding traitors against Church and State. Here, I very briefly take on three interacting colonial confusions: the "Jewish/mercantile problem," the "woman/witchcraft problem," and the "Indian problem." As illustrated, magistrates inevitably brought race thinking to bear on their judgments, just as they inevitably appealed to reasons of state to justify them. Further, inquisitors, like other state bureaucrats, did not have the only word on race and its meanings.

Debates over the character of New Christians—here defined as baptized women and men of Jewish ancestry—were debates that fused questions regarding Spain's emerging sense of nation with the new global, colonial order. The supporters of purity of blood laws believed that religious conversion could not erase the stains of a heretical religious past, and inquisitors who arrested New Christians on the assumption they were insidious Jewish merchants were making the case for a "racially" pure Spanish nation and for a "racially" pure definition of "Spanishness."[72] They were also participating in a vision of the world reminiscent of what we now call racial profiling.

Most inquisitors were dubious about the commitment of New Christians to Spain or to Catholicism (loyalty, after all, was in the blood), and their doubt became alarm in Peru, where magistrates were convinced that New Christians, internationalist merchants, were establishing subversive ties not only with indios and negros but also with Spain's enemies abroad (such as the Dutch). The remarkable transformations in political economy—the growth of merchant capital and the growth of colonialism—nurtured the tribunal's wildest fantasies of New Christian conspirators at the hub of a great conspiracy of oppressed colonial malcontents (Indians and blacks) and foreign (New Christian, Portuguese, Dutch, and British) political and economic interests.

New Christians were not the only ones to be accused of conspiratorial acts; colonial racial politics sired a new set of heretics whose treachery was attached, as well, to colonial racial politics. During the seventeenth century, when New Christians were sparking tribunal concerns, some non-Indian women were being arrested for heretically colluding with Peruvian natives. These women—heresy wore a gendered face—were charged with secretly practicing witchcraft, and one of their black art's most dangerous aspects had to do with Indians. By the middle of the seventeenth century, Peru's sorceresses were censured for going out to the countryside to learn Indian lore, employing coca leaf in their conjures, exhorting the Inca queen with Quechua words, and soliciting the Inca for help in their diabolic acts.[73] Non-Indian "witches" were charged with practicing an Inca-centered, nativist—possibly even an anticolonial and antiracialist—form of sorcery. These women, construing a miraculous Inca/Indian, were reinforcing colonial categories of rule but, like good witches, were also turning them upside down.[74] *Indian,* we must remember, was not a native word and had no bearing on how Andeans conceived of themselves before the Spanish conquest. *Indian* was part and parcel of the new global, colonial order. Yet by the seventeenth century, some native Peruvians were calling themselves by that very term.

The seventeenth century was a religious world, and native Peruvians constructed an array of religious stances: some became devout Catholics, others consciously or unconsciously took from both cultural traditions, and some from Peru's central sierra deliberately rejected the Spanish religion and became "Indian"—that is, their version of Indian. They refused to eat Spanish food, refused to wear Spanish dress, and refused to allow women to be contaminated by Spanish sex. This anti-Spanish idiom had a decades-long history. And even though "Indian" played no part—as category or identity—in earlier, sixteenth-century anti-Spanish movements, by the seventeenth century it was at the center of an indigenous political critique. *Indian,* originating as a formal term of colonial state making, could enter the broader cultural milieu and, to Spanish chagrin, take on—within limits—a life of its own.[75]

The fears inspired by "witches" who worshiped the Inca and by New Christian merchants who carried on with indios and negros were elaborated at the same time that some of Peru's native peoples, calling themselves Indian, were suspected of abandoning Catholicism for ancestral idolatries. This was the stuff of conspiracy; the "witch-woman problem," the "Jewish problem," and the "Indian problem" were mutually reinforcing, swelling authorities' anxieties over the brittleness of the social and political fabric—the cultural hierarchy—of the Spanish colonial state. Seventeenth-century Peru provides an extraordinary example of how such fears could coalesce, develop, and ultimately balloon into absurd theories of cultural blaming. Securing European state making to its moorings in global expansion helps explain the irrationalities that have accompanied the development of the modern age. The deep social contradictions of this modern world-in-the-making were, then, also about how some Spaniards, like Peru's mid-seventeenth-century inquisitors imagining conspiracies, were confronted by lifeways so profoundly different—morally, culturally, economically, and politically—from their perception of right that they felt their survival, and the survival of a world worth living in, to be at stake.

Hannah Arendt believed that the modern colonial world was the precedent for the savagery of the twentieth century: the "West's subterranean stream" of terror and violence that was to erupt in fascism. Nineteenth-century colonialism's governing principles—race thinking and bureaucratic rule—triggered the West's most barbaric acts and presaged, she argued, the extraordinary belief in one nation's destiny to command the world as a master race. Arendt's model was the nineteenth-century imperialism of England and France. But it was Spain's colonial efforts, not northern Europe's, that initiated the mix of "civilizing," bureaucracy, and race-thinking that was to brand modernity.

Our sense of modernity changes once we trace its elementary forms back from the nineteenth century to the seventeenth. We can better grasp how the convergence of colonialism, race thinking, and bureaucratic civilizing were at the heart of the emerging modern world. By virtue of our past, race thinking and state making were of a piece, and we have lost sight of their silent, chameleonlike exchanges because we have denied colonialism its rightful place at the core of modern life. From its birth, the modern world was global in scope and hierarchical in structure. By ignoring our foundation in colonialism, we ignore that the twinned hierarchies of global politics and racialized humanity are inherent to modern (civilized) life.

But blindness seems to be an unavoidable feature of modernity: we make sense of—we capture—many experiences of modern life by fetishizing them. Expanding "fetishism" from a critique of capitalism into a critique of politics demands a reappraisal of the bedrock of our common political sense—that "race" and "state" are objects, things, givens of human experience. "Fetishism" obscures our appreciation that Indian, New Christian, black, Spaniard, slave, tribute payer, bureaucrat, woman, and man are not "states of being" but social relations, inescapably part of one another and inescapably immersed in the swings of power. Turning these relations into fetishes stops us from seeing their history—our history—or even inquiring about it.

Like other papers in this volume, this essay, then, holds up our prevailing notions of modernity for critique and uses the mirror of colonial practices to do so. These practices suggest that we think broadly about the cultural dimensions of imperial politics and their signal ideologies of difference. The Spanish case underscores the need to remain sensitive to the insidious and confounding transformations of colonial and "national" ideologies—transformations that could, over time, morph religion and senses of nation, ethnicity, and race in "the space of the nation/empire-state."[76]

The essays in this volume, taken as a whole, suggest the importance of staying close to history and the social relations at the root of political and cultural life. For one, they cast that extraordinary term, "other," or, better said, the wanton use of "other," in a suspect light. There is no one "other" to emerge from the colonial experience; neither are all "others" the same. Imperial categories of rule encompass and emerge from a variety of social relations of power, and we gloss them in terms of categorical "others" at the risk of denying the human experience of empire. It is, after all, in the play of human histories, crafted in the social dynamics and exigencies of power, that these categories perform their cultural work.

The American goliath was behind much of the thinking that went into the essays of this volume: most are implicit, if not explicit, critiques of US endeavors in the realm of (neo) empire building. Furthering these concerns, this essay suggests disturbing venues joining Spanish colonialism and some of our colonizing practices. For one, it argues that the way we commonly brand the Inquisition as a premodern, barbaric, and un-American institution might encourage us to forget, ignore, or be blind to US actions that in fact, appear downright "Inquisitional": the rampant torture at Abu Ghraib Prison in Iraq, the detentions at Guantánamo, the domestic spying, the palpable intimidation of dissent. And haven't we offered similar rationale to justify these questionable practices—weren't all of these horrors performed in the name of state reason, all performed in homage to national security? Weren't they all vetted by state officials who were either adhering to rules of government or following orders?

Hannah Arendt searched for the precedent of fascism in the institutionalized relations of empire and the corresponding imperial categories of human being. She found the convergence of bureaucratic administration and race thinking a horrifying modern danger; and we can add, especially in these troubled times, so is our blinded ignorance of their history, their working, and their appeal.

Notes

Many, many thanks to Ann Stoler and Carole McGranahan for graciously and generously inviting me to contribute a chapter to this volume. I am truly honored to be a part of this effort. This chapter is based on my recently published *Modern Inquisitions: Peru and the Colonial Origins of the Civilized World.*

1. Arendt, *Origins of Totalitarianism,* ix.

2. Arendt, *Origins of Totalitarianism,* ix.

3. See Frederick Cooper, Nicholas Dirks, and Ussama Makdisi in this volume.

4. The phrasing of my argument here owes much to one of the volume's anonymous readers.

5. See Peter C. Perdue's essay in this volume for an example of this process in imperial China, as well as Fernando Coronil's important contribution.

6. A focus on the relation between the nation (imperial center) and empire (or periphery) was central to the conference. It is interesting to compare this relationship in different imperial settings. See Cooper and Dirks vis-à-vis Jane Burbank and Perdue in this volume.

7. Durkheim, *Elementary Forms of the Religious Life;* Comaroff and Comaroff, *Ethnography and the Historical Imagination.*

8. Bourdieu, *Practical Reason;* Burchell, Gordon, and Miller, *Foucault Effect;* Kamenka, *Bureaucracy.* For a pioneering study of the racial state based on a penetrating critique of Foucault, see Stoler, *Race and the Education of Desire.*

9. Burchell, Gordon, and Miller, *Foucault Effect,* 87-104.

10. Some historians would not use the term *state* to characterize the polities of early modern Europe, considering this term prematurely applied to the emerging bureaucratic institutions of the seventeenth century; see Feros, *Kingship and Favoritism.*

11. Burchell, Gordon, and Miller, *Foucault Effect,* 87-104.

12. Burchell, Gordon, and Miller, *Foucault Effect,* 87-104.

13. Bourdieu, *Practical Reason,* 35-74.

14. Bourdieu, *Practical Reason,* 35-74.

15. Abrams, "Notes on the Difficulty of Studying the State."

16. Abrams, "Notes on the Difficulty of Studying the State," 82.

17. Taussig, *Nervous System,* 1992.

18. Taussig, *Nervous System,* 111-40.

19. Coronil, "Beyond Occidentalism"; see also Coronil, this volume. Other examples of this important critical literature include Mignolo, *Local Histories/*

Global Designs; Amin, *Eurocentrism;* Dussel, "Beyond Eurocentrism"; Ribeiro, *Americas and Civilization;* Gilroy, *Black Atlantic;* and Cooper and Stoler, "Between Metropole and Colony." Césaire, *Discours sur le colonialisme,* and Fanon, *Wretched of the Earth* and *Black Skins, White Masks,* have pointed out the importance of "Africa" for defining "Europe." For a study of the contributions of radical black intellectuals to the global study of race, see also Robinson, *Black Marxism.*

20. There is a vast literature on "race" and Latin America, the Andes, and the colonial world. This essay has benefited from earlier studies of race and class in colonial Latin America, particularly Cahill, "Colour by Numbers," and Osorio, "El Callejón de la Soledad," and from a significant debate in the *Colonial Latin American Review;* see Kuznesof, "Ethnic and Gender Influences on 'Spanish Creole' Society," and Schwartz, "Colonial Identities and the 'Sociedad de Castas.'" Herman Bennett, in *Africans in Colonial Mexico,* notes the benignant treatment of Africans by Inquisition and church in colonial Mexico. Mary Weismantel has edited an important collection of articles about race and ethnicity in the contemporary Andes; see the *Bulletin of Latin American Research* 17, 2 (May 1998) and particularly Weismantel and Eisenman, "Race in the Andes"; Cadena, "Silent Racism"; Mendoza, "Defining Folklore"; and Orlove "Down to Earth." Also see two recently published monographs: Cadena, *Indigenous Mestizos,* and Poole, *Vision, Race, and Modernity.* One classic study is Morner, *Race Mixture in the History of Latin America.* For a recent literature review, see Warren and Twine, "Critical Race Studies in Latin America." For the relation between nation, race, and ethnicity after independence, see Larson, *Trials of Nation Making.*

21. Holt, *Problem of Race in the Twenty-First Century.*

22. I am indebted to so many scholars who have provided critical and historical views of race. Holt, *Problem of Race in the Twenty-First Century;* Stuart Hall, "Gramsci's Relevance for the Study of Race and Ethnicity"; Gilroy, *Black Atlantic* and *Against Race;* Trouillot, *Silencing the Past;* Baker, *From Savage to Negro;* Balibar and Wallerstein, *Race, Nation, Class;* Stoler, *Carnal Knowledge and Imperial Power;* Césaire, *Discours sur le colonialisme;* Fanon, *Wretched of the Earth* and *Black Skins, White Masks;* and Memmi, *Racisim,* among others, have reminded us of the African contribution to the making of Europe as well as the importance of colonialism for the construction of racial categories.

23. J. H. Elliott, "Spanish Conquest" and "Spain and America before 1700"; Gibson, "Indian Societies under Spanish Rule"; Spalding, *De indio a campesino.*

24. Gibson, "Indian Societies under Spanish Rule"; Elliott, "Spanish Conquest" and "Spain and America before 1700"; Spalding, *De indio a campesino,*

31-126; Morner, *Race Mixture in the History of Latin America.*

25. See Silverblatt, *Modern Inquisitions,* for a broader and more detailed discussion of the issues discussed below.

26. Kamen, *Spanish Inquisition.*

27. Silverblatt, *Modern Inquisitions.*

28. The Inquisition's jurisdiction did not extend to the colony's native populations. Their moral behavior and customs were monitored by church bishops; see Medina, *Historia del Tribunal del Santo Oficio de la Inquisición de Lima,* vol. 2, 27-28.

29. Kamen, *Spanish Inquisition.*

30. The Spanish Inquisition, unlike other European tribunals-Italy's, for example-was under the control of the Crown, not the pope. So even though the Inquisition had a religious purpose and therefore was tied indirectly to the church, the Spanish Crown oversaw the tribunal's functioning and appointed its members; Kamen, *Spanish Inquisition.*

31. Kamen, *Spanish Inquisition.*

32. Medina, *Historia del Tribunal del Santo Oficio de la Inquisición en Mexico,* 27, 41-51; Alberro, *Inquisición y sociedad en Mexico;* Splendiani, Sanchez Bohgorquez, and Luque de Salazar, *Cincuenta Años de Inquisition en el Tribunal de Cartagena de Indias.*

33. Castañeda Delgado and Hernández Aparicio, *La inquisición de Lima,* 101, 102.

34. Kamen, *Spanish Inquisition,* 101; Perez Villanueva and Bonet, *Historia de la Inquisición en España y America,* 12-13; Castañeda Delgado and Hernández Aparicio, *La inquisición de Lima,* 105-07, 126; see also Hampe-Martinez, *Santo Oficio e historia colonial.*

35. Castañeda Delgado and Hernández Aparicio, *La inquisición de Lima,* 12, 16, 50, 69, 114.

36. Castañeda Delgado and Hernández Aparicio, *La inquisición de Lima,* 3-9.

37. Kamen, *Spanish Inquisition,* 193.

38. Kamen, *Spanish Inquisition,* 193.

39. Kamen, *Spanish Inquisition,* 182-87.

40. Kamen, *Spanish Inquisition,* 193-213.

41. Archivo Histórico de la Nación, Madrid, Inq, Leg 1647, no. 13; Archivo Histórico de la Nación, Inq, Leg 1647, no. 11; Archivo Histórico de la Nación, Inq, Leg 1647 no. 3, ff. 46v-48.

42. Archivo Histórico de la Nación, Inq, Leg 1647, no. 5; Medina, *Historia del Tribunal del Santo Oficio de la Inquisición de Lima,* vol. 1, 57-110.

43. This perspective forces us to understand the Inquisition as a dynamic of interests and possibilities. It focuses on the context of decisions made by mid-level officials, on Lima magistrates' internal conflicts, and on conflicts between them and the accused and between them and their Madrid higher-ups. It challenges the common notion of the tribunal (or any bureaucracy or judicial system) as unified and monolithic.

44. Kamen, *Spanish Inquisition,* 187-91.

45. Archivo Histórico de la Nación, Inq, Lib 1031, f. 42-45; Archivo Histórico de la Nación, Inq, Lib 1028, f.502, 506v, 507-508, 511-511v, 515v-516; Archivo Histórico de la Nación, Inq, Lib 1030, f. 369v-373.

46. Kamen, *Spanish Inquisition,* 189; Escamilla-Colin, *Crimes et chatiments dans l'Espagne inquisitoriale,* 599.

47. See "Mysteries of State," in Silverblatt, *Modern Inquisitions,* 77-97, for greater detail and a broader overview of the issues discussed.

48. Montesinos, "Descripción del auto de fé de la 'complicidad grande,'" appendix 1, 160-61.

49. Archivo Histórico de la Nación, Inq, Leg 1647, no. 11, f. 58.

50. Archivo Histórico de la Nación, Inq, Leg 1647, no. 13, f. 249v, f. 279v; Archivo Histórico de la Nación, Inq, Leg 1647, no. 11, f. 58.

51. Archivo Histórico de la Nación, Inq, Leg 1647, no. 11, f. 91.

52. Archivo Histórico de la Nación, Inq, Leg 1647, no. 11, f. 91-91v. Montesinos, "Descripción del auto de fé de la 'complicidad grande,'" 183.

53. James C. Scott, *Seeing Like a State.*

54. Archivo Histórico de la Nación, Inq, lib. 1028, f. 384v, Leg. 1647, no. 13, f. 28, Lib. 1031, f. 162v-163; Quiroz 1986, "La expropiación inquisitorial de cristianos nuevos."

55. Perez Villanueva and Bonet, *Historia de la Inquisición en España y América,* 12-13; Castañeda Delgado and Hernández Aparicio, *La inquisición de Lima,* 6-9.

56. Anonimo Portugues, *Descripción del virreinato del Peru,* 13.

57. Archivo Histórico de la Nación, Inq, lib. 1032, f. 221.

58. Archivo Histórico de la Nación, Inq, Leg 1647, no. 11, f. 6; Archivo Histórico de la Nación, Inq, Leg 1647, f. 165.

59. Kamen, *Spanish Inquisition,* 255-82.

60. Archivo Histórico de la Nación, Inq, Lib 1031, f. 265v.

61. Medina, *Historia del Tribunal del Santo Oficio de la Inquisición de Lima,* vol. 1, 124-25.

62. Vázquez de Espinosa, *Compendium and Description of the West Indies,* 447-50.

63. Guaman Poma de Ayala, *El primer nueva corónica y buen gobierno,* 276, see also 279, 445, 538, 549, 585.

64. Medina, *Historia del Tribunal del Santo Oficio de la Inquisición de Lima,* vol. 1, 48-50.

65. See "States and Stains," in Silverblatt, *Modern Inquisitions,* 117-39, for greater detail and a broader overview of the issues discussed.

66. Beetham, *Bureaucracy;* Kamenka, *Bureaucracy.*

67. Cellorigo, *Memorial de la política necesaria y util restauración a la Republica de España y estados de ella;* Madera, *Excelencias de la monarchia y reyno de España.*

68. Pizarro, "Carta de Hernando Pizarro," 123, 124, 125, 127; Mena, "La conquista del Peru," 136, 138, 139, 141, 142, 145, 151, 153, 156; Arce, "Advertencia," 409, 410, 416, 419.

69. Archivo Histórico de la Nación, Inq, Leg 1647, no. 10, 11, 13; Archivo Histórico de la Nación, Inq, Leg 1647, no. 13, f. 86; Archivo Histórico de la Nación, Inq, Lib 1031, f. 31; Solorzano Pereira, "Politica Indiana."

70. Montenegro, *Itinerario para parrocos de indios,* 1678: f. 368-69; Solorzano Pereira, "Política Indiana," 336-38.

71. Montenegro, *Itinerario para parrocos de indios,* f. 368-72, 403-04.

72. Adler, "Contemporary Memorial." Note that Spaniards, who liked to see themselves as aristocrat-soldiers, were suspicious of the enormous changes in economic relations brought about by merchant capital. They associated Jews with merchandizing. See "New Christians and New World Fears," in Silverblatt, *Modern Inquisitions,* 141-60, for a fuller discussion of these questions.

73. See "Inca's Witches," in Silverblatt, *Modern Inquisitions,* 161-85, for a more detailed discussion of these issues.

74. Silverblatt, "Inca's Witches."

75. It is very difficult to assess the breadth or extent of these beliefs, and certainly they did not shape the vision of all Andeans. See "Becoming Indian," in Silverblatt, *Modern Inquisitions,* 187-213, for a fuller discussion of this argument. This dynamic was one dimension of the process of building colonial hegemony. During the last twenty years, students of the processes of nation-state building have been exploring the dynamics of class relations, state formation, and cultural practices. Nourished by Gramsci, they have complicated the meaning of "culture" and insisted on the ways that power permeates the living experiences of people in state-ruled societies. Although these studies have explored, for the most part, the

roads to nation-state building and capitalist development, I believe Gramscian insights are germane to the early colonial state as it drove the making of our modern world. The literature on these processes has grown enormously, and I cite here those works that most influenced my project: Corrigan and Sayers, *Great Arch;* E. P. Thompson, "Eighteenth-Century English Society"; Raymond Williams, *Marxism and Literature,* 75-144; Genovese, *Roll Jordan Roll;* Comaroff and Comaroff, *Ethnography and the Historical Imagination;* and Silverblatt, "Political Memories and Colonizing Symbols" and "Becoming Indian in the Central Andes of Seventeenth Century Peru."

76. See Cooper's paper in this volume.

10

Imperial Sovereignty

Nicholas Dirks

> There is a secret veil to be drawn over the beginnings of all governments. They had their origin, as the beginning of all such things have had, in some matters that had as good be covered by obscurity. Time in the origin of most governments has thrown this mysterious veil over them. Prudence and discretion make it necessary to throw something of that veil over a business in which otherwise the fortune, the genius, the talents and military virtue of this Nation never shone more conspicuously.
>
> —*Edmund Burke, February 16, 1788*[1]

This chapter returns us to the period imperial historians used to characterize as the founding of the "second British empire,"[2] when in the last decades of the eighteenth century Britain abandoned its experiment in American colonization and Asian trade in favor of a different kind of imperial ambition. The chapter does so, however, by drawing attention to the crisis in developing conceptions of sovereignty that empire began increasingly to represent, for reasons that had to do with changes both in metropolitan and colonial politics. Empire might have been brought to its ultimate test by colonial nationalism in the twentieth century, but it had already endured a major crisis when the European nation-state itself was formed two centuries earlier. During this formation, an uneasy break was made with earlier imperial forms, which, while they were often used to justify the new, were well known to have declined and fallen.[3] In the comparative genealogy of imperial formations, it is important to return to a time when the idea of empire was reinvented in Britain. This was also, not coincidentally, a critical time for the reinvention of ideas of sovereignty.

BRITISH SOVEREIGNTY

As Hobbes, Locke, and other theorists of the seventeenth century in Britain attempted to find ways to justify and anchor the rapidly changing claims of political leaders and institutions, they assumed that the people who would trade sovereignty for order and property rights would be members of a familiar, distinct, and shared political community. Although there was considerable debate, and ubiquitous uncertainty, about who could legitimately be part of this community, there were always unspoken limits. The limits and conditions of nationality were formed by the same histories of European states that gave rise to modern ideas of sovereignty, providing the ideological stakes for the formation of nations and empires alike. But for theorists as various as Locke, Hobbes, and Burke, there were also limits (however unspoken they were) that attended emergent ideas of community, nationality, and race. As Anderson has argued in his now classic formulation, nations were not only imagined, they were imagined in relation to notions of specific communities that were believed to be natural and primordial (however much they changed and grew over time). National imaginations were stretched as well as formed by print capitalism, state forms of governmentality, and the growing sense that only the nation could both realize and protect linguistic, social, cultural, religious, and political identities.[4] However, these same imaginations were produced as much by the encountering of difference as by consolidation and expansion.[5]

From the late sixteenth century at least, English preoccupations with nationhood were largely reactive, responses to travel in and experience of other worlds beyond Europe.[6] The racial and sectarian conditions of British nationality only became fixed once imperial expansion brought the English up against the terrifying perils of racial and cultural alterity.[7] If the American Revolution played out one contradiction of British sovereignty, it did so by using territory to distract attention from the far more significant contradictions of race, language, religion, and history. The fact that the British recognized their Britishness only when they were in danger of being mistaken for Native Americans or African slaves alerts us to the fundamental exclusions that are part of the history of western sovereignty. Even when these same British settlers claimed full political rights for themselves, the most enlightened seemed unconcerned about extending these rights to other communities.

For many political theorists in eighteenth-century Britain, the foundational crises of sovereignty were thought to have disappeared after the revolution and restoration of the seventeenth century. Debates over sovereignty after 1688 continued to focus on the relationship between the Crown and Parliament, but Filmer's famous defense of monarchy steadily lost any real authority. More importantly, debates about sovereignty became caught up in arguments over political imperatives and civic obligations, private interests and public good, national loyalty and religious belief, and the increasing importance of trade and mercantilism in politics and social life. Trade itself could be used to justify sovereignty even as sovereignty was used to protect and further trade, but convictions about national identity collided with sovereignty only in imperial domains. As a result, concerns about sovereignty came to crisis again in the eighteenth century because of empire. In colonial America, British settlers raised questions around representation, taxation, and local authority in ways that challenged the unquestioned reach of sovereignty at the same time they began to clarify some of the conditions of that sovereignty. Britain had claimed sovereignty over its own subjects wherever they traveled, but while it had to accept other national sovereignties in Europe, it assumed a virtual extension of its territorial claims in all imperial ventures. The flip side of this extensive extraterritoriality was the unbreakable connection between British settlers in the Americas and the British nation, a connection that was indeed broken, leading Britain to discourage settler colonization in its other imperial domains for the next hundred years. But if the American Revolution raised the question of the relationship of sovereignty and territory with a new sharpness, it also raised the stakes for imperial interests and acquisitions in other parts of the world.

BRITAIN AND INDIA

The East India Company began its career in 1600 but conducted its first century in India in relatively desultory fashion, establishing coastal forts, engaging in trade, forming alliances, contesting the Portuguese, the Dutch, and the French, and on occasion attempting to take on the Mughals themselves. Late in the century, the company tried to develop an imperial foothold, but without success. The Mughal empire was at its peak in the seventeenth century, a century that also saw the rise of Maratha power across western and southern India in the wake of the withdrawal of Vijayanagara rule. Fortunes were made, battles were fought, trade was expanded, and territories were claimed, but the seeds of empire were slow in germinating; the British imperial presence did not take on major significance until the long eighteenth century commenced in 1688. The Glorious Revolution might have been designed principally to alleviate the political turmoil of the previous century, but it also had important economic effects, not least in the establishment of the English stock market. And the most prominent stocks traded on Exchange Alley were shares of East India Company stock. Empire and capitalism were born hand in hand, and they both worked to spawn the modern British state.

Scandal, however, was the crucible in which both imperial and capitalist expansion was forged. When the East India Company's charter was technically forfeited in 1693, company shares were heavily used to influence parliamentary support for charter renewal. In 1695 the report of a parliamentary investigation into the developing scandal over quick fortunes made through bribery and insider trading led to the dismissal of the speaker of the Commons, the impeachment of the lord president of the council, and the imprisonment of the governor of the East India Company. If the company did, in the end, secure its renewal, it left a bad taste, suggesting to many that there was little to choose from between a licensed monopoly and a free-for-all in which pirate vessels could vie with East Indiamen for control over a new global marketplace, not to mention the possibilities of imperial acquisition. Nevertheless, the company not only survived into the new century, it soon became an engine that provided a steady source of wealth for parliamentarian and investor alike. The company also took much of the credit for—and the profit of—the new trade in tea. In the last years of the seventeenth and the first of the eighteenth century, China tea, laced with sugar from the West Indies, became the staple that it has remained in the English diet. Spices, silk, cotton, and an increasing array of other Asian commodities established Britain's dependence on the global economy even as it secured growing legitimacy for the role of the East India Company.

But scandal, and its deep association with mercantile trade and imperial venture, hardly disappeared. In fact, the eighteenth century could be said to be the long century of imperial scandal, a time when trade and empire led to successive crises around the fundaments of English politics, culture, and society. By 1788, when Edmund Burke delivered his impassioned denunciations of imperial excess in Parliament at the commencement of the spectacular impeachment trial of India's governor-general Warren Hastings, it was generally recognized throughout England that India had been pillaged by a growing succession of increasingly unscrupulous nabobs. *Nabob* was the term used for Englishmen who returned from the East with huge fortunes that allowed them to live like princes; *nabob* itself is an English corruption of *nawab,* the term used for the highest-ranking figures in the Mughal empire who ruled the provinces of Bengal, Awadh, and Madras. Imperial corruption had reached its highest point well before the time of Hastings, cresting during Robert Clive's years of greatest influence—from the 1750s through the 1770s. Clive, dubbed by many as the "founder of the British empire," used his imperial winnings to rise from his lowly origins as the son of a Shropshire grocer to become the richest man in England. Despite his own unsavory record, major concern about corruption in India came only later, finally preoccupying the metropolitan conscience in the 1780s, a new era of reform both at home and abroad. Nevertheless, before the India Act of 1784 and Burke's subsequent assault on Hastings, there had been two major and several minor parliamentary inquiries into Eastern scandal and a successful—if somewhat limited—attempt at regulatory legislation in 1773, amidst many other efforts to stem the rising tide of corruption.

It is thus small wonder that the growing number of company servants who returned to England with fortunes to invest in estates, titles, and seats in Parliament were denominated nabobs and roundly condemned and scorned by both older gentry and rising mercantile elites alike.[8] But if the servants of the company brought anxieties about both the place of commerce and the influence of Asia to a head, they also created a set of local political crises that made India central to debates over the nature of corruption, the need for public virtue, the character of the state, and the justifications as well as constituencies for claims of sovereignty. The company and its political activities in India represented a scandal of an even higher order. What once was a trading company with an Eastern monopoly vested by Parliament had become a virtual state: waging war, administering justice, minting coin, and collecting revenue over Indian territory. Company servants not only accumulated massive private fortunes, they engaged the British state in actions and commitments that occasioned considerable skepticism, disapproval, and on occasion outrage at home. The company waged almost constant warfare, both against the French and against a growing array of Indian armies.

Even the much heralded assumption of administrative and revenue rights (Diwani) in Bengal in 1765—which led to a negotiated commitment to pay Parliament a subvention of £400,000 a year—hardly compensated for company deficits, the result as well of the spectacular profiteering of company "servants." The subvention was in part a massive bribe to sustain the company monopoly, but it was also part of a compromise to stem the force of the assault on the company from the Chatham Ministry, concerned as it was with the statelike character of the company. Indeed, acceptance of the subvention effectively conceded sovereign rights over conquered territories to the company.[9] But it also increased financial pressure on the company, especially when it turned out that Clive's exuberant estimates were vastly exaggerated. Military victories had come at great cost to the company and the British state, and speculation in company shares after the assumption of the Diwani put unsustainable pressure on profits. Financial crises exerted pressure on company support at home at the same time they often led to greater exploitation in India, where new methods of revenue collection by the company led to the outbreak of grievous famine conditions throughout Bengal in 1770. An exploding bull market in company shares also developed, only to see the bubble burst by the end of the decade. Company shares lost much of their value after news of company military setbacks.[10] By 1772, the company had not only brought about a world credit crash, it had come close to bankruptcy, in both financial and political terms.

SOVEREIGNTY IN INDIA

Despite the critical importance of empire to Burke's concern that British sovereignty itself was being undermined by the company's mischievous duplicity, it has been for the most part forgotten that empire came to constitute a crisis for modern theories of sovereignty. The reforms of 1773 and 1784, while they bailed the company out of debt, attempted to resolve questions of its illicit sovereignty by appropriating as much of it as possible on behalf of the Crown as well as Parliament. In whatever way contemporaries defined the sovereignty of the Mughal emperor or the charter of the company, it was a necessary conceit of early colonial rule that the East India Company held its various rights and privileges in full acknowledgement of its dependence both on the Mughals and on Parliament. In the first instance, the company consistently ceded ultimate sovereignty in India to the Mughals, even after the assumption of full management over Bengal in 1765. That this concession was increasingly seen as a lie, a necessary fiction more than a political reality, first after the company's victory in Plassey in 1757 and certainly after 1765, was another matter. In the second instance, neither Clive nor Hastings had labored under any direct control by Parliament, let alone by the Board of Proprietors, and not only because it frequently took a year for correspondence to go back and forth between India and England. In both respects, the company frequently behaved as if it were an independent entity, a fully functioning state that acted as if it were sovereign and autonomous, for all practical purposes and even some symbolic ones too. In retrospect, it is not so surprising that the rumor spread quickly in 1784 that Hastings was about to declare formal independence for the company state. Far more widespread was the conviction that even the Mughal emperor ruled by the will of the company, under a rhetorical arrangement that allowed the company to control most of India at the same time it could directly take on the Marathas and the Mysoreans, the only two remaining obstacles to complete possession of the subcontinent.

Most imperial historians have argued that the East India Company was drawn reluctantly into political and military conflicts in India, only taking an interest in territorial power and revenue as a last-ditch effort to protect its trading activities. In fact, however, from the mid-seventeenth century, the company had the legal right and the military will to wage war in aggressive ways, securing greater and greater territorial and political claims within the subcontinent. Through intermittent negotiations with the Mughal state, as well as by a host of "subsidiary alliances" with regional powers, the company increasingly asserted its own sovereign position. As early as 1686, Josiah Childs, the company chairman who waged war against Emperor Aurangzeb in 1688, wrote that "[without territorial revenue] it is impossible to make the English nation's station sure and firm in India upon a sound political basis, and without which we shall always continue in the state of mere merchants subject to be turned out at the pleasure of the Dutch and abused at the discretion of the natives."[11] From 1668, the company in Bombay saw itself as sovereign, at least on behalf of the Crown. The company minted coins in Bombay in the name of the British Crown, even though its own coinage acquired limited currency outside the British settlement. It also established courts of judicature over both European and Indian subjects, a practice that in other parts of India usually had to await the formal grant of "Nizamut" rights.

Dominant official views asserted from the late seventeenth century that Mughal sovereignty, where it applied, was absolute and that Oriental despots owned all land, making the right to collect revenue into an entitlement to the land itself. But this official discourse came up against two other trajectories in company ideology concerning British status in India. In the first instance, the British were loath to concede any sovereignty to others, either to the Mughals or to other European powers. As C. A. Bayly notes, "the presumption in the Laws of England that 'Turkes and other infidels were not only excluded from being witnesses against Christians, but are deemed also to be perpetual enemies and capable of no property' was toned down but never entirely forgotten."[12] Indeed, the British systematically (and far more frequently than other European groups) refused to pay forced levies to Indian powers wherever they could get away with it, despite their formal rhetoric of subservience to Mughal sovereignty. In the second instance, the British construed every privilege they received from Indian powers, whether rights to territory, revenue collection, or use of certain honorary titles, as the transfer of full sovereign rights. Perhaps the first major example of this came in 1717, when the emperor Farrukhsiyar granted the right to trade freely within Bengal and its dependencies, providing the company with various tax exemptions as well.[13] When the British claimed sovereignty over the myriad chiefs and *poligars* of the southern countryside, many of whom had never either ceded sovereign rights or made tributary payments to the Mughals, they used a formal interpretation of Mughal sovereignty to give themselves the right of general conquest. Time after time, the British refused to accept that rights in India—and sovereignty itself—were not conceived in terms of simple, uniform, or exclusive proprietary dominion.[14]

This refusal, however, was far less about cultural misunderstanding than it was about the strategic use of cultural forms to explain and legitimate a relentless pattern of political and territorial conquest. The contradictions in company discourse were manifold. When the company exercised the right of landlord (*zamindar*) or local lord (*jagirdar*), it took upon itself powers that were hardly conceded to any of the other zamindars or jagirdars whose revenues it regularly assumed, lands it appropriated, or rights it absorbed. Even as the British saw fiscal dependency, taxation, and judicial rights of territoriality as incidents of sovereignty, they in fact adjudicated all questions of right in relation to a straightforward calculus of self-interest. Through the use of subsidiary alliances, the British were able to expand their territorial power in a variety of ways, taxing the lands of allies, requiring these allies to support garrisons of their own troops, and ultimately—as we have seen in the case of Hastings—forcing them to bail the company out of debt for unrelated military engagements or financial encumbrances of their own. When, for example, the company in Madras encouraged the nawab of Arcot to wage war against the rajah of Tanjore in the early 1770s, in large part to gain lucrative revenue assignments for company servants who had lent large sums of money at usurious interest rates to the nawab for his own obligations to support company military engagements, it argued that the rajah was a mere zamindar who was entirely dependent on a Mughal grant. Mughal sovereignty thus applied for the rajah of Tanjore in ways that had been entirely circumvented for the nawab, let alone the company itself.

SOVEREIGNTY AND THE BRITISH EMPIRE

It was within this larger context that Clive believed he was finally bringing some real political clarity to the unwieldy and often contradictory character of the company's political position as well as its self-representation. The Battle of Plassey was in fact the outcome of company assurance that it had been granted rights over Calcutta and its environs that made it independent of the governor (*nizam*) of Bengal, Siraj-ud Daulah. From the perspective of the nizam, however, the company's refusal to acknowledge his accession by the gifting of customary presents and its growing fortifications of its settlements no doubt seemed like open acts of rebellion.[15] Although subsequently justified by the largely mythological atrocity of the Black Hole (the alleged event in which 123 of 146 Englishmen and -women crammed in a tiny Calcutta cell died in 1756, the eighteenth-century version of weapons of mass destruction or the Gulf of Tonkin), British hostilities in 1756 and 1757 were crude and opportunistic efforts to gain greater power in Bengal. Some years later, when justifying his policies before the House of Commons in 1772, Clive spoke in what thereafter became the standard disavowal of imperial history. He observed that "ever since the year 1757 when we were roused to an offensive by the unprovoked injuries of the Tyrant Nabob Serajah Dowlah, an almost uninterrupted series of success has attended us. Perhaps it was not so much our choice as necessity that drove us progressively into the possessions we presently enjoy. One thing however is certain, that aggrandized as we are, we can never be less without ceasing to be at all."[16] But in the immediate aftermath of Plassey, he had advocated a far less cautious, or for that matter defensive, approach to empire. He observed that "so large a sovereignty may possibly be an object too extensive for a mercantile company; and it is to be feared they are not of themselves able, without the nation's assistance, to maintain so wide a dominion.... [But] I flatter myself I have made it pretty clear to you that there will be little or no difficulty in obtaining the absolute possession of these rich kingdoms; and that with the Moghul's own consent, on condition of paying him less than a fifth of the revenues thereof."[17] Six years later, when he finally accepted the Diwani, Clive in effect bribed Parliament into accepting his territorial ambitions with extravagant promises of endless riches.

After the decisive Battle of Baksar in 1765, Clive declared that "we have at last arrived at that critical Conjuncture, which I have long foreseen, I mean that Conjuncture which renders it necessary for us to determine, whether we can, or shall take the whole to ourselves." With the defeat of Shuja ud-Daula, the company had taken possession of his dominions, "and it is scarcely a Hyperbole to say that the whole Mogul Empire is in our hands."[18] He asserted that the "Princes of Indostan must conclude our Views to be boundless.... We must indeed become the Nabobs ourselves in Fact, if not in Name, perhaps totally without Disguise, but on this subject I cannot be positive until my arrival in Bengal."[19] In August 1765, having promised a huge financial windfall for the company, Clive negotiated the grant of Diwani rights from the Mughal emperor Shah Alam. The agreement formally recognized the emperor's authority over Bengal in the acceptance of a provision entitling the Mughals to an annual tribute of £325,000. Clive did not pursue his ambition to become the nabob in name,[20] preferring instead to inaugurate what came to be known as his "dual system." But the dual system was not merely the split between Mughal imperial authority and British administrative control, as contemporaries understood it, for Clive himself saw it as the resolution of the sham of dual sovereignty. As he wrote to the Court of Directors of the East India Company when he informed them of the assumption of the Diwani, the company "now became the Sovereigns of a rich and potent kingdom," not only the "collectors but the proprietors of the nawab's revenues."[21] Clive spelled this out in straightforward terms in his opening speech to the House of Commons in 1769 when he said, "the great Mogul (*de jure* Mogul, de facto nobody at all).... The Nabob (*de jure* Nabob, *de facto* the East India Company's most obedient humble servant)."[22]

If the grant of the Diwani changed the nature of the relationship between the company and the Mughal empire, it also changed the company's relations with the British state. It could hardly do otherwise. As Clive said in his speech to the House of Commons in 1769, "I was in India when the Company was established for the purposes of trade only, when their fortifications scarce deserved that name, when their possessions were within very narrow bounds.... The East India Company are at this time sovereigns of a rich, populous, fruitful country in extent beyond France and Spain united; they are in possession of the labour, industry, and manufactures of twenty million of subjects; they are in actual receipt of between five and six millions a year. They have an army of fifty thousand men."[23] In a dispatch of January 1767, the Select Committee declared that "the armies they maintained, the alliances they formed and the revenues they possessed procured them consideration as a sovereign and politic, as well as a commercial body."[24] Thomas Pownell put it bluntly when he analyzed Indian affairs in 1773: "the merchant is become the sovereign."[25] This transformation was viewed sympathetically, at least at first, because of Clive's estimates as to what the Diwani would be worth. Clive promised that the Diwani would yield close to £4 million a year, suggesting initially that the amount would increase dramatically once under company supervision. After the assumption of the Diwani, company servants certainly thought differently about the company's priorities and mandate. The Bengal Council noted to the directors in 1769 that "your trade from hence may be considered more as a channel for conveying your revenues to Britain than as only a mercantile system."[26] The only problem was that company debts kept mounting, and Clive's optimistic picture was not in fact borne out by subsequent events.

Clive's exuberance—and in turn that of many investors in company stock—ran aground against a steadily worsening financial picture, both for the company and for Bengal. The government quickly became aware that the company seemed to be a growing liability, however sovereignty was defined. Not only did Diwani collections plunge precipitously, Bengal underwent a serious famine in 1769–70, bringing collections in some areas to a virtual halt. When the ruthless means of collection were not judged to be at fault, the predatory character of British private trade provided a powerful explanation. Speculation in company stock, leading to substantial increases in dividend payments, further eroded the company's financial situation. Worst of all, increasing military expenditures put escalating pressure on company revenues, continuing the crisis that had, in effect, begun with the ascendancy of Clive a decade before. Parliament constituted a Select Committee in April 1772 to inquire into the "nature, state, and condition of the East India Company and of British affairs in India." The inquiries of the Select Committee were followed by those of a Secret Committee, empowered in part to investigate issues around corruption, private trade, and in particular Clive's own personal enrichment through the treaties he negotiated in India.

Clive was soon exonerated of all criminal behavior and instead praised by Parliament for having rendered "great and meritorious service to this country."[27] He was also allowed to keep a personal estate in

Bengal that had been granted him at the time of the conferral of Diwani rights. What did emerge out of the parliamentary fracas was the 1773 Regulating Act. If the Regulating Act was limited in its effects, it nevertheless set in place the principle, however abstract, that the company was to be under the ultimate control of Crown and Parliament. As Burke and others had recognized, this change entailed an important structural shift for a trading company that acted under a parliamentary charter as a monopoly firm. Empire had become a matter of official state interest.

CONTRADICTIONS OF EMPIRE

The company continued in many respects as a rogue state in its relations both to the Mughal empire and the British Crown. It was the fate of Warren Hastings to be governor-general during the tumultuous decade that saw these contradictions come to a head. In fact, Hastings was far more attentive to the contradictions of early British conquest and occupation than his predecessors, especially Clive, for whom sovereignty was to be seized along with treasure. Nevertheless, India's dangers seemed much more powerfully evidenced by the life and career of Warren Hastings than by others, in large part because Hastings sought both to systematize the company's relations with India and to embed his own rule within a subcontinental context. For this reason, Hastings was a more unlikely target than Clive might have been for Burke. Far more scrupulous than other nabobs, Hastings had greater political than financial ambition, and he made clear his deep frustration with the limits and contradictions of company authority in India.

His specific mandate in 1772 was to end Clive's system of dual rule, taking direct charge for the collection of the Diwani revenue. Hastings was ordered to "render the accounts of the revenue simple and intelligible, to establish fixed rules for collection, to make the mode of them uniform in all parts of the province, and to provide for an equal administration of justice."[28] However, in so elevating the company to the status of a state, Hastings was aware that he would eventually have to declare British sovereignty over all the company's possessions and that "the British sovereignty, through whatever channels it may pass into these provinces, should be all in all."[29] While Hastings achieved some success in the arena of law, he felt deeply frustrated in his larger ambition to reform company governance and to rationalize company sovereignty. When Hastings pursued aggressive military policies—whether they failed or succeeded—he ran into the limits of company financial policy. When Hastings declared that an Indian ruler was dependent on the company, a mere landlord or bureaucratic functionary, he collided with the rhetorical sham of company political theory, which was duplicitous both in sketching a formal feudal picture of Indian politics and in treating the Mughal emperor simultaneously as puppet and sovereign. Moreover, when Hastings argued that the company should buttress its own authority through establishing clearer ties with the Crown, he alienated both the Whig faction in Parliament and the company directors, who feared he was willing to give up company rights of territorial possession over the company's growing conquests.

Hastings's interest in clarifying company sovereignty was not unrelated to his political ambitions. In early 1773, he advocated that the "sovereignty of this country [be] wholly and absolutely vested in the Company" and that he be the sole "instrument" of this sovereignty. However, neither the regulating acts of 1773 or 1784 nor the steadily growing state apparatus changed the company's formal mandate. The Pitt Act of 1784 did clarify the Crown's formal control over the company's political policies, in particular its power to wage war. A Board of Control was set up to supervise both the directors at home and the governor-general in India, and the board was specifically put under royal direction. However, Parliament not only maintained its supervisory role—soon to be amply displayed in the Hastings trial—but the governor-general was given far greater powers than Hastings had previously had. And despite the recognition that the company would be steadily involved in revenue collection and local administration, it was told that its servants should concentrate more on the trading aspects of its operation. Pitt went so far as to insert a clause in the act stating "that to pursue schemes of conquest and extension of dominion in India, are measures repugnant to the wish, the honour, and the policy of this nation."[30] Cornwallis, who went to India as governor-general in 1786, did honor this stricture in formal terms, though his use of a political alliance with the Travancore rajah to justify his war against Tipu Sultan in 1792 echoed Hastings's own manipulations of treaties and feudal theories to cover his own aggressive actions. But in fulfilling the other mandates of the Pitt Act, Cornwallis by no means followed his instructions to return to trade.

On the one hand, he raised company salaries in order to impose full restrictions on private trade, regularizing the bureaucratic character of company service. On the other, he imposed the permanent revenue settlement on Bengal. Cornwallis got away with all this not just because of his upright image in Britain but because he arranged for £500,000 to be sent annually to the Exchequer in London, not just finally regularizing but increasing the earlier arrangement that had been made after the assumption of the Diwani. As significantly, Cornwallis set himself up as an imperial monarch of sorts, allowing himself to be represented with classical references as part of his own self-image of adhering to Roman civic virtue. Wellesley, when he became governor-general in 1798, not only abandoned the policy of nonexpansion but used the renewed warfare against France to justify his new policy of imperial aggression. In any case, by the 1790s there was an outpouring of patriotic and royal fervor and nationalist pride that was well suited to imperial expansion. Nevertheless, like all of his predecessors, Wellesley felt constrained to justify his conquests and politics in the complicated language of dual sovereignty. The sham of sovereignty—once again both in regard to the company's relationship to the Crown and its relationship to the Mughal—continued in the end unabated.

THE ANCIENT CONSTITUTION

As a productive fiction, dual sovereignty served multiple purposes, from disguising the extent and nature of imperial conquest to deferring British responsibility for imperial excesses. Burke's great anxiety was that the fiction of empire would potentially undermine the fiction of the ancient constitution in Britain itself. When Burke challenged his listeners to suspend their ideas of distance and difference in favor of sympathy for their fellow citizens of India, he implored them to realize that the crisis of legitimacy in India could lead to a crisis of legitimacy in Britain. In his speech on the Fox India Bill, he said, "I am certain that every means, effectual to preserve India from oppression, is a guard to preserve the British constitution from its worst corruption."[31] Thus it was that the French Revolution only heightened Burke's concern to press for Hastings's conviction. The upending of tradition and order in France was deeply threatening, taking place as it did just across a narrow channel of water. But the relentless duplicity, venality, and corruption of India were in some ways even worse, as these problems implicated the British imperial idea, and as a consequence British sovereignty itself, more centrally. Perhaps most troubling of all, the actions of Hastings, as governor-general and the sole representative of British authority in India (however the sovereignty of company or Mughal was conceived), threatened to draw back the veil over the beginning of imperial government. Hastings's support for the vicious attack on the Rohillas paid no heed to the need for prudence and discretion. Hastings's lack of concern for the maintenance of treaties with either the raja of Banares or the nawab of Awadh could undo the shining fortune, genius, talent, and military virtue of Britain in India. What Hastings defended as necessary for the maintenance of company rule in India was seen by Burke as likely to topple that very rule if not cleansed and exorcised. In an age of metropolitan crisis—one that was exacerbated by domestic political scandals, growing popular unrest, and the rapid influx of new money from imperial ventures—it seemed unwise to shine too penetrating a light on the beginnings of empire. In that context, Hastings's indiscretions threatened to call far too much attention to the scandal of imperial conquest.

Burke was perhaps correct to worry that Hastings's immediate legacy would be destabilizing for the expansion of empire, with the increased scrutiny concerning political as well as personal corruption in the years between the loss of America and the fall of old France. But in calling attention to Hastings's contradictions—his missteps as well as his achievements—Burke sought explicitly to separate the person of Hastings from the project of empire. The personalization of imperial excess was a deliberate effort to exorcise the evil from the imperial idea. When Burke made his first great speech in the impeachment trial of Warren Hastings, he made it clear that he was not condemning the idea of empire. In demonizing Hastings, Burke paved the way for the nationalist heroes who would follow Hastings. In fact, both Cornwallis and Wellesley continued Hastings's policies and inconsistencies, though they were better placed in Britain to maintain their domestic reputations, even as they rode the wave of a rising nationalist tide that, in the wake of the trial, increasingly took empire as a badge of Britain's honor. But by this time, the contradictions of sovereignty had ceased to cause much concern. On the one side, the sovereignty of the Mughal was seen as a mere rhetorical convenience. On the other, the company was now seen as performing the work of both Crown and Parliament (even if it still did so at great financial cost). Formally speaking, it was not until the great rebellion, and the final deposing of the Mughal king, that sovereignty in India was clarified. In one fell swoop, both the Mughal and the company were dethroned, and the British Crown became paramount.[32] Burke would have been proud. After all, he had made possible the apotheosis of British imperial sovereignty in India when the veil was finally drawn for good over the origins of empire in India. His achievement, however, was soon forgotten, erased along with Hastings's ignominy, for by 1858 there were none in Britain concerned that empire would compromise British sovereignty and the ancient constitution on which it rested, despite the general sigh of relief when Queen Victoria assumed Crown rule over India.

In drawing his veil, Burke had been most deeply concerned with the ancient constitution of Britain. His anxious desire to cleanse the imperial idea was not primarily related to his concern about India. Indeed, imperial and metropolitan claims to sovereignty were inseparable, making the trial of Warren Hastings a test not only of the ideal of empire but of state sovereignty at home as well. Empire could work to enhance the glory of, even as it could cruelly undermine, the ancient constitution. The story of sovereignty has always been told as a universal tale with origins (and frames of reference) in Europe. The modern idea of sovereignty emerged, so we are told, in the debates of European political theorists and activists—around the historical swirl of kings, revolutionaries, counterrevolutionaries, and demagogues, among others—in the seventeenth, eighteenth, and nineteenth centuries. Modern ideas of empire required a slight modification of the fundamental premise of sovereignty, but empire was always justified by the absence of sovereign forms—identities as well as institutions—in colonized territories and the ultimate export of these forms to them from the imperial metropole. Indeed, Third World nationalism has been seen as the great testimony to the universal value of this European idea, ultimate proof of the foundational originality of Europe and the intrinsic power of the nation-state. Successful entry to the world of nations has always reiterated what appears as a Western triumph, the birth of sovereignty out of the crucible of colonialism. Imperialism has justified itself over and again, in its heyday as well as in its shameful moments of demise, through the great narrative of sovereignty. This is a narrative that extends even to critiques that take colonial history into account. For example, a recent critical work that works to make empire central to the history of global sovereignty repeats key passages of this narrative. Michael Hardt and Antonio Negri assert that modern sovereignty "was born and developed in large part through Europe's relationship with the outside, and particularly through its colonial project and the resistance of the colonized."[33] But they write as if Third World nationalism only contributed the idea that sovereignty could be radicalized (and globalized) in the service of colonial resistance movements.[34] For them, as well as for most political theorists, "modern sovereignty is a European concept in the sense that it developed primarily in Europe in coordination with the evolution of modernity itself."[35] My argument here is that early imperial history was of rather more consequence than this. But to understand how empire was in fact of fundamental importance to the formation of both modernity and sovereignty, at least in the English case, we need to return to Burke's prosecution of Hastings, for it was precisely this concern that led Burke to use all his hard-earned political capital—and the last nine years of his political career—on a trial that failed in the end to impeach his enemy.

In 1782, Burke wrote a speech in connection with a parliamentary inquiry into the "State of the Representation of the Commons in Parliament." In this speech, he made one of his clearest statements about the nature of the nation, the meaning of sovereignty, and the relationship of both to the ancient constitution. Following Locke, Burke noted that government was chartered to protect property. But departing from Locke and other seventeenth-century theorists, he stressed even more the importance of the need to preserve a prescriptive constitution. Prescription is the claim sovereignty has to the future, or what he termed presumption: "It is a presumption in favour of any settled scheme of government against any untried project, that a nation has long existed and flourished under it. It is a better presumption even of the choice of a nation, far better than any sudden and temporary arrangement by actual election."[36] The nation itself was not merely an idea but the congealed effect of long historical experience. As he explained, "because a nation is not an idea only of local extent, and individual momentary aggregation; but it is an idea of continuity, which extends in time as well as in numbers and in space." For Burke, national sovereignty was a contract only in an abstract sense since it can hardly be based on a set of discrete, knowable choices. "And this is a choice, not of one day, or one set of people, not a tumultuary and giddy choice; it is a deliberate election of ages and generations; it is a constitution made by what is ten thousand times better than choice, it is made by the peculiar circumstances, occasions, tempers, dispositions, and moral, civil and social habitudes of the people, which disclose themselves only in a long space of time. It is a vestment which accommodates itself to the body."[37] Sovereignty, or the ancient constitution itself, has thus become naturalized as the necessary cover for the body politic, accustomed to its specific shapes and changing character. The principle of sovereignty is universal, but the specific form of sovereignty—and by implication any national constitution—is highly particular, the outcome of a specific if ancient history. Sovereignty may be the outcome of choice, but it reflects the agencies and agreements of a community forged through a long and established history.

Burke's views in 1782 had in fact changed greatly from those he held in younger years. In his first writings on law, he had been much more concerned to trace the contextual histories of legal development, arguing as he did against the opinions of Sir Matthew Hale, the great historian of the common law who held that the history of law was necessarily an inscrutable, "immemorial custom in perpetual adaptation." Now Burke seemed to agree with Hale, conceding that history's silences had foundational status for the idea of law.[38] Common wisdom has it that Burke had become more conservative as he aged and was giving vent here to the full traditionalism of his older reactionary years. But it cannot be accidental that in 1782 Burke was spending most of his time thinking about company abuses in India, wondering whether Warren Hastings was undermining universal principles and national reputations in his actions as chief of the East India Company. And in his opening speech on Hastings, he seemed preoccupied with matters concerning law and sovereignty, as if the conduct of Hastings was calling into question fundamental understandings of both. He praised Clive for arranging the transfer of Diwani rights: "For the Mogul, the head of the Mussulman religion there and likewise of the Empire, a head honoured and esteemed even in its ruins, he obtained recognition by all the persons that were concerned. He got from him the Dewanee, which is the great grand period of the constitutional entrance of the Company into the affairs of India. He quieted the minds of the people. He gave to the settlement of Bengal a constitutional form, and a legal right, acknowledged and recognized now for the first time by all the Princes of the Country, because given by the Charter of the Sovereign."[39] In Burke's view, dual sovereignty was necessary to accommodate difference, which for him had to be named as the ancient constitution of India. Clive's duplicity is rewritten as morality because of its apparent respect for sovereignty and the constitution of India, though the narrative of morality in conquest would not have borne the weight of Burke's critical scrutiny had he chosen that path.

SOVEREIGNTY ON TRIAL

Hastings, however, was a different matter. He was brought to trial under English law on the grounds that he had been a British governor. "My Lords, we contend that Mr. Hastings, as a British Governor, ought to govern upon British principles, not by British forms, God forbid. For if ever there was a case in which the letter kills and the spirit gives life, it would be an attempt to introduce British forms and the substance of despotic principles together into any Country. No. We call for that spirit of equity, that spirit of justice, that spirit of safety, that spirit of protection, that spirit of lenity, which ought to characterise every British subject in power; and upon these and these principles only, he will be tried."[40] The trial was thus an epic test of the ancient constitution of Britain, both because Hastings would be brought before justice in London and because he had been the agent of British justice in India. This is why Burke had railed against what he called a "geographical morality." In his oration, he said, "we are to let your Lordships know that these Gentlemen have formed a plan of Geographic morality, by which the duties of men in public and in private situations are not to be governed by their relations to the Great Governor of the Universe, or by their relations to men, but by climates, degrees of longitude and latitude, parallels not of life but of latitudes."[41] Burke was alarmed that relativism of this kind could be used in India to justify unparalleled corruption and abuse. Worse, however, this relativism cast the great law itself into doubt. Cultural relativism would in fact work to give an idea of choice, compact, or contract far too much importance, for the law had to rest on a more transcendental foundation. As he said in his speech on Hastings,

> this great law does not arise from our conventions or compacts. On the contrary, it gives to our conventions and compacts all the force and sanction they can have. It does not arise from our vain institutions. Every good gift is of God; all power is of God; and He who has given the power and from whom it alone originates, will never suffer the exercise of it to be practised upon any less solid foundation than the power itself. Therefore, will it be imagined, if this be true, that He will suffer this great gift of Government, the greatest, the best that was ever given by God to mankind, to be the play thing and the sport of the feeble will of a man, who, by a blasphemous, absurd, and petulant usurpation, would place his own feeble, contemptible, ridiculous will in the place of Divine wisdom and justice?[42]

By cheapening the idea of sovereignty by the use of arbitrary power and despotic action, and then justifying this by his account of India's history and culture, Hastings undermined the ancient constitutions of Britain and India alike.

Burke's commitment to a universal understanding of law was no less than an article of absolute faith in the sacrality of the constitution itself. Only a divine principle could provide the force and the sanction for law and sovereignty, at home and abroad. History, in the form of "tradition," would shape specific understandings and institutions of law, but the history of violent conquest had to be veiled. Conquest was for Burke the "state of exception," the term Carl Schmitt later coined to characterize the sovereign who was outside or above the very law he was charged to protect. Burke argued against Lockean commitments for a variety of reasons. He was worried that philosophical resort to contract would license popular revolution, as indeed it had in the context of seventeenth-century England. This worry became the source of particular anxiety around the events in France after 1789, but it was not a new concern for Burke, either in the English or the Indian context. Burke also argued against an emphasis on contract because he wanted to ground sovereignty in something other than natural right, a form of universal reason he soundly rejected in favor of history, law, and God. Burke's genius was to invoke the general culture of belief around English common law, especially its combination of ancient wisdom and contemporary custom, to construct his own theory of sovereignty. In this sense, the mandate of the divine was to simultaneously justify and transcend the historical actions of men, to cleanse the law from the tarnish of its historical origins. Clive was a hero because he acted out the charade of dual sovereignty, and indeed because the level of his own corruption was best forgotten if Britain were to seek to maintain its imperial mission. Yet Hastings was to be held accountable to Britain's own ancient constitution. At the very point that Burke came to hold that a prescriptive constitution had to be "immemorial,"[43] Hastings was to be judged wanting so that both England and empire might survive.

Burke's contemptuous condemnation of Hastings's invocation of cultural difference was thus in the service of an absolute idea of truth that slid, however uneasily, from the particularity of England's historical formation to the universality of an idea of law. But he did not leave his case at that, for he also argued that Hastings had misunderstood, and viciously violated, India's own ancient constitution. It was ironic that Hastings's own commitments to a rule of law—one that was in truth framed much like Burke's—would get him into such trouble, since it was widely believed that he had done himself particular harm when he used Nathaniel Halhed's defense of his record.[44] Halhed had used his understanding of Sanskrit legal texts—the basis of Hastings's major contribution in the area of codifying Hindu law—as well as his reckoning of Indian understandings of kingly authority to suggest that Hastings had to assume an Oriental mantle of despotic authority. Clive had simply acted as the despot, whereas Hastings, who at his worst was more considerate and more reasoned than Clive could ever be, sought to justify despotism under Indian conditions. When Hastings, quoting Halhed, had said in his defense that "the whole history of Asia is nothing more than precedents to prove the invariable exercise of arbitrary power," he had invoked a larger historical context. He had spoken about the great variety of "tenures, rights, and claims, in all cases of landed property and feudal jurisdiction in India from the informality, invalidity, and instability of all engagements in so divided and unsettled a state of society...as Hindoostan has been constantly exposed to...ever since the Mohomedan conquests."[45] Indeed, when he said that "rebellion itself is the parent and the promoter of despotism," he meant to imply, echoing Burke's own earlier critique of "Muhammedan" government in a tract he wrote with his cousin William, that Hindus rebelled for justifiable reasons.[46] But when he went on to say that "sovereignty in India implies nothing else [than despotism],"[47] he fell straight into the trap that Burke had set.

At the time of the great impeachment trial, Burke would hardly concede either the illegitimacy of Mughal rule or the essential rebelliousness of Hindus in the face of foreign rule. The stakes here had shifted far away from Tanjore and Arcot, let alone Bengal, and pertained to matters far more important than merely the future of imperial acquisitions in India. Burke's sense of the particularity of each historical formation of a prescriptive constitution could not countenance either arbitrary power or the language of despotism. The "mean and depraved state" said by Hastings to have been the fault of the Mughals was now turned to Hastings's own account. For Burke, the mandate of history was to transform necessarily iniquitous beginnings into something "better than choice," what he called "the peculiar circumstances...and...habitudes of the people."[48] History, in short, was about tradition and, by implication, about the sanctification of past contingency. When contrasting Britain and India, Burke used this idea of history to create the space for a difference that did not compromise morality. In the case of Britain's role in India, conquest was not about the original formation of the law but rather its appropriation of India's own law, an appropriation that transferred responsibility for the maintenance of another law rather than Britain's own: "For by conquest which is a more immediate designation of the hand of God, the conqueror only succeeds to all the painful duties and subordination to the power of God which belonged to the Sovereign that held the country before."[49] But even here, cultural relativity labored under the burden of Burke's absolutism.

It was in this context that Burke provided his extensive analysis of Islamic political and legal theory, demonstrating the extent to which law in India had been seen as transcendent in much the way it was in Britain. But he was ambivalent about the need for empirical demonstration, his ambivalence suggested as much by its awkwardness as by its careless scholarship. He asserted simply that "in Asia as well as in Europe the same Law of Nations prevails, the same principles are continually resorted to, and the same maxims sacredly held and strenuously maintained."[50] Historical analysis thus confirms the universality of the legal ideal, but it cannot capture the force of it. Tamerlane was a better man than Hastings, but in the end, "all power is of God." This was the primary puzzle of sovereignty, the war between the universal and the particular in the formation of Burke's sense of sovereign right and civic virtue. Burke attempted to use Mohammedan legal and theological texts to sustain an idea of an ancient constitution that was formed not only out of the specific historical experience of the British nation but in relation to a decidedly Christian idea of God's generative relationship to the law. Burke's call for sympathy for the fellow citizens of India was predicated both on sameness—the universal province and claim of law—and on difference, the distance as well as the distinctness of place.

THE UNIVERSAL CLAIM OF SOVEREIGNTY

In a recent analysis, Uday Mehta has emphasized Burke's commitment to the importance of place, or territory. Mehta shows how Burke was always careful to set up the mise-en-scène by emphasizing territorial and geographical markers as a way to frame his call to respect India's historical and political integrity. He reads Burke's treatment of Mohammedan law as a belief in Indian equivalence. Thus he sees Burke's defense of Indian sovereignty as a tacit acceptance of Indian nationality. And he suggests that Burke's emphasis on location or territory, combined with his use of territory to provide the experiential basis for collective or political identity, anticipates the anti-imperial nationalism of the next century.[51] He goes on to suggest that "Burke's defense of Indian history vindicates a social order in which freedom would not be 'solitary, unconnected, individual, selfish liberty, as if every man was to regulate the whole of his conduct by his own will.' It vindicates what subsequent nationalists might have called the conditions appropriate for the right of self-determination."[52] But in making this argument, Mehta underplays both the complementary emphasis Burke put on the theistic universality of the law and the degree to which Burke was not a critic of empire itself. Far from seeing in India an incipient nationhood that could compromise Britain's own nationhood,[53] Burke saw in British conduct in India a challenge to two different but allied forms of sovereignty that put at risk the sacrality of sovereignty itself. India's sovereignty did not constitute the basis of a claim for liberty so much as a second argument against the "absolute power," or despotism, of Hastings. And the French Revolution only brought more urgency, and proximity, to the danger.

In muting the defensiveness, as well as the reflexive character, of Burke's rhetoric about India, Mehta still makes a compelling argument that English political theory was significantly shaped by imperial connections.[54] But Burke's conservatism was hardly moderated by his concern for India. Burke believed that the ancient constitution was both primordial and shaped by shared history, even as he was committed to the idea that the law was universal in its principle if singular in its form. His paradoxical formulations were in the end clearly made in the service both of Britain and the idea of empire, rooted as they were in his sense that British justice was the most developed, and enlightened, in the world. His sympathy for India was the sympathy of a paternalist who believed his charge could only benefit from the relationship of dependency. His sense of Indian sovereignty, and nationhood, was itself always dependent on his greater concern for the past and future of Britain itself. If he could draw the veil on Clive's duplicitous conquest of India, he set the stage for the ultimate drawing of the veil on Hastings as well. In doing so, he played a vital role in the regeneration of the British imperial mission at a time of resurgent British nationalism and jingoism. Burke's attentiveness to place worked in the end to make one place sovereign and another place colonized. This was a contradiction that would require a different kind of political vision to undo.

Still, Burke's contradictory insistence on universality and specificity in the context of India did make clear the extent to which his own sense of sovereignty was both brought into crisis and yet unchallenged by difference. On the one hand, he needed to resist the cultural relativism that would both justify company despotism in India and call into question the absolute truth and universal provenance of England's own traditions. On the other hand, he needed to formulate a sense of history that was rooted in an ancient but still historical past that could provide the basis for a national claim to the ancient constitution. In this respect, India's alterity had to be simultaneously affirmed and disavowed. Ironically, imperial ideology made it possible for Burke to do this, though the thinly veiled fiction of dual sovereignty compromised the force of this complementary idea. For Burke, the contradictions of English, or British, sovereignty were highlighted by resort to empire, even if the greatest role of empire was to test the very transcendence of his commitment to the ancient constitution. Mehta is right to congratulate Burke for his acknowledgement of the role of empire—both its general significance and the excess of its corruption—as a necessary component of a national theory of sovereignty. Before Burke, most other English political theorists had systematically denied or ignored the presence of empire in their understanding of sovereignty, despite the obvious fact that modern sovereignty was born in an age of empire. Yet his genius lay less in the recognition of difference than in its use in his own critique of the social contract.[55]

For Britain, empire as an idea was examined only retrospectively, once the national character of claims about sovereignty made empire appear to be a problem. Empire began as an accidental extension of sovereign ambitions that survived largely by dissembling. The conceptual relations between empire and sovereignty could be left vague until they ran up against the anxieties that grew around the expansionist activities of the East India Company on the one hand and the recognition of racial and cultural difference on the other. The underlying national consensus required to make the claims of sovereignty carry weight only gradually became clear. Empire was fundamental to the history of British sovereignty, but not only in relation to the triumphal connection between English empire and American independence.[56] Instead, empire worked to crystallize the convictions of national sovereignty even as it helped garner the resources to make it possible. Empire also exposed the serious contradictions that emerged when economic interest, military might, and political expansion failed to secure cultural legitimation, whether at home or abroad. In either case, empire ultimately came to be of signal importance to the expanding cult of nationality in England during this same period. Linda Colley shows how an idea of Britishness was in the end triumphant in large part because of the growing collective sense of opposition to France (and the continent more generally). She also demonstrates that imperial ventures were especially useful for folding some Scots and Irish into the mix of Britishness by recruiting them to a project that highlighted differences between East and West.[57] While in some respects the loss of America only made the crisis of empire more pressing, posing a new set of national exclusions as fundamental to the problem of sovereignty, it also made the idea of empire all the more compelling. By the time Cornwallis had moved from the scene of his American failure to his Indian triumph, the contradictions of sovereignty were to be resolved by a new set of commitments around the importance of empire for Britain itself. The problems posed by imperial sovereignty became increasingly erased by the ambitions of national sovereignty.

Burke's role in the trial of Warren Hastings highlights the contradictions that were part of late eighteenth-century ideas of sovereignty. Yet it is ironic indeed that Burke's own understanding of sovereignty—given his commitment to the ancient constitution rather than the idea of contract—made empire ultimately less of a problem than it became for liberal theory, where contradictions outlived the trial.[58] For Burke, and indeed for most British historians of empire from at least the middle of the nineteenth century on, the trial brought closure to the crisis over sovereignty that empire in India had posed.[59] In bringing Hastings to scrutiny before the combined houses of Parliament, Burke had made empire safe for British sovereignty. And, whether in the hands of liberal or conservative theorists, empire could no longer threaten the foundations of political sovereignty until, in the end, nationalism appropriated the arguments of contract and ancient constitutions to make a different kind of territorial claim for self-rule. That, however, is a claim that has received only grudging, and to the present day still limited, acquiescence on the part of a West that still views sovereignty as fundamentally Western. The erasure of the role of empire continues to serve the interests of empire. It is now time for political theory, historical analysis, and political critique to join together to write empire back into the history of the West, where it has played such a foundational and constitutive role.

Notes

1. Burke, "Speech on Opening of Impeachment."

2. See Harlow, *Founding of the Second British Empire.*

3. See Edward Gibbon's monumental work, *Decline and Fall of the Roman Empire.* Published between 1776 and 1788, the work was widely seen as a parable of and for the British empire.

4. Anderson, *Imagined Communities.*

5. This was not only true in the early years, when modern nations emerged, but also in the late nineteenth and early twentieth centuries, when the European nations congealed around even more narrowly defined cultural identities; see, for example, Stoler, *Race and the Education of Desire.*

6. See Helgerson, *Forms of Nationhood.*

7. Armitage, *Ideological Origins of the British Empire.*

8. *Nabob,* Samuel Foote's popular Haymarket play, exemplified the public image of these returned India men.

9. See the discussion of this in Bowen, *Revenue and Reform,* 64-66.

10. See Bowen, *Revenue and Reform,* 76-77.

11. Despatch Book, June 9, 1686, vol. 91: 142, 145, India Office Records, cited in Chaudhuri, *The Trading World of Asia and the English East India Company,* 454.

12. Bayly, "British Military-Fiscal State and Indigenous Resistance," 205.

13. Dodwell, *Cambridge History of India,* 591.

14. For my own analysis of shared sovereignty and notions of proprietary rights in precolonial India, see my *Hollow Crown.*

15. Bayly, "British Military-Fiscal State and Indigenous Resistance," 206.

16. British Library, Home Miscellaneous, Vol. 211, speech dated November 24, 1772.

17. Letter from Robert Clive to William Pitt, Principal Secretary of State, January 7, 1759, quoted in George Forrest, *Life of Lord Clive,* 413.

18. Quoted in Spear, *Master of Bengal,* 145.

19. Quoted in Forrest, *Life of Lord Clive,* 256-58.

20. As Percival Spear approvingly put it, "the dominion of Bengal was not desired in itself, but only as a safeguard for peaceful commercial operations....

Rule by legal fiction and by deputy was both safer and cheaper in the conditions of the time." *Master of Bengal,* 156.

21. Quoted in Cohn, *Colonialism and Its Forms of Knowledge,* 59.

22. Quoted in Bowen, *Revenue and Reform, 10.*

23. British Library, Eg. Mss 218, ff. 149-51.

24. Quoted in Bowen, *Revenue and Reform,* 9-10.

25. Pownall, Right, *Interest, and Duty of Government.*

26. Bowen, *Revenue and Reform,* 12.

27. Quoted in Bowen, *Revenue and Reform,* 173. George III was upset at the about-face, writing to North, "I own I am amazed that private interest could make so many forget what they owe to their country." Quoted in Sutherland, *East India Company in Eighteenth Century Politics,* 258.

28. Quoted in Bowen, *Revenue and Reform,* 113.

29. Gleig, *Memoirs of the Life of the Right Honorable Warren Hastings,* 534-44.

30. Quoted in Lawson, *East India Company,* 128.

31. Burke, "Fox's Indian Bill Speech."

32. Cohn, "Representing Authority in Victorian India."

33. Hardt and Negri, *Empire,* 70.

34. Hardt and Negri, *Empire,* 105-09.

35. Hardt and Negri, *Empire,* 70.

36. Speech on a motion made in the House of Commons, May 7, 1782, for a committee to inquire into the state of the representation of the Commons in Parliament, in Marshall, *Works of the Right Honorable Edmund Burke,* vol. 7, 94-95.

37. Marshall, *Works of the Right Honorable Edmund Burke,* vol. 7, 95.

38. See Pocock, "Burke and the Ancient Constitution," 202-32.

39. Burke's speech of February 16, 1788, quoted in Marshall, *Writings and Speeches of Edmund Burke,* vol. 6, 341.

40. Burke's speech of February 16, 1788, quoted in Marshall, *Writings and Speeches of Edmund Burke,* vol. 6, 345-46.

41. Quoted in Marshall, *Writings and Speeches of Edmund Burke,* vol. 6, 346.

42. Quoted in Marshall, *Writings and Speeches of Edmund Burke,* vol. 6, 350-51.

43. Quoted in Pocock, "Burke and the Ancient Constitution," 227.

44. Nathaniel Halhed, noted Orientalist and compiler of Hindu law codes. See Rocher, *Orientalism, Poetry, and the Millennium,* 48.

45. Quoted in Marshall, *Writings and Speeches of Edmund Burke,* vol. 6, 348-49.

46. Burke, "Policy of Making Conquests for the Mahometans."

47. Quoted in Marshall, *Writings and Speeches of Edmund Burke,* vol. 6, 348.

48. Quoted in Pocock, "Burke and the Ancient Constitution," 227.

49. Quoted in Marshall, *Writings and Speeches of Edmund Burke,* vol. 6, 351.

50. Quoted in Marshall, *Writings and Speeches of Edmund Burke,* vol. 6, 367.

51. Mehta, *Liberalism and Empire,* 149.

52. Mehta, *Liberalism and Empire,* 186.

53. Mehta, *Liberalism and Empire,* 189.

54. Mehta writes that "this neglect is evident in both historical political theory and contemporary normative scholarship. Historically, the fact that most British political theorists of the 18th and 19th centuries were deeply involved with the empire in their writings and often in its administration is seldom given any significance or even mentioned in the framing of this intellectual tradition." Mehta, *Liberalism and Empire,* 6.

55. See also O'Brien, *Great Melody.*

56. Armitage, *Ideological Origins of the British Empire,* 3.

57. Colley, *Britons: Forging the Nation.*

58. I do not mean to exonerate the liberal political tradition, for Mehta and other critics are clearly correct to note the ways in which liberal theory depends on exclusions to its universal claims. But this does not mean that Burke's peculiar commitments to universalism and particularity escape the very same anthropological conundrum.

59. Burke, of course, would have preferred a successful prosecution, and he was deeply embittered by the failure of the trial. Yet he had made his argument in such a way that even though Hastings was let off, his passion became redundant after Lord Cornwallis had succeeded Hastings and begun the reforms of the 1784 Pitt Act. In this sense, despite his own intentions, Burke's fevered rhetoric served as a brilliant means to exorcise the past of corrupt and despotic nabobs.

11

Provincializing France

Frederick Cooper

Léopold Sédar Senghor, the Franco-Senegalese intellectual and political activist who was to become Senegal's first president, wrote in 1945, "the colonial problem is fundamentally nothing but a provincial problem, a human problem." Leading luminaries of the French colonial establishment, like René Pleven, were saying something similar: "the French colonies, like the other provinces of France, wish to help rebuild the house of France."[1]

The critical intellectual and the colonial officials both had their reasons for trying to blur the line between the European and the African provinces of France. The latter were trying to justify their political system to a world becoming more skeptical of the claims of some people to rule over others, and they were combating colleagues who saw colonies as mere zones of extraction and exploitation, possessions of France, but not integral to the polity. The former was trying to position colonized people firmly within the political space of a Greater France—as citizens of empire—so as to make claims on that system for a fuller, more meaningful, and more respectful inclusion in the polity. Part of Senghor's article was an effort to tell French people about

African history and culture and to convince them that Africa, like France, had much to contribute to world civilization as well as to a heterogeneous France. Another part was a plea to Africans: "assimilate but do not be assimilated." Africans should not make themselves into black French people, and they should not hold themselves aloof from French culture and proclaim their cultural authenticity.[2] They should be critical, adaptive, and selective as they seek to better understand what French and African cultures have to offer them in the future.

In 1945, both Senghor and the ascendant progressive wing of the colonial establishment were anxious to shed the term *empire* without replacing it with a culturally homogenized polity, and they acknowledged what Senghor called the "historic fact" of colonization while seeking to turn the tide of history toward another form of multinational polity.[3] Both were trying to provincialize France. Both understood well that empire, nation, and province were all constructs—ways of representing a system of power whose lines were not so clear—and they made use of them to try to adapt political structures to conform better to the constructs they favored.

A couple of generations later, the idea of "provincializing Europe" has come back into academic circles, but not in so dynamic a form. The argument, in Dipesh Chakrabarty's formulation among others, turns the thought that Europe could be like an ordinarily place among other ordinary places into an ironic demonstration that Europe cannot be provincialized. The stumbling block is that Europe has passed off its particularity as universal, obscuring not least how much its pretension to be the source of global civilization is in fact the story of colonialism. European colonialism was not just about economic exploitation or geopolitical domination but about configuring an "other" that would underscore Europe's position as the font of social progress, democracy, and rationality. This approach suggests that even when colonialism came into question, Europe could still determine the forms in which opposition could gain a foothold and the terms in which analysis of colonization, including by historians, could be articulated. Colonized societies always seemed to "lack" something that Europe possessed, to be "behind" in whatever trajectory Europe seemed to be following, not least the trajectory that seemed to make the nation-state the only possible outcome of political mobilization.[4]

Such arguments reflect the political dilemmas that colonial activists had to confront but could not always overcome, and they reveal the frustrations of non-European intellectuals today who willingly engage the theoretical propositions of European social thought without finding their European colleagues willing to reciprocate. The danger, however, is that the critique perpetuates what is being criticized. Europe remains the reference point to which everyone else has to point. Enlightenment, rationality, modernity, and the nation-state remain on their pedestal, now emblematic of European arrogance instead of universal civilization, but still quintessentially European. But one might ask instead whether Europe itself "lacked" what India or Africa is said to lack.

In this chapter I hope to contribute to the goal of provincializing Europe, but in a different way. I question whether concepts such as modernity or the narrative of the rise of the nation-state tell us very much about French history in the nineteenth and twentieth centuries. Their widespread deployment keeps bouncing French history from its provincial stage to a metanarrative of the post-Enlightenment West. Instead, I want to look at France not as a French "nation" extending its power and sense of destiny outward, but from uncertainty and conflict over what sort of polity France actually was, from the revolution through the final crisis of the French colonial empire in the 1950s. I want to get away from a double narrative that has dominated discussion of the nineteenth and twentieth centuries, a narrative to which many postcolonial critiques have conformed rather than challenged. The postcolonial critique posits a period of two centuries defined by "post-Enlightenment rationality," "modern governmentality," and "colonial modernity." The supposed transition from empire to nation-state within this time frame is an integral part of what modernity is supposed to mean.[5] Postrevolutionary France seems like the archetype of how this metahistory actually played out: the founding point of the genealogy of the modern state, the modern nation, and the export of those concepts to parts of the world that had not asked to receive them.

My plan is to focus on two points at the beginning and end of the era from the French Revolution to decolonization. The concepts of "nation-state" and "modern" pop in and out of this story, but they give it no coherence and little means of understanding the way in which both the leaders of state and the critics of state power understood the terms in which they made decisions and asserted claims. But the concept of empire—as a polity that conjugates incorporation and differentiation—does some useful work in helping us understand how France was defined as a polity and what it meant for people in Greater France to work within and against those terms.[6]

THE IMPERIAL POLITY AFTER THE REVOLUTION

Scholars wishing to tell the story of the postrevolutionary advance of the nation-state would have had an easier task if Napoleon's accession to power in 1799 had not attached to France the label of empire, complete with symbolic appeals to the models of Rome and Charlemagne. It is tempting to save France for the categories of modern nation and post-Enlightenment rationality by portraying Napoleonic conquests as the work of a patriotic citizen army, extending the power of the nation over foreign lands, sweeping from most of Europe aristocratic privilege in favor of the scientific and bureaucratic modes of governance. But Napoleon's story is ambiguous on all these counts, partly a reflection of the revolutionary changes of the era that immediately proceeded him, partly a reaction against those same trends, and partly an indication of how powerful a concept, structurally and ideologically, empire has been. The imperial imaginary contained both the new and old elements in Napoleonic thinking, and it was in such terms that Europeans reacted to him.

The French Revolution had indeed inspired its early leaders to turn to a voluntary army of citizen-soldiers to fight for *la patrie en danger,* but the government gave up this idea before Napoleon took power. Mass levies of soldiers began in 1793, and systematic conscription in 1798. Napoleon further systematized conscription. Even within the boundaries of pre- (or post-) Napoleonic France, draft evasion and desertion were common and persistent. Organizing the draft and repressing resistance to it was at the core of the Napoleonic project of building a state apparatus capable of tracking and punishing recalcitrant individuals. Napoleon achieved grudging consent to conscription rather than willing participation in a national effort and national glory.[7] Conscription is more a story about state than it is about nation.

Most important, the story is not very different outside the "national" borders of France than inside. Conscription was imposed from Italy through Holland, Westphalia, and the Hanseatic cities, and in such places it too was the key to the building up of a state apparatus—especially the prefects and the gendarmes—structured in the same way as that of the older areas of the empire. Only a third of the army that attacked Russia in 1812 came from places that had been part of France before the Revolution; it consisted of people who later would be called Germans, Italians, Poles, and Swiss. Napoleon's some-time allies, Austria-Hungary and Prussia, were part of the military apparatus as well. Beyond as well as within French-speaking parts of the empire, resistance to recruitment and desertion were considerable problems; that they diminished over time reflects less the triumph of a national order of things than the routinization of state power throughout the empire.[8]

Michael Broers rejects the idea of the Napoleonic empire as a "pure and simple extension of France, la Grande Nation" and argues instead that some parts of what is now France, such as the Vendée or the Pyrenées, lay outside the core, while Napoleon's "inner empire" included parts of western Germany, northern Italy, and the Low Countries—reflecting a territorial conception rooted in the earlier empire of Charlemagne.[9] Outside of this historic space of European empire, expectations of integration and conformity to Napoleonic norms could be less. The empire—which at its height encompassed 40 percent of Europe's population[10]—was differentiated space, and it was governed in differentiated ways: parts of the core were turned into departments like those of France; in other regions a dynastic principle prevailed, with members of Napoleon's family installed as local rulers presiding over territories that were still presumed to remain intact; and in others Napoleon maintained a subordinate, allied dynasty and the fiction of distinct states under his overrule. In Stuart Woolf's words, "this imperial system was a political, military, dynastic and economic federation of very unequal states."[11]

Whether the empire was fundamentally French, European, or a personal and dynastic dominion is not a simple question. Napoleon himself looked backward to the Holy Roman Empire to assert his view of the common traditions and religion of France, Spain, England, Italy, and Germany, and after his fall he claimed that his goal had been to found "a European system, a European code, a Supreme Court for all

Europe; there would have been a single European people."[12] Napoleon had for a time an appeal to forward-looking European elites, from Italy to Germany and eastern Europe, because he seemed a useful counterpoint to the arbitrary authoritarianism of local rulers and the lethargy of local aristocracies. If the prefectural system of administration remained dominated by "old Frenchmen," "new Frenchmen," from Italy, Belgium, Holland, and Germany were represented in the legislative bodies in Paris.[13]

The military machine required feeding, and that meant conscription and revenue extraction, while the army was not nearly as disciplined in reality as in theory, meaning pillage. The army's demands for men and supplies made expansion a goal in itself, compromising the reformist side of Napoleonic ventures in favor of a pattern more typical of empires in the past: making deals with local magnates, allowing soldiers and allies to have a share of spoils, distributing estates in conquered territories to French generals and incorporated notables.[14]

The mechanics of ruling an empire undermined any project of constructing a progressive Europe but not the arrogance behind such a project. Broers points to the "orientalizing" dimension of Napoleonic rule over Italy—a place associated with the glory that was Rome, but a glory long dissipated. Napoleon was bringing to Italy and to the rest of conquered Europe the accomplishments France achieved in breaking with the *ancien régime:* legal equality of citizens, a separation of public finance from officials' fortunes, well-defined property rights, secularization of the state, and the opening of civil service to qualified people of all origins.[15] Napoleon's officials "proved arrogant and inflexible in their dealings with those who, unlike them, had failed to 'liberate themselves.'" In parts of Germany, officials thought that local political culture was compatible with the notions of administration that Napoleon's men were imposing, but in others feudal arrangements seemed deeply entrenched.[16]

The idea of French cultural imperialism itself needs to be qualified on two grounds. First, the Napoleonic structure was not a projection of France but a system built up in France at the same time as in non-French-speaking conquered territories. Napoleon's prefects were trying to understand the cultural and social characteristics of French peasants and their relations to provincial elites, whose power had been diminished by revolutionary enthusiasm but reinforced by official sanction given to private property.[17] Second, the politics of empire forced compromises in the generalization of the administrative and legal system at the heart of the acculturative project. Outside the inner core of the empire, the Napoleonic law code was diluted, and serf obligations and seigneurial dues were at times maintained in order to keep local elites within the system. As Woolf put it, "the price of collaboration was acceptance of limits."[18]

Following where he could the principle of dynastic affiliation, Napoleon incorporated kingdoms and principalities into his empire, keeping their rulers as long as they acceded to his wishes, reorganizing them into larger and more efficient units when he saw fit. In some places, notably Spain and Holland, he installed his brothers. He put much effort into wooing local aristocracies, giving notables imperial titles and a place in the administrative hierarchy. But dynastic ideas were compromised as well by Napoleon's desire for centralized administration, by his officials' Francocentric views of society and politics, and most importantly by the imperatives of imperial defense and expansion. He replaced his own brother in Spain when Joseph was ineffective. When allied kingdoms did not support his expansionist plans in central and eastern Europe, he fought them, forging in such places a more incorporative, authoritarian empire.[19]

For all of Napoleon's interest in harnessing geography, ethnography, and other forms of scientific knowledge to the cause of administration, his thinking was also shaped by a much older vision of empire, hence his fascination with Rome and Charlemagne. And Napoleon retained important aspects of an old regime empire. He made many of his generals and top supporters into nobles, and he did likewise with some of the elites in conquered regions. The most favored of these were awarded principalities and duchies as grand fiefs, heritable under primogeniture. His armies, like those of old, were allowed to engage in undisciplined extraction. His famous legal code was certainly systematic, but it rolled back the revolutionary notion of the equivalence of citizens into a more patriarchal vision of family, and its implementation was compromised when incorporated elites had to be placated. Napoleon did achieve a greater penetration of state into society than prior European monarchs had, but the social significance of that process was quite ambiguous, for conscription and extraction, the distribution of booty and estates, remained crucial to the militaristic nature of the enterprise, even as rational administration, the rule of law, the destruction of intermediary statuses between citizen and state, and the secularization of authority were part of the Napoleonic vision.[20]

Resistance to Napoleon's conquest and rule in Europe does not fit the nation/empire dichotomy. Although Napoleon lost initial support of local patriots, he gained support by his strategies of co-optation of elites into an imperial, rather than French, nobility. There was armed opposition, most notably in Spain, Calabria, and Tyrol, but it was as much opposition to elites who were both collaborating with Napoleon and expropriating local resources as it was opposition to "foreign" rule.[21] Some intellectuals counterposed to Napoleon's militarism and destructiveness a vision of nations peacefully trading and interacting with each other.[22] But what stopped Napoleon was other empires, most notably the two supranational empires on the edges of Europe's central continental space, Britain and Russia, both of which could draw resources from outside the contested region.[23] Neither by the French example and regime building across Europe nor by providing a locus of opposition did Napoleon help make Europe a continent of nations, although both by the institutional changes he instituted and the pressure he put on rival empires he can be said to have contributed to the strengthening and consolidation of states. Post-Napoleonic Europe was dominated by a small number of empire-states (Britain, Russia, Austro-Hungary, Prussia/Germany, and France), whose competition with each other lasted through World War I and in different form through 1945; France itself went through a monarchical phase, a short-lived republic, a longer-lasting Second Empire, and only after 1871 a durable, if still contested, form of republican rule.

EMPIRE AS POLITICAL AND MORAL SPACE: OVERSEAS COLONIES AFTER THE REVOLUTION

One might at first glance consider Napoleon's regime a continental empire distinguished from an overseas one. Yet it was not for lack of effort overseas. Napoleon inherited the old empire of the Caribbean, and some of his old regime supporters, as well as his wife Josephine, had their roots in colonial society. The Caribbean, for Napoleon, was another aspect of the differentiated imperial space; it was a resource to be used (see below). His conquest of Egypt in 1798 reflected a peculiar combination of motives: a desire to push his imperial genealogy back to the pharaohs and an effort to bring science and rational rule to a piece of the backward Ottoman empire.[24] He intrigued in South America and hoped to incorporate parts of that region, as well as Louisiana, into a Caribbean-centered counterpoint to British and North American dominance of the Atlantic; he tried to preserve French colonial outposts in India.[25] Napoleon specialists tend not to make much of all this for a simple reason: he failed.

But we need to back up to appreciate the most important part of the overseas picture. Especially after the loss of much overseas territory to Great Britain in 1763, the sugar grown by slaves on Saint Domingue, and to a lesser extent Martinique and Guadeloupe, was the most lucrative part of the empire. How to interpret the significance of the revolution for the colonies has been a point of controversy among scholars and activists, for some the source of a liberating ideology, for others evidence of a fundamental hypocrisy in European emancipatory projects, and for still others the source of the very concepts of racial classification that underlined the exclusion of colonized people from the "civilized" world.[26] But beginning with the concept of empire allows us to look at such questions from a different angle: not the immanent consequences of revolutionary logic but the way politics played out over the space of empire.

There is little indication that the authors of the *Declaration of the Rights of Man and of the Citizen* thought about its implications in the Caribbean. Some Enlightenment thinkers, Diderot most notably, deduced from their principles that slavery and conquest were unjust. Europe—whose political institutions were the targets of Diderot's writing—had no business imposing its way of life on the diverse cultures of the world.[27] The Abbé Grégoire and others organized in 1788 the Société des Amis des Noirs, which put a clear antislavery position before the public. Others tried to define minimum standards for admission to the *cité,* the domain of citizenship, standards that excluded most imperial subjects while acknowledging their potential entry. But the boundedness of the revolutionary "nation" was thrown open by events in the empire.

First, slave owners, represented in the Paris assemblies and connected to commercial interests in the ports, insisted that citizenship meant that French colonists deserved a voice in their own affairs. Then, the substantial Caribbean category of *gens de couleur*, people of mixed origin who had acquired property and slaves, claimed the rights of other free property owners, calling into question any racial classification of admission to the cité. They were received in Paris, found allies among the Paris leadership, and made sure that the relationship of citizenship and race could not be avoided in discussion of rights. The planters defended their racial privileges, and their allies in the metropole did not want to compromise a system that brought in sugar and profits.[28]

The revolution that broke out in Saint Domingue in 1791 and the less successful revolts on other islands do not fit neatly in the category of "slave revolt." They were movements that crossed categories and changed in character as they unfolded; Toussaint Louverture, the famous leader of a largely slave army, was a free person of color. The revolts indicate the importance of imperial networks and the difficulty of isolating categories within them. The gens de couleur were well aware of the revolutionary currents coming from Paris.[29] Many slaves, sailors and servants most obviously, were also following events, and they knew not only of the state's vulnerability, which a revolutionary situation exposed, but also of possible allies.[30] Like most revolutions that go very far, the one in Saint Domingue developed through efforts to mobilize people across social categories.[31]

The revolutionary category of citizenship—and the political strategies it entailed—took on a particular importance in this context because citizenship implies a reciprocal relationship of rights and obligations: the state's recognition of claims upon it legitimizes its capacity to make claims on citizens, and vice versa. How sincere intellectuals and leaders in Paris were about applying universal principles is not the major question. What is crucial is how the resonance of principles across the space of empire and the practice of politics in that space extended a revolutionary dynamic.

Fighting in Saint Domingue pitted patriots against royalists, and French against British and Spanish armies trying to take lucrative territory for their own empires, with the representatives of the French government in Saint Domingue trying to mobilize whomever it could to the patriotic cause. Paris assemblies now had to take seriously the question they had initially avoided: gens de couleur should be treated as citizens independent of their race not only because of principle but for the needs of state; gens de couleur acceded to citizenship in 1792. In 1793, in a more desperate situation of slave rebellion and British invasion, the French government abolished slavery in Saint Domingue. Similarly, in Guadeloupe and Martinique, the governor hoped that freeing slaves would give him an army of black citizens with which to preserve the colony for France. France therefore abolished slavery in its remaining colonies in 1794.[32]

As tactics, these moves were typical of empires, which often brought under arms nobles, commoners, and servile populations to fight other empires with their nobles, commoners, and servile populations.[33] But in the revolutionary situation, their significance was different, and the Paris leaders understood this quite well. The repudiation of discrimination against property-holding nonwhites and the freeing of slaves were portrayed in Paris as matters of revolutionary ideology, while in the Caribbean, many ex-slaves hoped that if they fulfilled one of the central obligations of the citizen, other aspects of citizenship would come their way.

Toussaint Louverture was not an anti-imperialist. His goal was to end slavery and acquire a degree of autonomy within the French empire; he served for a time as *commissaire* for the revolutionary government in Saint Domingue. This imperial perspective later proved his undoing, for he miscalculated Napoleon's willingness to deal with him on such terms and allowed himself to be duped into surrender. But the dynamics of the Saint Domingue revolution had moved beyond this personage and this strategy. As Michel-Rolph Trouillot has argued, the "Black Jacobin" dimension of the revolution was not the only one, and much of the mobilization of slaves—vast numbers of whom had been recently imported from Africa—came through religious affinity and a vision of re-creating on Caribbean soil something like an African polity. For them, remaining in the French empire, even an empire of rights, citizenship, and freedom, was not the point.[34] Such a vision was not neatly distinguished from the more Jacobin variety, for the interplay of the two was as shifting as the alliances and betrayals that characterized the revolution between 1791 and 1804.

Back to Napoleon. Whereas the revolutionary government had sought to maintain an imperial structure while arguing over the relationship of national and imperial citizenship, Napoleon, after his accession to power, sent a powerful expedition to reconquer Haiti, restored slavery in the colonies in 1802, and tricked Toussaint into surrender. But—with a little help from other imperialists and a lot more from the microbes that decimated Napoleon's army—the Haitian Revolution prevailed. Haiti became a republic in 1804. It should have been the vanguard of liberation in world history, but Haiti's revolutionaries were premature anticolonialists and premature abolitionists. The French and other imperial governments needed to quarantine Haiti, to portray it as an example of black mischief rather than emancipatory progress, and more sedate abolitionists did not want such a radical example of the consequences of abolishing slavery to inhibit their own efforts at persuasion.

But what does the reinstatement of slavery in 1802 say about Napoleon's vision of empire?[35] This was a restorationist move in the fullest sense of the word: it reflected Napoleon's links to an ancien-régime set of planters in the islands and an old regime view of colonies as exceptional places from which resources could be drawn for the sole benefit of the metropole against the revolution's tendency at least to debate the universality of its principles and laws.[36] It would be a mistake to go too far in the other direction and see a seamless web of revolutionary ideology linking Haiti's slaves to the masses in the Paris streets of 1789. The issues of slavery and race were thrust upon political actors in France. From the attempts of representatives of the gens de couleur to claim their rights as citizens irrespective of race to the triumph of the Haitian revolutionaries, empire was the space of political mobilization and the assertion of moral claims.

Napoleon's only major defeat at the hands of what became a national liberation movement occurred at the hands of Haiti's often-divided armies of slaves, ex-slaves, and free people of color. Napoleon's previous overseas venture, the conquest of Egypt in 1798, proved short-lived, with British intervention playing a role in leaving this territory to another imperial system, the Ottoman. In 1803, Napoleon was reputed to say, "damn sugar, damn coffee, damn colonies!" as he decided to sell Louisiana to the United States for cash to finance his other imperial dreams.[37] We are left with a picture of one of the great state-building projects of the postrevolutionary era shaping a state that was by no means a nation or a type of empire neatly divided between a national core and a subordinate periphery. Napoleon's empire was a more finely differentiated entity, whose Frenchness was both narrower (personal, dynastic, Paris-centered) than France and wider (European, universalistic).

The appeal of empire did not disappear with Napoleon's defeat in 1814. It was echoed later in a regime that called itself the Second Empire (1852–71) and whose ruler called himself Napoleon III. The first Napoleon's juridical and administrative innovations also had a wide influence in Europe, in rival empires as well as his own. But the Europe of the nineteenth century was not a Europe of nation-states. It was a Europe with a small number of serious players, interacting, competing, and at times fighting with each other, each needing supranational resources to survive.

But even in the most explosively powerful empire of the postrevolutionary era, the limits of power were crucial: the understandings and compromises with conquered elites throughout Europe and the uneven imposition of the kind of centralized, bureaucraticized administration for which Napoleon is—not quite accurately—remembered, the failures in Haiti and Egypt. Even in Guadeloupe and Martinique, where colonial rule was maintained and slavery reimposed in 1802, the short-lived opening to slaves of the possibility of freedom and citizenship did not disappear from social consciousness. Laurent Dubois argues that the Haitian Revolution "'universalized' the idea of rights." It "outran the imagination of the metropole, transforming the possibilities embodied in the idea of citizenship."[38] It did this because empire was not simply out there, a place from which to extract resources but that did not need to trouble the political consciousness of people at home. The Haitian revolutionaries made themselves matter and showed that moral and political questions affected the entire space of empire.

CITIZENS, SUBJECTS, AND EMPIRE

Let me quickly bridge the space between the two stories of empire that I am telling in some detail, the period just after the revolution and the one just before the collapse of empire. Both are stories about how politics were conducted in empire space, in an ambiguous space that was neither sharply differentiated nor wholly unitary. The very question of what kinds of political principles applied where was at the center of conflict in both extremes. In the middle, I will argue briefly, the French state did try to make clear the distinction between colonial subject and metropolitan citizen, but such a distinction never became stable, was never fully adequate for the needs of the state, and was always contested. At times, the French state was more "national" in its language of politics and its forms of administration than in others, but national and imperial thinking kept getting in the way of each other, keeping in the fore both the possibility of an order divided into colonizer and colonized and the possibility of its becoming something else.

It was in Algeria, conquered in 1830, that the distinction between subject and citizen was worked out. Algerian territory was conceived of as an extension of France, while its people were too numerous and too well integrated into Islamic and Ottoman institutions developed by previous conquerors, Arabs and Ottomans, to be safely incorporated without overwhelming "Europeans." Algeria's European settlers had to be made "French" at the same time as its more long-term inhabitants had to be kept at some distance. As Benjamin Stora points out, Algeria was a very Mediterranean territory, and its settlers came much more from Malta, Italy, and other pan-Mediterranean areas than from France. To French jurists, the crucial distinction was in terms of civil status, the regulatory regime for marriage, inheritance, and other civil matters. Muslims had their legal status based on the sharia, enforced by Islamic courts. Jews also had a distinct civil status, based on Mosaic law. Christians came under the French civil code, as did all citizens in metropolitan France. Coming under Islamic or Mosaic civil status implied that the individual was not truly autonomous—just as since the revolution, women, considered subject to their husbands, were denied the vote. Whereas women in European France were considered passive citizens—with rights but not the vote—in Algeria, Muslims and Jews were not citizens at all. Jews resident in Algeria only became eligible for citizenship, over opposition, in 1870.[39]

A government decision of 1865, during the rule of Napoleon III, made clear that Muslim Algerians were French *nationals* and could serve in the army or civil service, but they could become citizens only if the government accepted them as such and only if they gave up Muslim civil status. The government saw the decision as generous, opening a door to Muslims to become French citizens. Few wanted to give up Islamic civil status to do so. Fewer still were accepted into the cité. Under the Third Republic, it was the white settlers who seized the institutions of citizenship and used them to ensure that the barriers for Muslims to enter would be high. The legislature, in the 1880s and again during World War I, debated widening to door to allow at least some Muslims to acquire citizenship while keeping their civil status—*citoyenneté dans le statut,* as it was called. The proposals did not pass. Nevertheless, citizenship was an available category, familiar to those who could not have it, and it would be a sore point until the Algerian Revolution.[40]

The subject–citizen distinction was not a fixed essence of empire but a policy that could be and was debated, in terms of both principle and pragmatism. In 1848, after revolution in France and slave revolt in the Caribbean, France abolished slavery for good in its colonies, a reminder that the unit in which political and moral discourse took place, as in 1789, was the empire-state and not just the nation-state. Freed slaves entered directly into the category of citizen. The citizenship construct in the Antillies cut two ways: emphasizing that formal equivalence of ex-slaves to other French citizens as if their lives had begun anew—rejecting the prejudices attached to their former status and their African origins but also occluding memories of a history of enslavement and claims that might derive from that past.[41]

In the French colonies in India, there was also no neat subject–citizen distinction, nor was such a distinction found in the earliest outposts of French Africa, the eighteenth-century trading posts on the mouth of the Senegal River and on the peninsula that includes Dakar: the Four Communes.[42] It was not made clear that the *originaires* of these colonies *were* citizens, but after 1848 it was clear that they had the qualities of citizens, particularly the right to vote for local assemblies and to elect a deputy to the Paris legislature. Unlike the case of Algeria, the originaires of the Four Communes did not have to renounce Muslim civil status; marriage, inheritance, and family law remained for citizens under the jurisdiction of Islamic courts. The difference was in part structural: the Four Communes were bastions of France in a remote, largely unconquered space, and the state needed more people on its side, whereas the fear in Algeria was of a population of European origin being swallowed up by a much larger one that was Arab and Berber, and most importantly Muslim.

With the later conquests of the interior of Africa, especially after the 1870s, the ideological and juridical awkwardness of colonization in a republic of citizens became more acute. Leaders of the Third Republic were aware that colonization smacked of adventurism to a bourgeois society and of oppression to republicans. The republican case for empire rested on an evolutionist concept and hence an unstable one: the civilizing mission. According to the ideologues of the Third Republic, citizenship should open before "subjects" as they attained civilization, and the colonial regimes did make gestures in this direction—a series of rules, quite hard to meet, for how the conversion could be made. The separate judicial regime for noncitizens, the *indigénat,* was treated as a regime of exception, always temporary but continuously renewed.[43]

Inside the Four Communes, citizens had to use every resource citizenship offered to hold onto their rights in the face of white traders and officials who wanted to treat all Africans as subjects, as they did in the newly conquered interior. There were a few openings to citizenship in the interior: education, the status of a "local notable," and in some circumstances military service. But in most of French West Africa, citizenship was something many Africans knew but could not have.

These arrangements were more than a gesture to appease a certain republican rigor in Paris. The colonial administration needed educated subalterns; it needed collaborators in the rural areas. The republic needed military help from its subjects. This small fissure opened wider in World War I, when manpower needs escalated. The Senegalese citizen-politician Blaise Diagne took advantage of the French need for soldiers. Diagne in 1914 became the first black African to be elected to a seat in the legislature in Paris (in distinction to the métis who had previously served in this post). He was willing to serve as an effective broker to help recruit African soldiers and smooth over conflict, as long as the French government affirmed, without the previous ambiguity, that the originaires were indeed citizens, with full political and civil rights regardless of their civil status. The Blaise Diagne Law of 1916 proved important to France's recruitment efforts and crucial to the political history of Senegal.

Diagne turned this opening into the creation of a political machine in Senegal.[44] The postwar years in Senegal witnessed a small explosion of citizen activism—and a reaction to it. The French government in the 1920s turned to a more traditionalist policy precisely because citizenship claims were getting all too real. The government promoted chiefs—not the citizens of towns—as the intermediaries best able to represent "their" people with "their" customs. The 1931 Colonial Exhibition in Paris celebrated the cultural richness of the peoples France had colonized, vividly asserting France's genius in preserving and appreciating their integrity and in making them part of Greater France. The view of a united but differentiated space of empire entailed complex discussions over how to classify the large number of people whose place was unclear, notably children born of mixed relationships, distinguishing cases where the father recognized the child, where he did not, and in the latter case whether the child partook of enough "French" characteristics to be a useful recruit to the "citizen" side. Such a question took on new political as well as juridical meaning after the 1920s, when challenges to the regime in places such as Vietnam began to mount.[45]

Even the self-consciously progressive leaders of the Popular Front government in France (1936–38) saw the future of the large majority of Africans within a traditional or customary milieu, rescued from the abuses of past governments and predatory settlers. They accepted that a small number of *évolués,* both educated Africans and long-term workers, could benefit from the institutions and social policies applied to people of metropolitan origin, and the Popular Front government worked calmly with African leaders of trade unions and political parties allied to the French Socialist Party. The vision of authentic African communities evolving within their own customary structure contained nostalgic echoes of a rural France that had all but disappeared, but it implied that Africans would continue to follow separate paths, a select few being accepted without great qualms as potential citizens.[46]

Eugen Weber has emphasized how long it took to make French "peasants" into Frenchmen, into people whose "provincial" perspective had given way to participation in a national political culture. Particularity was not solely a colonial feature. Weber puts the army and the school at the center of the mechanisms that, slowly, made Frenchmen at long last (and not quite fully) by the time of World War I. French historians have questioned his timing and his formulations, but most relevant to our purposes is that the same institutions that Weber sees as national, the army and the school, were also operating in the French empire.[47] They produced not a homogenous Frenchness but varying levels of acculturation, different forms of service to French interests, powerful and volatile sentiments of connection to Greater France among segments of the population—and, most important of all, claims upon the state from veterans and the évolués. The Frenchman that institutions of state produced was thus only sometimes national.

FROM EMPIRE TO UNION TO COMMUNITY

General Charles de Gaulle, speaking in Normandy on June 16, 1946, asserted that here "on the soil of the ancestors the State reappeared." After the nightmare of defeat, the French state would now reestablish "national unity and imperial unity." This dualism within what de Gaulle referred to both as the empire and (the new term) the French Union recurred throughout the speech. De Gaulle spoke of the future of "100 million men and women," less than half of whom lived in European France, the rest in "the overseas territories attached to the French Union by very diverse ties."[48]

The French state was not the French nation, and the nation was not the state. What de Gaulle variously called the nation, *la patrie,* and the republic was one part of the state. The other consisted of overseas territories, whose full membership in the French state was reaffirmed, whose loyalty to France during the war was celebrated, but whose relationships to French culture and society were varied and whose administrative and political status was in 1946 the object of intense debate. France, in 1946, was not a nation-state but an empire-state.

Between 1946 and 1962, French leaders tried a series of organizational initiatives to preserve France as a single but differentiated entity. Throughout this period, the French political establishment was agreed that invidious distinction between metropole and colony had to be eliminated, but that only raised the stakes on the precise institutional arrangements that would exist within Greater France.

Equally important—with echoes of the Haitian Revolution—the unit of Greater France was also crucial to the people and movements who challenged the French government in this period. Secession and creating new nations was one strand of opposition politics, but it was not the only one and in some places not the most salient. This section will pursue two themes: first, the efforts of political actors—including elected representatives from throughout the union—to work out constitutional and juridical rules for this undefined multinational polity that was no longer "colonial" but not yet a community of equals; and second, the ways in which social and political movements in the overseas territories turned the notion of citizenship into a language of claim making. In the end, the discourses and institutions by which French leaders hoped to tie France's diverse components together helped convince its leaders that the price of the new imperial France could not be paid.

Both the underlying continuity of 1946—the insistence that all components of the empire remain under French sovereignty—and the willingness to erase long-lasting distinctions are consistent with the politics of ruling an empire. Just how incorporation and difference could be conjugated was subject to change without compromising sovereignty or the imperial nature of the polity. At war's end, the existence of France as a worldwide actor was under threat because France was severely damaged economically and politically by the war and occupation, because the fight against Hitler had opened many eyes to the dangers of racial and cultural distinctions within a polity, because new actors and organizations were seizing wider forums in which to question colonial rule and racial distinction, and because active political conflicts in Vietnam and North Africa were raising independence as an alternative to empire.

As the end of the war came in sight, colonial specialists in the French leadership were putting on the table an agenda that leaned much further in the direction of inclusion than anything seen since the uncertainties of the revolution. In March 1945, the Minister of the Colonies, in a proclamation regarding Indochina, used for the first time the phrase "Union Française" to replace the term "French Empire." Colonies were renamed Overseas Territories, and the ministry in charge of them the Ministry of Overseas France.[49] France was to be, a Free French spokesman asserted, "a more or less federal ensemble in which each French country, morally equal to each other, including the metropole, will be capable of following its distinct vocation, while sharing in the rights and obligations of the same human society."[50] Heady words —but consistent with a view of an emancipatory but imperial France that had never quite gone away since the revolution. While some tried to defer equality and maintain hierarchy, other political activists soon claimed equality immediately within this imperial conception of France. Officials in the overseas territories were made aware that overt racial discrimination, including distinct judicial regimes for subjects and citizens, could no longer be sanctioned. Officials in Paris accepted that France would at last have to get serious about funding social and economic development.[51]

Just how far an empire that had combined centralized authority with the notion of colonial tutelage could move toward becoming a union of equals would depend on the outcome of much pushing and shoving, in streets and in legislative assemblies. But the imperial framework—the idea of a multinational France—was itself used in making claims to equality.

As the National Constituent Assembly debated a new constitution, it used its legislative powers to put in place key elements of the new picture. Between December 1945 and May 1946, the assembly passed legislation that dismantled one of the most hated features of colonial rule: the indigénat, the separate judicial system that allowed officials to inflict arbitrary punishment on subjects; it acceded to a campaign long waged by Aimé Césaire that Martinique, Guadeloupe, Guyana, and Réunion become French departments, equivalent to those of the metropole; it made forced labor for public or private purposes illegal; and, in May, in a bill submitted by the Senegalese deputy Lamine Guèye, it abolished the distinction between subject and citizen and proclaimed that all people in all parts of the empire now had the "qualities" of French citizens. The law eliminated at a stroke the issue that had bedeviled the citizenship issue since the 1860s: people were citizens regardless of their civil status, and their personal and private affairs could be regulated under Islamic or other "local" codes.[52]

While this was going on, events in the colonies pushed legislators to find new solutions to the relationship of incorporation and differentiation. In Vietnam, Japanese dominance during the war meant that rather than defend the territory, France virtually had to recapture it, and it never fully did so in the face of the Viet Minh. Conflicts in North

Africa threatened after the Sétif massacre of 1945 to degenerate into a cycle of repression and revolution, and full-scale war erupted in Algeria in 1954. Also revealing were the lessons of the many smaller-scale conflicts that could not be managed within older frameworks of "tribal" subjects under the eyes of administrators who knew their natives. The Senegalese general strike movement, which lasted from December 1945 through February 1946, shutting down for a time the major port and administrative center of French West Africa, was a case in point. A range of workers, from civil servants, many long residents of Dakar and hence citizens, to manual workers, mostly subjects who had migrated to the city, participated. The slogan "equal pay for equal work" was at the heart of the mobilization, which took on the tone of a mass urban movement as much as an industrial action.

Officials in Paris realized that the distinction between subject and citizen did not correspond to reality in Senegal, and it offered no help in figuring out how to restore the urban order. Instead, French officials turned to their metropolitan models of settling industrial disputes, and they negotiated with the unions, giving each major category of worker concessions until the general strike peeled back. The fiction that African workers were like any other workers and could be handled as workers were in France proved far more useful than the fiction of unbridgeable otherness. Further strikes—including a railway strike that engulfed all of French West Africa for five months in 1947 and 1948—widened this opening.[53]

The strategies of African social movements as well as of the government point to the overlapping territory on which a French reference point could be put to use, notably by Africans to claim higher wages and benefits. Officials were caught up in these terms, not just because they could not repudiate the postwar rationale for French power but because they hoped that Africans would perhaps become the productive, orderly, predictable contributors to the new French society that they wanted to see.

The constitutional debates focused on the balance between autonomy for individual territories and central control, on separate voting for different categories of citizens versus a single college for all. The African and Caribbean delegates, including Senghor, Guèye, and Césaire, played leading roles in legislative debates over the new constitution.

The result was a series of compromises: the territories got less autonomy than they sought but guarantees of equal civil rights for colonial and metropolitan citizens in all the empire. Algerian delegates were the least successful of all, for reconciling their demands for autonomy, European settlers' insistence on dominance, and French notions of an indissoluble union was all but impossible. Debates over the details of the franchise and elected assemblies went on through the summer of 1946, through two constitutional referenda.

The most revealing exchange occurred in August, when an advocate of a strong republican France, Edouard Herriot, cut to the heart of the contradiction between a colonizing state and a federation of different peoples, warning that if one took literally the notion of all citizens participating equally in electoral institutions and if one looked at population figures, then France could become "the colony of its former colonies." At this, Senghor jumped up to reply, "this is racism!"[54] The exchange revealed the limits of equivalence within the idea of imperial citizenship: power was not going to be distributed evenly.

In the end, political institutions, following Herriot's logic, ensured the participation of colonial citizens but not control by an overseas majority.[55] The franchise was at first restricted but gradually expanded. Voting would be in separate colleges, loosely for people of French civil status and those of "personal" or "special" (Islamic "customary") civil status. Ultimate authority rested with the parliament in Paris, where all citizens were represented but not in proportion to population. The assemblies in individual territories and the federations of West and equatorial Africa were more representative but much weaker, and the Assemblée de l'Union Française, specifically intended for overseas citizens, was consultative only.

But the legislative accomplishments of the spring of 1946 had already shown that even a minority of colonial deputies could have considerable influence on matters about which they cared deeply.[56] Just as in metropolitan France, it took from 1789 until 1848 for citizenship to translate into universal male suffrage and until 1944 for the vote to be extended to women; suffrage was gradually extended from people meeting educational qualifications or having served in the army toward more openness, until suffrage in the colonies became universal in 1956.[57]

For all the compromises, the message that African leaders took away was that aspirations for equality had a basis in constitutional texts and official ideology. Everyone would be under the same regime of criminal justice but would have the right to have family and other matters of personal status come under "customary" or "Islamic" legal jurisdiction; terms like indigène were banned from official publications; any citizen could enter European France and seek any job within the French civil service; all French citizens were supposed to carry equivalent identification cards.[58] Equality could be claimed without giving up difference, since the citizenship law was independent of the civil code under which personal life was administered. Senghor, in the assembly, had noted the advance over the notion of citizenship at the time of the revolution. Citizenship in the 1790s, even as extended to the Caribbean, reflected the "Jacobin tradition"—of a unified France—but after that, "France discovered bit by bit the diverse civilizations overseas." Such a recognition lay behind the 1946 constitution's acceptance that the new citizens of the overseas territories did not have to give up their civil status under Islamic or customary law to exercise their rights. As the Overseas Ministry's political bureau concluded, "the legislature wanted to mark the perfect equality of all in public life, but not the perfect identity of the French of the metropole and the overseas French."[59]

The preamble to the constitution used the plural in setting out a France "composed of nations and peoples." The French Union consisted of the French Republic, including Algeria, overseas departments, and "overseas territories" (as colonies were renamed); associated states (former "protectorates" such as Morocco, Vietnam, and Tunisia, which were technically sovereign states that had ceded part of their power to France); and mandated territories, notably Cameroon and Togo. Inhabitants of the French Republic, in Europe and overseas, were French nationals. The constitution was deliberately vague on what residents of the overseas territories and Algeria were citizens of—the union or the republic—but by giving them the "qualities" of the citizen, it gave them the legal basis to claim equal rights.[60] The authors may not have realized just how intense claim making would become, especially for social and economic equivalence, for the citizens of the French Republic.

Moroccans, Vietnamese, and others from Associated States were French citizens within the French Union, but they had Moroccan or Vietnamese nationality; they did not elect members of the Assemblée Nationale as did voters from the Overseas Territories. There was a special body for considering affairs that applied to the Associated States generally and their relation to the republic, but it was weakened by the refusal of Morocco and Tunisia to participate.[61] People from the mandated territories were treated in most respects like those from the Overseas Territories but were not French nationals because France was acting on behalf of the United Nations as a trustee charged with their advancement. They did vote for deputies to the Assemblée, but that was considered a generous concession, mainly intended to bring them closer to their neighbors in the Overseas Territories.

Then there was Algeria, technically part of the metropole, divided into three departments, but administered as a special case and in reality a politically dysfunctional organization, whose representative institutions had been hijacked by settlers and whose legitimacy was not accepted by Muslim Algerians, whose accession to citizenship in 1946 was too little too late.[62] Juridical treatises and government discussions of institutions and the application of principles of citizenship go on for pages about the intricacies of these arrangements, but the necessity to balance inclusion and differentiation with the French Union was clear at the time and should not now be obscured by thinking of nation-state and subordinated colony as the only two alternatives available.[63] The decade and a half after the war was a time of uncertainty—and possibility. In the aftermath of war, the state became an increasingly active agent in shaping the social and economic lives of its citizens, and the stakes involved in such debates were high—higher no doubt than the writers of the constitution of 1946 had realized.

The institutional house of cards began to come apart with the independence of Vietnam in 1954, the less blood-ridden accession to independence of Morocco and Tunisia in 1956, and the Algerian War. But French leaders did not give up, and during the writing of the constitution of 1958, which brought in the Fifth Republic, much of the debate over the union was repeated, this time in relation to the French Community. The terms had clearly changed, and the intentions were more federal. Overseas Territories were now termed "member states," and the constitution provided terms for promotion to a new form of association or for independence at the territory's behest. As jurists noted, these rules were murky, and negotiations and bilateral treaties—under duress in the crucial case of Algeria—were the forms in which status changes took place.[64] But there is no question that the French elite put a great deal of effort into maintaining the notion of France as a multinational entity.

To some observers, all this was window dressing. The reality of French policy was of centralized control and an insistence that the only route for personal or collective advancement lay in assimilation and conformity to French norms. At most, they would argue, France conceded diluted representation in central legislative bodies in order to prevent territorial bodies from having any real power or autonomy. There is more than a little truth in criticisms of legislative institutions and French leaders' belief that they were best equipped to shape a "development" process. Indeed, the idea of France as model and tutor enabled many French people to accept Africans' willing participation in French institutions.[65]

But the critique neglects the power of the citizenship construct when combined with mobilizing organizations and leadership at various levels and the important dynamic unleashed by rising aspirations. The issue is not only what citizenship *was* but also how it was *used*. And citizenship in the French Union, far from being a containment device to hold people's aspirations in check, soon proved to provide a language of claims with considerable power. Even officials' evolutionary notions took on a new form when it became less a matter of static classification—"civilized" versus "primitive"—than a serious program for economic and social change and a basis for claims by African leaders for resources in order to advance.

For some leaders of African political movements, the range of possibilities was not limited to the quest for the nation-state. Senghor and his associate Mamadou Dia were among those who—until very late in the game—sought to make French citizenship meaningful and convert the institutions of the French Union into a federal structure, in which component "states" would have a high degree of autonomy and equal status, with an administrative and legislative apparatus at the Union/ Community level exercising a set of common functions.

It was the very success of social and political movements in Africa in using the rhetoric and institutions of the postwar empire-state to claim equivalence with other French citizens that eventually convinced the French government that its attempt at an empire of citizens was unaffordable.[66] Well-organized social movements posed demands in the language in which imperial hegemony was now proclaimed. Trade unionists and political leaders insisted that the equivalence of citizens meant that workers in French Africa should have the same wages and benefits as workers in France, and they played on officials' hopes to create a predictable and orderly African working class. The labor movement demanded, above all, the passage of a labor code that would forbid racial discrimination in employment, provide the same social guarantees to all workers, and set out a framework for trade union recognition and collective bargaining. The debate over the code took six years and was the focus of intense mobilization and strikes, but in 1952 the code was passed. During the struggle, major Africa unions affiliated with the French communist trade union federation, and through it with the World Federation of Trade Unions. These positionings of Africans as an exploited working class, as citizens of France, and as part of an assertive black population reinforced rather than contradicted each other.

In one of the many legislative debates on the code, Léopold Senghor remarked, "as you know, Africans now have a mystique of equality. In this domain, as in others, they want the same principles to be applied from the first in the overseas territories as in the metropole."[67] The social claims seemed to dig Africans deeper into French institutions, and it was in reference to France and the French standard of living that claims of equality were being posed. For a time, even when things were going badly for France in Vietnam and heating up in Algeria, the institutions of the French Union seemed to be working well in sub-Saharan Africa, with conflict mostly contained within industrial relations and legislative mechanisms. One official concluded from the long 1947–48 strike that "social peace can only profit from such a crystalization of forces around two poles, certainly opposed but knowing each other better and accepting to keep contact to discuss collective bargaining agreements and conditions of work."[68]

Yet the unions and the African political parties were using impeccable logic to show that anything short of complete equality in every sphere of political, social, and economic life was incompatible with the very justification for the French Union.[69] By the mid-1950s, French officials were thoroughly fed up with the demands being made upon them in the language of citizenship. The costs of modernizing imperialism in sub-Saharan Africa were high, and the promised transformation of the African economy was proving a more difficult goal than expected. An influential report on the modernization of colonial territories in 1953 warned of the danger that the process might result in the "exhaustion of the Metropole." A French minister in 1956 put it bluntly: citizenship had come to mean "equality in wages, equality in labor legislation, in social security benefits, equality in family allowances, in brief, equality in standard of living."[70]

But if the costs of modernizing imperialism in sub-Saharan Africa were high, in Algeria the costs of not modernizing imperialism were even higher. The French army fought the Algerian liberation movement with terror and torture, but by 1956 the government was introducing programs of *promotion sociale* (affirmative action) in the civil service of both Algerian and European France in an effort to give the "Muslim French people of Algeria" a fuller stake in the system that many were rebelling against.[71] In sub-Saharan Africa, French officials were by 1956 looking for a way to back out of the endless demands of an inclusive imperialism without running into a stone wall that could become a second Algeria.

The formula they found was "territorialization." It meant devolution of power, away from the Assemblée Nationale in Paris and toward individual colonial territories. It was a strategy of divide and not rule. Each territorial assembly would be elected under universal suffrage and choose a cabinet that would work with a French governor. The leader would be a kind of junior prime minister, and the assembly would have real budgetary authority. That meant that political leaders who depended on the vote of taxpayers would decide whether to answer demands for higher wages for government workers, more state schools, more health clinics, more paved roads. The framework for the equivalence of the citizen would not be Greater France—whose resources seemed enormous when viewed from Africa and limited when viewed from Paris—but the resources of the territory itself. The federation of French West Africa was stripped of much of its power and resources.

Criticism of territorialization came from civil servants' unions, which realized that the territorial treasury would be much less able to meet their pay claims than the French one, and most powerfully from Senghor and Dia. Dia expressed his "profound and sad conviction of committing one of those major historical errors that can inflect the destiny of a people....In spite of us, West Africa was balkanized, cut into fragments." Dia and Senghor persisted, trying to turn the French Community defined by the new constitution of 1958 into the "Franco-African Community" they wanted.[72]

Their argument was in part practical—fearing the weakness of small, poor states—and it was in part cultural, focused on people whom Senghor and Dia repeatedly referred to as the "négro-africains de l'Union Française." Under the umbrella of the French Community, they argued, West Africans should cooperate in their own federation, which would be both a strong actor within the wider Franco-African Community and an expression of an African national will. They were emphatic that their notion of "national" was not focused on territorial units like Senegal but on a federal French West Africa—and through that on Africa as a whole. In the late 1950s then, Senghor and Dia were advocating not the replacement of colonialism by the territorial nation-state but a layered sovereignty of territory, African federation, and Franco-African Community. As Dia proclaimed, "it is necessary in the final analysis that the imperialist conception of the nation-state give way to the modern conception of the multinational state."[73]

The post-1958 French Community proved as unworkable as its predecessor. It was an association of states that were theoretically equal and in reality anything but, still creating dangers of claim making that France was trying to avoid without giving Africans the control of their destiny that they sought. For most African leaders, the temptations of territorialization, autonomy, and independence were greater—and certainly more immediately realizable—than the promise of greater economic integration and more political clout that federation seemed to offer. The efforts of Senghor and some of his colleagues to persuade the newly installed heads of partly self-governing territories to transform rather than abandon the federation of French West Africa succeeded only in regard to Senegal and the Sudan, which for a brief period formed the Mali Federation.

Senghor, Dia, and Mamadou Keita of the Sudan formed the federation within the French Community and then negotiated independence as the state of Mali, but with bilateral treaties with France that continued much of what imperial citizenship had previously offered, including the right of nationals of each state to reside and work in the other. But the Mali Federation could not overcome the temptations of its leaders to protect their own territorial base from potential competition from the other unit, and in August 1960, two months after independence, the two federated states, with much acrimony, went their separate ways, as territorial states claiming their distinct nationalities. Thinking only of Mali's failure—and not the attempt—misses the tragedy of African decolonization. And assuming the futility of any attempt at building supranational polities with shared sovereignties and overlapping citizenries makes it harder to understand that Europeans eventually came around to seeing the virtues in something like what Dia and Senghor wanted—but only for themselves.[74]

The reality of territorialization in 1956 and the recognition of former colonies as "states" in the constitution of 1958 was that they destroyed precisely what the French government had tried to make invincible after the war: the notion that France was the only unit in which real power was vested and toward which aspirations could be directed. If in 1946 the idea of national independence was to French leaders an anathema and the politics of citizenship a game they were willing to play, a decade later the costs of social and economic equivalence had become so threatening that the alternative of claims to national autonomy was greeted by French officials with something akin to relief.

If imperial citizenship was too much citizenship for France, it was too imperial for many Africans, a humiliation for some who saw the French reference point held up before them, irrelevant for others who saw no equivalent to anything metropolitan in their conditions of life. There were vigorous debates at trade union meetings, at political gatherings, and in newspapers over these issues. People later termed "fathers of the nation," such as Senghor and Félix Houphouët-Boigny, were among those who continued to assert French citizenship, while Sékou Touré, most dramatically, shifted from a position of demanding equality with a Greater France to one that specifically repudiated such demands in favor of national assertion. In 1958, only Sékou Touré's Guinea voted to make a clean break to independence; the other African territories tried for a few more years to work out a formula for federation among themselves and some form of Franco-African Community. With territorialization making it more difficult for African territories to claim social and economic equality within the French Community, with conflict among African leaders inhibiting African federation and a community umbrella, and with France at last seeing that the community was offering it less and less, the member states moved in 1960 to negotiate terms of their independence via bilateral agreements with the French government. Among political and social movements challenging an imperial France after World War II, sovereignty was only one goal, but it was what France, in the end, was willing to concede.[75]

Looking back on the postwar decade, the emergence of the fiction of equivalence among all citizens in an indissoluble empire was an important step in enabling French leaders in the late 1950s to imagine how they could give up the empire and how Africans could govern themselves. Such an imaginative leap was inconceivable from the ideological perspectives predominant before World War II. The acknowledgment of Africans as at least potentially within the realm of citizenship made it possible to think of them as exercising sovereignty. The fiction of the formal equivalence of sovereign nations could then help get France out of the social and economic implications of the equivalence of citizens. For African leaders, the same framework produced alternative possibilities, and the idea that turning empire into federation could allow for the expression of an African personality was pursued by Senghor and others with great persistence, until they were left in 1960 with little choice but to make the best of the remaining option, a territorial vision of the nation-state.

NATIONAL FRANCE

The same contingent process that left Senegal and other colonies in Africa as nation-states made France more national than it had ever been. However, even that statement has to be qualified by the importance France attached to its former colonies after they became independent: efforts to propagate the French language and French culture (*francophonie*) within the former French empire; aid programs focused on ex-colonies; military bases remaining in former colonies; personal, commercial, and political relations between French elites and former colonial leaders; and—for a time—bilateral agreements setting up favorable conditions for people born in ex-colonies before the date of independence to gain access to immigration and acquisition of French nationality (as usual, with complications in the case of Algeria).[76]

The citizenship construct, as adapted in 1946 to people who defined their personal status in different ways, had seemed to open the possibility that people of diverse origins could be incorporated within France. But ideas of French particularity and notions of France as a tutelary, civilizing society did not end with decolonization either, shaping a still ongoing debate across much of the political spectrum over what it means to be French. On the French far right, the national framework has shaped forms of reracialization, which escalated in the 1980s. If imperial racism implied that colonized subjects had to be held within the polity in a position of inferiority, so as to be useful, national racism implied exclusion. One cannot understand the Front National simply as an imperial hangover; it emerges out of a *national* reconfiguration of French politics. It competes with an egalitarian, republican conception of French nationality, one that posits an undifferentiated French citizen projected backward to the French Revolution, a version that also skips over the struggles over different forms of inclusion and differentiation that have been the subject of this chapter. Those who accept neither position and argue that cultural differentiation and affinity are compatible with citizenship are not helped by intellectuals who project backward the concept of the nation-state into an essential attribute of "modernity" or to an essential attribute of the "republican model" stretching back to the revolution.

My goal has been to probe the nature and the limits of an imperial perspective on a polity and on the social issues within that polity. Other chapters in this volume have widened our perspective on empires by looking beyond western Europe, and this one has attempted to take that broadened vision back to Europe itself. The familiar narrative of French imperialism—the construction of a French nation-state that then holds itself as a model that others must emulate but cannot attain—is inadequate for describing the kind of polity France actually was, in the years after World War II as much as in the years of the Franco-Haitian Revolution of 1789–1804. The politics of difference, conjugated with the politics of incorporation into an imperial polity, implied a series of possible strategies, among them Napoleon's complex continental and overseas empire, France's inconsistent attempts to distinguish citizen and subject, and the 1946 decision to generalize citizenship.[77] Difference was not dichotomy, and empires tried to attach collectivities to the state in a mix of ways. Critics and opponents of empire, from Toussaint Louverture to Léopold Senghor, took up different aspects of an imperial perspective to make their claims and to try to reconfigure incorporation and differentiation in ways that tested and revealed the limits of possibility within imperial formations. To work through this history helps us comprehend the limits of power and imagination within empires and the peculiarities of national ideas as well.

Acknowledgments

My thanks to Mamadou Diouf, Emmanuelle Saada, Peter Perdue, and Ann Stoler for comments on drafts of this paper and to Prasenjit Duara for introducing a valuable discussion of the paper at the Santa Fe conference. The second half of the paper is an early version of an ongoing research project on imperial citizenship in France and French Africa after 1946.

Notes

1. Senghor, "Vues sur l'Afrique Noire," 58; Pleven, "Préface," to a section of articles on colonial affairs. Senghor mentioned Marshal Lyautey and his contemporary Robert Delavignette among those who shared his conception of provincial France.

2. Senghor, "Vues sur l'Afrique Noire," 84.

3. Senghor, "Vues sur l'Afrique Noire," 59.

4. Chakrabarty, *Provincializing Europe.*

5. For a collection of my critical essays on the concepts mentioned here, see Cooper, *Colonialism in Question.* See in particular ch. 5, "Modernity," and ch. 6, "States, Empires, and Political Imagination."

6. If not a precise definition, we can set out a family description of "empire": a political unit that is large and expansionist (or with memories of an expansionist past) and that reproduces differentiation and inequality among the people it

incorporates. Empires, like nation-states, are first of all states. All states entail inequality and distinction, but if nation-states operate under the fiction of a single people, empire-states institutionalize difference among component populations.

7. Alan Forrest, *Conscripts and Deserters and Napoleon's Men,* 18-19; Woloch, *New Regime,* esp. 433.

8. Forrest, *Napoleon's Men,* 18-19; Grab, "Army, State, and Society."

9. Broers, "Napoleon, Charlemagne, and Lotharingia," 136.

10. Pagden, *Peoples and Empires,* 136.

11. Stuart Woolf, *Napoleon's Integration of Europe,* 27, 40-41.

12. Quoted in Martyn P. Thompson, "Ideas of Europe," 38-39.

13. Woolf, *Napoleon's Integration of Europe,* 43.

14. Woolf, *Napoleon's Integration of Europe,* 197; Dwyer, *Napoleon and Europe,* 10; Geoffrey Ellis, "The Nature of Napoleonic Imperialism," 111; Broers, "Napoleon, Charlemagne, and Lotharingia."

15. Woolf, *Napoleon's Integration of Europe,* 125.

16. Broers, "Cultural Imperialism in a European Context?" 157.

17. Broers, "Europe under Napoleon." On Napoleon's conception of rural France as itself in effect an object of ethnographic observation, see Bourguet, *Déchiffrer la France.*

18. Woolf, *Napoleon's Integration of Europe,* 109, 118, 115, 129.

19. Woolf, *Napoleon's Integration of Europe,* 30, 49-50.

20. Woolf, *Napoleon's Integration of Europe,* 17, 20, 27, 43, 152, 178-81, 197; Dwyer, *Napoleon and Europe,* 3, 5.

21. Woolf, *Napoleon's Integration of Europe,* 226-37.

22. Fontana, "Napoleonic Empire and the Europe of Nations," 124-27.

23. Lieven, "Empire's Place in International Relations."

24. Cole, "Empires of Liberty?"

25. Sloane, "Napoleon's Plan for a Colonial System."

26. The emancipatory project is recuperated most famously in James, *Black Jacobins.* See also Blackburn, *Overthrow of Colonial Slavery,* and Bénot, *La révolution française et la fin des colonies.* Enlightenment bashing is a favorite sport of postmodern and postcolonial theorists, a point of view examined critically in Cooper, *Colonialism in Question.*

27. Muthu, *Enlightenment against Empire.*

28. Forster, "French Revolution, People of Color, and Slavery"; Tarrade, "Les colonies et les principes de 1789"; Geggus, "Racial Equality, Slavery, and Colonial Secession."

29. Gens de couleur owned one-third of the plantations and one-fourth of the slaves on the eve of the revolution. Fick, "French Revolution in Saint Domingue," 56.

30. Geggus, "Slavery, War, and Revolution in the Greater Caribbean," 5, 12-13, 17. On communication networks among slaves and people of color, see Julius Scott, "Common Wind."

31. The most gripping narrative of the revolution remains James, *Black Jacobins.* For more recent scholarship, see Fick, *Making of Haiti,* and Dubois, *Avengers of the New World.*

32. Dubois, *Colony of Citizens.*

33. The presence of blacks, mulattoes, and whites in opposing factions within the Saint Domingue war is mentioned in Geggus, "Slavery, War, and Revolution," 11.

34. Trouillot, *Silencing the Past.*

35. This is one of the most embarrassing moments in French history, and attempts by French ideologues to claim credit for the emancipation of slaves are made difficult by the fact that France had to do it twice. See Bénot and Dorigny, *Rétablissement de l'esclavage dans les colonies françaises.*

36. The regression to the ancien régime is emphasized in Bénot, *La démence coloniale sous Napoléon,* esp. 11-12.

37. Quoted in Kukla, *Wilderness So Immense,* 249.

38. Dubois, "La République Métissée," 22.

39. Stora, "'Southern' World of the Pieds-noirs"; Ruedy, *Modern Algeria.*

40. Blévis, "Sociologie d'un droit colonial."

41. Cottias, "Le silence de la nation."

42. The following section is based on Conklin, *Mission to Civilize;* Dickens, "Defining French Citizenship Policy in West Africa"; and Diouf, "French Colonial Policy of Assimilation."

43. Merle, "Retour sur le régime de l'indigénat."

44. G. Wesley Johnson, *Emergence of Black Politics in Senegal.*

45. Saada, "La 'question des métis' dans les colonies françaises."

46. Bernard-Duquenet, *Le Sénégal et le front populaire.*

47. Weber, *Peasants into Frenchmen.*

48. Speech at Bayeux, June 16, 1946, reprinted in Comité national chargé de la publication des travaux préparatoires des institutions de la Ve République, *Documents pour servir à l'élaboration de la constitution du 4 octobre 1958,* 3-7.

49. Borella, *L'évolution politique et juridique de l'Union Française depuis 1946,*

33. The Third Republic had not liked to use the word *empire* but had no trouble with *colony*. The Vichy government had no trouble with *empire*. In the early post-Vichy years, even republican-minded officials used *empire* occasionally and *colony* consistently. Both words had been dropped by 1946.

50. Laurentie, "Pour ou contre le colonialism?" 10. On the repudiation of "colonies in the old sense of the word," see also Delavignette, "Union Française," 230.

51. Such sentiments had been articulated at the famous Brazzaville Conference of 1944, at which French officials set out a new colonial policy for Africa while reaffirming the indissolubility of the French empire.

52. See Borella, *L'évolution politique et juridique de l'Union Française depuis 1946* for a summary of the debates and the legislation. The most extensive treatment of the constitutional debates comes from Bruce Marshall, *French Colonial Myth.*

53. Cooper, "Senegalese General Strike of 1946" and "'Our Strike.'"

54. Assemblée Nationale Constituante, *Annales,* August 27, 1946, 3334.

55. Borella (*L'évolution politique et juridique de l'Union Française depuis 1946,* 442) sees as the constitution's biggest weakness that it was "put in place unilaterally by France." The referendum that approved the constitution in September (like the one that rejected the previous draft in June) was voted on by the old electorate, even though the Assemblée that drafted the constitution included colonial representatives elected under a limited franchise.

56. Metropolitan France was represented by 544 deputies, the overseas territories and departments and Algeria by 83, which translates to one deputy per 79,000 people in Europe and one per 520,000 overseas. Borella, *L'évolution politique et juridique de l'Union Française depuis 1946,* 188.

57. The constitution gave the legislature authority to define voting rights; Borella, *L'évolution politique et juridique de l'Union Française depuis 1946,* 182. On the ambiguous relationship throughout French history between citizenship and suffrage, see Pierre Rosanvallon, *Le sacre du citoyen: Histoire du suffrage universel en France* (Paris: Gillmard, 1992). The 1944 enfranchisement of female citizens applied to the female originaires of the Four Communes (even before citizenship was generalized in 1946), but officials tried to block its implementation on the grounds that women were less educated and more backward than men. Quick mobilization by political leaders and mass assemblies of men and women in the Four Communes forced the government to back down. See the official correspondence, reports on meetings, and protests from Senegalese leaders from June 1944 to April 1945 in dossier 20G 25, Archives du Sénégal.

58. Minister of Interior circular letter to Commissaires de la République and Préfets, February 20, 1946, Centre d'Archives Contemporaines, Fontainebleau, France, 770623/83; Decrees of December 23, 1945, February 20, 1946, and April 30, 1946, ending restrictions on personal liberty and the separate judicial regime. On the difficulties of organizing a unitary penal system and multiple civil systems, see "Situation de la Justice en Afrique: Rapport de M. le Président Sedille, Membre du Conseil Supérieure de la Magistrature," 1952, Centre d'Archives Contemporaines, Fontainebleau, France, 940167/7.

59. Senghor in Assemblée Nationale Constituante, *Annales,* April 11, 1946, 1714; Afrique Occidental Française(AOF), Directeur Général des Affaires Politiques, Administratives et Sociales (Berlan), note, July 46, Archives of Senegal, 17G 152.

60. Senghor did not consider it important that former subjects became citizens of the French Republic or the French Union, as long as they had the same rights as citizens. Assemblée Nationale Constituante, Annales, April 11, 1946, 1714.

61. Peureux, *Le Haut-Conseil de l'Union Française.* On its failure, see pages 165-69, 172.

62. The Algerian Revolution can too easily be read as the prototypical "national" revolution. Political forces were in fact divided: some wanted to make French citizenship meaningful; some looked to an internationalist, communist revolution in both France and Algeria; others favored Islamist mobilization throughout the Arab world. The Front de Libération Nationale (FLN) tried to channel these tendencies into an effort focused specifically on the nation, only partly succeeding. The FLN purged its leaders so often that it became a "revolution without a face." The French left wavered between backing the revolution and hoping to make a *colonialisme du progrès* actually work. Frantz Fanon's vision of a Manichean French colonialism and a purified anticolonialism is best read not as an embodiment of the Algerian Revolution but as a valiant effort to make it into something it was not. See Connelly, *Diplomatic Revolution,* and Stora, *La gangrène et l'oubli.*

63. For an example of the complexity in which jurists were engaged, see Rolland and Lampué, *Précis de droit des pays d'outre-mer.*

64. Gonidec, "La Communaute et les voies d'indépendance."

65. For a thoughtful analysis of the contradictions within the 1946 constitution, see Borella, *L'évolution politique et juridique de l'Union Française depuis 1946.*

66. For this argument and what follows in the next paragraphs, see Cooper, *Decolonization and African Society.*

67. Assemblée Nationale, *Débats,* November 22, 1952, 5502-05. Senghor used the phrase in print as well in *Marchés Coloniaux.*

68. "La vie syndicale en AOF," January 31, 1949, AP 3406/1, Archives d'Outre-Mer, France.

69. Similar arguments for equality were made in regard to education and equitable treatment of war veterans. Chafer, *End of Empire in French West Africa,* 97; Mann, *Native Sons.*

70. Commission de modernisation et d'équipement des Territoires d'Outre-Mer, "Rapport général de la sous-Commission de l'intégration métropole Outre-Mer," 1953, PA 19/3/38, France, Archives d'Outre-Mer; quote by Pierre-Henri Teitgen in Assemblée Nationale, *Débats,* March 20, 1956: 1072-73.

71. Shepard, *Invention of Decolonization.*

72. Discours d'ouverture du President Mamadou Dia au premier seminaire national d'études pour les responsables politiques, parlementaires, gouvernementaux, October 26, 1959, "sur la construction nationale," Archives du Sénégal, VP 93.

73. Senghor, "Rapport sur le méthode du Parti"; Dia, "L'Afrique Noire devant le nouveau destin de l'Union Francaise"; Mamadou Dia to the first national study seminar for political, parliamentary, and government leaders, opening and closing speeches on national construction, October 26, 1959, VP 93, Archives du Sénégal. This part of my analysis is being developed much more fully in ongoing work.

74. The minutes of the Council of Ministers of Mali are especially revealing of the effort to build a shared sovereignty and overlapping notions of nationality-Senegalese, Sudanese, Malian, and French-compatible with a citizenship that could be exercised anywhere in the French Community. See dossiers FM 37 and FM 38 (1959-60), housed in the Archives du Sénégal, and Foltz, *From French West Africa to the Mali Federation.*

75. After all attempts to forge a "Franco-African," "West African," or "Malian" nationality failed, in February 1961 Senegalese leaders passed a law defining a "Senegalese" nationality, emphasizing either birth from Senegalese parents or residence combined with *enracinement* in Senegalese society. It was a nation-state kind of nationality. See drafts and analyses from the minister of justice and others in early 1961 in Archives du Sénégal, VP 226.

76. Weil, *Qu'est-ce qu'un Français?*

77. I prefer the expression "politics of difference" to Partha Chatterjee's "rule of difference," for the politics were too contentious and conflicting to constitute a stable rule. For Chatterjee's formulation, see *Nation and Its Fragments,* 16.

References

Abdurakhimova, Nadira A. "The Colonial System of Power in Turkistan." *International Journal of Middle East Studies* 34, no. 2 (May 2002): 239–62.

Abdurakhimova, Nadira A., and G. Rustamova. *Kolonial'naia sistema vlasti v Turkestane vo vtoroi polovine XIX–pervoi chetverti XX v.v.* Tashkent, Uzbekistan: Universitet, 1999.

Abrahamian, Ervand. *Iran between Two Revolutions.* Princeton, NJ: Princeton University Press, 1982.

Abrams, Philip. "Notes on the Difficulty of Studying the State." 1977. *Journal of Historical Sociology* 1, no. 1 (March 1988): 58–89.

Adas, Michael. "The Great War and the Decline of the Civilizing Mission." In *Autonomous Histories: Particular Truths,* edited by Laurie Sears, 101–21. Madison: University of Wisconsin Press, 1993.

Adler, Cyrus, ed. and trans. "A Contemporary Memorial Relating to Damages to Spanish Interests in America Done by Jews of Holland." 1634. *American Jewish Historical Society* 17 (1909): 45–51.

Agamben, Giorgio. *Homo Sacer: Sovereign Power and Bare Life.* Stanford, CA: Stanford University Press, 1998.

Agishev, N. M., and V. D. Bushen, eds. *Materialy po obozreniiu gorskikh i narodnykh sudov kavkazkogo kraia.* Saint Petersburg: Senatskai tipografiia, 1912.

Ahlstrom, Sydney E. *A Religious History of the American People.* New Haven, CT: Yale University Press, 1972.

Alberro, Solange. *Inquisición y sociedad en México, 1571–1700.* Mexico City: Fondo de Cultura Económica, 1988.

Alder, Ken. *The Measure of Things: The Seven-Year Odyssey and Hidden Error That Transformed the World.* New York: Free Press, 2002.

References

Aldrich, Robert, and John Connell. *The Last Colonies.* Cambridge: Cambridge University Press, 1998.

Aleinikoff, Alexander T. *Semblances of Sovereignty: The Constitution, the State, and American Citizenship.* Cambridge, MA: Harvard University Press, 2002.

Allison, Robert J. *The Crescent Obscured: The United States and the Muslim World, 1776–1815.* New York: Oxford University Press, 1995.

Althusser, Louis, and Etienne Balibar. *Reading Capital.* New York: Pantheon Books, 1971.

American Board of Commissioners for Foreign Missions. *Instructions to the Missionaries About to Embark for the Sandwich Islands and to the Rev. Messrs. William Goodell, & Isaac Bird, Attached to the Palestine Mission: Delivered by the Corresponding Secretary of the American Board of Commissioners for Foreign Missions.* Boston: Crocker and Brewster, 1823.

Amin, Samir. *Eurocentrism.* Translated by Russell Moore. New York: Monthly Review Press, 1989.

Anagnost, Ann. "Constructing the Civilized Community." In *Culture and State in Chinese History: Conventions, Accommodations, and Critiques.* Edited by Theodore Huters, R. Bin Wong, and Pauline Yu, 346–68. Stanford, CA: Stanford University Press, 1997.

Anderson, Benedict. *Imagined Communities: Reflections on the Origins and Spread of Nationalism.* New York: Verso, 1991.

Anderson, Warwick. "States of Hygiene: Race 'Improvement' and Biomedical Citizenship in Australia and Colonial Philippines." In *Haunted by Empire.* Edited by Ann Laura Stoler, 94–115. Durham, NC: Duke University Press, 2006.

Andrew, John A., III. "Educating the Heathen: The Foreign Missionary School Controversy and American Ideal." *Journal of American Studies* 12 (1978): 331–42.

———. *From Revivals to Removal: Jeremiah Evarts, the Cherokee Nation, and the Search for the Soul of America.* Athens: University of Georgia Press, 1992.

Anónimo Portugues. *Descripcion del virreinato del Peru. 1610.* Edited by Boleslao Lewin. Rosario, Argentina: Imprenta de La Universidad Nacional del Litoral Santa Fe, 1958.

Ansart, Pierre. *Le ressentiment.* Brussels: Bruylant, 2002.

Appadurai, Arjun. "Globalization and the Rush to History." Unpublished manuscript, Sawyer Seminar, Columbia University, October 28, 1999.

Arce, Juan Ruiz de. "Advertencia," 1545, in *Biblioteca Peruana.* Ser. 1, vol 1., 407–37. Lima: Editores Técnicos Asociados, 1968.

Arendt, Hannah. *The Origins of Totalitarianism.* New York: Harcourt Brace Jovanovich, 1973.

Armitage, David. *The Ideological Origins of the British Empire.* New York: Cambridge University Press, 2000.

Arrighi, Giovanni. *The Long Twentieth Century: Money, Power, and the Origins of Our Times.* New York: Verso, 1994.

Arrighi, Giovanni, Po-keung Hui, Ho-Fung Hung, and Mark Selden. "Historical Capitalism, East and West." In *The Resurgence of East Asia: 500, 150 and 50 Year Perspectives.* Edited by Giovanni Arrighi, Takeshi Hamashita, and Mark Selden, 259–333. London: Routledge, 2003.

Assemblée Nationale. *Débats,* November 22, 1952; March 20, 1956.

Assemblée Nationale Constituante. *Annales,* April, 11, 1946; August 27, 1946.

Atabaki, Touraj, and Erik J. Zürcher, eds. *Men of Order: Authoritarian Modernization under Atatürk and Reza Shah.* London: I. B. Tauris, 2004.

Babich, Irina. *Evoliutsiia pravovoi kul'tury adygov (1860–1990-e gody).* Moscow: Institut etnologii i antropologii, RAN: 1999.

Bacevich, Andrew J. *American Empire: The Realities and Consequences of US Diplomacy.* Cambridge, MA: Harvard University Press, 2002.

Baker, Lee D. *From Savage to Negro: Anthropology and the Construction of Race, 1896–1954.* Berkeley: University of California Press, 1998.

Balibar, Etienne, and Immanuel Wallerstein. *Race, Nation, Class: Ambiguous Identities.* London: Verso, 1991.

Ballantyne, Tony, and Antoinette Burton, eds. *Bodies in Contact: Rethinking Colonial Encounters in World History.* Durham, NC: Duke University Press, 2005.

Barfield, Thomas J. *The Perilous Frontier: Nomadic Empires and China.* Cambridge: Blackwell, 1989.

Barkey, Karen, and Mark von Hagen, eds. *After Empire: Multiethnic Societies and Nation-Building: The Soviet Union and the Russian, Ottoman, and Habsburg Empires.* Boulder, CO: Westview Press, 1997.

Barlow, Tani E. "Colonialism's Career in Postwar China Studies." *Positions: East Asia Cultures Critique* 1, no. 1 (Spring 1993): 224–67.

Barth, Frederick. *Ethnic Groups and Boundaries: The Social Organization of Culture Difference.* London: George Allen and Unwin, 1969.

Bassin, Mark. *Imperial Visions: Nationalist Imagination and Geographical Expansion in the Russian Far East, 1840–1865.* Cambridge: Cambridge University Press, 1999.

———. "Inventing Siberia: Visions of the Russian East in the Early Nineteenth Century." *American Historical Review* 96 (June 1991): 763–94.

Bayly, C. A. "The British Military-Fiscal State and Indigenous Resistance: India 1750–1820." In *The East India Company: 1600–1858.* Vol. 5. Edited by Patrick Tuck. London: Routledge, 1998.

References

Beetham, David. *Bureaucracy.* Minneapolis: University of Minnesota Press, 1996.

Beissinger, Mark. "Demise of the Empire-State: Identity, Legitimacy, and the Deconstruction of Soviet Politics." In *The Rising Tide of Cultural Pluralism: The Nation-State at Bay?* Edited by Crawford Young, 93–115. Madison: University of Wisconsin Press, 1993.

———. "Soviet Empire as 'Family Resemblance.'" *Slavic Review* 65, no. 2 (Summer 2006): 294–303.

Belvaude, Catherine. *L'Algérie.* Paris: Editions Karthala, 1991.

Bencherif, Osman. *The Image of Algeria in Anglo-American Writings 1785–1962.* Lanham, MD: University Press of America, 1997.

Bender, Thomas, ed. *Rethinking American History in a Global Age.* Berkeley: University of California Press, 2002.

Ben-Ghiat, Ruth, and Mia Fuller, eds. *Italian Colonialism.* New York: Palgrave Macmillan, 2005.

Bennett, Herman L. *Africans in Colonial Mexico: Absolutism, Christianity, and Afro-Creole Consciousness.* Bloomington: University of Indiana Press, 2003.

Bennigsen, Alexandre, and Chantal Lemercier-Quelquejay. *Sultan Galiev, le père de la révolution tiers-mondiste.* Paris: Fayard, 1986.

Bénot, Yves. *La démence coloniale sous Napoléon.* Paris: Editions la Découverte, 1992.

———. *La révolution française et la fin des colonies.* Paris: Editions la Découverte, 1988.

Bénot, Yves, and Marcel Dorigny, eds. *Rétablissement de l'esclavage dans les colonies françaises.* Paris: Maisonnevue et Larose, 2003.

Bernard-Duquenet, Nicole. *Le Sénégal et le front populaire.* Paris: Harmattan, 1985.

Bhabha, Homi. *The Location of Culture.* London: Routledge, 1994.

Bird, Isaac. *Bible Work in Bible Lands, or Events in the History of Syria Mission.* Philadelphia: Presbyterian Board of Publication, 1872.

Bishop, Peter. *The Myth of Shangri-la: Tibet, Travel Writing, and the Creation of a Sacred Landscape.* Berkeley: University of California Press, 1989.

Blackburn, Robin. *The Overthrow of Colonial Slavery, 1776–1848.* London: Verso, 1988.

Blévis, Laure. "Sociologie d'un droit colonial: Citoyenneté et nationalité en Algérie (1865–1947): une exception républicaine?" Doctoral thesis, Institut d'Etudes Politiques, Aix-en-Provence, 2004.

Blitstein, Peter. "Cultural Diversity and the Interwar Conjuncture: Soviet Nationality Policy in its Comparative Context." *Slavic Review* 65, no. 2 (Summer 2006): 273–93.

———. "Nation and Empire in Soviet History, 1917–1953." *Ab Imperio* 1 (2006): 216–17.

Blum, William. *Killing Hope: US Military and CIA Interventions since World War II.* Monroe, ME: Common Courage Press, 1995.

Bobrovnikov, Vladimir. "Bandits and the State: Designing a 'Traditional' Culture of Violence in the Russian Caucasus." In *Russian Empire: Space, People, Power, 1700–1930.* Edited by Jane Burbank, Mark von Hagen, and Anatolyi Remnev. Bloomington: Indiana University Press, 2007.

———. *Musul'mane severnogo kavkaz: Obychai pravo nasilie.* Moscow: Vostochnaia literatura, 2002.

———. "Sud po adatu v dorevoliutsionnom Dagestane (1860–1917)." *Etnograficheskoe obozrenie* 2 (March–April 1999): 31–45.

Bod mi dmangs gsar skye thob pa [Rebirth of the Tibetan People]. Beijing: Beijing Nationalities Publishing House, 1960.

Borella, François. *L'évolution politique et juridique de l'Union Française depuis 1946.* Paris: Librarie Générale de Droit et de Jurisprudence, 1958.

Borneman, John. "State, Anthropological Aspects." In *International Encyclopedia of Behavioral and Social Sciences.* Edited by Neil J. Smelser and Paul B. Bates. Amsterdam: Elsevier, 2001.

Bose, Sugata, and Aysha Jalal. *Modern South Asia: History, Culture, Political Economy.* London: Routledge, 1997.

Bourdieu, Pierre. *Outline of a Theory of Practice.* Translated by Richard Nice. Cambridge: Cambridge University Press, 1977.

———. *Practical Reason.* Stanford, CA: Stanford University Press, 1998.

Bourguet, Marie-Noëlle. *Déchiffrer la France: la statistique départementale à l'époque napoléonienne.* Paris: Editions des archives contemporaines, 1988.

Bowen, H. V. *Revenue and Reform: The Indian Problem in British Politics, 1757–1773.* Cambridge: Cambridge University Press, 1991.

Brandenberger, David. *National Bolshevism: Stalinist Mass Culture and the Formation of Modern Russian National Identity, 1931–1956.* Cambridge, MA: Harvard University Press, 2002.

Brennan, Timothy. "From Development to Globalization: Postcolonial Studies and Globalization Theory." In *The Cambridge Companion to Postcolonial Literary Studies.* Edited by Neil Lazarus, 120–38. Cambridge: Cambridge University Press, 2004.

Brenner, Robert. *The Boom and the Bubble: The US in the World Economy.* New York: Verso, 2002.

———. "The Origins of Capitalist Development: A Critique of Neo-Smithian Marxism." *New Left Review* 1, no. 104 (July–August 1977): 25–92.

Breyfogle, Nicholas, B. *Heretics and Colonizers: Forging Russia's Empire in the South Caucasus.* Ithaca, NY: Cornell University Press, 2005.

Briggs, Laura. *Reproducing Empire: Race, Sex, Science, and US Imperialism in Puerto Rico.* Berkeley: University of California Press, 2002.

References

Broers, Michael. "Cultural Imperialism in a European Context? Political Culture and Cultural Politics in Napoleonic Italy." *Past and Present* 170, no. 1 (2001): 152–80.

———. "Europe under Napoleon." Paper presented at the Empires in Modern Times conference, Institut des Hautes Etudes Internationales, Geneva, March 2003.

———. "Napoleon, Charlemagne, and Lotharingia: Acculturation and the Boundaries of Napoleonic Europe." *Historical Journal* 44, 1 (2001): 135–54.

Browder, Robert Paul, and Alexander F. Kerensky, eds. *The Russian Provisional Government 1917.* Vol 1. Stanford, CA: Stanford University Press, 1961.

Brower, Daniel. *Turkestan and the Fate of the Russian Empire.* London: RoutledgeCurzon, 2003.

Brower, Daniel, and Edward J. Lazzerini, eds. *Russia's Orient: Imperial Borderlands and Peoples, 1700–1917.* Bloomington: Indiana University Press, 1997.

Bukharin, Nikolai I. *Imperialism and World Economy. 1918.* New York: International Publishers, 1929.

Bulag, Uradyn Erden. *The Mongols at China's Edge: History and the Politics of National Unity.* Lanham, MD: Rowman & Littlefield Publishers, 2002.

Burbank, Jane. "Discipline and Punish in the Moscow Bar Association." *Russian Review* 54, no. 1 (January 1995): 44–64.

———. *Intelligentsia and Revolution: Russian Views of Bolshevism, 1917–1922.* New York: Oxford University Press, 1986.

———. "Legal Culture, Citizenship, and Peasant Jurisprudence: Perspectives from the Early Twentieth Century." In *Reforming Justice in Russia, 1864–1994: Power, Culture, and the Limits of Legal Order.* Edited by Peter Solomon Jr., 82–106. Armonk, NY: M. E. Sharp, 1997.

———. *Russian Peasants Go to Court: Legal Culture in the Countryside, 1905–1917.* Bloomington: Indiana University Press, 2004.

Burbank, Jane, and David L. Ransel, eds. *Imperial Russia: New Histories for the Empire.* Bloomington: Indiana University Press, 1998.

Burbank, Jane, and Mark von Hagen. "Coming into the Territory: Uncertainty and Empire." In *Russian Empire: Space, People, Power, 1700–1930.* Edited by Jane Burbank, Mark von Hagen, and Anatolyi Remnev. Bloomington: Indiana University Press, 2007.

Burbank, Jane, Mark von Hagen, and Anatolyi Remnev, eds. *Russian Empire: Space, People, Power, 1700–1930.* Bloomington: Indiana University Press, 2007.

Burchell, Graham, Colin Gordon, and Peter Miller, eds. *The Foucault Effect: Studies in Govermentality.* Chicago: University of Chicago Press, 1991.

Burke, Edmund. "Fox's Indian Bill Speech." In *Writings and Speeches of Edmund Burke.* Vol 5. Edited by Peter J. Marshall, 385, Oxford: Clarendon Press, 1981.

———. "Policy of Making Conquests for the Mahometans." In *The Writings and Speeches of Edmund Burke*. Vol. 5. Edited by Peter J. Marshall, 41–123. Oxford: Clarendon Press, 1981.

———. "Speech on Opening of Impeachment, 1788." In *The Writings and Speeches of Edmund Burke*. Vol. 6. Edited by Peter Marshall, 316–17. Oxford: Clarendon Press, 1981.

Burnett, Christina Duffy, and Burke Marshall, eds. *Foreign in a Domestic Sense: Puerto Rico, American Expansion and the Constitution*. Durham, NC: Duke University Press, 2001.

Burton, Antoinette, ed. *After the Imperial Turn: Thinking with and through the Nation*. Durham, NC: Duke University Press, 2003.

Bury, J. P. T. *France 1814–1940*. London: Routledge, 1989.

al-Bustani, Butrus. *Qissat As'ad al-Shidyaq*. 1860. Beirut: Dar al-Hamra, 1992.

Cadena, Marisol de la. *Indigenous Mestizos: The Politics of Race and Culture in Cuzco, 1919–1991*. Durham, NC: Duke University Press, 2000.

———. "Silent Racism and Intellectual Superiority in Peru." *Bulletin of Latin American Research* 17, no. 2 (May 1998): 143–64.

Cagaptay, Soner. *Islam, Secularism, and Nationalism in Modern Turkey: Who Is a Turk?* London: Routledge, 2006.

Cahill, David. "Colour by Numbers: Racial and Ethnic Categories in the Viceroyalty of Peru: 1552–1824." *Journal of Latin American Studies* 26, no. 2 (May 1994): 325–46.

Calhoun, Craig, Frederick Cooper, and Kevin W. Moore, eds. *Lessons of Empire: Imperial Histories and American Power.* New York: New Press, 2006.

Caplan, Lionel. *Warrior Gentleman: "Gurkhas" in the Western Imagination*. Providence, RI: Berghahn Books, 1995.

Cardoso, Fernando Henrique, and Enzo Faletto. *Dependency and Development in Latin America*. Berkeley: University of California Press, 1979.

Carl, George Edmund. "First Among Equals: Great Britain and Venezuela, 1810–1910." *American Historical Review* 86, no. 2 (April 1981): 483–84.

Castañeda Delgado, Paulino, and Pilar Hernández Aparicio. *La inquisición de Lima*. Vol. 1. Madrid: Demos, 1989.

Cavanaugh, Cassandra. "Backwardness and Biology: Medicine and Power in Russian and Soviet Central Asia, 1868–1934." PhD dissertation, Columbia University, 2001.

Cellorigo, Martin Gonzalez de. *Memorial de la política necesaria y util restauración a la República de España y estados de ella, y del desempeño universal de estos reinos*. 1600. Madrid: Instituto de Cooperación Iberoamericana, 1991.

Césaire, Aimé. *Discours sur le colonialisme*. Paris: Presence Africaine, 1955.

Chafer, Tony. *The End of Empire in French West Africa*. Oxford: Berg, 2002.

References

Chakrabarty, Dipesh. *Provincializing Europe: Postcolonial Thought and Historical Difference.* Princeton, NJ: Princeton University Press, 2000.

Chamberlain, Muriel E. *Decolonization: The Fall of the European Empires.* 2nd ed. Oxford: Blackwell, 1999.

———. *The Longman Companion to European Decolonization in the Twentieth Century.* London: Longman, 1998.

Chang, Michael. "A Court on Horseback: Constructing Manchu Ethno-Dynastic Rule in China, 1751–84." PhD dissertation, University of California–San Diego, 2001.

Chatterjee, Partha. "Empire and Nation Revisited: 50 Years after Bandung." *Inter-Asia Cultural Studies* 6, no. 4 (December 2005): 487–96.

———. *The Nation and Its Fragments: Colonial and Postcolonial Histories.* Princeton, NJ: Princeton University Press, 1993.

———. *Nationalist Thought and the Colonial World.* 1986. Minneapolis: University of Minnesota Press, 1993.

Chatterjee, Pratap. *Iraq, Inc.: A Profitable Occupation.* New York: Seven Stories Press, 2004.

Chaturvedi, Vinayak, ed. *Mapping Subaltern Studies and the Postcolonial.* London: Verso, 2000.

Chaudhuri, K. N. *The Trading World of Asia and the English East India Company, 1600–1760.* Cambridge: Cambridge University Press, 1978.

Ching, Leo T. S. *Becoming "Japanese": Colonial Taiwan and the Politics of Identity Formation.* Berkeley: University of California Press, 2001.

Chun, Allen. "Introduction: (Post)Colonialism and Its Discontents, or the Future of Practice." *Cultural Studies* 14, nos. 3–4 (July 2000): 379–84.

Coates, Timothy J. *Convicts and Orphans: Forced and State-Sponsored Colonizers in the Portuguese Empire, 1550–1775.* Stanford, CA: Stanford University Press, 2001.

Coatsworth, John. *Central America and the United States: The Clients and the Colossus.* New York: Twayne, 1994.

———. "United States Interventions. What For?" *ReVista, Harvard Review of Latin America* (Spring 2005): 6–9.

Cohen, Paul. *Discovering History in China: American Historical Writing on the Recent Chinese Past.* New York: Columbia University Press, 1984.

Cohn, Bernard S. *Colonialism and Its Forms of Knowledge.* Princeton, NJ: Princeton University Press, 1996.

———. "Representing Authority in Victorian India." In *The Invention of Tradition.* Edited by Eric Hobsbawm and Terence Ranger. Cambridge: Cambridge University Press, 1983.

Cole, Juan R. "Empires of Liberty? Democracy and Conquest in French Egypt, British Egypt, and American Iraq." In *Lessons of Empire.* Edited by Craig Calhoun, Frederick Cooper, and Kevin Moore, 94–115. New York: New Press, 2006.

Colley, Linda. *Britons: Forging the Nation, 1707–1837.* New Haven, CT: Yale University Press, 1992.

Comaroff, Jean, and John Comaroff. *Ethnography and the Historical Imagination.* Boulder, CO: Westview Press, 1992.

———. *Of Revolution and Revelation.* Vol. 1, *Christianity, Colonialism, and Consciousness.* Chicago: University of Chicago Press, 1991

———. *Of Revolution and Revelation.* Vol. 2, *The Dialectics of Modernity on a South African Frontier.* Chicago: University of Chicago Press, 1997.

Comité national chargé de la publication des travaux préparatoires des institutions de la Ve République. *Documents pour servir à l'élaboration de la constitution du 4 octobre 1958.* Vol. 1. Paris: Documentation Française, 1987.

Conboy, Kenneth, and James Morrison. *The CIA's Secret War in Tibet.* Lawrence: University of Kansas Press, 2002.

Conklin, Alice. *A Mission to Civilize: The Republican Idea of Empire in France and West Africa, 1895–1930.* Stanford, CA: Stanford University Press, 1998.

Connelly, Matthew. *A Diplomatic Revolution: Algeria's Fight for Independence and the Origins of the Post–Cold War Era.* New York: Oxford University Press, 2002.

Constantine, Stephen. *The Making of British Colonial Development Policy, 1914–1940.* London: Frank Cass, 1984.

Cooper, Frederick. *Colonialism in Question: Theory, Knowledge, History.* Berkeley: University of California Press, 2005.

———. *Decolonization and African Society: The Labor Question in French and British Africa.* Cambridge: Cambridge University Press, 1996.

———. "Empire Multiplied: A Review Essay." *Comparative Studies in Society and History* 46, no. 2 (April 2004): 247–72.

———. "Modernizing Colonialism and the Limits of Empire." In *Lessons of Empire: Imperial Histories and American Power.* Edited by Craig Calhoun, Frederick Cooper, and Kevin W. Moore, 73–93. New York: New Press, 2006.

———. "'Our Strike': Equality, Anticolonial Politics, and the French West African Railway Strike of 1947–48." *Journal of African History* 37, no. 1 (1996): 81–118.

———. "The Senegalese General Strike of 1946 and the Labor Question in Post-War French Africa." *Canadian Journal of African Studies* 24, no. 2 (1990): 165–215.

References

Cooper, Frederick, and Ann Laura Stoler. "Between Metropole and Colony: Rethinking a Research Agenda." In *Tensions of Empire: Colonial Cultures in a Bourgeois World.* Edited by Frederick Cooper and Ann Laura Stoler, 1–58. Berkeley: University of California Press, 1997.

———, ed. *Tensions of Empire: Colonial Cultures in a Bourgeois World.* Berkeley: University of California Press, 1997.

Coronil, Fernando. "Beyond Occidentalism: Toward Nonimperial Geohistorical Categories." *Cultural Anthropology* 11, no. 1 (February 1996): 51–87.

———. "Latin American Postcolonial Studies and Global Decolonisation." In *Postcolonial Literary Studies.* Edited by Neil Lazarus, 221–41. London: Cambridge University Press, 2004.

———. *The Magical State: Nature, Money and Modernity in Venezuela.* Chicago: University of Chicago Press, 1997.

———. "Nación y estado durante el golpe contra Hugo Chávez." *Anuario de Estudios Americanos* 62, no. 1 (2005): 87–112.

———. "Towards a Critique of Globalcentrism: Speculations on Capitalism's Nature." *Public Culture* 12, 2 (Spring 2000): 351–374.

———. "Transculturation and the Politics of Theory: Countering the Center, Cuban Counterpoint." In *Cuban Counterpoint: Tobacco and Sugar,* 1947, by Fernando Ortiz, ix–lvi. Durham, NC: Duke University Press, 1995.

Corrigan, Philip, and Derek Sayers. *The Great Arch: English State Formation as Cultural Revolution.* Oxford: Basil Blackwell, 1985.

Cottias, Myriam. "Le silence de la nation: Les 'vielles colonies' comme lieu de definition des dogmes républicains (1848–1905)." *Outre-Mers* 90, nos. 338–39 (2003): 21–45.

Cronin, Stephanie, ed. *The Making of Modern Iran: State and Society under Riza Shah, 1921–1941.* London: Routledge, 2003.

Crossley, Pamela Kyle. *A Translucent Mirror: History and Identity in Qing Imperial Ideology.* Berkeley: University of California Press, 1999.

Cumings, Bruce. "Global Realm with No Limit, Global Realm with No Name." *Radical History Review* 57 (Fall 1993): 46–59.

Curzon, G. N. *Frontiers.* Oxford: Romanes lectures, 1907.

Daalder, Hans. "Imperialism." In *International Encyclopedia of the Social Sciences.* Vol. 7. Edited by David L. Sills, 101–09. New York: Macmillan and Free Press, 1968.

Das, Veena, and Deborah Poole. "State and Its Margins: Comparative Ethnographies." In *Anthropology in the Margins of the State.* Edited by Veena Das and Deborah Poole, 3–33. Santa Fe, NM: SAR Press, 2004.

Dawisha, Karen, and Bruce Parrott, eds. *The End of Empire? The Transformation of the USSR in Comparative Perspective.* Armonk, NY: M. E. Sharpe, 1997.

DeConde, Alexander. *A History of American Foreign Policy.* New York: Scribner, 1971.

Delavignette, Robert. "Union Française, à l'échelle du monde, à la mesure de l'homme." *Esprit* 112 (July 1945): 214–36.

Deringil, Selim. "'There Is No Compulsion in Religion': On Conversion and Apostasy in the Late Ottoman Empire: 1839–1856." *Comparative Studies in Society and History* 42, no. 3 (July 2000): 547–75.

———. "'They Live in a State of Nomadism and Savagery': The Late Ottoman Empire and the Post-Colonial Debate." *Comparative Studies in Society and History* 45, no. 2 (April 2003): 311–42.

———. *The Well Protected Domains: Ideology and the Legitimation of Power in the Ottoman Empire, 1876–1909.* New York: St. Martin's Press, 1998.

DesChene, Mary. "Relics of Empire: A Cultural History of the Gurkhas, 1815–1987." PhD dissertation, Stanford University, 1991.

Dia, Mamadou. "L'Afrique Noire devant le nouveau destin de l'Union Française." *La Condition Humaine,* August 29, 1955.

Diamond, Norma. "The Miao and Poison: Interactions on China's Southwest Frontier." *Ethnology* 27, no. 1 (1988): 1–25.

Dib, Pierre. *Histoire de l'Eglise Maronite.* Beirut: La Sagesse, 1962.

Dickens, Ruth H. L. "Defining French Citizenship Policy in West Africa, 1895–1956." PhD dissertation, Emory University, 2001.

Diouf, Mamadou. "The French Colonial Policy of Assimilation and the Civility of the Originaires of the Four Communes (Senegal): A Nineteenth Century Globalization Project." *Development and Change* 29, no. 4 (October 1998): 671–96.

Dirks, Nicholas. *Castes of Mind: Colonialism and the Making of Modern India.* Princeton, NJ: Princeton University Press, 2001.

———, ed. *Colonialism and Culture.* Ann Arbor: University of Michigan Press, 1992.

———. "History as a Sign of the Modern." *Public Culture* 2, no. 2 (1990): 25–32.

———. *The Hollow Crown: Ethnohistory of an Indian Kingdom.* Cambridge: Cambridge University Press, 1987.

Dobb, Maurice. *Studies in the Development of Capitalism.* New York: International Publishers, 1946.

Dodin, Thierry, and Heinz Rather, eds. *Imagining Tibet: Perceptions, Projections, and Fantasies.* Boston: Wisdom Press, 2001.

Dodwell, H. H., ed. *The Cambridge History of India.* Vol. 5: *British India.* Delhi: S. Chand & Co., 1968.

Donnan, Hastings, and Thomas M. Wilson. *Borders: Frontiers of Identity, Nation and State.* Oxford: Berg, 1999.

Du Bois, W. E. B. *The Souls of Black Folk.* New York: Washington Square Press, 1970.

Duara, Prasenjit, ed. *Decolonization: Perspectives from Now and Then.* New York: Routledge, 2004.

Duara, Prasenjit. "The Discourse of Civilization and Pan-Asianism." *Journal of World History* 12, no. 1 (Spring 2001): 99–130.

———. "Nationalism, Imperialism, Federalism and the Example of Manchukuo: A Response to Anthony Pagden." *Common Knowledge* 12, no. 1(Winter 2006): 47–65.

———. *Rescuing History from the Nation: Questioning Narratives of Modern China.* Chicago: University of Chicago Press, 1995.

———. *Sovereignty and Authenticity: Manchukuo and the East Asian Modern.* Lanham, MD: Rowman and Littlefield, 2003.

Dubois, Laurent. *Avengers of the New World: The Story of the Haitian Revolution.* Cambridge: Harvard University Press, 2004.

———. *A Colony of Citizens: Revolution and Slave Emancipation in the French Caribbean, 1787–1804.* Chapel Hill: University of North Carolina Press, 2004.

———. "La République Métissée: Citizenship, Colonialism, and the Borders of French History." *Cultural Studies* 14, no. 1 (January 2000): 14–34.

Dudden, Alexis. *Japan's Colonization of Korea: Discourse and Power.* Honolulu: University of Hawai'i Press, 2005.

Dunbar-Ortiz, Roxanne. "The Grid of History: Cowboys and Indians." In *Pox Americana: Exposing the American Empire.* Edited by John Bellamy Foster and Robert W. McChesney, 31–40. New York: Monthly Review Press, 2004.

Dupret, Baudouin, Maurits Berger, and Laila al-Zwaini, eds. *Legal Pluralism in the Arab World.* The Hague: Kluwer Law International, 1999.

Durkheim, Emile. *The Elementary Forms of the Religious Life.* Translated by John Ward Swain. New York: Free Press, 1965.

Dussel, Enrique D. "Beyond Eurocentrism: The World System and the Limits of Modernity." In *The Cultures of Globalization.* Edited by Fredric Jameson and Masao Miyoshi, 3–31. Durham, NC: Duke University Press, 1998.

———. *Essays: The Underside of Modernity: Apel, Ricouer, Rorty, and Taylor, and the Philosophy of Liberation.* Translated and edited by Eduardo Mendieta. Atlantic Highlands, NJ: Humanities Press, 1996.

Dwyer, Philip G., ed. *Napoleon and Europe.* Harlow, UK: Longman, 2001.

Edgar, Adrienne. "Bolshevism, Patriarchy, and the Nation: The Soviet 'Emancipation' of Muslim Women in Pan-Islamic Perspective." *Slavic Review* 65, no. 2 (Summer 2006): 252–72.

———. "Emancipation of the Unveiled: Turkmen Women under Soviet Rule, 1924–29." *Russian Review* 62, no. 1 (January 2003): 132–49.

Edney, Matthew H. *Mapping an Empire: The Geographical Construction of British India, 1765–1843.* Chicago: University of Chicago Press, 1997.

Eichengreen, Barry, and Jeffrey A. Frankel. "Economic Regionalism: Evidence from Two Twentieth-Century Episodes." *North American Journal of Economics and Finance* 6, no. 2 (1995): 89–106.

Eisenstadt, Shmuel. "Empire." In *International Encyclopedia of the Social Sciences.* Vol. 5. Edited by David Sills, 41–48, New York: Macmillan Company and Free Press, 1968.

Elliott, J. H. "Spain and America before 1700." In *Colonial Spanish America.* Edited by Leslie Bethell, 59–111. Cambridge: Cambridge University Press, 1987.

———. "The Spanish Conquest." In *Colonial Spanish America.* Edited by Leslie Bethell, 1–59. Cambridge: Cambridge University Press, 1987.

Elliott, Mark C. *The Manchu Way: The Eight Banners and Ethnic Identity in Late Imperial China.* Stanford, CA: Stanford University Press, 2001.

Ellis, Geoffrey, "The Nature of Napoleonic Imperialism," in *Napoleon and Europe,* ed. Philip G. Dwyer, chapter 5, Harlow, UK: Longman, 2001.

Elsbree, Oliver Wendell. *The Rise of the Missionary Spirit in America, 1700–1815.* Williamsport, PA: Williamsport Printing and Binding Co., 1928.

Emerson, Rupert. *From Empire to Nation: The Rise to Self-Assertion of Asian and African Peoples.* Boston: Beacon Press, 1962.

Eroshkin, N. P. *Istoriia gosudarstvennykh uchrezhdenii dorevoliutsionnoi Rossii.* 4th rev. ed. Moscow: Tretii rim, 1997.

Escamilla-Colin, Michele. *Crimes et chatiments dans l'Espagne inquisitoriale.* Vol. 1. Paris: Berg International, 1992.

Escobar, Arturo. *Encountering Development: The Making and Unmaking of the Third World.* Princeton, NJ: Princeton University Press, 1995.

Evans, Peter. *Dependent Development: The Alliance of Multinational, State, and Local Capital in Brazil.* Princeton, NJ: Princeton University Press, 1979.

Fanon, Frantz. *Black Skins, White Masks.* New York: Grove, 1991.

———. *The Wretched of the Earth.* New York: Grove Press, 1968.

Feros, Antonio. *Kingship and Favoritism in the Spain of Philip III: 1598–1621.* Cambridge: Cambridge University Press, 2000.

Fick, Carolyn. "The French Revolution in Saint Domingue: A Triumph or a Failure." In *A Turbulent Time: The French Revolution and the Greater Caribbean.* Edited by David Barry Gaspar and David Patrick Geggus, 51–77. Bloomington: Indiana University Press, 1997.

———. *The Making of Haiti: The Saint Domingue Revolution from Below.* Knoxville: University of Tennessee Press, 1990.

Field, James A., Jr. *America and the Mediterranean World.* Princeton, NJ: Princeton University Press, 1969.

REFERENCES

Foltz, William. *From French West Africa to the Mali Federation.* New Haven, CT: Yale University Press, 1965.

Fontana, Biancamaria. "The Napoleonic Empire and the Europe of Nations." In *The Idea of Europe: From Antiquity to the European Union.* Edited by Anthony Pagden, 116–28, Cambridge: Cambridge University Press, 2002.

Foote, Samuel. *Nabob, A Comedy, in Three Acts. As It Is Performed at the Theatre-Royal in the Haymarket.* London: Printed by T. Sherlock for T. Cadell, 1778.

Foreign Relations of the United States. *Diplomatic Papers, 1943: China.* Washington, DC: United States Government Printing Office, 1957.

Forrest, Alan. *Conscripts and Deserters: The Army and French Society during the Revolution and Empire.* New York: Oxford University Press, 1989.

———. *Napoleon's Men: The Soldiers of the Revolution and Empire.* London: Hambledon and London, 2002.

Forrest, George. *The Life of Lord Clive.* Vol. 2. London: Cassell and Co., 1918.

Forster, Robert. "The French Revolution, People of Color, and Slavery." In *The Global Ramifications of the French Revolution.* Edited by Joseph Klaits and Michael Haltzel, 89–104. Cambridge: Cambridge University Press, 1994.

Foster, John Bellamy. "The New Age of Imperialism." In *Pox Americana: Exposing the American Empire.* Edited by John Bellamy Foster and Robert W. McChesney, 161–74. New York: Monthly Review Press, 2004.

Foster, John Bellamy, and Robert W. McChesney, eds. *Pox Americana: Exposing the American Empire.* New York: Monthly Review Press, 2004.

Frank, Andre Gunder. "The Development of Underdevelopment." *Monthly Review* 18, no. 4 (1966): 17–31.

Frederickson, George M. *Racism: A Short History.* Princeton, NJ: Princeton University Press, 2002.

Frierson, Cathy A. "Rural Justice in Public Opinion: The Volost' Court Debate." *Slavonic and East European Review* 64, no. 4 (October 1986): 526–45.

Fuentes, Carlos. "Prologue." In *Ariel,* by José Enrique Rodó. Austin: University of Texas Press, 1988.

Gaddis, John Lewis, and Paul Kennedy. "Kill the Empire! (Or Not)." *New York Times Book Review,* July 25, 2004.

Gallagher, John, and Ronald Robinson. "The Imperialism of Free Trade." *The Economic History Review,* 2nd ser., 6, no. 1 (1953): 1–15.

Gaspar, David Barry, and David Patrick Geggus, eds. *A Turbulent Time: The French Revolution and the Greater Caribbean.* Bloomington: Indiana University Press, 1997.

Gasster, Michael. *Chinese Intellectuals and the Revolution of 1911: The Birth of Modern Chinese Radicalism.* Seattle: University of Washington Press, 1969.

Geggus, David. "Racial Equality, Slavery, and Colonial Secession during the Constituent Assembly." *American Historical Review* 95, no. 5 (December 1989): 1290–1308.

———. "Slavery, War, and Revolution in the Greater Caribbean, 1789–1815." *In A Turbulent Time: The French Revolution and the Greater Caribbean.* Edited by David Barry Gaspar and David Patric Geggus, 1–50. Bloomington: Indiana University Press, 1997.

Genis, V. L. *"S Bukharoi nado konchat'...": k istorii butaforskikh revoliutsii.* Moscow: MNPI, 2001.

Genovese, Eugene D. *Roll Jordan Roll: The World the Slaves Made.* New York: Pantheon, 1974.

Geraci, Robert P. "Russian Orientalism at an Impasse: Tsarist Education Policy and the 1910 Conference on Islam." In *Russia's Orient: Imperial Borderlands and Peoples, 1700–1917.* Edited by Daniel R. Brower and Edward J. Lazzerini, 138–61. Bloomington: Indiana University Press, 1997.

———. *Window on the East: National and Imperial Identities in Late Tsarist Russia.* Ithaca, NY: Cornell University Press, 2001.

Gersimov, Ilya, Serguei Glebov, Alexander Kaplunovski, Marina Mogilner, and Alexander Semyonov. "In Search of a New Imperial History." *Ab Imperio* 1 (2005): 33–56.

Gibbon, Edward. *The Decline and Fall of the Roman Empire. 1776–1788.* Edited by J. B. Bury. New York: Heritage Press, 1946.

Gibson, Charles. "Indian Societies under Spanish Rule." In *Colonial Spanish America.* Edited by Leslie Bethell, 361–99. Cambridge: Cambridge University Press, 1987.

Gill, Lesley. *The School of the Americas: Military Training and Political Violence in the Americas.* Durham, NC: Duke University Press, 2004.

Gilroy, Paul. *Against Race: Imagining Political Culture beyond the Color Line.* Cambridge, MA: Harvard University Press, 2002.

———. *The Black Atlantic: Modernity and Double Consciousness.* Cambridge, MA: Harvard University Press, 1993.

Gitlin, Semën. *Natsional'nye otnosheniia v Uzbekistane: illiuzii i real'nost'.* Tel Aviv: privately printed, 1998.

Gladney, Dru C. *Dislocating China: Reflections on Muslims, Minorities, and other Subaltern Subjects.* Durham, NC: Duke University Press, 2004.

Gleig, G. R. *Memoirs of the Life of the Right Honorable Warren Hastings, First Governor General of Bengal.* Vol. 1. London: Richard Bentley, 1841.

Go, Julian, and Anne Foster, eds. *The American Colonial State in the Philippines: Global Perspectives.* Durham, NC: Duke University Press, 2003.

Goldstein, Melvyn C. *A History of Modern Tibet, 1913–1951: The Demise of the Lamaist State.* Berkeley: University of California Press, 1991.

Goldstein, Melvyn C., Dawei Sherap, and William Siebenschuh, eds. *A Tibetan Revolutionary: The Political Life and Times of Bapa Phuntso Wangye.* Berkeley: University of California Press, 2004.

Golinger, Eva. *El Código Chávez: Descifrando la intervención de los Estados Unidos en Venezuela.* Caracas: Editorial Melvin, 2005.

Gonidec, P.-F. "La Communaute et les voies d'indépendance." *Recueil Penant* 70 (1960): 1–14.

Gorilovskaya, Nonna. "Imperial Denial." Interview with Niall Ferguson. *Mother Jones,* May–June 2004. http://motherjones.com/news/qa/2004/05/05_400.html.

Goswami, Manu. *Producing India: From Colonial Economy to National Space.* Chicago: University of Chicago Press, 2004.

Grab, Alexander. "Army, State, and Society: Conscription and Desertion in Napoleonic Italy (1801–1814)." *Journal of Modern History* 67, no. 1 (March 1995): 25–54.

Graham, Richard. *Britain and the Onset of Modernization in Brazil, 1850–1914.* London: Cambridge University Press, 1968.

Gravil, Roger. *The Anglo-Argentine Connection, 1900–1939.* Boulder, CO: Westview Press, 1985.

Gregorian, Vartan. *The Emergence of Modern Afghanistan: Politics of Reform and Modernization, 1880–1946.* Stanford, CA: Stanford University Press, 1969.

Gregory, Brad S. *Salvation at Stake: Christian Martyrdom in Early Modern Europe.* Cambridge: Harvard University Press, 1999.

Grewal, Inderpal. *Transnational America: Feminisms, Diasporas, Neoliberalisms.* Durham, NC: Duke University Press, 2005.

Grunfeld, A. Tom. *The Making of Modern Tibet.* Armonk, NY: M. E. Sharpe, 1996.

Guaman Poma de Ayala, Felipe. *El primer nueva corónica y buen gobierno.* Edited by John V. Murra and Rolena Adorna. Mexico City: Siglo Veintiuno, 1980.

Guha, Ranajit. *Dominance without Hegemony: History and Power in Colonial India.* Cambridge, MA: Harvard University Press, 1997.

———. *History at the Limit of World-History.* New York: Columbia University Press, 2003.

Gupta, Akhil, and James Ferguson. "Beyond 'Culture': Space, Identity, and the Politics of Difference." *Cultural Anthropology* 7, no. 1 (February 1992): 6–23.

Haass, Richard N. "Imperial America." Paper presented at the Atlanta Conference, November 11, 2000. *http://www.brook.edu/views/articles/haass/19990909 primacy_FA.htm.*

Haboush, JaHyun Kim. "Contesting Chinese Time, Nationalizing Temporal Space: Temporal Inscription in Late Chosôn Korea." In *Time, Temporality, and Imperial Transition: East Asia from Ming to Qing*. Edited by Lynn A. Struve, 115–41. Honolulu: Association for Asian Studies and University of Hawai`i Press, 2005.

Hacking, Ian. *Historical Ontology*. Cambridge, MA: Harvard University Press, 2002.

Hall, Catherine. *Civilising Subjects: Colony and Metropole in the English Imagination*. Chicago: University of Chicago Press, 2003.

———. *Cultures of Empire: Colonizers in Britain and the Empire in the Nineteenth and Twentieth Centuries: A Reader*. Manchester, UK: Manchester University Press, 2000.

Hall, Stuart. "Gramsci's Relevance for the Study of Race and Ethnicity." *Journal of Communication Inquiry* 10, no. 2 (April 1983): 5–27.

Hampe-Martinez, Teodoro. *Santo Oficio e historia colonial: Aproximaciones al Tribunal de la Inquisición de Lima (1570–1820)*. Lima: Ediciones del Congreso del Peru, 2000.

Hamza, Alavi. "Imperialism Old and New." *Socialist Register* 1 (1964): 105–26.

Han, Suk-jung. "Puppet Sovereignty: The State Effect of Manchukuo, from 1932 to 1936." PhD dissertation, University of Chicago, 1995.

Hancok, William K. *The Wealth of Colonies*. London: Cambridge University Press, 1950.

Hansen, Peter. "Why Is There No Subaltern Studies for Tibet?" *Tibet Journal* 28, no. 4 (Winter 2003): 7–22.

Hansen, Thomas Blom, and Finn Stepputat. "Introduction: States of Imagination." In *States of Imagination: Ethnographic Explorations of the Postcolonial State*. Edited by Thomas Blom Hansen and Finn Stepputat, 1–38. Durham, NC: Duke University Press, 2001.

———, eds. *States of Imagination: Ethnographic Explorations of the Postcolonial State*. Durham, NC: Duke University Press, 2001.

Hardt, Michael, and Antonio Negri. *Empire*. Cambridge, MA: Harvard University Press, 2000.

Harlow, Vincent T. *The Founding of the Second British Empire, 1763–1793*. 2 vols. London: Longmans, 1952.

Harrell, Stevan, ed. *Cultural Encounters on China's Ethnic Frontiers*. Seattle: University of Washington Press, 1995.

Harris, Sheldon H. *Factories of Death: Japanese Biological Warfare 1932–45 and the American Cover-Up*. New York: Routledge, 1994.

Havinden, Michael, and David Meredith. *Colonialism and Development: Britain and Its Tropical Colonies, 1850–1960*. London: Routledge, 1993.

References

Haya de la Torre, Victor. *El imperialismo y el Apra.* Santiago de Chile: Ediciones Ercilla, 1936.

Helgerson, Richard. *Forms of Nationhood: The Elizabethan Writing of England.* Chicago: University of Chicago Press, 1992.

Hernon, Ian. "The Falklands, 1833." In *Massacre and Retribution: Forgotten Wars of the Nineteenth Century.* Edited by Ian Hernon, 43–48. Gloucestershire, UK: Sutton, 1998.

Hess, Robert L. *Italian Colonialism in Somalia.* Chicago: University of Chicago Press, 1966.

Hevia, James. *Cherishing Men from Afar: Qing Guest Ritual and the Macartney Embassy of 1793.* Durham, NC: Duke University Press, 1995.

———. *English Lessons: The Pedagogy of Imperialism in Nineteenth-Century China.* Durham, NC: Duke University Press, 2003.

———. "Lamas, Emperors, and Rituals: Political Implications in Qing Ritual Ceremonies." *Journal of the International Association of Buddhist Studies* 16, no. 2 (1993): 243–78.

Heyberger, Bernard. *Les Chrétiens du Proche-Orient au temps de la Réforme Catholique.* Rome: École Française, 1994.

Hilferding, Rudolf. *Finance Capital: A Study of the Latest Phase Capitalist Development.* 1910. London: Routledge & Kegan Paul, 1981.

Hillman, Ben. "Paradise under Construction: Minorities, Myths and Modernity in Northwest Yunnan." *Asian Ethnicity* 4, no. 2 (June 2003): 175–88.

Hirsch, Francine. *Empire of Nations: Ethnographic Knowledge and the Making of the Soviet Union.* Ithaca, NY: Cornell University Press, 2005.

———. "Toward an Empire of Nations: Border-Making and the Formation of Soviet National Identities." *Russian Review* 59, no. 2 (April 2000): 201–26.

Ho, Engseng. "Empire through Diasporic Eyes: A View from the Other Boat." *Comparative Studies in Society and History* 46, no. 2 (April 2004): 210–46.

Hobsbawm, Eric. "Addressing the Questions." *Radical History Review* 57 (Fall 1993): 73–75.

———. *Nations and Nationalism since 1780: Program, Myth, Reality.* Cambridge: Cambridge University Press, 1990.

Hobson, John Atkinson. *Imperialism: A Study.* 1902. London: George Allen & Unwin, 1961.

Holt, Thomas C. *The Problem of Race in the Twenty-First Century.* Cambridge, MA: Harvard University Press, 2000.

Horsman, Reginald. *Race and Manifest Destiny: The Origins of American Racial Anglo-Saxonism.* Cambridge, MA: Harvard University Press, 1981.

Hostetler, Laura. *Qing Colonial Enterprise: Ethnography and Cartography in Early Modern China.* Chicago: University of Chicago Press, 2001.

———. "Qing Connections to the Early Modern World: Ethnography and Cartography in Eighteenth-Century China." *Modern Asian Studies* 34 (July 2000): 623–62.

Hubbert, Jennifer. "(Re)Collecting Mao: Memory and Fetish in Contemporary China." *American Ethnologist* 33, no. 2 (May 2006): 145–61.

Hughes, Langston. "Letter to the Academy." In *The Collected Poems of Langston Hughes.* Edited by Arnold Rampersad and David Roessel, 169. New York: Knopf, 1994.

———. *A Negro Looks at Soviet Central Asia.* Moscow: Co-Operative Publishing Society of Foreign Workers in the USSR, 1934.

Hutchison, William R. *Errand to the World: American Protestant Thought and Foreign Mission.* Chicago: University of Chicago Press, 1987.

Ignatieff, Michael. "The Burden." *New York Times Magazine,* January 5, 2003.

Inda, Jonathan Xavier. "A Flexible World: Capitalism, Citizenship, and Postnational Zones." *PoLAR: Political and Legal Anthropology Review* 23, no. 1 (May 2000): 86–102.

Ingerflom, Claudio Sergio. "Entre le mythe et la parole: l'action Naissance de la conception politique du pouvoir en Russie." *Annales HSS* 4 (July–August 1996): 733–57.

James, Cyril Lionel Robert. *The Black Jacobins: Toussaint L'Ouverture and the San Domingo Revolution.* 1938. New York: Vintage, 1989.

Jersild, Austin. *Orientalism and Empire: North Caucasus Mountain People and the Georgian Frontier, 1845–1917.* Montreal and Kingston: McGill-Queen's University Press, 2002.

Johnson, Chalmers. *The Sorrows of Empire: Militarism, Secrecy, and the End of the Republic.* New York: Metropolitan Books, 2004.

Johnson, G. Wesley. *The Emergence of Black Politics in Senegal: The Struggle for Power in the Four Communes, 1890–1920.* Stanford, CA: Stanford University Press, 1971.

Jones, Eric L. *The European Miracle: Environments, Economies, and Geopolitics in the History of Europe and Asia.* Cambridge: Cambridge University Press, 1987.

Jones, Francis Clifford. *Manchuria since 1931.* London: Royal Institute of International Affairs, 1949.

Joseph, Gilbert. "Close Encounters: Toward a New Cultural History of US–Latin American Relations." In *Close Encounters of Empire: Writing the Cultural History of US–Latin American Relations.* Edited by Gilbert Joseph, Catherine C. Legrand, and Ricardo D. Salvatore, 3–46. Durham, NC: Duke University Press, 1998.

Joseph, Gilbert M., Catherine C. Legrand, and Ricardo D. Salvatore, eds. *Close Encounters of Empire: Writing the Cultural History of US–Latin American Relations.* Durham, NC: Duke University Press, 1998.

Kamen, Henry. *The Spanish Inquisition: A Historical Revision.* New Haven, CT: Yale University Press, 1998.

Kamenka, Eugene. Bureaucracy: *The Career of a Concept.* New York: St. Martin's Press, 1979.

Kamp, Marianne R. *The New Woman in Central Asia: Islam, the Soviet Project, and the Unveiling of Uzbek Women.* Seattle: University of Washington Press, 2006.

Kaplan, Amy. *The Anarchy of Empire in the Making of US Culture.* Cambridge, MA: Harvard University Press, 2002.

———. "'Left Alone with America': The Absence of Empire in the Study of American Culture." In *Cultures of United States Imperialism.* Edited by Amy Kaplan and Donald E. Pease, 3–21. Durham, NC: Duke University Press, 1993.

Kaplan, Amy, and Donald E. Pease, eds. *Cultures of United States Imperialism.* Durham, NC: Duke University Press, 1993.

Kappeler, Andreas. *The Russian Empire: A Multiethnic History.* Harlow, UK: Pearson Education Limited, 2001.

Karal, Enver Ziya. *Selim III. ün Hatt-ı Hümayunlari.* Ankara: Türk Tarih Kurumu Basımevi, 1942.

Karl, Rebecca E. "'Slavery,' Citizenship, and Gender in late Qing China's Global Context." In *Rethinking the 1898 Reform Period: Political and Cultural Change in Late Qing China.* Edited by Rebecca E. Karl and Peter Zarrow, 212–44. Cambridge, MA: Harvard University Asia Center, 2002.

———. *Staging the World: Chinese Nationalism at the Turn of the Twentieth Century,* Durham, NC: Duke University Press, 2002.

Kaufman, Michael T. "What Does the Pentagon See in 'Battle of Algiers'?" *New York Times,* September 7, 2003.

Kautsky, Karl. *Die Internationalitat und der Krieg.* Berlin: Vorwats, 1915.

Keller, Shoshana. *To Moscow, not Mecca: The Soviet Campaign against Islam in Central Asia, 1917–1941.* Westport, CT: Praeger, 2001.

———. "Trapped between State and Society: Women's Liberation and Islam in Soviet Uzbekistan, 1926–1941." *Journal of Women's History* 10, no. 1 (Spring 1998): 20–44.

Kelly, John. "US Power, after 9/11 and before It: If Not an Empire, Then What?" *Public Culture* 15, no. 2 (Spring 2003): 347–69.

Kelly, John, and Martha Kaplan. *Represented Communities: Fiji and World Decolonization.* Chicago: University of Chicago Press, 2001.

Khalid, Adeeb. "Backwardness and the Quest for Civilization: Early Soviet Central

Asia in Comparative Perspective." *Slavic Review* 65, no. 2 (Summer 2006): 231–51.

———. "Nationalizing the Revolution: The Transformation of Jadidism, 1917–1920." In *A State of Nations: Empire and Nation-Making in the Age of Lenin and Stalin.* Edited by Ronald Grigor Suny and Terry Martin, 145–62. New York: Oxford University Press, 2001.

———. *The Politics of Muslim Cultural Reform: Jadidism in Central Asia.* Berkeley: University of California Press, 1998.

Kimerling Wirtschafter, Elise. "Legal Identity and the Possession of Serfs in Imperial Russia." *Journal of Modern History* 70 (September 1998): 561–87.

King, Jonas. *Extraits d'un ouvrage écrit vers la fin de l'année 1826 et au commencement de 1827, sous le titre de Coup d"Oeil sur la Palestine et la Syrie, accompagné de quelques reflexions sur les missions évangeliques par Jonas King.* Athens: C. Nicolaidès Philadelphien, 1859.

Kivelson, Valerie. "Kinship Politics, Autocratic Politics: A Reconsideration of Early-Eighteenth-Century Political Culture." In *Imperial Russia: New Histories for the Empire.* Edited by Jane Burbank and David Ransel, 5–31. Bloomington: Indiana University Press, 1998.

———. "Muscovite 'Citizenship': Rights without Freedom." *Journal of Modern History* 74, no. 3 (September 2002): 465–89.

Klein, Christina. *Cold War Orientalism: Asia in the Middlebrow Imagination.* Berkeley: University of California Press, 2003.

Klein, Naomi. "Baghdad Year Zero: Pillaging Iraq in Pursuit of a Neocon Utopia." *Harper's Magazine,* September 2004: 43–53.

Knaus, John Kenneth. *Orphans of the Cold War: America and the Tibetan Struggle for Survival.* New York: Public Affairs, 1999.

Knight, Nathaniel. "Science, Empire and Nationality: Ethnography in the Russian Geographical Society, 1845–1855." In *Imperial Russia: New Histories for the Empire.* Edited by Jane Burbank and David Ransel, 108–42. Bloomington: Indiana University Press, 1998.

Kohn, Hans. "Reflections on Colonialism." In *The Idea of Colonialism.* Edited by Robert Strausz-Hupé and Harry W. Hazard, 2–16. New York: Frederick A. Praeger, 1958.

Kollmann, Nancy. *By Honor Bound: State and Society in Early Modern Russia.* Ithaca, NY: Cornell University Press, 1999.

Kolmas, Josef. *Tibet and Imperial China: A Survey of Sino-Tibetan Relations up to the End of the Manchu Dynasty in 1912.* Canberra: Australian National University, 1967.

Komagome, Takeshi. *Shokuminchi Teikoku Nihon no Bunka Tōgō* [The Cultural Integration of the Japanese Colonial Empire]. Tokyo: Iwanami Shoten, 1996.

Kōmin [citizen], ed. *Chianbu keisatsushi* [Law and Order Ministry, Police Deparment]. Xinkyō, China: Manshōkoku toshō kabushiki geisha, 1940.

Kornbluh, Peter. *The Pinochet File: A Declassified Dossier on Atrocity and Accountability.* New York: Free Press, 2003.

Koroteyeva, V. V., and Ekaterina Makarova. "Money and Social Connections in the Soviet and Post-Soviet Uzbek City." *Central Asian Survey* 17, no. 4 (December 1998): 579–96.

Kramer, Paul. "Empires, Exceptions, and Anglo-Saxons: Race and Rule between the British and United States Empires, 1880–1910." *Journal of American History* 88, no. 4 (March 2002): 1315–53.

Kukla, Jon. *A Wilderness So Immense: The Louisiana Purchase and the Destiny of America.* New York: Knopf, 2003.

Kunitz, Joshua. *Dawn over Samarkand: The Rebirth of Central Asia.* New York: Covici Friede, 1935.

Kuznesof, Elizabeth Anne. "Ethnic and Gender Influences on 'Spanish Creole' Society in Colonial Spanish America." *Colonial Latin American Review* 4, no. 1 (June 1995): 153–75.

Lafeber, Walter. *Inevitable Revolutions: The United States in Central America.* New York: W. W. Norton, 1992.

Landes, David. *The Wealth and Poverty of Nations: Why Some Are So Rich and Some So Poor.* New York: W. W. Norton & Company, 1998.

Larson, Brooke. *Trials of Nation Making: Liberalism, Race, and Ethnicity in the Andes, 1810–1910.* Cambridge: Cambridge University Press, 2004.

Latyshev, S. "Volost'." In *Entsiklopedicheskii slovar'.* Vol. 13. Edited by F. A. Brokgaus and I. A. Efron, 95. Saint Petersburg: Tipo-litografiia I. A. Efrona, 1890–1907.

Laurentie, Henri. "Pour ou contre le colonialism? Les colonies françaises devant le monde nouveau." *Renaissances* (October 1944): 3–13.

Lawson, Philip. *The East India Company: A History.* New York: Longman, 1993.

Le Sueur, James, ed. *The Decolonization Reader.* New York: Routledge, 2003.

LeDonne, John P. *Absolutism and Ruling Class: The Formation of the Russian Political Order, 1700–1825.* New York: Oxford University Press, 1991.

———. *The Russian Empire and the World: The Geopolitics of Expansion and Containment.* New York: Oxford University Press, 1997.

Lenin, V. I. *Imperialism: The Highest Stage of Capitalism.* 1917. New York: International Publishers, 1963.

———. *Polnoe sobranie sochinenii.* Vol. 53. 5th ed. Moscow: Gos. izd. Politicheskoi literatury, 1965.

Levitin, Leonid. *Uzbekistan na istoricheskom povorote: kriticheskie zametki storonnika Prezidenta Islama Karimova.* Moscow: Vagrius, 2001.

Lewis, Laura. *Hall of Mirrors: Power, Witchcraft, and Caste in Colonial Mexico.* Durham, NC: Duke University Press, 2003.

Lieven, Dominic. *Empire: The Russian Empire and Its Rivals.* New Haven, CT: Yale University Press, 2000.

———. "Empire's Place in International Relations." Paper presented at the Empires in Modern Times conference, Institut des Hautes Etudes Internationales, Geneva, March 20–23, 2003.

———. *Russian Rulers under the Old Regime.* New Haven, CT: Yale University Press, 1989.

Liu, Morgan. "Recognizing the Khan: Authority, Space and Political Imagination among Uzbek Men in Post-Soviet Osh, Kyrgyzstan." PhD dissertation, University of Michigan, 2002.

Lopez, Donald S., Jr. *Prisoners of Shangri-la: Tibetan Buddhism and the West.* Chicago: University of Chicago Press, 1998.

Louis, William Roger. *Imperialism at Bay: The United States and the Decolonization of the British Empire.* New York: Oxford University Press, 1978.

Louis, William Roger, and Ronald Robinson. "Empire Preserv'd: How the Americans Put Anti-Communism before Anti-Imperialism." In *Decolonization: Perspectives from Now and Then.* Edited by Prasenjit Duara, 152–61. New York: Routledge, 2004.

———. "The Imperialism of Decolonization." *Journal of Imperial and Commonwealth History* 22, no. 3 (1994): 462–511.

Love, Eric T. L. *Race over Empire: Racism and US Imperialism, 1865–1900.* Chapel Hill: University of North Carolina Press, 2004.

Lubin, Nancy. *Labour and Nationality in Soviet Central Asia: An Uneasy Compromise.* London: Macmillan, 1984.

Ludden, David, ed. *Reading Subaltern Studies: Critical History, Contested Meaning and the Globalization of South Asia.* London: Anthem, 2002.

Lustick, Ian, *Unsettled States, Disputed Lands: Britain and Ireland, France and Algeria, Israel and West Bank–Gaza.* Ithaca, NY: Cornell University Press, 1993.

Lutz, Catherine. "Empire Is in the Details." *American Ethnologist* 33, no. 4 (November 2006): 593–611.

———. *Homefront: A Military City and the American 20th Century.* Boston: Beacon Press, 2001.

Luxemburg, Rosa. *The Accumulation of Capital.* 1913. New York: Monthly Review Press, 1964.

Macey, David A. J. *Government and Peasant in Russia, 1861–1906.* DeKalb: Northern Illinois University Press, 1987.

MacFarquhar, Roderick. *The Politics of China, 1949–1989.* Cambridge: Cambridge University Press, 1993.

Macmaster, Neil. "Torture: From Algiers to Abu Ghraib." *Race and Class* 46, no. 2 (October 2004): 1–21.

Madera, Gregorio López. *Excelencias de la monarchia y reyno de España.* Valladolid, Mexico, 1597.

Magdoff, Harry. *Imperialism: From the Colonial Age to the Present.* New York: Monthly Review Press, 1978.

Makdisi, Ussama. *The Culture of Sectarianism: Community, History, and Violence in Nineteenth-Century Ottoman Lebanon.* Berkeley: University of California Press, 2000.

———. "Ottoman Orientalism." *American Historical Review* 107, no. 3 (June 2002): 768–96.

Makley, Charlene. "On the Edge of Respectability: Sexual Politics in China's Tibet." *Positions: East Asia Cultures Critique* 10, no. 3 (Winter 2002): 575–630.

———. "'Speaking Bitterness': Autobiography, History, and Mnemonic Politics on the Sino-Tibetan Frontier." *Comparative Studies in Society and History* 47, no. 1 (January 2005): 40–78.

Mallon, Florencia. *Peasant and Nation: The Making of Postcolonial Mexico and Peru.* Berkeley: University of California Press, 1995.

Mann, Gregory. *Native Sons: West African Veterans and France in the Twentieth Century.* Durham, NC: Duke University Press, 2006.

Marer, Paul, and Kazimierz Z. Poznanski. "Costs of Domination, Benefits of Subordination." In *Dominant Powers and Subordinate States: The United States in Latin America and the Soviet Union in Eastern Europe.* Edited by Jan F. Triska, 371–99. Durham, NC: Duke University Press, 1986.

Marshall, Bruce. *The French Colonial Myth and Constitution-Making in the Fourth Republic.* New Haven, CT: Yale University Press, 1973.

Marshall, Peter J., ed. *Works of the Right Honorable Edmund Burke.* Vols. 5, 6, and 7. Oxford: Clarendon Press, 1981.

Martin, Terry. *The Affirmative Action Empire: Nations and Nationalism in the Soviet Union, 1923–1939.* Ithaca, NY: Cornell University Press, 2001.

Martin, Virginia. "Barïmta: Nomadic Custom, Imperial Crime." In *Russia's Orient: Imperial Borderlands and Peoples, 1700–1917.* Edited by Daniel R. Brower and Edward J. Lazzerini, 254–57. Bloomington: Indiana University Press, 1997.

———. *Law and Custom in the Steppe: The Kazakhs of the Middle Horde and Russian Colonialism in the Nineteenth Century.* London: Curzon, 2001.

Marx, Karl. *Capital.* Vol. 3. New York: Vintage Books, 1981.

Masters, Bruce. *Christians and Jews in the Ottoman Arab World: The Roots of Sectarianism.* Cambridge: Cambridge University Press, 2001.

Matsusaka, Yoshihisa Tak. *The Making of Japanese Manchuria, 1904–1932.* Cambridge, MA: Harvard University Press, 2001.

Maxwell, Kenneth. "The Case of the Missing Letter in Foreign Affairs: Kissinger, Pinochet and Operation Condor." Working paper, David Rockefeller Center of Latin American Studies, Harvard University, 2004.

McAlister, Melani. *Epic Encounters: Culture, Media, and US Interests in the Middle East, 1945–2000.* Berkeley: University of California Press, 2001.

McClintock, Anne. "The Angel of Progress: Pitfalls of the Term Postcolonial." *Social Text* 31–32 (1992): 84–98.

McCormack, Gavan. *Chang Tso-lin in Northeast China, 1911–1928: China, Japan, and the Manchurian Idea.* Stanford, CA: Stanford University Press, 1977.

McGranahan, Carole. "Empire and the Status of Tibet: British, Chinese, and Tibetan Negotiations, 1913–1934." In *The History of Tibet.* Vol. 3: *The Tibetan Encounter with Modernity.* Edited by Alex McKay, 267–95. Richmond, UK: Curzon Press, 2003.

———. "In Rapga's Library: The Texts and Times of a Rebel Tibetan Intellectual." *Les Cahiers d'Extreme-Asie* 15 (2005): 255–76.

———. "Tibet's Cold War: The CIA and the Chushi Gangdrug Resistance, 1956–1974." *Journal of Cold War Studies* 8, no. 3 (Summer 2006): 102–30.

———. "Truth, Fear, and Lies: Exile Politics and Arrested Histories of the Tibetan Resistance." *Cultural Anthropology* 20, no. 4 (November 2005): 570–600.

McGranahan, Carole, and Ann Laura Stoler. "Empires: Thinking Colonial Studies beyond Europe." Unpublished proposal for a School of American Research advanced seminar, April 2002.

McKay, Alex. *Tibet and the British Raj: The Frontier Cadre, 1904–1947.* Richmond, UK: Curzon, 1997.

Medani, Khalid Mustafa. "State Rebuilding in Reverse: The Neoliberal 'Reconstruction' of Iraq." *Middle East Report* 232 (Fall 2004): 28–35.

Medina, Jose Toribio. *Historia del Tribunal del Santo Oficio de la Inquisición de Lima. Vols.* 1 and 2. Santiago: Impr. Gutenberg, 1887.

———. *Historia del Tribunal del Santo Oficio de la Inquisición en Mexico.* Mexico City: Consejo Nacional de la Cultura y Artes, 1991.

Mehta, Uday Singh. *Liberalism and Empire: A Study in Nineteenth-Century British Liberal Thought.* Chicago: University of Chicago Press, 1999.

Meinig, D. W. *The Shaping of America: A Geographical Perspective on 500 Years of History.* Vol. 2: *Continental America, 1800–1867.* New Haven, CT: Yale University Press, 1993.

Memmi, Albert. *Racism.* Translated by Steve Martinot. Minneapolis: University of Minnesota Press, 2000.

Mena, Cristóbal de. "La conquista del Peru." In *Biblioteca Peruana.* Ser. 1, vol. 1. 135–69. Lima: Editores Técnicos Asociados, 1968.

Mendoza, Zoila. "Defining Folklore: Indigenous and Mestizo Identities on the Move." *Bulletin of Latin American Research* 17, no. 2 (May 1998): 165–84.

Merle, Isabelle. "Retour sur le régime de l'indigénat: genèse et contradictions des principes répressifs dans l'empire français." *French Politics, Culture and Society* 20, no. 2 (Summer 2002): 77–97.

Michaels, Paula. *Curative Powers: Medicine and Empire in Stalin's Central Asia.* Pittsburgh: Pittsburgh University Press, 2003.

Mignolo, Walter. *Local Histories/Global Designs: Coloniality, Subaltern Knowledges, and Border Thinking.* Princeton, NJ: Princeton University Press, 2000.

Miles, William F. S. *Imperial Burdens: Countercolonialism in Former French India.* Boulder, CO: Lynne Rienner Publishers, 1995.

Miller, Perry. *Errand into the Wilderness.* Cambridge, MA: Belknap Press, 1956.

Millward, James A. *Beyond the Pass: Economy, Ethnicity, and Empire in Qing Central Asia, 1759–1864.* Stanford, CA: Stanford University Press, 1998.

Min Tu-ki, "Ch'ôngcho ûi hwangche sasang t'ongche ûi silche" [Imperial Thought Control and Practice in the Qing Dynasty]. In *Chungkuk Kûntaesa Yônku.* Edited by Min Tuki, 2–53. Seoul: Ichokak, 1973.

———. *National Polity and Local Power: The Transformation of Late Imperial China.* Cambridge, MA: Harvard University Press, 1989.

Mintz, Sidney. *Sweetness and Power: The Place of Sugar in the Modern World.* New York: Penguin Books, 1985.

Montagnon, Pierre. *Histoire d'Algérie.* Paris: Pygmalion, 1998.

Montenegro, Alonso de la Pena. *Itinerario para parrocos de indios, en que se tratan las materias....* Lyon: Joan A. Hugetan, 1678.

Monteón, Michael. "The British in the Atacama Desert: The Cultural Bases of Economic Imperialism." *Journal of Economic History* 25, no. 1 (March 1975): 117–33.

Montesinos, Fernando de. "Descripción del auto de fé de la 'complicidad grande'" ("Auto de la fé celebrado en Lima a 23 de enero de 1639"). In *El Santo Oficio en America y el mas grande proces inquisitorial en el Peru.* Edited by Boleslao Lewin, 155–89. Buenos Aires: Sociedad Hebraica Argentina, 1950.

Moore, David Chioni. "Colored Dispatches from the Uzbek Border: Langston Hughes' Relevance, 1933–2002." *Callaloo* 25, no. 4 (Autumn 2002): 1115–35.

Mordukhai-Boltovskii, I. D., ed. *Svod Zakonov Rossiiskoi Imperii* [Collected Laws of the Russian Empire]. Saint Petersburg: Russkoe Knizhnoe Tovarishchestvo "Deiatel'," 1912.

Morillo-Alicea, Javier. "Uncharted Landscapes of 'Latin America': The Philippines in the Spanish Imperial Archipelago." In *Interpreting Spanish Colonialism: Empires, Nations, and Legends.* Edited by Christopher Schmidt-Nowara and John Nieto-Phillips, 25–54. Albuquerque: University of New Mexico Press, 2005.

Morner, Magnus. *Race Mixture in the History of Latin America.* Boston: Little Brown, 1967.

Morrison, Alexander. "Russian Rule in Samarkand 1868–1910: A Comparison with British India." D.Phil. thesis, Oxford University, 2005.

Morris-Suzuki, Tessa. *Reinventing Japan: Time, Space, Nation.* Armonk, NY: M. E. Sharpe, 1998.

Motyl, Alexander J. *Revolutions, Nations, Empires: Conceptual Limits and Theoretical Possibilities.* New York: Columbia University Press, 1999.

———. *Will the Non-Russians Rebel? State, Ethnicity, and Stability in the USSR.* Ithaca, NY: Cornell University Press, 1987.

Muthu, Sankar. *Enlightenment against Empire.* Princeton, NJ: Princeton University Press, 2003.

Myers, Ramon H. "Customary Law, Markets, and Resource Transactions in Late Imperial China." In *Explorations in the New Economic History.* Edited by Roger L. Ransom, Richard Sutch, and Gary M. Walton, 273–98. New York: Academic Press, 1982.

Nawid, Senzil K. *Religious Response to Social Change in Afghanistan, 1919–1929.* Costa Mesa, CA: Mazda, 1999.

Negash, Tekeste. *Italian Colonialism in Eritrea, 1882–1941: Policies, Praxis, and Impact.* Uppsala, Sweden: Uppsala University Press, 1987.

Nkrumah, Kwame. *Neo-colonialism: The Last Stage of Imperialism.* New York: International Publishers, 1965.

Nol'de, B. E. "Edinstvo i nerazdel'nost' Rossii." In *Ocherki russkogo gosudarstvennogo prava.* Edited by B. E. Nol'de, 223–554. Saint Petersburg: Pravda, 1911.

———. *La formation de l'empire russe: etudes, notes et documents.* Vol. 1. Paris: Institut d'etudes slaves, 1952.

Norbu, Dawa. *China's Tibet Policy.* Richmond, UK: Curzon Press, 2001.

Norbu, Jamyang. "Dances with Yaks: Tibet in Film, Fiction, and Fantasy of the West." *Tibetan Review* 33, no. 1 (1998): 18–23.

———. *Warriors of Tibet: The Story of Aten and the Khapas' Fight for the Freedom of Their Country.* Ithaca, NY: Snow Lion Publications, 1987.

North, Douglass C. "The Paradox of the West." In *The Origins of Modern Freedom in the West.* Edited by Richard W. Davis. Stanford, CA: Stanford University Press, 1995.

Northrop, Douglas T. *Veiled Empire: Gender and Power in Stalinist Central Asia.* Ithaca, NY: Cornell University Press, 2004.

Obenzinger, Hilton. *American Palestine: Melville, Twain, and the Holy Land Mania.* Princeton, NJ: Princeton University Press, 1999.

O'Brien, Conor Cruise. *Great Melody: A Thematic Biography and Commented Anthology of Edmund Burke.* Chicago: University of Chicago Press, 1993.

"Obshchee polozhenie o krest'ianakh" [The General Regulation on Peasants]. In *Svod Zakonov Rossiiskoi Imperii.* Edited by I. D. Mordukhai-Boltovskii. Saint Petersburg: Russkoe Knizhnoe Tovarishchestvo "Deiatel'," 1912.

Oguma, Eiji. *A Genealogy of "Japanese" Self-images.* Translated by David Askew. Melbourne: Trans Pacific Press, 2002.

Ong, Aihwa. *Flexible Citizenship: The Cultural Logics of Transnationality.* Durham, NC: Duke University Press, 1999.

Onogawa Hidemi. "Cho heilin no haiman shisô" [Zhang Binglin's Ideology of Expelling the Manchus]. In *Shinmatsu Seiji Shisô Kenkyû.* Edited by Onogawa Hidemi, 285–338. Tokyo: Misuzu, 1969.

Orlove, Ben. "Down to Earth: Race and Substance in the Andes." *Bulletin of Latin American Research* 17, no. 2 (May 1998): 207–22.

Ortiz, Fernando. *Cuban Counterpoint: Tobacco and Sugar.* Durham: Duke University Press, 1995.

Osborne, Thomas J. *"Empire Can Wait": American Opposition to Hawaiian Annexation, 1893–1898.* Kent, OH: Kent State University Press, 1981.

Osorio, Alejandra. "El Callejón de la Soledad: Vectors of Cultural Hybridity in Seventeenth Century Lima." In *Spiritual Encounters: Interactions between Christianity and Native Religions in Colonial America.* Edited by Fernando Cervantes and Nicolas Griffiths, 198–229. Lincoln: University of Nebraska Press, 1999.

Osterhammel, Jürgen. *Colonialism: A Theoretical Overview.* Princeton, NJ: Markus Wiener Publishers, 1997.

Overy, Richard. "World Trade and World Economy." In *The Oxford Companion to World War II.* Edited by Ian C. B. Dear and M. R. D. Foot, 1002–07. Oxford: Oxford University Press, 2001.

O'zbekistonning yangi tarixi. Vol. 2: *O'zbekiston sovet mustamlikachiligi davrida.* Tashkent, Uzbekistan: Sharq, 2000.

Pachen, Ani, and Adelaide Donnelly. *Sorrow Mountain: The Journey of a Tibetan Warrior Nun.* New York: Kodansha America, 2002.

Pagden, Anthony. "The Empire's New Clothes: From Empire to Federation, Yesterday and Today." *Common Knowledge* 12, no. 1 (Winter 2006): 36–46.

———, ed. *The Idea of Europe: From Antiquity to the European Union.* Cambridge: Cambridge University Press, 2002.

———. *Peoples and Empires: A Short History of European Migration, Exploration, and Conquest, from Greece to the Present.* New York: Modern Library, 2001.

Palumbo, Patrizia, ed. *A Place in the Sun: Africa in Italian Colonial Culture from Post-Unification to the Present.* Berkeley: University of California Press, 2003.

Panitch, Leo. "The New Imperial State." *New Left Review* 2 (March–April 2000): 5–20.

Panitch, Leo, and Sam Gindin. "Global Capitalism and American Empire." *Socialist Register* (2004): 1–42.

Park, Sub. "Exploitation and Development in Colony: Korea and India." *Korean Journal of Political Economy* 1, no. 1 (2003): 3–31.

Parrini, Carl. "The Age of Ultraimperialism." *Radical History Review* 57 (Fall 1993): 7–20.

Peattie, Mark R. *Ishiwara Kanji and Japan's Confrontation with the West.* Princeton, NJ: Princeton University Press, 1975.

Perdue, Peter C. *China Marches West: The Qing Conquest of Central Eurasia.* Cambridge, MA: Belknap Press of Harvard University Press, 2005.

———. "Constructing Chinese Property Rights, East and West." In *Constituting Modernity: Private Property in the East and West.* Edited by Huri Islamoglu, 35–68. New York: I. B. Tauris, 2004.

———. "Culture, History, and Imperial Chinese Strategy: Legacies of the Qing Conquests." In *Warfare in Chinese History.* Edited by Hans van de Ven, 252–87. Leiden: Brill, 2000.

———. "Identifying China's Northwest, for Nation and Empire." In *Locating China: Space, Place, and Popular Culture.* Edited by Jing Wang, 94–114. New York: Routledge, 2005.

Pérez Villanueva, Joaquín, and Bartolome Escandell Bonet, eds. *Historia de la Inquisición en España y América.* Vol. 2. Madrid: Biblioteca de Autores Cristianos, Centro de Estudios Inquisitoriales, 1984.

Petech, Luciano. *China and Tibet in the Early XVIIIth Century.* Leiden: Brill, 1972.

Peters, Edward. *Inquisition.* New York: Free Press, 1988.

Petrone, Karen. *Life Has Become More Joyous, Comrades: Celebrations in the Time of Stalin.* Bloomington: Indiana University Press, 2000.

Peureux, Gérard. *Le Haut-Conseil de l'Union Française.* Paris: Librarie de Droit et de Jurisprudence, 1960.

Phillips, Clifton Jackson. *Protestant America and the Pagan World: The First Half Century of the American Board of Commissioners for Foreign Missions, 1810–1860.* Cambridge, MA: Harvard University Press, 1969.

Pizarro, Hernando. "Carta de Hernando Pizarro." 1553. In *Biblioteca Peruana.* Ser. 1, vol. 1. 119–30. Lima: Editores Técnicos Asociados, 1968.

"A Pleasure Garden for Blossoming the Tibetan People's Wisdom to Reestablish an Independent Republic of Tibet." Unpublished manuscript, 1960.

Pleven, René. "Préface." *Renaissances* (October 1944): 8.

Pocock, J. G. A. "Burke and the Ancient Constitution." In *Politics, Language and Time: Essays on Political Thought and History.* New York: Atheneum, 1973.

Polnoe sobranie zakonov Rossiiskoi imperii, Sobranie tretie. Vol. 26, 1906 (Saint Petersburg, 1909), 28392, I, October 5, 1906.

Pomeranz, Kenneth. *The Great Divergence: China, Europe, and the Making of the Modern World Economy.* Princeton, NJ: Princeton University Press, 2000.

Poole, Deborah. *Vision, Race, and Modernity: A Visual Economy of the Andean Image World.* Princeton, NJ: Princeton University Press, 1997.

Popkins, Gareth. "Peasant Experiences of the Late Tsarist State: District Congresses of Land Captains, Provincial Boards and the Legal Appeals Process," *Slavonic and East European Review* 78, no. 1 (January 2000): 90–114.

Poullada, Leon B. *Reform and Rebellion in Afghanistan, 1919–1929: King Amanullah's Failure to Modernize a Tribal Society.* Ithaca, NY: Cornell University Press, 1973.

Powell, Eve Troutt. *A Different Shade of Colonialism: Egypt, Great Britain, and the Mastery of the Sudan.* Berkeley: University of California Press, 2003.

Powers, John. *History as Propaganda: Tibetan Exiles versus the Peoples' Republic of China.* Oxford: Oxford University Press, 2004.

Pownall, T. *The Right, Interest, and Duty of Government, as Concerned in the Affairs of the East Indies.* London, 1773.

Prakash, Gyan, ed. *After Colonialism: Imperialism and the Postcolonial Aftermath.* Princeton, NJ: Princeton University Press, 1995.

———. *Another Reason: Science and the Imagination of Modern India.* Princeton, NJ: Princeton University Press, 1999.

Pravilova, E. A. *Zakonnost' i prava lichnosti: Administrativnaia iustitsiia v Rossii (vtoraia polovina XIX v.-oktiabr' 1917 g.).* Saint Petersburg: SZAGS "Obrazovanie-kul'tura," 2000.

Price, Richard. *Convict and Colonel.* Boston: Beacon Press, 1998.

Quiroz, Alfonso W. "La expropiación inquisitorial de cristianos nuevos portugueses en Los Reyes, Cartagena, y México (1635–1649)." *Histórica* 10 (1986): 237–303.

Rafael, Vicente L. *White Love and Other Events in Filipino History.* Durham, NC: Duke University Press, 2000.

Rai, Amit. *The Rule of Sympathy.* New York: Palgrave, 2002.

Ram, Harsha. "Imagining Eurasia: The Poetics and Ideology of Olzhas Suleimenov's Az i Ia." *Slavic Review* 60, no. 2 (Summer 2001): 289–311.

Redfield, Peter. *Space in the Tropics: From Convicts to Rockets in French Guiana.* Berkeley: University of California Press, 2000.

Remnev, Anatolyi. "Siberia and the Russian Far East in the Imperial Geography of Power." In *Russian Empire: Space, People, Power, 1700–1930.* Edited by Jane Burbank, Mark von Hagen, and Anatolyi Remnev. Bloomington: Indiana University Press, 2007.

Reynolds, Nancy. "Difference and Tolerance in the Ottoman Empire." Interview with Aron Rodrigue. *Stanford Humanities Review* 5, no. 1 (Fall 1995): 81–92. http://www.stanford.edu/group/SHR/5-1/text/rodrigue.html.

Rhoads, Edward J. *Manchus and Han: Ethnic Relations and Political Power in Late Qing and Early Republican China, 1861–1928.* Seattle: University of Washington Press, 2000.

Ribeiro, Darcy. *The Americas and Civilization.* Translated by L. Barrett and M. Barrett. New York: Dutton, 1971.

Richards, Thomas. *The Imperial Archive: Knowledge and the Fantasy of Empire.* London: Verso, 1993.

Richardson, Louise. *When Allies Differ: Anglo-American Relations During the Suez and Falklands Crisis.* New York: St. Martins, 1996.

Robinson, Cedric J. *Black Marxism: The Making of the Black Radical Tradition.* London: Zed Press, 1983.

Rocher, Rosanne. *Orientalism, Poetry, and the Millennium: The Checkered Life of Nathaniel Brassey Halhed, 1751–1830.* Delhi: Motilal Banarasidass, 1983.

Rolland, Louis, and Pierre Lampué. *Précis de droit des pays d'outre-mer (territoires, départements, états associés).* Paris: Dalloz, 1952.

Rosaldo, Renato. *Culture and Truth: The Remaking of Social Analysis.* Boston: Beacon Press, 1989.

Rosen, Stephen Peter. "An Empire, If You Can Keep It." *National Interest* 71 (Spring 2003): 51–61.

Ruedy, John. *Modern Algeria: The Origins and Development of a Nation.* Bloomington: Indiana University Press, 1992.

Ryan, David, and Victor Pungong, eds. *The United States and Decolonization: Power and Freedom.* New York: St. Martin's Press, 2000.

Rycaut, Paul. *The Present State of the Ottoman Empire.* 1688. New York: Arno Press, 1971.

Saada, Emmanuelle. "La 'question des métis' dans les colonies françaises: socio-histoire d'une catégorie juridique (Indochine et autres territories de l'Empire français; années 1890-années 1950)." Doctoral thesis, École des Hautes Études en Sciences Sociales, 2001.

Sahadeo, Jeffrey. *Russian Colonial Society in Tashkent, 1865–1923.* Bloomington: Indiana University Press, 2007.

Sahlins, Peter. *Boundaries: The Making of France and Spain in the Pyrenees.* Berkeley: University of California Press, 1998.

Said, Edward. *Culture and Imperialism.* New York: Vintage, 1994.

———. *Orientalism.* New York: Vintage, 1978.

———. *Orientalism.* Twenty-fifth anniversary edition. New York: Vintage, 2003.

———. *Reflections on Exile and Other Essays.* Cambridge, MA: Harvard University Press, 2000.

Salibi, Kamal, and Yusuf K. Khoury, eds. *The Missionary Herald: Reports from Ottoman Syria, 1819–1870.* 5 vols. Amman: Royal Institute for Inter-Faith Studies, 1995.

Salvatore, Ricardo. "The Enterprise of Knowledge: Representational Machines of Informal Empire." In *Close Encounters of Empire: Writing the Cultural History of US–Latin American Relations.* Edited by Gilbert Joseph, Catherine C. Legrand, and Ricardo D. Salvatore, 69–106, Durham, NC: Duke University Press, 1998.

Sandars, C. T. *America's Overseas Garrisons: The Leasehold Empire.* Oxford: Oxford University Press, 2000.

Sbornik ukazov i postanovlenii Vremennogo pravitel'stva. Vyp. 1. Petrograd: Gosudarstvennaia tipografiia, 1917.

Schein, Louisa. "Gender and Internal Orientalism in China." *Modern China* 23, no. 1 (January 1997): 69–98.

———. *Minority Rules: The Miao and the Feminine in China's Cultural Politics.* Durham, NC: Duke University Press, 2000.

Schell, Jonathan. "Imperialism without Empire." *Global Policy* Forum, August 26, *2004. http://www.globalpolicy.org/empire/analysis/2004/0826imperialism.htm.*

Schmid, Andre. *Korea between Empires, 1895–1919.* New York: Columbia University Press, 2002.

Schmitt, Carl. *The Nomos of the Earth in the International Law of the Jus Publicum Europaeum.* New York: Telos, 2003.

Schneider, Michael A. "The Limits of Cultural Rule: Internationalism and Identity in Japanese Responses to Korean Rice." In *Colonial Modernity in Korea.* Edited by Gi-wook Shin and Michael Robinson, 97–127. Cambridge, MA: Harvard University Asia Center, 1999.

Schwartz, Stuart B. "Colonial Identities and the 'Sociedad de Castas.'" *Colonial Latin American Review* 4, no. 1 (June 1995): 185–201.

Scott, James C. *Seeing Like a State: How Certain Schemes to Improve the Human Condition Have Failed.* New Haven, CT: Yale University Press, 1998.

Scott, Julius. "The Common Wind: Currents of Afro-American Communication in the Era of the Haitain Revolution." PhD dissertation, Duke University, 1986.

Scully, Eileen. *Bargaining with the State from Afar: American Citizenship in Treaty Port China, 1844–1942.* New York: Columbia University Press, 2001.

Seed, Patricia. *American Pentimento: The Invention of Indians and the Pursuit of Riches.* Minneapolis: University of Minnesota Press, 2001.

———. *Ceremonies of Possession in Europe's Conquest of the New World, 1492–1640.* Cambridge: Cambridge University Press, 1995.

———. "Taking Possession and Reading Texts: Establishing the Authority of Overseas Empires." *William and Mary Quarterly* 49, no. 2 (April 1992): 183–209.

Senghor, Léopold Sédar. *Marchés Coloniaux* 375 (January 17, 1953): 124.

———. "Rapport sur le méthode du Parti." *La Condition Humaine,* April 26, 1949.

———. "Vues sur l'Afrique Noire, ou assimiler, non être assimilés." In *La communauté impériale française.* Edited by Robert Lemaignen, Léopold Sédar Senghor, and Prince Sisonath Youtévong, 57–98. Paris: Alsatia, 1945.

Sha'ban, Fuad. *Islam and Arabs in Early American Thought: The Roots of Orientalism in America.* Durham, NC: Acorn Press, 1991.

Shakabpa, Tsepon W. D. *Tibet: A Political History.* New Haven, CT: Yale University Press, 1967.

Shakya, Tsering. *The Dragon in the Land of Snows: A History of Modern Tibet since 1947.* London: Pimlico, 1999.

———. "Tibet and the Occident: The Myth of Shangri-la." *Tibetan Review* 27, no. 1 (1992): 13–16.

Sharkey, Heather J. *Living with Colonialism: Nationalism and Culture in the Anglo-Egyptian Sudan.* Berkeley: University of California Press, 2003.

Shein, V. "K istorii voprosa o smeshannykh brakakh." *Zhurnal Ministerstva iustitsii* (1907): 231–73.

Shepard, Todd. *The Invention of Decolonization: The Algerian War and the Remaking of France.* Ithaca: Cornell University Press, 2006.

al-Shidyaq, Tannus. *Kitab Akhbar al-a'yan fi Jabal Lubnan.* 2 vols. 1859. Beirut: Publications de l'université libanaise, 1970.

Shimada, Kenji. *Pioneer of the Chinese Revolution: Zhang Binglin and Confucianism.* Translated by Joshua A. Fogel. Stanford, CA: Stanford University Press, 1990.

Shin, Gi-Wook, and Michael Robinson, eds. *Colonial Modernity in Korea.* Cambridge, MA: Harvard University Press, 2001.

Shohat, Ella. "Notes on the Postcolonial." *Social Text* 31–32 (1992): 99–113.

Silverblatt, Irene. "Becoming Indian in the Central Andes of Seventeenth Century Peru." In *After Colonialism: Imperialism and the Postcolonial Aftermath.* Edited by Gyan Prakash, 279–98. Princeton, NJ: Princeton University Press, 1995.

———. *Modern Inquisitions: Peru and the Colonial Origins of the Civilized World.* Durham, NC: Duke University Press, 2004.

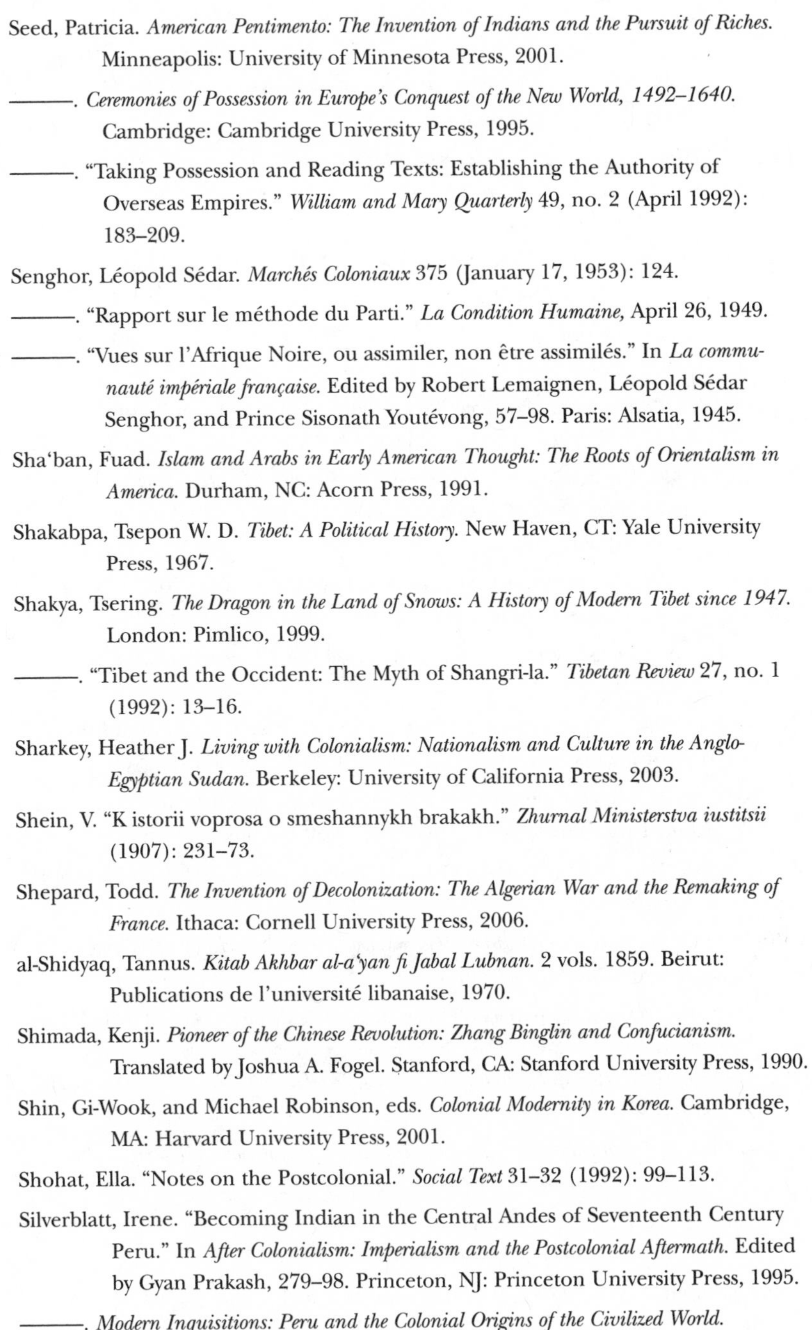

———. "Political Memories and Colonizing Symbols: Santiago and the Mountain Gods of Colonial Peru." In *Rethinking History and Myth: Indigenous South American Perspectives on the Past.* Edited by Jonathan D. Hill, 174–94. Urbana: University of Illinois Press, 1988.

Sinha, Mrinalini. *Colonial Masculinity: The "Manly Englishman" and the "Effeminate Bengali" in the Late Nineteenth Century.* Manchester, UK: Manchester University Press, 1995.

———. "Mapping the Imperial Social Formation: A Modest Proposal for Feminist History." *Signs* 25, no. 4 (Summer 2000): 1077–82.

———. "Teaching Imperialism as a Social Formation." *Radical History Review* 67 (Winter 1997): 175–86.

Siqueira, Alito. "Postcolonial Portugal, Postcolonial Goa: A Note on Portuguese Identity and Its Resonance in Goa and India." *Lusotopie* 2 (2002): 211–13.

Sklar, Richard L. *Corporate Power in an African State: The Political Impact of Multinational Mining Companies in Zambia.* Berkeley: University of California Press, 1975.

Slezkine, Yuri. *Arctic Mirrors: Russia and the Small Peoples of the North.* Ithaca, NY: Cornell University Press, 1994.

———. "Imperialism as the Highest Stage of Socialism." *Russian Review* 59, no. 2 (April 2000): 227–34.

———. "Naturalists versus Nations: Eighteenth-Century Scholars Confront Ethnic Diversity." *Representations* 47 (Summer 1994): 170–95.

———. "The USSR as a Communal Apartment, or How a Socialist State Promoted Ethnic Particularism." *Slavic Review* 53, no. 2 (Summer 1994): 414–52.

Sloane, W. M. "Napoleon's Plan for a Colonial System." *American Historical Review* 4 (1899): 439–55.

Smith, Neil. *American Empire: Roosevelt's Geographer and the Prelude to Globalization.* Berkeley: University of California Press, 2003.

Smith, Robert Freeman. "Republican Policy and the Pax Americana, 1921–1932." In *From Colony to Empire: Essays in the History of American Foreign Relations.* Edited by William Appleman Williams, 253–92. New York: John Wiley and Sons, 1972.

———. *The United States and the Latin American Sphere of Influence,* Malabar, India: Krieger Publication Co., 1981.

Solorzano Pereira, Juan de. "Política Indiana." 1647. In *Biblioteca de autores españoles.* Vols 252–56, 436–38. Madrid: Ediciones Atlas, 1972.

Spalding, Karen. *De indio a campesino.* Lima: Instituto de Estudios Peruanos, 1974.

Spear, Percival. *Master of Bengal: Clive and His India.* London: Thames and Hudson, 1975.

Spence, Jonathan. *Treason by the Book.* New York: Viking, 2001.

Spengler, Oswald. *The Decline of the West.* An abridged edition by Helmut Werner; English abridged edition prepared by Arthur Helps from the translation by Charles Francis Atkinson. New York: Alfred A. Knopf, 1962.

Sperling, Eliot. "Awe and Submission: A Tibetan Aristocrat at the Court of Qianlong," *International History Review* 20, no. 2 (June 1998): 325–35.

Spivak, Gayatri Chakravorty. *A Critique of Postcolonial Reason: Toward a History of the Vanishing Present.* Cambridge, MA: Harvard University Press, 1999.

Splendiani, Anna Maria, José Enrique Sánchez Bohgorquez, and Emma Cecilia Luque de Salazar. *Cincuenta Años de Inquisición en el Tribunal de Cartagena de Indias 1610–1660.* 4 vols. Bogota: Centro Editorial Javeriano, 1997.

Springhall, John. *Decolonization since 1945.* New York: Palgrave, 2001.

Stalin, Josef. "Our Tasks in the East." In *Works.* Vol. 4. Moscow: Foreign Languages Publishing House, 1952.

Steel, Ronald. *Pax Americana.* New York: Viking Press, 1967.

Steiner, George. *Lessons of the Masters.* Cambridge, MA: Harvard University Press, 2003.

Steinmetz, George. *The Devil's Handwriting: Precoloniality and the German Colonial State in Qingdao, Samoa, and Southwest Africa.* Chicago: University of Chicago Press, forthcoming.

———. "Odious Comparisons: Incommensurability, the Case Study, and 'Small N's' in Sociology." *Sociological Theory* 22, no. 3 (September 2004): 371–400.

———. "Return to Empire: The New US Imperialism in Comparative Historical Perspective." *Sociological Theory* 23, no. 4 (December 2005): 339–67.

———. "State of Emergency and the Revival of American Imperialism: Towards an Authoritarian Post-Fordism." *Public Culture* 15, no. 2 (2003): 333–45.

Stoddard, Heather. *Le Mendiant d'Amdo.* Paris: Societe d'Ethnographie, 1985.

Stoler, Ann Laura. *Carnal Knowledge and Imperial Power: Race and the Intimate in Colonial Rule.* Berkeley: University of California Press, 2002.

———. "Degrees of Imperial Sovereignty." *Public Culture* 18, no. 1 (Winter 2006): 125–46.

———. *Haunted by Empire: Geographies of Intimacy in North American History.* Durham, NC: Duke University Press, 2006.

———. "Imperial Formations and the Opacity of Rule." In *Lessons of Empire: Imperial Histories and American Power.* Edited by Craig Calhoun, Frederick Cooper, and Kevin W. Moore, 48–60. New York: New Press, 2006.

———. "In Cold Blood: Hierarchies of Credibility and the Politics of Colonial Narratives." *Representations* 37 (Winter 1992): 151–89.

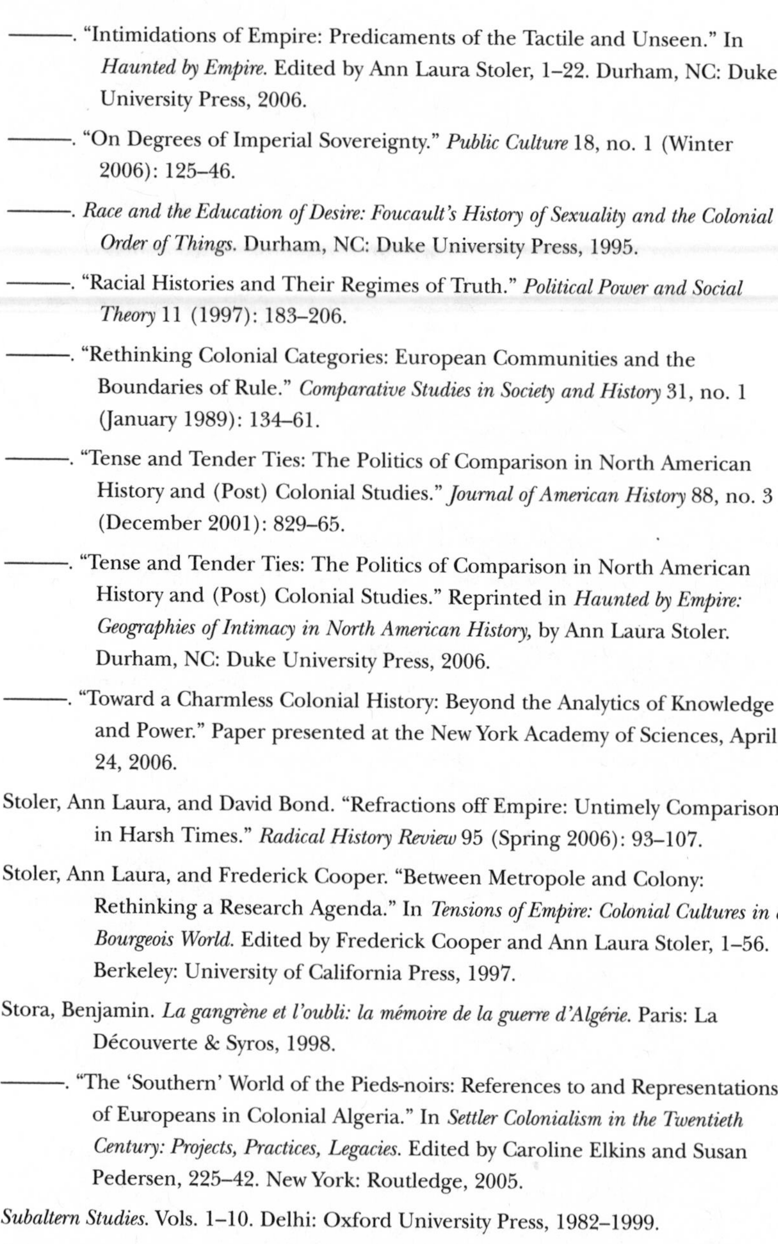

———. "Intimidations of Empire: Predicaments of the Tactile and Unseen." In *Haunted by Empire*. Edited by Ann Laura Stoler, 1–22. Durham, NC: Duke University Press, 2006.

———. "On Degrees of Imperial Sovereignty." *Public Culture* 18, no. 1 (Winter 2006): 125–46.

———. *Race and the Education of Desire: Foucault's History of Sexuality and the Colonial Order of Things*. Durham, NC: Duke University Press, 1995.

———. "Racial Histories and Their Regimes of Truth." *Political Power and Social Theory* 11 (1997): 183–206.

———. "Rethinking Colonial Categories: European Communities and the Boundaries of Rule." *Comparative Studies in Society and History* 31, no. 1 (January 1989): 134–61.

———. "Tense and Tender Ties: The Politics of Comparison in North American History and (Post) Colonial Studies." *Journal of American History* 88, no. 3 (December 2001): 829–65.

———. "Tense and Tender Ties: The Politics of Comparison in North American History and (Post) Colonial Studies." Reprinted in *Haunted by Empire: Geographies of Intimacy in North American History*, by Ann Laura Stoler. Durham, NC: Duke University Press, 2006.

———. "Toward a Charmless Colonial History: Beyond the Analytics of Knowledge and Power." Paper presented at the New York Academy of Sciences, April 24, 2006.

Stoler, Ann Laura, and David Bond. "Refractions off Empire: Untimely Comparisons in Harsh Times." *Radical History Review* 95 (Spring 2006): 93–107.

Stoler, Ann Laura, and Frederick Cooper. "Between Metropole and Colony: Rethinking a Research Agenda." In *Tensions of Empire: Colonial Cultures in a Bourgeois World*. Edited by Frederick Cooper and Ann Laura Stoler, 1–56. Berkeley: University of California Press, 1997.

Stora, Benjamin. *La gangrène et l'oubli: la mémoire de la guerre d'Algérie*. Paris: La Découverte & Syros, 1998.

———. "The 'Southern' World of the Pieds-noirs: References to and Representations of Europeans in Colonial Algeria." In *Settler Colonialism in the Twentieth Century: Projects, Practices, Legacies*. Edited by Caroline Elkins and Susan Pedersen, 225–42. New York: Routledge, 2005.

Subaltern Studies. Vols. 1–10. Delhi: Oxford University Press, 1982–1999.

Subaltern Studies. Vol. 11. New York: Columbia University Press, 2000.

Suleimenov, Olzhas. *Az i Ia: kniga blagonamerennogo chitatelia*. Alma-Ata, Kazakhstan: Zhazushy, 1975. http://www.geocities.com/plt_2000plt_us/azia/

Sun, Kungtu C. *The Economic Development of Manchuria in the First Half of the Twentieth*

Century. Edited by Ralph W. Huenemann. Cambridge, MA: East Asian Research Center, Harvard University, 1969.

Sun Yat-sen. "Da Yaxiyazhuyi" [Great Asianism]. *Xinyaxiya* 1, no. 1 (1930): 2–7.

Sunderland, Willard. *Taming the Wild Field*. Ithaca, NY: Cornell University Press, 2004.

———. "Imperial Space: Territorial Thought and Practice in the Eighteenth Century." In *Russian Empire: Space, People, Power, 1700–1930*. Edited by Jane Burbank, Mark von Hagen, and Anatolyi Remnev. Bloomington: Indiana University Press, 2007.

Suny, Ronald Grigor. "Ambiguous Categories: States, Empires, and Nations." *Post-Soviet Affairs* 11, no. 2 (April–June 1995): 185–96.

———. "Learning from Empire: Russia and the Soviet Union." In *Lessons of Empire: Imperial Histories and American Power*. Edited by Craig Calhoun, Frederick Cooper, and Kevin W. Moore, 73–93. New York: New Press, 2006.

Sutherland, Lucy. *East India Company in Eighteenth Century Politics*. Oxford: Clarendon Press, 1952.

"Svod zakonov grazhdanskikh." In *Svod Zakonov Rossiiskoi Imperii* [Collected Laws of the Russian Empire]. Vol. 10, part 1. Edited by I. D. Mordukhai-Boltovskii. Saint Petersburg: Russkoe Knizhnoe Tovarishchestvo "Deiatel'," 1912.

Sweezy, Paul. *The Theory of Capitalist Development*. Oxford: Oxford University Press, 1946.

Sweezy, Paul, and Paul Baran. *Monopoly Capital: An Essay on the American Economic and Social Order*. New York: Monthly Review Press, 1966.

Tamanoi, Mariko. *Crossed Histories: A New Approach to Manchuria in the Age of Empires*. Honolulu: University of Hawai'i Press, 2005.

———. *Dreaming Manchuria: Migration, Colonization, Repatriation and Nostalgia*. Berkeley: University of California Press, forthcoming.

Tapontsang, Adhe. *Ama Adhe: The Voice That Remembers*. As told to Joy Blakeslee. Boston: Wisdom Press, 1997.

Tarrade, Jean. "Les colonies et les principes de 1789: Les assemblées révolutionaire face au problème de l'esclavage." *Revue Française d'Histoire d'Outre-Mer* 282–83 (1989): 9–34.

Taussig, Michael. "Culture of Terror—Space of Death: Roger Casement's Putumayo Report and the Explanation of Torture." *Comparative Studies in Society and History* 26, no. 3 (July 1984): 467–97.

———. *Defacement: Public Secrets and the Labor of the Negative*. Stanford, CA: Stanford University Press, 1999.

———. *The Nervous System*. New York: Routledge, 1992.

Temas 33–34 (April–September 2003).

Teng, Emma Jinhua. *Taiwan's Imagined Geography: Chinese Colonial Travel Writing and Pictures, 1683–1895.* Cambridge, MA: Harvard University Asia Center, 2004.

Thomas, Kevin Tyner. "Collecting the Fatherland: Early-Nineteenth-Century Proposals for a Russian National Museum." In *Imperial Russia: New Histories for the Empire.* Edited by Jane Burbank and David Ransel, 91–107. Bloomington: Indiana University Press, 1998.

Thompson, E. P. "Eighteenth-Century English Society: Class Structure without Class?" *Social History* 3, no. 2 (May 1978): 133–65.

Thompson, Martyn P. "Ideas of Europe during the French Revolution and Napoleonic Wars." *Journal of the History of Ideas* 55, no. 1 (January 1994): 37–58.

Thomson, William M. *The Land and the Book or Biblical Illustrations Drawn from the Manners and Customs, the Scenes and the Scenery, of the Holy Land.* Vol. 3: Lebanon, Damascus, and beyond Jordan. Hartford, CT: S. S. Scranton Co., 1910.

Thurner, Mark. *From Two Republics to One Divided: Contradictions of Postcolonial Nationmaking in Andean Peru.* Durham, NC: Duke University Press, 1997.

Thurner, Mark, and Andres Guerrero, eds. *After Spanish Rule: Postcolonial Predicaments of the Americas.* Durham, NC: Duke University Press, 2003.

Tibawi, A. L. *American Interests in Syria 1800–1901: A Study of Educational, Literary, and Religious Work.* Oxford: Clarendon Press, 1966.

Todorov, Tzvetan. *The Conquest of America: The Question of the Other.* New York: Harper Perennial, 1984.

Tominaga, Tadashi. *Manshūkoku no Minzoku Mondai.* Shinkyō: Manshu Tomiyamabo, 1943.

Torke, Hans-Joachim. "From Muscovy towards St. Petersburg 1598–1689." In *Russia: A History.* Edited by Gregory Freeze, 56–63. New York: Oxford University Press, 1997.

Tourdonnet, Le Comte A. *de Essais sur l'éducation des enfants pauvres: des colonies agricoles d'éducation.* Vols. 1 and 2. Paris: P. Brunet, 1862.

Trask, Haunani-Kay. *From a Native Daughter: Colonialism and Sovereignty in Hawai'i.* Honolulu: University of Hawai'i Press, 1999.

Trouillot, Michel-Rolph. "The Anthropology of the State in the Age of Globalization: Close Encounters of the Deceptive Kind." *Current Anthropology* 42, no. 1 (February 2001): 121–38.

———. *Silencing the Past: Power and the Production of History.* Boston: Beacon Press, 1995.

Tsering, Tsongkha Lhamo. *bsTan rgol rgyal skyob* [Resistance]. Vols. 1–4. Translated and edited by Tashi Tsering. Dharamsala, India: Amnye Machen Institute, 1992–2002.

Tsiunchuk, Rustem. "Peoples, Regions and Electoral Politics: The State Duma and the Constitution of New National Elites." In *Russian Empire: Space, People, Power, 1700–1930.* Edited by Jane Burbank, Mark von Hagen, and Anatolyi Remnev. Bloomington: Indiana University Press, 2007.

Tsou, Jung (Zou Rong). *The Revolutionary Army: A Chinese Nationalist Tract of 1903.* Translated by John Lust. Paris: Mouton, 1968.

Tsu, Jing. *Failure, Nationalism, and Literature: The Making of Modern Chinese Identity, 1895–1937.* Stanford, CA: Stanford University Press, 2005.

Tuttle, Grey. *Tibetan Buddhists in the Making of Modern China.* New York: Columbia University Press, 2005.

Tyrell, Ian. "American Exceptionalism in an Age of International History." *American Historical Review* (October 1991): 1031–55.

Ukaz ob ustroistve krest'ian. February 19/March 2, 1864.

Ulysse, Gina. "I Came of Age Colonized Now My Soul Is Tired and I Am Feeling All This Rage." *Jouvert: A Journal of Postcolonial Studies* 7, no. 1 (Autumn 2002): http://social.chass.ncsu.edu/jouvert/v7is1/con71.htm

Urquhart, David. *The Lebanon: A History and a Diary.* 2 vols. 1860. Farnborough, UK: Gregg International Publishers, 1972.

Ustav grazhdanskogo sudoproizvodsta. Compiled by I. M. Tiutriumov. Saint Petersburg: Zakonovedenie, 1916.

Ustrialov, N. *Istoricheskoe obozrenie tsarstvovaniia gosudaria imperatora Nikolaia I.* Saint Petersburg: Ekspeditsiia zagotovleniia gosudarstvannykh bumag, 1847.

van Goor, Jurriaan. "Imperialisme in de Marge?" In *Imperialisme in de Marge: De afronding van Nederlands-Indie.* Edited by Jurriaan van Goor, 9–19. Utrecht: Hes uitgevers, 1986.

Vázquez de Espinosa, Antonio. *Compendium and Description of the West Indies.* Washington, DC: Smithsonian Institution, 1942.

Verdes-Leroux, Jeannine. *Les Français d'Algérie.* Paris: Fayard, 2001.

Vishniak, Mark V. "Ideia uchreditel'nogo sobraniia." *Griadushchaia Rossiia* (1920): 1: 270–92; 2: 182–216.

von Hagen, Mark. "Federalisms and Pan-movements: Re-imagining Empire." In *Russian Empire: Space, People, Power, 1700–1930.* Edited by Jane Burbank, Mark von Hagen, and Anatolyi Remnev. Bloomington: Indiana University Press, 2007.

Wagner, William. *Marriage, Property, and Law in Late Imperial Russia.* Oxford: Clarendon Press, 1994.

Walker, Barbara. "Kruzhok Culture and the Meaning of Patronage in the Early Soviet Literary World." Special issue, *Contemporary European History* 11, no. 1 (February 2002): 107–23.

Wallace, Anthony F. C. *Jefferson and the Indians: The Tragic Fate of the First Americans.* Cambridge, MA: Belknap Press of Harvard University Press, 1999.

Wallerstein, Immanuel. "The Construction of Peoplehood: Racism, Nationalism, Ethnicity." In *Race, Nation, Class: Ambiguous Identities.* Edited by Etienne Balibar and Immanuel Wallerstein, 71–85. London: Verso, 1991.

Wang, Lixiong. "Tibet Facing Imperialism of Two Kinds: An Analysis of the Woeser Incident." *World Tibet Network News,* December 20, 2004.

Warren, Jonathan, and France Winddance Twine. "Critical Race Studies in Latin America: Recent Advances and Recent Weaknesses." In *A Companion to Racial and Ethnic Studies.* Edited by John Solomos and David Theo Goldberg, 538–60. Malden, MA: Blackwell, 2002.

Weber, Eugen. *Peasants into Frenchmen: the Modernization of Rural France, 1870–1914.* Stanford, CA: Stanford University Press, 1976.

Weil, Patrick. *Qu'est-ce qu'un Français? Histoire de la nationalité française depuis la Révolution.* Paris: Grasset, 2002.

Weismantel, Mary, and Stephen F. Eisenman. "Race in the Andes: Global Movements and Popular Ontologies." *Bulletin of Latin American Research* 17, no. 2 (May 1998): 121–42.

Weldes, Jutta, Mark Laffey, Hugh Gusterson, and Raymond Duvall, eds. *Cultures of Insecurity: States, Communities, and the Production of Danger.* Minneapolis: University of Minnesota Press, 1999.

Werth, Paul W. *At the Margins of Orthodoxy: Missions, Governance, and Confessional Politics in Russia's Volga-Kama Region, 1827–1905.* Ithaca, NY: Cornell University Press, 2002

———. "Big Candles and 'Internal Conversion': The Mari Pagan Reformation and Its Russian Appropriations." In *Of Religion and Identity: Missions, Conversion, and Tolerance in the Russian Empire.* Edited by Michael Khodarkovsky and Robert Geraci, 144–72. Ithaca, NY: Cornell University Press, 2001.

———. "Changing Conceptions of Difference, Assimilation, and Faith in the Volga-Kama Region, 1740–1870." In *Russian Empire: Space, People, Power, 1700–1930.* Edited by Jane Burbank, Mark von Hagen, and Anatolyi Remnev. Bloomington: Indiana University Press, 2007.

Weyrich, Paul M. "Contemporary Slavery." *CNS News.com. http://www.cnsnews.com/ViewCommentary.asp?Page=%5CCommentary%5Carchive%5C200401%5CCOM20040116b.html.*

Wildenthal, Lora. *German Women for Empire, 1884–1945.* Durham, NC: Duke University Press, 2001.

Williams, Eric. *Capitalism and Slavery.* Chapel Hill: North Carolina University Press, 1961.

Williams, Frances. "Half the World's Workers Earn Less Than $2 a Day." *Financial Times,* December 8, 2004: 6.

Williams, Raymond. *Marxism and Literature.* New York: Oxford University Press, 1978.

———. *Keywords: A Vocabulary of Culture and Society.* London: Fontana, 1976.

Williams, William Appleman. *Empire as a Way of Life: An Essay on the Causes and Character of America's Present Predicament, Along with a Few Thoughts about an Alternative.* New York: Oxford University Press, 1980

Winichakul, Thongchai. *Siam Mapped: A History of the Geo-Body of a Nation.* Honolulu: University of Hawai'i Press, 1994.

Winn, Peter. "Britain's Informal Empire in Uruguay during the Nineteenth Century." *Past and Present* 73 (November 1976): 100–26.

Wirtschafter, Elise Kimerling. "Legal Identity and the Possession of Serfs in Imperial Russia." *Journal of Modern History* 70 (September 1998): 561–63.

———. *Social Identity in Imperial Russia.* DeKalb: Northern Illinois University Press, 1997

Wolfe, Patrick. "History and Imperialism: A Century of Theory, from Marx to Postcolonialism." *American Historical Review* 102, no. 2 (April 1997): 388–420.

Woloch, Isser. *The New Regime: Transformations of the French Civic Order, 1789–1820s.* New York: Norton, 1994.

Wong, R. Bin. *China Transformed: Historical Change and the Limits of European Experience.* Ithaca, NY: Cornell University Press, 1997.

Wood, Bryce. *The Making of the Good Neighbor Policy.* New York: Columbia University Press, 1961.

Woolf, Leonard. *Economic Imperialism.* London: Swarthmore, 1920.

Woolf, Stuart. *Napoleon's Integration of Europe.* London: Routledge, 1991.

Wright, Gwendolyn. "Tradition in the Service of Modernity: Architecture and Urbanism in French Colonial Policy, 1900–1930." *Journal of Modern History* 59, no. 2 (June 1987): 291–316.

Xinhua News Agency, March 14, 2001.

Yamamuro, Shinichi. *Kimera: Manshūkoku no Shōzō* [Chimera: A Portrait of Manzhouguo]. Tokyo: Chūo koronsha, 1993.

Yaney, George L. *The Systematization of Russian Government: Social Evolution in the Domestic Administration of Imperial Russia, 1711–1905.* Urbana: University of Illinois Press, 1973.

Yekelchyk, Serhy. *Stalin's Empire of Memory: Russian-Ukrainian Relations in the Soviet Historical Imagination.* Toronto: University of Toronto Press, 2004.

Yong Shao. *Zhongguo Huidaomen* [China's Religious Societies]. Shanghai: Renmin chubanse, 1997.

Young, C. Walter. *The International Relations of Manchuria: A Digest and Analysis of Treaties, Agreements, and Negotiations Concerning the Three Eastern Provinces of China.* Chicago: University of Chicago Press, 1929.

Young, Crawford. *Imperial Ends: The Decay, Collapse, and Revival of Empires.* New York: Columbia University Press, 2001.

Young, Louise. *Japan's Total Empire: Manchuria and the Culture of Wartime Imperialism.* Berkeley: University of California Press, 1998.

Young, Robert. *White Mythologies: Writing History and the West.* London: Routledge, 1990.

———. *Colonial Desire: Hybridity in Culture, Theory, and Race.* London: Routledge, 1995.

Zhang Binglin [Taiyan]. "Shehui tongquan shangdui" ["A Discussion of Social Groupings"], *Minbao* 12 (1907): 17–18.

———. "Letter Opposing Kang Youwei's Views on Revolution." In *Sources of Chinese Tradition,* ed. William T. De Bary, 308–313. New York: Columbia University Press, 2000.

Zhang Yushu comp. *Qinzheng Pingding Shuomo Fanglue* [Chronicle of the Emperor's Personal Expeditions to Pacify the Northwest Frontier]. Beijing: Zhongguo Shudian, 1708.

Index

School of American Research Advanced Seminar Series

Published by SAR Press

Chaco & Hohokam: Prehistoric Regional Systems in the American Southwest
Patricia L. Crown & W. James Judge, eds.

Recapturing Anthropology: Working in the Present
Richard G. Fox, ed.

War in the Tribal Zone: Expanding States and Indigenous Warfare
R. Brian Ferguson & Neil L. Whitehead, eds.

Ideology and Pre-Columbian Civilizations
Arthur A. Demarest & Geoffrey W. Conrad, eds.

Dreaming: Anthropological and Psychological Interpretations
Barbara Tedlock, ed.

Historical Ecology: Cultural Knowledge and Changing Landscapes
Carole L. Crumley, ed.

Themes in Southwest Prehistory
George J. Gumerman, ed.

Memory, History, and Opposition under State Socialism
Rubie S. Watson, ed.

Other Intentions: Cultural Contexts and the Attribution of Inner States
Lawrence Rosen, ed.

Last Hunters–First Farmers: New Perspectives on the Prehistoric Transition to Agriculture
T. Douglas Price & Anne Birgitte Gebauer, eds.

Making Alternative Histories: The Practice of Archaeology and History in Non-Western Settings
Peter R. Schmidt & Thomas C. Patterson, eds.

Senses of Place
Steven Feld & Keith H. Basso, eds.

Cyborgs & Citadels: Anthropological Interventions in Emerging Sciences and Technologies
Gary Lee Downey & Joseph Dumit, eds.

Archaic States
Gary M. Feinman & Joyce Marcus, eds.

Critical Anthropology Now: Unexpected Contexts, Shifting Constituencies, Changing Agendas
George E. Marcus, ed.

The Origins of Language: What Nonhuman Primates Can Tell Us
Barbara J. King, ed.

Regimes of Language: Ideologies, Polities, and Identities
Paul V. Kroskrity, ed.

Biology, Brains, and Behavior: The Evolution of Human Development
Sue Taylor Parker, Jonas Langer, & Michael L. McKinney, eds.

Women & Men in the Prehispanic Southwest: Labor, Power, & Prestige
Patricia L. Crown, ed.

History in Person: Enduring Struggles, Contentious Practice, Intimate Identities
Dorothy Holland & Jean Lave, eds.

The Empire of Things: Regimes of Value and Material Culture
Fred R. Myers, ed.

Catastrophe & Culture: The Anthropology of Disaster
Susanna M. Hoffman & Anthony Oliver-Smith, eds.

Uruk Mesopotamia & Its Neighbors: Cross-Cultural Interactions in the Era of State Formation
Mitchell S. Rothman, ed.

Remaking Life & Death: Toward an Anthropology of the Biosciences
Sarah Franklin & Margaret Lock, eds.

Tikal: Dynasties, Foreigners, & Affairs of State: Advancing Maya Archaeology
Jeremy A. Sabloff, ed.

Gray Areas: Ethnographic Encounters with Nursing Home Culture
Philip B. Stafford, ed.

Published by SAR Press

American Arrivals: Anthropology Engages the New Immigration
Nancy Foner, ed.

Violence
Neil L. Whitehead, ed.

Law & Empire in the Pacific: Fiji and Hawai'i
Sally Engle Merry & Donald Brenneis, eds.

Anthropology in the Margins of the State
Veena Das & Deborah Poole, eds.

Pluralizing Ethnography: Comparison and Representation in Maya Cultures, Histories, and Identities
John M. Watanabe & Edward F. Fischer, eds.

The Archaeology of Colonial Encounters: Comparative Perspectives
Gil J. Stein, ed.

Community Building in the Twenty-First Century
Stanley E. Hyland, ed.

Copán: The History of an Ancient Maya Kingdom
E. Wyllys Andrews & William L. Fash, eds.

Globalization, Water, & Health: Resource Management in Times of Scarcity
Linda Whiteford & Scott Whteford, eds.

A Catalyst for Ideas: Anthropological Archaeology and the Legacy of Douglas W. Schwartz
Vernon L. Scarborough, ed.

Afro-Atlantic Dialogues: Anthropology in the Diaspora
Kevin A. Yelvington, ed.

The Archaeology of Chaco Canyon: An eleventh-Century Pueblo Regional Center
Stephen H. Lekson, ed.

The Seductions of Community: Emancipations, Oppressions, Quandaries
Gerald W. Creed, ed.

The Evolution of Human Life History
Kristen Hawkes & Richard R. Paine, eds.

Published by Cambridge University Press

The Anasazi in a Changing Environment
George J. Gumerman, ed.

Regional Perspectives on the Olmec
Robert J. Sharer & David C. Grove, eds.

The Chemistry of Prehistoric Human Bone
T. Douglas Price, ed.

The Emergence of Modern Humans: Biocultural Adaptations in the Later Pleistocene
Erik Trinkaus, ed.

The Anthropology of War
Jonathan Haas, ed.

The Evolution of Political Systems
Steadman Upham, ed.

Classic Maya Political History: Hieroglyphic and Archaeological Evidence
T. Patrick Culbert, ed.

Turko-Persia in Historical Perspective
Robert L. Canfield, ed.

Chiefdoms: Power, Economy, and Ideology
Timothy Earle, ed.

Reconstructing Prehistoric Pueblo Societies
William A. Longacre, ed.

Published by University of California Press

Writing Culture: The Poetics and Politics of Ethnography
James Clifford & George E. Marcus, eds.

Published by University of Arizona Press

The Collapse of Ancient States and Civilizations
Norman Yoffee & George L. Cowgill, eds.

Published by University of New Mexico Press

New Perspectives on the Pueblos
Alfonso Ortiz, ed.

Structure and Process in Latin America
Arnold Strickon & Sidney M. Greenfield, eds.

The Classic Maya Collapse
T. Patrick Culbert, ed.

Methods and Theories of Anthropological Genetics
M. H. Crawford & P. L. Workman, eds.

Sixteenth-Century Mexico: The Work of Sahagun
Munro S. Edmonson, ed.

Ancient Civilization and Trade
Jeremy A. Sabloff & C. C. Lamberg-Karlovsky, eds.

Photography in Archaeological Research
Elmer Harp, Jr., ed.

Meaning in Anthropology
Keith H. Basso & Henry A. Selby, eds.

The Valley of Mexico: Studies in Pre-Hispanic Ecology and Society
Eric R. Wolf, ed.

Demographic Anthropology: Quantitative Approaches
Ezra B. W. Zubrow, ed.

The Origins of Maya Civilization
Richard E. W. Adams, ed.

Explanation of Prehistoric Change
James N. Hill, ed.

Explorations in Ethnoarchaeology
Richard A. Gould, ed.

Entrepreneurs in Cultural Context
Sidney M. Greenfield, Arnold Strickon, & Robert T. Aubey, eds.

The Dying Community
Art Gallaher, Jr. & Harlan Padfield, eds.

Southwestern Indian Ritual Drama
Charlotte J. Frisbie, ed.

Lowland Maya Settlement Patterns
Wendy Ashmore, ed.

Simulations in Archaeology
Jeremy A. Sabloff, ed.

Chan Chan: Andean Desert City
Michael E. Moseley & Kent C. Day, eds.

Shipwreck Anthropology
Richard A. Gould, ed.

Elites: Ethnographic Issues
George E. Marcus, ed.

The Archaeology of Lower Central America
Frederick W. Lange & Doris Z. Stone, eds.

Late Lowland Maya Civilization: Classic to Postclassic
Jeremy A. Sabloff & E. Wyllys Andrews V, eds.

Photo by Katrina Lasko

Participants in the School for Advanced Research advanced seminar "Empires: Thinking Colonial Studies Beyond Europe," Santa Fe, New Mexico, October 26–30, 2003. Standing (from left): Nicholas Dirks, Ann Laura Stoler, Ussama Makdisi, Frederick Cooper, Peter C. Perdue, Adeeb Khalid, Prasenjit Duara. Seated (from left): Patricia Seed, Carole McGranahan, Fernando Coronil, Jane Burbank.